BUYING POWER

BUYING POWER

THE POLITICAL ECONOMY
OF JAPAN'S FOREIGN AID

David Arase

LYNNE
RIENNER
PUBLISHERS

BOULDER
LONDON

Published in the United States of America in 1995 by
Lynne Rienner Publishers, Inc.
1800 30th Street, Boulder, Colorado 80301

and in the United Kingdom by
Lynne Rienner Publishers, Inc.
3 Henrietta Street, Covent Garden, London WC2E 8LU

Library of Congress Cataloging-in-Publication Data
Arase, David.
  Buying power : the political economy of Japan's foreign aid / by
David Arase.
    p. cm.
  Includes bibliographical references and index.
  ISBN 1-55587-447-9 (cloth : alk. paper)
  1. Economic assistance, Japanese. 2. Japan—Foreign economic
relations. I. Title.
HC60.A697 1995
338.9'152—dc20   94-34471
                                                            CIP

British Cataloguing in Publication Data
A Cataloguing in Publication record for this book
is available from the British Library.

Printed and bound in the United States of America

 The paper used in this publication meets the requirements
of the American National Standard for Permanence of
Paper for Printed Library Materials Z39.48–1984.

5 4 3 2 1

To my parents,
who have seen me through everything

Contents

Tables and Figures

Acknowledgments

I first acknowledge Chalmers Johnson and Robert A. Scalapino, whose advice and encouragement were tremendously helpful as I researched this topic. I owe gratitude as well to Seizaburo Sato for his assistance at early stages of this work. Thanks also to my friend Wes Young, who gave valuable comments on early chapter drafts. Needless to say, the views and any errors in this book are entirely my own.

I must also thank the Japan Institute of International Affairs (JIIA) for accepting me as a visiting researcher between 1986 and 1988 and including me in a variety of policy research activities, including ODA-related conferences and seminars. A special debt is owed to the Overseas Economic Cooperation Fund (OECF), which gave me a desk in their research bureau for over a year. OECF generously allowed me free access not only to its personnel but also to its specialized library and to its overseas offices in Thailand and Indonesia. The individuals who extended friendly cooperation at JIIA, OECF, the Japan International Cooperation Agency (JICA), the Institute of Developing Economies (IDE), the Ministry of Foreign Affairs, and other organizations in Japan both public and private are too numerous to list, but without their assistance this book would not have been possible. Thanks are also due to the Thai, Indonesian, and Philippine officials and academics whom I encountered in Japan and on visits to their countries.

I am also grateful for financial support received during the research and writing of this volume. The Japan Foundation financed research of this topic in Tokyo from 1986 to 1988, and the Steele Foundation financed a year-long leave for further research and writing after I began teaching at Pomona College. During that leave Joyce Kallgren of the Institute of East Asian Studies at the University of California at Berkeley provided a cheerful place for me to work, and Dan Okimoto enabled me to have access to the Hoover Institution library as well as to seminars at Stanford University's Asia Pacific Research Center. As I entered the final stages of writing and editing, David Chadwick supplied outstanding research assistance.

Finally, I wish to acknowledge my wife, Judy, whose patience and support allowed me to bring this work to fruition.

David Arase

1

Introduction

At first glance Japan's foreign aid effort may seem to be relatively uncomplicated and straightforward. The foreign policy of Japan, which most Western observers take to be the main context for aid activity, has been relatively modest in its goals, seeking to keep its international political and security commitments to a strict minimum. Viewed superficially this foreign policy might explain why Japanese aid consists solely of official development assistance (ODA), which has as its ostensible aim the economic development of recipient countries. In contrast to Japan, U.S. foreign policy after World War II created overseas political and military commitments as it sought to attract allies and to punish its enemies in the Cold War. This gave a complex role to U.S. foreign aid, which then had to reconcile aid for economic development with other types of aid aimed at sustaining client regimes against internal and external threats. Thus, at least when compared with the United States, Japan might seem to be a straightforward donor of foreign aid.

As a general proposition, however, donor and recipient governments are rarely uninterested in how and why their money is spent, even if it is "aid." The result is that economic aid is rarely straightforward and always politicized. As Charles Kindleberger says about foreign aid in general: "Its purposes remain political even when the proximate purpose of aid is economic growth—a hypothesized relationship of doubtful validity."[1] These considerations raise the question of what Japan actually is buying with the roughly $10 billion it now spends annually on foreign aid.

This study is concerned primarily with Japan's interests in giving aid bilaterally, i.e., giving grants and concessional loans directly to developing country governments, as opposed to making financial contributions to multilateral organizations such as the World Bank or the United Nations Development Programme (UNDP). The point of contributing to multilateral agencies is to pool rich country resources and remove the element of donor self-interest from aid policy making. What is of interest in the study of bilateral aid, however, is precisely the element of donor self-interest: how it intrudes in policymaking and what this might tell us about the international orientation of the donor nation.

In previous studies of Japan's ODA, models of bureaucratic politics,[2] of the state as a rational actor responding to a changing security environment,[3] or of the foreign ministry responding to U.S. pressure have been used to explain policy.[4] This traditional foreign policy approach to analyzing Japan's

1

ODA policy is also followed in some recent edited volumes on Japan's ODA.[5] This approach naturally highlights the policymaking role of the Ministry of Foreign Affairs (MFA) and foregrounds political policy motivations such as continued good relations with the United States and the developing world. Because the traditional foreign policy approach tends to discount economic and commercial aspects of policymaking, it can lead to mistaken assessments of Japan's ODA by foreign-policy–oriented analysts such as the following: "There is still a commercial element in some current aid programs, but such examples are now the exception rather than the rule."[6]

The traditional foreign policy approach is good at developing an understanding of the MFA agenda in Japan's ODA, but it shortchanges the more complex and difficult issue of how Japan's ODA serves the agendas of Japan's economic planning bureaucracies as well as the interests of private sector actors. To put Japan's ODA into a broader and more meaningful context requires a study that focuses on how domestic economic interests link up with political and state bureaucratic actors to design and implement policy. A more balanced approach that takes account of the full range of domestic structures and interests that shape Japanese ODA policy shows that economic and commercial interests are at least as important as diplomatic and security interests.

In assessing the relative importance of economic and commercial motives in ODA policy, one must be careful to choose appropriate indicators. This study relies on institutional structures in policymaking and implementation to provide an indication of the relative influence of actors in Japan's ODA, and a narrative of institutional development complemented by several case studies will indicate how structurally included economic and commercial actors have played a central policymaking role up to the present. In this view policy is the product of institutionalized structures and relations that link state and societal interests.

Previous studies of Japanese ODA have tended to focus on aid tying as the measure of economic and commercial interests in ODA.[7] This implies that the percentage of ODA that is officially tied measures the degree of commercial motivation. Aid tying by itself is too narrow an indicator, however. Virtually all ODA donors tie their aid in one way or another, but this does not mean their policies are mercantilist. Consider the case of France, which spends a large share of its ODA on the provision of French language instruction by French citizens. Such aid may be tied but it is not commercial. Conversely, aid can be officially untied, but still mercantilist. For example, a donor can offer program assistance to win changes in recipient government regulations that will benefit donor commercial and economic interests; recipients can be influenced by donors to request projects that serve donor interests; or informal procedures can manipulate open bidding procedures to ensure certain outcomes. The basic point is that donors have economic and commercial interests besides the simple export of goods and services that is the objective of tied aid procurement. Nontied ODA schemes can still serve a donor's interest in access to vital energy, food, and resource supplies in the developing world; in the restructuring of a donor's domestic industries; or in influencing recipient government policies to benefit donor country trade and investment activities. 2-3

A better way to evaluate the role of economic and commercial interests in a donor's ODA policy is to examine the position of economic planners and commercial actors relative to others within the policy making system. What distinguishes Japan's policymaking system is the centrality of powerful economic policymaking actors and the systematic informal incorporation of commercial interests in its ODA-related institutions and practices. This organizational structure yields a predictable result: ODA that is designed to advance Japan's economic and commercial interests. This means not only overt and covert tied aid schemes, but it also entails economic information gathering, investment promotion, and policy to improve the competitiveness of Japanese industry and finance.

That Japan's ODA advances a commercial and economic agenda does not make it unique. The United States has required its food aid be shipped in U.S.-registered ships to benefit its shipping industry, and Australia's minister for development cooperation has drawn attention to the fact that Australia gets three dollars in commercial sales for every one dollar of ODA given to China.[8] ODA is a flexible policy instrument that normally incorporates a wide range of donor interests and motivations, and it would be unusual not to find some element of economic self-interest in donor policies.

One theme that sets apart this effort from most previous studies of Japanese aid written in English is the identification of Japan's foreign economic policy as still the most relevant context for Japan's ODA—rather than that of traditional foreign policy or developmental economics. The distinction between foreign economic policy and foreign policy is a subtle one, but it is important for analyzing Japan's foreign aid. Foreign economic policy seeks to regulate (or perhaps not regulate at all, depending on whether one subscribes to mercantilist or free trade principles) cross-border flows of economic resources to enhance the wealth of the nation. Foreign policy encompasses a good deal of this and more in using the nation's resources to ensure the nation's security and political standing in a competitive—and sometimes dangerous—international system. Although the differences between these two policy areas may be overdrawn by those who see an inherent conflict between the pursuit of wealth and the pursuit of national power, there are still key variations in emphasis.

One difference between these areas of policymaking is in the implied policymaking community. The sources of economic policy are usually found in the interests of powerful domestic actors that are involved in the creation and allocation of wealth. Thus, policymaking does not exclude societal interests such as agriculture, labor, industry, or finance, though the degree of access to policymaking may differ among them. In contrast, foreign policy springs from the collective fear of a nation for its survival in an anarchic international system. This implies that policy should be in the hands of those who are relatively autonomous from domestic pressure groups and able to act in the "national interest" (i.e., anything that on balance increases the nation's power for survival in the face of existing threats). In practice this has meant state officials, diplomats, military officials, and only to a much lesser extent business executives and economic experts.

This leads to another implied difference in the relative priority of the dictates of these policies. Economic rationality is a powerful justification when policy serves the needs of an economy or those of its most powerful actors. When policy is meant to meet the threats to a nation's survival, however, economic rationality is transcended by political realism. On this subject Adam Smith comments, "Defense is of much more importance than opulence."[9]

Finally, analysis of these related areas reveals different emphases that are to some extent complementary. Studies of foreign policy tend to discuss decisionmaking in terms of intragovernmental dynamics (e.g., bureaucratic politics), if not a unitary rational actor model, driven by constraints and imperatives imposed by international conditions. In contrast, studies of political economy often focus on societal determinants, i.e., how private interests link up with political parties and government agencies to determine the policy agenda. In the case of Japan's ODA—which is a hybrid policy area, the axis of which runs between economic policy, and foreign policy with its center traditionally closer to economic policy—one needs an analytical approach that allows one to put societal, state, and international sources of policy in proper perspective.

There has been discussion inside Japan of using aid as a discriminating tool for advancing Japan's post–Cold War political and security objectives. How far this change will go is a question for the future, and in its conclusion this book will have more to say about the prospects. For now three impediments to change need only be noted: Japan's entrenched ideological and institutional bias for using aid as an integral part of its foreign economic policies; Japan's ability to rely on the United States for its security; and Japan's weakness in those institutions central to the conduct of an independent foreign policy.

The approach taken here is to clarify policy through institutional analysis. In this view the root of policy is not found in the immediate intention of any particular actor. Individual actors tend to be cognitively and behaviorally constrained by their membership in institutionalized structures in periods of political stability, and these structures can be expected to give a consistent thrust to policy outcomes. It follows that any satisfactory treatment of the sources of policy or the motivation of particular actors must address the issue of what the relevant framework of institutional structures is designed to achieve or is authorized to protect.

JAPANESE AID:
COORDINATION WITH TRADE AND INVESTMENT

Although the idea of foreign aid originated with the United States, any investigation of its start and subsequent development in Japan requires one to take note of circumstances peculiar to Japan that gave it a special character. Unlike the United States, which from the beginning took up foreign aid as a weapon against the spread of communist influence in the decolonizing world, Japan undertook what would only in retrospect be called foreign aid because of its obligation to make war reparations to neighboring developing countries victimized in World War II. Confronted by its own need for recovery and development, Japan invented a distinctive pattern of economic cooperation with the developing world that at its core is intended to contribute to Japan's own developmental plans.

This book will use the term *keizai kyōryoku* (the Japanese term for "economic cooperation") for two reasons: first, to call attention to the subject heading for those who can access the considerable literature in Japanese; and second, to emphasize a distinctive policy orientation that utilizes ODA as one kind of official policy instrument among others that complement the trade and investment activities of private sector actors. The immediate effect of keizai kyō ryoku is to accelerate the "advance" *(shinshutsu)* of Japanese private sector actors into the developing world. The government's strategic intention behind keizai kyōryoku is to utilize private sector actors to serve Japan's national interests, whereas the Japanese private sector seeks profits and pursues its own competitive strategies. What creates the basis for governmental guidance of private sector activity today is ODA and other incentives such as trade credits, investment insurance, and loan guarantees. Upon this basis has been built a densely institutionalized network for information exchange and policy coordination *(chōsei)* among the relevant governmental and private sector actors, the development of which will be illustrated by several case studies. The institutional and conceptual innovations that went into keizai kyōryoku stemmed from the priority given to issues of economic security and industrial development by the post-Occupation domestic reorganization of Japan's political economy. What is underappreciated some thirty to forty years later is the stability of these basic institutional arrangements and the integration of ODA into the keizai kyōryoku policy orientation.

Overlaying this basic continuity in institutional arrangements and policy orientation is a narrative of incremental development in Japan's aid policies and practices. This narrative can be valuable for what it tells us about how

Japan responds to changing external and internal pressures and constraints. The nature and degree of responsiveness can suggest who has access to policymaking and how this access is secured, and these questions bear directly on current debates about Japanese politics and political economy. Beyond this the pattern of change also reveals the complex influences acting on Japanese aid policy. External factors include the changing structure of international politics and global economic relations as well as instances of acute pressure and criticism from external actors *(gaiatsu)*. Domestic factors include the changing interests of public and private actors within the institutionalized context of aid policy making and implementation, as well as the broader issues of Japan's changing economic structure and political attitudes, especially those relating to Japan's role in the world. $\downarrow$ 5~6

In order to point out the dynamic of incremental change but the underlying structural continuity in Japan's aid policies, this book will focus on Japan's orientation toward Southeast Asia. This region was the first target of Japanese aid, and it remains at the center of Japan's aid even today. The reasons for this regional focus have to do with the constraints imposed by the structure of postwar international relations, geography, and Japan's resource endowments, but not to be overlooked are domestic institutional factors that operationalize the successive aid initiatives to develop this region for Japanese economic activities.

How to View Aid Policy

There are good reasons for viewing ODA in the context of Japan's foreign economic policy. Aid policy in Japan is jointly administered by four ministries, three of which are responsible for formulating economic policy. The Economic Planning Agency (EPA) coordinates the policies of government ministries to establish a broad strategy for national economic and social development, and the other two, the Ministry of International Trade and Industry (MITI) and the Ministry of Finance (MOF), develop and implement the nation's industrial and financial policies, respectively. Although the EPA does not function as an autonomous power center, both MITI and MOF do, and they are regarded as being more powerful and prestigious than the Ministry of Foreign Affairs, and they attract more ambitious and able administrative talent. They also marshal powerful natural constituencies in Japanese industry and finance. In contrast, the MFA can call on no powerful domestic constituency for political support in bureaucratic turf battles. Its most powerful allies often are external actors who demand change from the MFA. Although MITI and MOF have their own disagreements over policy priorities, they have successfully contested efforts by the MFA to take away their power over ODA policy making.

As one might expect from the preponderance of economic ministries involved in the making and implementation of Japanese aid policy, Japan's ODA tends to serve the needs of the Japanese economy. Thus, the influence of the economic ministries in managing aid policy explains the coordination of ODA with financial policies, trade and investment policies, and industrial policy. It also explains the intimate involvement of Japanese business and financial interests in ODA activities that will be explored in this volume. The concentration of Japan's most important developing country trade and investment markets, such as China, Indonesia, Thailand, Malaysia, and the Philippines, among the top ten of its ODA recipients over the 1985–1989 period is therefore not surprising. In contrast, U.S. foreign aid policy is not deeply influenced by economic ministries in the policy process, and as a result in 1985 only one country among the top ten recipients of U.S. ODA appeared among the lists of the top ten developing country export or investment markets of the United States. That "developing country" was Israel!

Finally, Japanese ODA mobilizes several billions of dollars of national resources and distributes them through bilateral aid programs to Japanese official agencies and private firms located both domestically and overseas. The manner of distribution affects powerful domestic interests, and accordingly ODA policy making is an intensely political process. The outputs of this policy process are clothed in the authority and legitimacy of the state, as well as in the rhetoric of aid, but they are the inevitable result of the mixture of interests, values, and operating procedures that dominate the policymaking system.

As a result of these considerations it makes more sense to view Japanese ODA in the context of foreign economic policy than in that of foreign policy if one wishes to explain persistent characteristics such as the predominant types of aid, its low concessionality, and its coordination with commercial interests in Japan. This is not to say that aid does not play a key role in Japan's diplomacy. It is certainly true that aid serves Japan's diplomatic needs. Through bilateral aid Japan is able to build strong relations with the governments of the developing world, a form of political capital that will be increasingly important as Japan pursues an independent foreign policy agenda in the post–Cold War period. In addition, Japan's aid has been increased and extended to regions outside of Asia in order to satisfy criticism by the advanced Western countries of Japan's weak contributions to sustaining the international order. The purely political aspect of Japan's aid policy is well known and easily understood, but what is less well understood is how Japanese aid is implemented to advance Japan's economic interests after the announcement of quantitative aid increases have had the desired political impact.

Another basic point about the decentralized administration of Japan's ODA is that the system was determined by preexisting bureaucratic structures and new postwar political arrangements. This cumbersome administrative architecture was set during the reparations era to ensure the coordination of the state's diplomatic, financial, and industrial objectives, as well as the promotion of its commercial interests. This leads to the following two points. First, the system's architecture constrains the efforts of even central actors like

MITI or the MFA to reorganize institutionalized networks and policies by unilateral initiative. Second, keizai kyōryoku—as well as ODA—is an administrative area where *coordination,* and not *command,* is the key characteristic. Conflict among institutionally linked actors with diverging interests is certainly predictable and important, but on balance the degree of successful coordination—both interministerial and public-private sector—is what prevents administrative gridlock and makes Japan's economic cooperation pay multiple dividends. ODA offers a case of coordination that has wider significance for understanding how Japan manages its producer-oriented political economy in an international environment.

As implied in the foregoing discussion, there are a variety of factors going into the determination of Japanese aid policy arising from societal, state, and international levels of analysis. This complexity makes it unlikely that any reductionist approach can make adequate sense of policy. In any particular case ODA will appear to be misoriented, confused, or irrational if it is assessed from the viewpoint of any single actor or criterion. Multiple causal factors exist at each level of analysis, and donor motives are complex. This does not mean, however, that complex and competing pressures cannot be managed by institutional arrangements to produce a modal pattern or generative principle that distinguishes a particular donor's policy.

The thesis of this book is that Japanese ODA cannot be adequately understood until its place in keizai kyōryoku is recognized. Of course Japan's aid has utility in advancing its diplomacy, but it also is designed to advance its international economic competitiveness. Japan's success in this effort translates into more status and influence in the international system. The use of aid for these purposes grows out of an approach to statecraft that is familiar to the West in certain doctrines of mercantilism,[10] but its actual operation is less well understood. > 8

WHY GIVE FOREIGN AID?

To understand how Japanese aid can serve both economic and foreign policy objectives, one must have some understanding of the unusual flexibility of foreign aid as a policy instrument. Foreign aid as a concessional transfer of resources between governments for the declared purpose of economic development is a postwar innovation in international affairs. Although it is true that before World War II governments often encouraged lending abroad, this usually was done by private investors on market terms; and although outright gifts of wealth were regularly made, these usually were bribes, tribute, or reparations intended on balance to benefit the powerful rather than the weak.[11] What is unprecedented about foreign aid as a policy concept is that a powerful state would want to transfer resources on concessional terms to poor states in order to raise their standards of living.

If we recognize that the broad concept of foreign aid includes military and other forms of security assistance, we might see something traditional in the effort of a rich state to strengthen weaker states who are, or may in the future become, strategic allies. The novel and problematic nature of foreign aid is clearer when we consider the concessional transfer of resources from donor to recipient governments ostensibly aimed at speeding the development of the recipient economy—a kind of foreign aid otherwise known as ODA. The core notion behind ODA (as a normative concept developed by international aid organizations) is that rich governments should grant economic resources to poor ones while leaving aside any commercial, political, and strategic considerations in order to maximize their developmental impact.[12]

What ODA is, or ought to be, as a technical enterprise can be defined by type of resource transferred and method of financing. But when one takes account of prevailing theories of international politics and foreign policy, exactly *why* rich states assist poor ones is less clear. There are at least three sources of confusion: the semantics of the term aid, the many different and conflicting rationales offered for aid activity, and the nature of public policy making.

The Semantics of Aid

What the terms *aid* or *development assistance* connote in the minds of laypersons often obscure what they denote in reality. The terms imply altruistic efforts to improve the lives of the truly poor, and although this conveys the spirit of charitable activity sponsored by private individuals and groups, it is often misleading with regard to official bilateral aid. The reality is that ODA involves the transfer of public resources from one government to another. A certain logic is inevitably imposed on the process by the political nature of the transfer mechanism, and regrettably, as students of international relations point out, humanitarianism is a principle difficult to operationalize when states are acting in the international arena, even in the area of aid.[13] In the case of U.S. aid, Charles Wolf, for example, concludes that "humanitarian objectives are not, nor do they appear likely to be, prominent among the continuing objectives of US foreign aid;"[14] and another candid study of U.S. foreign aid by Edward S. Mason states that "it is doubtful that humanitarianism . . . can be considered important either in explaining the actions of this country since 1947 or in laying the basis for a reasonable expectation of future action."[15]

Even accepting the premise that aid is given only to help the recipient's poorest population segments, donor and recipient are not likely to agree on what the recipient most needs to do, and many economists even doubt whether governments *can* know or do what is most needed. In reality there are further conundrums because donors have other priorities to factor into aid programs such as: "trade interests, foreign policy, military, strategic, security, employment, output . . . and many other variables."[16] It should not surprise anyone that bilateral foreign aid cannot be divorced from a donor nation's own interests and priorities, yet many volumes about aid have been written over the years to remind the world of this fact.

Governments and aid agencies continue to justify their aid activities by appeals to compassion and images of the poor being fed because these are most effective with mass publics. Recognizing the false image being constructed of U.S. aid, which actually was being guided more by security and political considerations, and properly so in his opinion, Hans Morgenthau complains, "Economic development has become an ideology by which the transfer of money and services from one government to another is rationalized and justified."[17] Another unpersuaded critic of economic aid points out: "To call these transfers aid simultaneously disarms criticism, prejudges the effects of the policy and also obscures its realities and results."[18] In other words, the rhetoric of compassion can make it difficult to question the authenticity or effectiveness of aid in reaching its ostensible goals.[19]

This gap between aid rhetoric and reality also explains why aid often does not generate much genuine gratitude and friendship toward donors:

> When the rhetoric of aid is confronted with the facts of aid, when promises do not materialize and the supposed generosity appears more like parsimony, then, hardly surprisingly, the expected friendship frequently does not manifest itself or appears muted.[20]

Those who look for empirical proof of the effectiveness of ODA argue that it has promoted growth, but only when other more important factors were working in the same direction. One recent study that seeks "to purge the case for aid of these excesses of claim and counter claim and to rebuild it on more secure, if more modest foundations," admits that a gap between rhetoric and results exists and proposes that governments not oversell their aid programs and focus more on developmental effectiveness. "Stripped of its essentials, then, the case for foreign aid is that it increases growth rates in some developing countries, improves the living standards of some poor people, and offers the prospect of doing better in the future on both counts. That is all."[21] A large intergovernmental effort to study aid effectiveness sponsored jointly by the World Bank and the International Monetary Fund (IMF) comes to a similar conclusion. It finds the impact on poverty to be only marginal, and the impact on growth to be "not a demonstrable fact." Nonetheless, it claims that based on a "well-educated assessment" one could conclude that "most aid does indeed work."[22]

The Arguments For and Against Foreign Aid

The second source of confusion over why aid is given has to do with the multitude of rationales that observers either discern in practice or advocate in theory, whether we consider aid as a general proposition or in a particular case. The arguments for and against ODA have proliferated ever since the start of development assistance in Truman's Fourth Point in his inaugural address of January 20, 1949, in which he called for a "bold new program" for "the improvement and growth of underdeveloped areas." Today the newest proposed aims include preservation of the environment and enhancement of the status of women. The range of traditional Western motivations may be summarized by the matrix and explanatory key presented below:

	Donor motivation			
	Strategic	Economic	Humanitarian	Commercial
Short term	S_1	E_1	H_1	C_1
Long term	S_2, S_3	E_2	H_2	C_2

S_1 The use of aid to win short-term political concessions from, or to provide support to, a particular client regime of strategic value to the donor. [23]

S_2 The long-term use of aid to economic promote development in countries who then will come to share the political values of the donor and favor peace. [24]

S_3 The use of aid to manage North-South tensions. Aid reduces tension created by the chronic inequitable distribution of global wealth and facilitates continued North-South cooperation and stable access to vital resources and markets.

E_1 Generally speaking, the economic rationale arises out of an interest in raising the efficiency of developing economies and improving the operations of the global economy. Donors may expect an indirect, deferred benefit from this. In the short run such aid is used to remove impediments to self-sustaining growth such as savings or foreign exchange shortages, public infrastructure bottlenecks, or recipient economic policies. [25]

E_2 As expressed in UN and Organization for Economic Cooperation and Development (OECD) reports, long-term aid is needed to rationalize the international economy and achieve global growth and equity goals.

H_1 Emergency relief for the victims of human-made and natural disasters. [26]

H_2 Long-term aid commitments reflect compassion for the poor,[27] which is sometimes criticized for being "liberal guilt" over persisting poverty in former colonial areas and in other backward areas.[28] Proposals for large-scale North-South resource transfers to eradicate poverty and improve global equity are often justified on humanitarian as well as economic grounds.[29]

C_1 The commercial motive is to earn the donor an immediate and direct economic benefit from aid. Aid usually is not publicly justified on short-term commercial grounds, but such considerations often explain the selection of questionable aid projects or the tying of aid to commercial benefits for special interest groups or sectors in the donor and recipient countries.

C_2 Aid used to develop new markets for donor exports and investment, and to protect those that already exist. This motive is more central to donors other than the United States. For example, in defense of aid giving the British government reported: "The prosperity of Britain is closely bound up with that of the developing world, which in turn is bound up with the international aid effort. . . . Commercial considerations alone would suffice to justify participation in the aid effort, both bilaterally and through international agencies."[30]

Searching criticisms directed against each type of motivation outlined above have kept the debate over aid energetic.

Political realists such as Hans Morgenthau have questioned S_2. Morgenthau doubts whether in fact peace and democracy are actually promoted by propping up status quo regimes in the Third World. As he so colorfully puts it, "A team of efficiency experts and public accountants might well have improved the operations of the Al Capone gang, yet by doing so, it would have aggravated the social and political evils which the operations of that gang brought forth." Alternatively, if rapid economic development was the true consideration, success could destabilize the client regime that one presumably wished to preserve.[31] George Liska echoes this view and doubts those who "assert necessary connections between foreign aid, economic development, and this or that political order, economic order, and international order."[32]

Conservative economists such as Milton Friedman have questioned the economic rationale for ODA on the grounds that it facilitates excessive and counterproductive government intervention in the economic growth process and wastefully substitutes foreign capital for domestic saving. He states that "in the long run it will almost surely retard economic development and promote the triumph of communism."[33] Others argue, "If the conditions for development other than capital are present, the capital required will either be generated locally or be available commercially from abroad to governments or businesses. If the required conditions are not present, then aid will be ineffective and wasted."[34] Even more moderate economists such as Kindleberger doubt the economic case for aid.[35] Finally, it is argued that if the development of the poorer countries is truly the policy objective, the most effective policy would not be aid but unrestricted trade.[36]

The often professed humanitarian rationale for aid is usually not categorically rejected except by die-hard realists, but some experts argue that except in the case of large-scale disaster situations the mobilization and allocation of resources through private voluntary organizations (PVOs) would be both a more genuine demonstration of concern and a more effective means of reaching the truly needy. In this view the problem is that primary reliance on donor and recipient government bureaucracies means that resource allocation regularly serves political elites, bureaucratic interests, or organized private interests more than genuine humanitarian principle.

Finally, although there is no doubt that the commercial rationale has been an important part of many donor programs, it is criticized for blunting aid's effectiveness in the other three areas, and economists regularly point out that as an instrument designed to enhance a nation's wealth, it is not an optimal policy choice. Nonetheless, such criticisms fail to explain why donors persist in using aid as a commercial instrument. One must take account of the institutional characteristics of public policy making (indicated below) that will inject commercial interests even into programs intended for other purposes. It should be added, however, that states have a rational incentive to gain a direct economic return from aid, instead of gaining nothing at all, other things being equal. Viewed in this light, criticizing the commercial use of aid because it is not the most efficient way to benefit the donor's economy simply misses the point. The point of using aid commercially is to gain some direct economic return where otherwise there would be none. Using rational criteria a donor may seek commercial returns up to the point where the marginal cost to its other objectives begins to exceed the marginal benefit to its purse.

This is not the place to resolve the debate over which motives should, or actually do, drive ODA; rather the point of the foregoing discussion is to indicate the wide range of objectives that foreign aid can plausibly serve. Perhaps the safest generalization to make is that foreign aid, when used alone or in combination with other policy instruments, has a unique ability to allow the donor to demonstrate compassion while simultaneously pursuing a variety of other objectives.

Public Policymaking

Finally, the nature of policymaking under conditions of mass democracy makes clarification of policy motives and objectives difficult. One could argue that to the extent a policy process characterized by legislative logrolling and bureaucratic bargaining is inclusive of different interests, the motives and objectives served by a policy multiply if it is to be funded and effectively implemented. As Ohlin puts it in the case of aid:

Public policy in a democratic society necessarily finds its support in a variety of motives and purposes. The task of generating effective agreement does not require that all must agree for the same reason. Foreign aid policies will be approached and interpreted differently, first of all by the various branches of government—departments of foreign affairs, finance, commerce, defense—and secondly by the electorate and its representatives to whom foreign aid policies, even when well understood, will necessarily mean many and different things and be approved or rejected for different reasons.[37]

John D. Montgomery makes the same point about the case of congressional approval of U.S. foreign aid:

Even supporters of foreign aid were divided by peripheral issues, such as the disposal of agricultural surpluses or the use of aid funds to promote private enterprises abroad or support small business at home. The administration was beset with internal conflict between the economizing forces, centered in the Treasury and the Bureau of the Budget, and the overseas operational groups, mainly supported by the Defense Department, the State Department, and ICA, which struggled for funds they believed to be essential for national security.[38]

The foregoing discussion shows that foreign aid is a flexible but widely misunderstood policy instrument. In actual practice it can serve a multitude of donor purposes. Ironically, because it is so flexible, it is impossible to determine without reference to a donor's broader interests which purpose, or priority of purposes, will likely motivate that donor's aid program.

2

Foundations of
Economic Cooperation

JAPAN AFTER DEFEAT

Defeat and Occupation created a strategic opportunity to restructure and re-orient Japan for the U.S. Occupation authorities. In essence their initial objective was to turn Japan into a demilitarized democratic society with limited industrial capacity. They started first by imposing the new Peace Constitution that renounced the use of force to settle international disputes and also incorporated democratic principles informing the U.S. Constitution. The Occupation dismantled Japan's prewar military and security structures and banished their leadership from public office; reformed education; and created a more competitive, decentralized political system by lifting the ban on leftist parties and creating elected local and prefectural governments. Land reform freed the rural population from poverty and broke the political power of small landholding elites; labor reform laws allowed unionization, strikes, and collective bargaining; and antitrust laws broke up the prewar *zaibatsu*. The Occupation authorities also intended to impose punitive reparations on Japan that would have limited Japan's industrial development to prewar levels.

The "loss" of China in 1949 and the Korean War (1950–1953) forced a "reverse course" in Occupation policy. In the interest of resisting communist subterfuges and demonstrating the superiority of democratic capitalism, the United States allowed the partial rollback of democratizing reforms. In particular, Occupation authorities forbade public employees to strike, purged the labor movement of leftist leaders, and allowed the rehabilitation of many conservatives initially purged by the Occupation. The U.S. attempt to move Prime Minister Yoshida Shigeru (1946–1947, 1948–1954) toward revision of the Constitution and remilitarization was not, however, successful for reasons mentioned below. [39]

INTERNATIONAL CONSTRAINTS
ON JAPANESE POSTWAR STRATEGY

The reentry of Japan as a sovereign actor in the international system was marked by the San Francisco Peace Treaty, which was signed in September

1951 and entered into force on April 28, 1952. The U.S.-Japan Security Treaty signed in May 1952 gave U.S. forces extensive base facilities in Japan and consolidated Japan's role in the U.S. alliance system. In the same month Japan was admitted to the International Monetary Fund and the International Bank for Reconstruction and Development (The World Bank), thus smoothing the way for Japan's participation in the international economy. If Japan had not provided base facilities, the United States could have obstructed Japan's full participation in the U.S.-sponsored Bretton Woods system. In the Yoshida-Dulles talks and the Robertson-Ikeda talks on these two treaties, the real choice Yoshida had was limited to the degree of support Japan would give U.S. containment strategy.

If Yoshida's strategic bargain of political subservience to the United States in exchange for inclusion in the U.S.-sponsored economic and security structure constrained Japan, so did Japan's poor natural resource endowment. Widespread hunger and shortages of housing, clothing, fuel, and industrial materials in the years immediately following defeat reminded all Japanese of the nation's dependence on imports. Beyond simple food sufficiency and industrial recovery, conservative business and bureaucratic elites wished to achieve parity with the advanced Western nations. To do so Japan would have to secure access to far more energy and raw materials than it possessed, and because of its small domestic market and the need to pay for imports, the development of export markets would be a strategic necessity. These factors had helped to push prewar Japan into reckless imperialism, and they still had to be resolved in postwar Japan. If the orientation of Meiji Japan was, as E. H. Norman put it, "*Internally,* . . . to hasten industrialization and the development of the home market, and *internationally,* to win recognition as a Great Power,"[40] then postwar Japan retained a familiar outlook on the world. Of Japan's postwar strategic orientation, the pragmatic Yoshida wrote:

> A maritime nation, Japan has no choice but to engage in overseas trade if she is to support her ninety million inhabitants. This being the case, her chief partners should be the United States and Great Britain, countries whose relations with Japan, in trade as well as in history, have been closest, countries that are economically prosperous and technologically advanced. This is not essentially a question of either dogma or philosophy, nor need it lead to a subservient relationship; it is merely the quickest and most effective way—indeed the only way—to promote the prosperity of the Japanese people.[41]

Accordingly, the choice Yoshida made for postwar Japan was passive support for U.S. hegemonic leadership, i.e., to provide little more than military bases and diplomatic support for U.S. Cold War strategy. This choice was supported by the postwar civilian bureaucracies for they had no wish to revive the military as a domestic political rival. By interpreting the postwar Constitution as ruling out any overseas use of force even in defense of an ally or in support of a UN-authorized collective security operation, Japan would avoid entanglement in overseas military affairs and could then focus better on the critical issue of rapid economic recovery and development. Thus, at an early stage the role of postwar Japanese diplomacy was clear: it would be to preserve the U.S. security guarantee and promote access to markets while avoiding overinvolvement in U.S. strategic designs. What was less clear, however, was how the political economy would be organized in the aftermath of the Occupation's reforms.

Yoshida's postwar strategy was a necessary, but not sufficient, condition for the subsequent concentrated effort to organize Japan's political economy for speedy economic recovery and development. In the end the postwar recovery of Japan was built upon prewar civilian structures and personnel that could contribute to Japan's industrial growth and development without straying outside the boundaries set by Yoshida's basic strategic design.

CONTINUITIES IN STATE INSTITUTIONS

Although it was shaped by Occupation reforms, the organization of postwar Japan's political economy still owed much to the legacy of prewar structures, personnel, and ideological factors. If the genius for this reorganization is to be found anywhere, it would be in the prewar and wartime planning experiences. This was possible because the Occupation chose to rule Japan indirectly through the Japanese civilian bureaucracies. Occupation authorities incorrectly assumed that like U.S. bureaucracies, Japanese economic bureaucracies were politically neutral instruments, and so the Occupation purge and reform efforts never targeted them. Instead Occupation attention was given to the powerful home affairs ministry (Naimushō), which integrated police and political repression functions into all aspects of domestic administration. Therefore, of the 1,800 civilian bureaucrats purged, about 70 percent were police and other officials from the home affairs ministry, and this bureaucratic actor was then cut up to form the postwar ministries of construction, labor, and health and welfare; the local autonomy; police agencies. Thus, the substantially untouched civilian economic bureaucracies had their military and home affairs rivals cut down by Occupation reforms, and they found themselves with unprecedented preeminence within the Japanese government. Nevertheless, they still constituted a central medium for the transmission of certain prewar institutional and ideological legacies.

It was pointed out during the Occupation that the unreformed civilian ministries were a potential threat to Occupation reforms in other areas. John Maki wrote, "It is a striking fact that nowhere in either American or Allied basic policy is the bureaucracy as a class mentioned as a target for the reforms necessary to achieve the establishment of a 'peaceful and responsible government' in Japan."[42] A famous editorial in the August 1947 issue of *Chūō Kōron* quoted at length by Chalmers Johnson elaborates this point:

The problem of the bureaucracy under present conditions is both complex and paradoxical. On the one hand, the responsibility for the war clearly must be placed on the bureaucracy, as well as on the military and the zaibatsu. From the outbreak of the war through its unfolding to the end, we know that the bureaucracy's influence was great and that it was evil. Many people have already censured the bureaucrats for their responsibility and their sins. On the other hand, given that under the present circumstances of defeat it is impossible to return to a *laissez-faire* economy, and that every aspect of economic life necessarily requires an expansion of planning and control, the functions and significance of the bureaucracy are expanding with each passing day. It is not possible to imagine the dissolution of the bureaucracy in the same sense as the dissolution of the military or the zaibatsu, since the bureaucracy as a concentration of technical expertise must grow as the administrative sector broadens and becomes more complex.[43]

The means and effects of continuity may be illustrated by the career of Okita Saburō, a key architect of Japan's postwar economic miracle, during this transition period. Okita was born in 1915 in Dairen, Manchuria, the son of a Japanese intellectual who published a newspaper for Japanese colonists. Okita was trained as an engineer at Tokyo University and entered the Ministry of Communications. He subsequently transferred to the Greater East Asia Ministry, where he turned his skills to economic planning for colonial development and the war effort. Outside of work he participated in Prince Konoe Fumimaro's brain trust, the Shōwa Research Association (Shōwa Kenkyūkai). At the end of the war economic bureaucrats such as Okita moved quickly to start planning Japan's postwar recovery and development. When defeat was imminent he and others in the Greater East Asia Ministry organized the ad hoc Research Committee on Postwar Economic Problems that brought together prominent economists and economic planners in the closing days of the war. The work of this group would help to formulate a consensus over the basic economic strategies and objectives that postwar Japan would adopt.

When the Greater East Asia Ministry was dissolved within days of Japan's defeat, Okita was invited into the research bureau of the MFA.[44] There he found support for the continuing work of the committee, which met some forty times, and he succeeded in distributing 10,000 copies of its report to government and business leaders in March 1946.[45] He describes it as "a kind of harbinger of the postwar economic plans; a forerunner, if you like, of the first Economic White Paper published some years later."[46] Others writing Japan's postwar economic history have pointed to its significance as a touchstone to Japan's postwar political economy. Looking beyond defeat, the report focuses on four basic directions of the world economy: (1) the expansion of the proportion of economic problems in politics, (2) the increasing management of the international economy, (3) the expansion of planning in economic management, and (4) the need for shared effort and guarantees to national welfare. According to the report Japan's postwar aim should be to become an exporter of capital equipment to serve the industrialization of Asia. Interestingly enough, when the report was translated and presented to the Occupation authorities the response was that Japan should develop export capacity in textiles, where Japan then had comparative advantage, and not in capital equipment.

The Japanese report also emphasizes the need for economic planning: "[The] implementation of a conscientious and wise planned economy is becoming necessary. . . . Experience with the failures of wartime economic controls can give us guidelines for a better planned economy."[47] Although the report favors democratization qua demilitarization, it does not embrace economic laissez-faire: "Open and free competition is not the only way. With regard to the democratization of the Japanese economy, public ownership and economic planning of financial organs and important basic industries, as well as a considerable strengthening of state controls, are probably necessary." The bias of the report was summarized by the well-known economist Iida Tsuneo, who comments: "The report did not call for rebuilding the economy to have a genuine private sector–led style of capitalism. . . . It is significant that at this time both the leading economists and technocratic bureaucrats were asking for a common conception."[48]

Okita subsequently wrote key reports helping to limit the impact of reparations policy and participated in regular informal meetings with Prime Minister Yoshida to brief him on economic policy. When Yoshida brushed aside advice to create a powerful economic planning bureaucracy Okita resigned from government service in early 1947, but he returned to service later that year when Yoshida fell from office. Okita was then put in charge of writing the first Economic White Papers for the Economic Stabilization Board. When Yoshida returned to power, Okita resigned but again later returned to head research and planning bureaus in the Economic Planning Agency, which formulated the first postwar long-term development plans and the Income-Doubling Plan.

As in the case of Okita, prewar civilian bureaucrats moved into key positions in the postwar economic bureaucracies planning Japan's economic recovery and development.[49] It followed that the postwar government would retain faith in the kind of centralization of state and private sector institutions that had facilitated the operation of Japan's prewar and wartime economic performance. This orientation inspired the formation of postwar Japan's state-guided capitalist political economy.[50]

THE ORGANIZATION OF POSTWAR JAPAN'S POLITICAL ECONOMY

Although prewar bureaucratic elements made the transition into the postwar era, this alone cannot explain postwar Japan's political economy. Occupation reforms and parliamentary politics did change the course of Japan's institutional development and create new possibilities. But in the final analysis these reforms did not succeed in reconfiguring Japan's politics and economy according to the U.S. model. Some of the difficulties may be illustrated by Yoshida's unsuccessful battle against the reinstatement of economic planning.

Prime Minister Yoshida, who favored a comparatively liberal approach to economic policy and administration, resisted the early advice of Arisawa Hirōmi and his followers (among them Okita) to turn the Economic Stabilization Board (ESB) into an economic rationing and control organ reminiscent of the Cabinet Planning Board created in 1937 to mobilize Japan's economy for war. Only when Yoshida left office for the first time in 1947 could the ESB implement a rationing system along the lines recommended by Arisawa.[51] Ironically, it was a Socialist government under Wada Hirō that allowed the ESB to implement the so-called priority production plan, with successful results for industry but severe hardships for households. After his return to power Yoshida eviscerated the ESB and turned it into the smaller and weaker Economic Deliberation Agency (Keizai Shingi Chō). MITI took this opportunity to turn its Industrial Rationalization Council (Sangyō Gōrika Shingikai) under Arisawa's chairmanship into the focus for industrial policy. After Yoshida was replaced as prime minister in 1954 by Hatoyama Ichirō, a depurged prewar conservative politician, the Economic Deliberation Agency was permanently upgraded and renamed the Economic Planning Agency (EPA) in 1955, but by then most of its rationing and control powers had been appropriated by MITI, leaving the EPA with broader macrolevel research and indicative planning functions, and this path of institutionalization explains the present division of labor between the two. But the broader point is that even though bureaucratic efforts to establish economic planning functions were delayed and deflected by Yoshida, they eventually succeeded.

Here we may point to certain historical contingencies, domestic institutional characteristics, and international factors that gave the economic bureaucracies power, which they used to organize a system of coordinated state–private sector developmental activity. First, as indicated above, if the Occupation had understood how to reform the civilian bureaucracies to achieve a liberal state orientation, things might have been radically different. But this was not to be, and so Yoshida had to battle unsuccessfully against the economic bureaucrats. When he lost effective leadership in 1954 to conservatives such as Hatoyama Ichirō, Kishi Nobusuke, and Ikeda Hayato, all of whom supported national planning and close public-private sector coordination, the last hope for a liberal Japanese political economy disappeared.

The possibility of societally driven change was narrowed even more by developments in the party system. Early Occupation political reforms encouraged parties to form along a wide political spectrum and open their ranks to new blood. However, elected politicians were inexperienced in actual matters of governance because the military and civilian bureaucracies had always drafted and implemented national policies. It was not surprising, therefore, that postwar parties recruited bureaucrats to help them govern. For example, in the 1949 general election forty-two first-time representatives were bureaucrats, many of whom were persuaded to run by Yoshida. The return to political life of prewar politicians at the end of the Occupation introduced factional rifts among conservatives based on career background and party affiliations. Recognizing that the imminent consolidation of the socialist parties endangered conservative predominance, the two main conservative parties rooted in the prewar Jiyūtō and Minseitō formed the LDP—the Liberal Democratic Party (Jiyūminshutō)—in 1955, which from the beginning was hegemonial in size and solidly backed by business and bureaucratic interests. From its inception the LDP recruited bureaucrats to give it influence within the bureaucracy, and because it was heavily penetrated by bureaucrats it did not attempt to displace the bureaucracy from its traditional role of formulating basic national policies. Instead the LDP focused on winning elections, and it blocked attempts in the Diet to check the discretionary power of the bureaucracy.

It should also be noted that the private sector had neither the inclination nor the means of breaking free of state supervision because Japanese industry, commerce, and finance had come to rely on government measures to revive and develop them. Huge prewar zaibatsu assets that had given the private sector considerable autonomy from the state were gone. To facilitate the revival of the industrial economy after the Occupation ended, the Japanese government relaxed antimonopoly policy and actively encouraged the formation of *keiretsu* (financial lineages). By encouraging their formation the government created a successor to the prewar zaibatsu, which had concentrated scarce resources in priority areas. Keiretsu differed from the prewar zaibatsu in that there was no holding company, although cross-shareholding knit group members together. At the core of each group was a large bank, and the main business of the group's bank was to finance group members. This role was enhanced by the system of overloaning devised by the government to ensure the survival of key industries during the financial crisis brought on by the anti-inflationary Dodge Line. The main bank was allowed to lend over the borrower's capitalization, and the keiretsu bank was given direct borrowing privileges from the Bank of Japan in return for responding to bureaucratic guidance (window guidance). This system of policy-based, indirect financing gave modern large-scale firms in commerce and industry priority access to national savings, but in return the private sector became dependent on the Japanese state.

As was the case in zaibatsu groupings, the role of the general trading company in the keiretsu was to procure raw materials and sell the group's products overseas, as well as to organize member firms for collective overseas projects. Because of their effectiveness in this role, the government viewed the trading company as a strategic asset. It reduced the number of trading companies from some 2,800 during the Occupation to around 20 and assigned each to a keiretsu or a group of small producers.[52]

The horizontal keiretsu that emerged from this post-Occupation reorganization of the private sector not only facilitate relations with the state, but they also give the economy strength and resilience. Constituent firms represent a cross section of industrial, financial, and commercial sectors. To some extent keiretsu members can spread costs and benefits within the group, as when a firm in dire straits is able to draw capital, technology, or personnel from others at below market rates; and in more prosperous times, the firm can share with others newly acquired business. Competition between keiretsu promotes efficiency, but in certain cases there can be cooperation through, for example, state-sponsored recession cartels or technology development projects.

Because keiretsu tend to include large firms in each major sector, and because each large firm will have smaller subsidiaries and subcontractors, each group is able to generate a sense of collective welfare and a strategic view of Japan's economy. This helps the private sector give the government critical information and policy advice. Institutionalized networks of state–private sector interaction ranging from peak organizations such as the Keidanren (Keizai Dantai Rengōkai) to sectoral trade associations and policy deliberation councils can facilitate policy dialogue that leads to growth-oriented policies within a statist framework. For example, the Steel Federation and the Keidanren successfully pressed to amend the Anti-Monopoly Law in 1953 to allow the state to sponsor recession and rationalization cartels.[53]

A fourth factor contributing to a state-led, developmentally oriented postwar political economy was the passivity of public opinion in the face of continuing autonomous bureaucratic power. The deference paid to prewar bureaucrats as servants of the exalted emperor continued into the postwar period. This continuity of attitude and habit is at odds with the fact that the postwar Constitution disestablished Shinto, transferred sovereignty from the emperor to the people, and made the Diet the highest organ of state. It must be recalled, however, that the Constitution was promulgated in 1946 by the Occupation authorities without even a popular referendum. Thus, the Constitution did not follow from a changed popular consciousness, but instead was intended to promote a change in political culture.

Finally, a fifth permissive factor allowing the economic bureaucracies to shape the postwar political economy was the role of the United States. It defended Japan's security without requiring a reciprocal obligation from Japan, supported Japan's ambitious economic plans, and accordingly allowed Japan to implement controls until it had recovered. What the United States did not understand was that the measures to accelerate the growth of industrial capacity taken at the end of the Occupation indicated briefly below were neither temporary nor easily remedied aberrations from the norm. Instead, they reestablished a prewar norm of state-guided capitalist development built on partially restored prewar state and private sector institutions.

ROLLBACK OF OCCUPATION REFORMS

The Purge of Public Officials Law was revised in 1951 in order to depurge approximately 170,000 of the roughly 200,000 persons previously barred from public service by the Occupation authorities. In 1951 the Japanese government also announced the end of the zaibatsu dissolution campaign. In March 1952 the Enterprises Rationalization Promotion Law was introduced which authorized the government to form depression cartels and rationalization cartels. In the same year new additions to the Special Tax Measures Law created a set of flexible tax measures, reserve funds, and special depreciation systems to be implemented by MITI to promote export industries, technology imports, and industrial development. The revision of the Anti-Monopoly Law in 1953 is also noteworthy because it allowed recession and rationalization cartels and it let former zaibatsu firms use their old trademarks and regroup into new "financial lineages," or keiretsu.

In this early postwar process of economic restructuring for rapid industrial growth and export expansion, a key task was the creation of a system to guide accelerated investment. One of the most central actors was MITI, which, with the cooperation of MOF, guided investment funds, scarce foreign exchange, and special tax measures to targeted industrial sectors; at the same time the EPA oriented the public and private sector decisionmakers by keeping track of Japan's economic position in the world economy and by identifying new strategic needs and goals for the nation.

Important structures created to augment this system include the Japan Development Bank, established in March 1951 to promote lending to key industrial sectors and infrastructure projects; the Fiscal Investment and Loan Plan (Zaisei Tōyūshi Keikaku), established in July 1952 by combining separate postal savings accounts into a single pool of government-controlled investment funds; and of particular importance to the development of Japan's economic cooperation, the Export Bank of Japan, established in 1950 to channel credit to export industries. The Export Bank was reorganized into the Export-Import Bank (Ex-Im Bank) in 1952 in order to better finance imports of key raw materials. As a step to promote Japanese exports, MITI encouraged private firms to form the Japan Export Trade Research Organization in 1951, which later was raised to semiofficial status as the Japan External Trade Recovery Organization in 1954.

THE START OF *KEIZAI KYŌRYOKU*

The need to establish raw material import sources and export markets gave birth to keizai kyōryoku. The seminal initiatives were taken just after the return of sovereignty when Japan, cut off from prewar markets in China and Korea by geopolitical events, had to look to relatively unfamiliar regions of Asia and Latin America for raw materials and strategic export opportunities. At the time the Japanese government strictly controlled the allocation of foreign exchange in order to finance critical imports. This made the government's approval of a foreign currency allocation for Japan's first postwar foreign direct investment, an iron ore development project in India in 1951, a starting point in its economic cooperation.

The measure was justified on the grounds that it was a "development investment" *(kaihatsu tōshi)*, meaning an investment in developing a supply of strategic raw materials for Japan. Imports from such projects came to be called "development imports" *(kaihatsu yunyū)* because they were developed to supply Japanese industry. This policy concept was soon reinforced by other investments in resource extraction in Malaya, the Philippines, and other areas in Asia. Development investments were also directed at this early date to Brazil, where stable supplies of cotton for Japan's textile industries and iron for Japan's steel industries could be found. Japan's first act of export promotion to the developing world was an export trade credit extended by the Ex-Im Bank in 1952 to facilitate the sale of railway locomotives to Chile.[54]

The private sector identified these projects and subsequently approached the Japanese government for policy support. These first instances of development imports and export promotion set the pattern for Japan's economic cooperation with the developing world. From these seminal first initiatives the government's role in keizai kyōryoku has been to subsidize those private sector project proposals that would enhance Japan's economic security and development, whereas the private sector's role has been to identify profitable ways of achieving state-defined priorities. The first extended opportunity to develop this approach to economic cooperation was provided by Japan's war reparations activities.

Japan's War Reparations Obligations

Article 11 of the Potsdam Declaration issued on July 28, 1945, called for Japan to demilitarize and pay punitive war reparations. Ambassador Edwin W. Pauley, head of the first reparations mission to Japan, which identified over 1,000 factories to be transferred abroad as reparations, issued a final report in November 1946 calling for Japan's return to the level of industrialization it had in the early 1930s. This became the basis of the original reparations policy of the Far Eastern Commission, the highest legal authority in Occupied Japan.

Implementation of this policy became difficult, however, when disputes between the Soviet Union and the United States arose over the distribution of the designated factories. To break the deadlock, in April 1947 the United States unilaterally declared that 30 percent of the designated assets would be handed over, half going to the Republic of China, with the balance to be evenly divided among the Philippines, Holland, and England. By the end of 1950 the transfer of these assets was largely completed and was valued at $45 million. But as the situation in East Asia changed, the Draper-Johnston mission of March 1948 pointed out that if the reparations policy were fully carried out, it would put Japan's recovery in grave doubt. This led to the U.S. announcement in May 1949 that no more designated reparations assets would be transferred abroad, and it became clear that the United States would not allow the reparations issue to hinder a peace treaty or the ending of the Occupation.

The revised U.S. policy is articulated in Article 14 of the San Francisco Peace Treaty, where it was stipulated that reparations claimants were limited to those countries suffering losses from Japanese occupation, and that reparations would be limited to the provision of Japanese services and would not impose foreign exchange burdens on Japan.[55] The peace treaty left the reparations issue to be settled through bilateral negotiations between Japan and remaining claimants. Before the end of 1951 an Indonesian delegation had arrived in Tokyo presenting demands for $18 billion, and in January 1952 a Philippine delegation arrived demanding $8 billion in cash. In response to the latter demand Japan offered to pay $200 million. Substantial progress on the reparations issue was not made until after the Korean War, when Japan turned to developing markets in Asia.

THE IMPACT OF THE POST–KOREAN WAR ECONOMIC CRISIS

During the Korean War special U.S. procurements in Japan caused an economic boom that allowed many key industries such as steel, autos, synthetic fibers, and electrical machinery to modernize and expand production. Exports actually declined and unit production costs rose, even as imports increased to feed the expanding Japanese economy. U.S. war procurements in Japan, which came to $800 million per year in 1952–1953, balanced Japan's external account.

When the Korean War ended in 1953, Japan's balance of payments went into a tailspin and currency reserves fell from over $2 billion in November 1953 to $600 million in seven months. To cut imports and save foreign exchange, the Bank of Japan instituted window guidance in which monthly new-lending ceilings were set for each city bank (i.e., banks with direct borrowing privileges from the Bank of Japan), with punitive interest rates applied if targets were exceeded. Fiscal brakes were also applied as the Yoshida government made sharp reductions in the 1954 budget. This brought on a sharp recession in 1954 in which the Yoshida government fell and was replaced by a Cabinet under Hatoyama Ichirō.

As economic planners considered the situation, it became clear that Japan would have to promote exports if it was to continue its postwar recovery and growth.[56] The recovery and development of the economy during the Korean War had been good, but in 1954 Japan's exports were only 46.3 percent and imports were 76.6 percent of prewar levels, and Japan had only 2.1 percent of world trade in 1954 as opposed to 5.4 percent in 1938. Loss of empire helped to explain this, as did the fact that the Occupation had cut off direct contacts with foreign countries and had disabled Japan's large trading companies. Japan's trade was also impaired by the process of decolonization, which created newly independent states, many of which favored import substitution policies. These factors were brought into focus during the 1954 balance-of-payments crisis when Japan was forced to borrow from the IMF three times to finance imports (see Table 2.1).[57]

If Japan needed to promote exports, exactly what exports to promote was not clear until the Economic Deliberation Agency issued a paper in 1953 entitled "On making our economy independent" *(Waga kuni keizai no jiritsu ni tsuite)*. It called for restored ties with South and East Asia, but more important, it called for the development of Japan's heavy and chemical industries to sustain import growth. The reason was that the world's demand for advanced machinery would increase faster than would its demand for food or textiles, and so Japan should become an exporter of capital goods, despite the fact that its comparative advantage then was its low wages.[58] The policy recommendation was rejected by Yoshida as an instance of unwarranted planning, but after he was replaced as prime minister in December 1954 it was adopted as Japan's basic policy up to the 1970s.

The year 1954 therefore became the year for export promotion during which the Supreme Export Council (Saikō Yushutsu Kaigi) chaired by the prime minister, was created to draw attention to the strategic importance of exports. The Japan External Trade Recovery Organization (JETRO) was also

Table 2.1 Japan's Trade Dependence by Region (percent of total trade)

	1934–1936		1954	
	Export	Import	Export	Import
Asia	64	53	49	31
North America	17	25	21	46
Others	19	22	30	23

Source: MFA, 1956.[59]

upgraded into a commercial intelligence organization. To broaden access to markets in noncommunist Asia, Japan joined the Columbo Plan for technical cooperation among Britain's Asian Commonwealth members. This was the Japanese government's first voluntary and entirely self-financed commitment to aid the Third World, and as such it has been retrospectively identified as the start of Japan's ODA. The above steps alone, however, could not suffice because Japan's economic relations in Asia could not be normalized until the festering reparations issue was resolved. Asia-oriented planners such as Okita Saburo and Hara Kakuten warned even during the Korean War that "with regard to 'natural resources' and 'markets' we cannot expect the development we desire unless we put value on goodwill and trust with the peoples and governments in this region."[60]

As the Korean War came to an end the MFA invited private sector leaders to form an advisory council to formulate a coordinated public-private sector approach to economic cooperation with the countries of Asia. This advisory body, the Asian Economic Deliberation Council (Ajia Keizai Kondankai), was established in June 1953 under the chairmanship of Hara Yasusaburo, an eminent Asia-oriented business leader from the Mitsui group. This officially sponsored policy deliberation council composed of business executives and government officials helped to institutionalize the close linkage of the government and private sector in keizai kyōryoku.

One key innovation originating in this body's deliberations was the proposal to consolidate thirty-five private sector groups promoting Japan's Asian interests by establishing the Ajia Kyōkai, or Asia Association.[61] Through the joint sponsorship of the MFA and MITI, it was legally incorporated as a semiofficial body *(zaidan hōjin),* and it was originally capitalized at ¥60 million, with ¥30 million provided by the MFA, ¥5 million provided by MITI, and the balance provided by the private sector. The Asia Association was given the responsibility of handling Japan's participation in the Columbo Plan and of surveying the economies of Asia. It was staffed by retired bureaucrats, active and retired government economists, engineers, and professionals, many from the old South Manchurian Railroad Research Department. Its most visible activity was publishing a journal in Japanese and another in English. Through technical cooperation it supported the export of equipment and whole plants through the reparations program. Other institutional changes were made in preparation for reparations. In 1952 a small Asian Economic Cooperation Office was added to the MFA's Asia Bureau to supervise the Asia Association. In 1953 MITI established an economic cooperation section in its Trade Bureau while MOF tasked the investment division of the Foreign Exchange Bureau to coordinate economic cooperation policy.

The most significant long-term product of the Asian Economic Deliberation Council was the government's first comprehensive policy statement on economic cooperation which was issued in December 1953. This Cabinet-approved statement entitled "Policy on economic cooperation with the countries of Asia" ("Kakugi kettei—Ajia shokoku ni tai-suru keizai kyōryoku ni kan-suru ken") establishes the basic principle governing keizai kyōryoku that lasts to this day. Aside from recommending early settlement of the reparations issue, it states that "in principle, economic cooperation is carried out through private sector initiative, and the government is to render the necessary assistance."[62] This policy statement made explicit what had been only implicit in Japan's initial steps in economic cooperation.

Reparations Agreements

As Japan turned urgently to promoting exports to Asia, it signed its first reparations agreement in November 1954 with Burma. This reparations agreement had two precedent-setting differences from the provisions of the San Francisco Peace Treaty. First, it allowed Japan to provide goods in fulfilling its reparations obligations. This would allow Japan to turn the reparations obligation into a subsidy for Japanese capital goods exports. Second, it shifted the rationale for the transfer of goods from Japan's war guilt to concern for Burma's "economic recovery and development" and for "the improvement of social welfare." This developmental rationale for reparations allowed Japanese reparations *(baishō)* and reparations-like payments *(junbaishō)* to be incorporated in Western statistics on ODA.

Japan had slower going in dealing with other claimants in part because then–Prime Minister Yoshida was inclined to put first priority on the developed West in economic as well as political affairs. After returning from an official trip to Southeast Asia in 1954, he derided those who pressed for economic cooperation with Asia by commenting, "You have to trade with rich men; you can't trade with beggars."[63] This orientation changed after Hatoyama took over later in 1954, and it became clear at the 1955 Bandung Conference that Japan would have to make faster progress in improving relations with the developing world.

A final total of thirteen countries and areas accepted either reparations or war compensation payments from Japan. Four countries demanded formal reparations: the Philippines, Indonesia, Burma, and South Vietnam. After months and years of difficult negotiations, the original demands of these countries, totaling some $30 billion, were scaled back to roughly $1.5 billion. The remaining countries and areas that accepted reparations-like grants were Cambodia, Laos, Malaysia, South Korea, Singapore, Thailand, Micronesia, Mongolia, and the Democratic People's Republic of Vietnam (grants to the latter two were war compensation in all but name and were pledged when relations were normalized with these countries). In addition, South Vietnam and Burma gained additional grants of this type beyond their previously negotiated reparations totals. The Republic of China (Taiwan) and the People's Republic of China both renounced their right to war reparations or compensation, as did India. Formal reparations payments ended in 1976, and war compensation payments ended in 1977. Table 2.2 summarizes reparations and reparations-like grants.

Table 2.2 Reparations and Grants

Country	Year of Agreement	Settlement	Payment Period
Burma	1954	$340 million	1955–1965
Thailand	1955	$26.7 million	1962–1970
Philippines	1956	$550 million	1956–1966
Indonesia	1958	$223 million	1958–1970
Laos	1958	$2.8 million	1959–1961
Cambodia	1959	$4.2 million	1959–1961
South Vietnam	1959	$390 million	1960–1965
South Korea	1965	$300 million	1965–1975
Singapore	1967	$8.2 million	1968–1972
Malaysia	1967	$8.2 million	1968–1972
Micronesia	1969	$5.9 million	1973–1976
Vietnam	1975	¥ 8.5 billion	1975–1978
Mongolia	1977	¥ 5.0 billion	1977–1981

Source: Tsushosangyosho (MITI), *Kokusai Kyōryuku no Genjō to Mondaiten 1986,* 320–322.

In total, the amount Japan paid, excluding loans, came to a sum of roughly $1.9 billion, or somewhat over ¥6,000 per capita. Other measures of reparations show that as a percentage of GNP they peaked at 0.17 in 1959, and as a percentage of exports they peaked at 2.5 in 1960.[64] It should also be noted that many of these agreements contained a loan element not included in the above figures. For example, the 1954 Burma reparations agreement included a Japanese government pledge to provide $50 million in "private" loans at low interest to finance purchases from Japan. The same formula was followed in the Philippine settlement, in which Japan promised $250 million in "private" loans, and also in the Indonesian settlement, in which $400 million in such loans was pledged.

Keizai Kyōryoku *and Reparations Policy*

Japan developed economic cooperation techniques that partially turned its reparations obligations to Japan's own developmental advantage. Reparations could not be an optimal way to promote Japan's economic interests, but that it was used effectively for these ends at all is the result of the private sector–led, government-backed techniques of keizai kyōryoku. Ushiba Nobuhiko, a diplomatic councilor who helped to negotiate the Burma reparations agreement (and who subsequently became a special cabinet minister for economic cooperation in the 1970s), stated that "in reparations by no means did Japan suffer losses."[65] A major multivolume Japanese study of keizai kyōryoku describes how Japanese reparations policy was designed to achieve Japan's interests:

> Provisions were put in the reparations agreements stipulating such things as that reparations should not obstruct [Japan's] normal exports, or that reparations commodities would not be reexported to third countries. With the provision of reparations, both the bureaucracy and business were united in paying scrupulous attention to see these would not obstruct, even in the smallest degree, their efforts to increase exports.
>
> It was, however, insufficient merely to ensure that reparations would not hinder exports; it was also necessary to see that reparations would be used as a vanguard for exports. At the time, most of our country's exports were textiles and sundry goods, and steel exports to the United States had just begun, and the emphasis had turned to developing heavy and chemical industrial products with calls for upgrading our exports. In this context, it was expected that reparations would push high-grade manufactured exports into Southeast Asia and widen the scope for ordinary exports.[66]

Thus, key points of Japan's reparations agreements were as follows: (a) reparations were not to interfere with "normal" trade; (b) procurement contracts would be signed between Japanese firms and recipient governments; (c) only goods or services would be transferred to recipients; (d) one party in reparations deals must be Japanese; (e) transactions would be in yen; and (e) normal commercial procedures would be followed.

Another key innovation was the request-based system to guide Japan's reparations activity. The pattern was set early in the reparations period and may be illustrated by a brief case study. Reparations payments to Burma began in 1955, and the single largest item by far was the Balu Chuang hydroelectric power project located midway between Rangoon and Mandalay. This first major aid infrastructure project built by Japan set a standard pattern for the many other projects to follow.

The project was identified in 1953 when Yutaka Kubota, president of Nihon Kōei (who had been president of Chōsen Dengyō, The Korean Electric Power Co., in prewar days and had planned and built almost all of the power dams in Korea, including the largest ones on the Yalu River), visited Burma in search of business opportunities.[67] After Kubota sold the Burma Electricity Supply Board on the idea of a power dam supplying electricity to Rangoon and Mandalay, this Burmese government agency made a formal request to the Japanese government for reparations funds to build the project. The Japanese government approved the request, and Nihon Kōei was hired as the consulting engineer; Nihon Kōei then hired Kajima Construction Company as the main contractor, which in turn subcontracted pieces of the project out among various Japanese suppliers.

The request-based implementation system was such that if a Japanese business executive could motivate a reparations recipient to make an official request for Japanese goods or services, with Japanese government approval of the request, the Japanese executive could gain a lucrative contract. (Open bidding for reparations procurements was not part of the implementation system.) In fact, reparations activity has been called "business diplomacy" *(zaikai gaikō)* because of the fact that Keidanren missions often conducted the actual reparations negotiations with foreign governments.[68] In other words, the request-based system worked to induce Japanese business activity in recipient economies and gave the Japanese government the ability to approve only projects that would subsidize targeted Japanese industries. This system marked an important step forward in articulating the principle of private sector initiative and government backing in the service of Japan's strategic interests.

A survey of the Showa period's economic history supervised by one of the chief architects of Japan's postwar economic strategy, Arisawa Hirōmi, sums up reparations as follows: "Reparations that began in 1955 and continued for the next twenty years gave postwar Japan its first foothold in advancing into Southeast Asia."[69] The key role reparations and other forms of keizai kyōryoku played in rebuilding Japan's economic ascendancy in Asia is put in the following way: "If one were to indicate on a map the projects built by reparations, grant aid, and yen loans, with the exception of China, North Korea, and North Vietnam, within the entire region previously held by [Japanese] force, one can see postwar Japan's economic power extending outward step-by-step."[70]

The Arisawa study also indicates those Japanese industrial sectors subsidized by Japan's reparations, as well as the managing firms benefiting from reparations contracts:

> Looking briefly at the details of the content of reparations, the core in Burma was the Balu Chuang hydroelectric dam and railroad renovation with much provision of vehicles (Tōyō Kōgyo, Hino), electrical equipment (Matsushita), pumps (Kubota), and other whole plants, as well as transportation equipment such as trucks, trains, rails, and ships. . . . Reparations to Indonesia included ships, automobiles, agricultural machinery, as well as many paper, cotton textile, plywood plants (Kanematsu, Itoh-Chu, Tōmen, and others), with special efforts in general development plans for the Brantas River in Eastern Java and Riamukanan in Southern Borneo (Nihon Kōei, Kajima Kensetsu, Hazamagumi); and hotel construction (Kinoshita, Daisei Kensetsu, Tōnichi, and others).[71]

The effectiveness of reparations procurements in nurturing *(ikusei)* Japan's capital goods industries was marginal relative to the size of domestic demand or total exports, but they were of strategic importance in cracking new overseas markets for Japanese firms. The industries benefiting the most were shipbuilding, automobiles, electrical machinery, steel, construction, and

engineering consulting, but more broadly, in the view of Arisawa, "As a practical result the effect of opening markets for normal exports was large."[72]
Instead of displacing commercial exports, reparations enhanced them.
Although the burden on the government budget reached 1 to 2 percent, this
actually represented a subsidy to targeted industrial sectors, and the growth of
revenue during the period of high-speed growth eased the fiscal burden.

The creation of new governmental structures and institutionalized networks of public-private sector interaction kept pace with the expanding size
and scope of Japan's reparations activity. The first formal governmental bureaucracy administering reparations was the Reparations Agency established
in February 1948. With the actual start of reparations payments, this agency
became the Provisional Reparations Office within the Asian Bureau of the
MFA in February 1955. This Reparations Office was quickly upgraded to
department *(bu)* status and lasted until 1964, when it was absorbed by the
Economic Cooperation Bureau within the MFA.

The role of the MFA was to coordinate *(chōsei)* implementation and to
act as a transmission belt between the bureaucracy and recipient governments.[73] The operation of the review system within the government was
described as follows:

> For example, when a claimant wants to obtain a ship as reparations, the
> reparations mission and a Japanese shipbuilder will conclude a contract and
> refer it to the Reparations Division of the Foreign Ministry. The Reparations
> division will refer the contract to the Transportation Ministry. The
> Transportation Ministry will study the contract from the standpoint of ship-
> ping administration, the Finance Ministry will look into monetary aspects,
> and the Ministry of International Trade and Industry will examine it from
> the standpoint of the export trade administration. Only when these three
> ministries approve the contract, the Reparations Division, at the request of
> the reparations mission, will pay money into mission designated banks such
> as the Bank of Tokyo and the Fuji Bank, and the reparations mission will
> pay the bill to the shipbuilder.[74]

Decisionmaking power was formally vested in the government-wide
Reparations Implementation Council (Baishō Jisshi Renraku Ky ōgikai)
chaired by the foreign minister and consisting of the administrative vice-
ministers of the following ministries: EPA, MFA, MOF, the Ministry of
Education (MEd), the Ministry of Health and Welfare (MHW), MAFF
(Ministry of Agriculture, Forestry, Fisheries), MITI, MOT (Ministry of
Transportation), MPT (Ministry of Posts and Telecommunications), MOL
(Ministry of Labor), and MOC (Ministry of Commerce). This council deliberated negotiating stances and broad policy and approved reparations requests. By the early 1960s this cumbersome system was streamlined until
only the *yonshōchō* (the MFA, MITI, MOF, and EPA) regularly attended to
all aspects of economic cooperation, and they coordinated with the other
ministries and agencies on a case-by-case basis.

Private sector leaders gave policy advice to the government through the Baishō Jisshi Kondankai, an advisory council created by the Foreign Ministry. There was also the Baishō Jisshi Renraku-bu, a lower-level coordinating group of division and department heads meeting weekly that handled routine planning and implementation issues. MITI controlled approval of reparations exports.

The Japanese government was careful to choose an indirect rather than direct relationship with recipient governments in the implementation of reparations (see Figure 2.1). Parties to procurement contracts would be a Japanese firm and a recipient government. This would allow Japanese business to develop relations with recipient governments. And reparations monies would be held in private Japanese banks in Tokyo from which Japanese contractors would draw payment. Thus, Japanese banks would earn interest and transaction fees from reparations, and the Japanese government would have better control over the actual use of funds. The deliberately constructed intermediary role played by the Japanese private sector, as well as the principle of request-based assistance *(yōseishugi)* and the system of interministerial coordination through case-by-case decisionmaking, provided the basis upon which Japanese ODA would develop.

On balance, reparations cleared away roadblocks to Japanese political

Figure 2.1 Reparations Payment Model

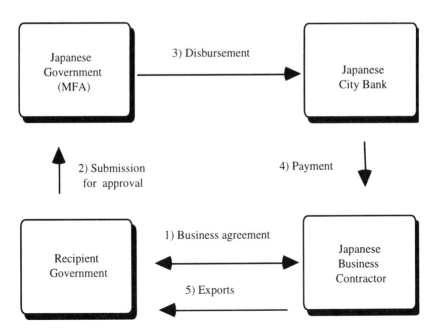

and economic relations with Southeast Asia left by World War II. Perhaps the key achievement for Japan was to use reparations as a mechanism for subsidizing targeted industries and promoting exports to neighboring countries. This was critical because economic expansion without export growth would put the international payments balance through the ceiling.[75] Japan's reparations were intended to help Japan's structural development by increasing economies of scale for heavy industries, upgrading Japan's export structure, and sustaining high-speed growth.[76]

3

The Development
of *Keizai Kyōryoku*

Early postwar Japan's conservatively ruled, producer-oriented, and bureaucratically coordinated political economy would require that Japan's external relations, like its domestic policies, be managed to promote commercial industrial development above all else. Keizai kyōryoku gained its strategic orientation from this broad institutional setting. What brought the system to maturity were the challenges of actual policy implementation. This required reasonably smooth interministerial and public-private sector coordination to ensure that Japan's diplomats, economic planners, and business executives remained oriented toward a strategic goal, even if this was not always apparent or uppermost in the minds of individuals. Japan found answers as it first used reparations to expand capital goods exports, as indicated previously, and then inaugurated yen loans to augment export promotion as well as develop stable supplies of strategic energy and raw materials for itself in the face of growing Third World resource nationalism.

KEIZAI KYŌRYOKU BEYOND REPARATIONS

The year 1955 marked the end of Japan's postwar recovery phase. The formation of the LDP consolidated conservative control over postwar Japan's political agenda, and a strong economic recovery from the post–Korean War recession and balance-of-payments crisis created optimism. In the same year Japan joined the General Agreement on Tariffs and Trade (GATT), as well as the United Nations in 1956. It is in this context that the 1956 Economic White Paper states: "The postwar period is over. Future economic growth must be supported by modernization."[77]

The structure of Japan's economy in 1955 was such that it had modern industrial sectors approaching Western standards but a small domestic market with wages and living conditions closer to those of the developing world. This put Japan in an intermediate position in the international division of labor, with a comparative advantage over the developing world in capital-intensive goods and an advantage over the developed West in labor-intensive goods. Japanese planners hoped to structure trade such that capital goods exported to the developing world would pay for raw materials imports, whereas exports of cheap consumer goods to advanced countries would pay for imports of Western capital goods and technology.

The need for raw materials and export markets in the developing world made penetration of Southeast Asian markets a focus of attention. A 1956 paper on economic cooperation published in English by the MFA noted that these countries could be expected to buy Japanese capital goods and could also supply Japan's growing need for food, lumber, and mineral resources. Japan would accordingly promote "a gradual changeover of the sources of imports of the principal raw materials from the dollar area to the Asian Area."[78] At this time the center of the MFA's Asian policy was trade promotion. If the MFA had been interested in a substantially different agenda in Asia, keizai kyōryoku would not have developed as it did. But the attitude of the MFA at this time gave priority to trade interests. In January 1956 a major conference of foreign ministry officials concerned with Asian policy focused on economic cooperation. The vice-minister of foreign affairs articulated the basic policy concern by stating, "It goes without saying that Japan should place emphasis on machinery and chemical products in its future export drive."[79]

Because Japan was also seeking political rehabilitation, MFA policy at this time stressed the so-called three great principles, or *san dai-gensoku*: faithful membership in the UN, membership in the Western alliance, and membership in Asia.[80] Japan was, however, unable to pursue an independent political agenda as a U.S. satellite during the Cold War. It was also unable to make new overseas political or military commitments because of domestic factors, and it had weak or nonexistent ties to its Asian neighbors because of bitter war experiences and the intervention of the Cold War. By focusing on economic cooperation in Asia, Japan could move within these constraints. A Japanese expert gives the following interpretation of MFA policy (the phrase in quotes in the following translated passage is taken from the 1957 *Diplomatic Blue Book*):

> There was a complementary relationship between on the one hand, Asia, which had enormous natural resources but whose development was still to come, and on the other, Japan, which had advanced technologies and industrial strength. Moreover, Japan had an obligation to facilitate the inflow of capital and technology from outside. Thus, "economic cooperation that combines *(ittai to natte)* the government and private sector in a planned, high-priority, and flexible way" was required. It went without saying that capital and technology from outside would come from America for the time being. This corresponded to the political concept of Japan being linked to the Western alliance while standing as a member of Asia. Thus, a strategy for economic diplomacy was self-consciously formed taking advantage of Japan's placement at the point where American capital and Asian resources met, while promoting the "peaceful overseas advance" of the Japanese economy.[81]

The Need for New Measures

To support future rapid industrial growth and development, Japan needed more than reparations. Japan needed to access nonreparations countries, and it also needed new sources of raw materials that export-promoting reparations were unable to develop. The task of economic cooperation was expressed most clearly by the chief of MITI's international trade bureau, who wrote in 1958:

> As we search for a stable market for the exports of the products of the heavy and chemical industries, on the basis of the growing height of domestic industrial structure, the significance of the market of Southeast Asia may be said to be greatest, especially when there is but a limited possibility of expanding our trade with the prewar neighboring markets in the Far East. The Southeast Asian countries intend to free themselves from their backwardness through industrialization and, therefore, have a great demand for capital goods; moreover, Southeast Asia is the exclusive source of supply in the world for some of its indigenous products, many of which are important industrial raw materials for our country, and its supplying capacity is expandable remarkably [sic] through its future development.
>   As the supplier of capital goods or the importer of raw materials, our country is at greatest geographical advantage in this region over any of the advanced countries.[82]

He went on to conclude:

> It is necessary to expand our capital-goods exports to this region and at the same time to exploit raw material resources on a far greater scale. Concrete measures for these purposes have for some time been loudly discussed in the various quarters concerned. What is in question today is how to put them into practice as early as possible.[83]

What made new economic cooperation instruments critical was the disturbing fact that the United States and Europe were scoring faster export growth to Southeast Asia than Japan. The 1958 report on the foreign trade of Japan states:

> To compete with the US and Europe in trade with East Asia and Southeast Asia under these conditions, Japan must further develop its capacity to export capital goods. At the same time, Japan must help these areas bolster their importing capacity by extending credits to them.[84]

This same report goes on to state:

> Greater significance will be attached to the kind of economic cooperation whereby we can secure both stabilized export markets for our capital goods . . . and imports of various sorts of materials. . . . We must take cognizance of the grim fact that once the capital goods produced by one country find a stabilized market in an underdeveloped country, it is very difficult for those

produced by another to squeeze themselves into the same market. This fact
is all the more significant for Japan which has to seek expanded export of
her capital goods in the future.[85]

In designing new economic cooperation instruments there were certain
problems that needed recognition. First, Japan had weak ties with the newly
independent countries of the Third World, especially the former European
colonies. Second, those countries that would buy Japanese equipment for resource development projects often had neither the money nor the technical
expertise to use it effectively. Finally, the quality of Japanese equipment for
large-scale projects often fell below Western standards. These problems
could be overcome by offering longer-term, concessional financing tied to
procurement from Japan, but the keizai kyōryoku system did not have this
capacity.

Japan dealt with this impasse with the premiership of Kishi Nobusuke
from February 1957. With his prewar background as an economic planning
bureaucrat in Manchuria and a wartime minister of commerce and industry,
Kishi was acutely aware of the need to develop raw material sources and export markets in Asia to accommodate the expansion of Japan's heavy industrial sectors. In his first year Kishi made two trips through noncommunist
Asia visiting a total of twelve countries, and in each he made efforts both to
resolve war reparations issues and to develop new forms of economic cooperation. He strengthened Japan's capabilities in information gathering and analysis by supporting the creation of the Ajia Keizai Kenkyūjo (the English
language name for which is the Institute of Developing Economies, or IDE)
in 1958 to survey the Asian economies. In addition, the Japan External Trade
Organization (previously the Japan External Trade Recovery Organization)
was strengthened with the addition of overseas offices and technical cooperation activities. Both were under MITI supervision.

Also significant was the start of publication by MITI of the annual White
Paper on Economic Cooperation in 1958. The widening significance and
scope of keizai kyōryoku required a more detailed definition and statement of
purpose, and so this report offers the first indication of what Japan intended
to accomplish. The first report states:

> Economic cooperation between less developed countries and industrialized
> countries can be categorized according to the content of cooperation in
> overseas [direct] investment, capital cooperation, technical cooperation, and
> trade transactions. One special point about economic cooperation is that al-
> though the role of the state is gradually expanding, it is normally private
> sector based.[86]

The different types of cooperation are defined as follows:

> Overseas investment introduces foreign capital into less developed
> countries, and by conforming to their development plans, it can promote de-

velopment through the development and effective use of natural resources, industrial construction, or diversification of the economy; while for industrialized countries it can effectively employ excess capital and secure needed raw materials.

Capital cooperation alleviates the capital shortage of less developed countries, and it is carried out through grants, loans, investment, export credits, and import credits. Reparations have the same effect as capital cooperation, but they are analytically different. Of the types of capital cooperation, investment, export credits for capital goods, and import credits for industrial raw materials are especially noteworthy. . . .

Technical cooperation is the despatch of experts from industrialized countries, or in special cases from developing countries, or the training of developing country experts.

For industrialized countries to procure primary products from developing countries on a long-term and large-scale basis requires not only measures to help developing countries through direct infusions of foreign exchange, capital goods imports, and expanded domestic investment, but also the stabilization of production. Economic cooperation assisting import and export transactions is especially good at respecting the views of the developing countries and achieving the importing industrialized country's goal of securing sources of food and industrial raw materials. [87]

Finally, the relationship between private sector and public sector in keizai kyōryoku is reiterated:

Economic cooperation has been promoted primarily on a private sector basis, and this should continue.

It goes without saying that private sector economic cooperation has been on a commercial basis. As a result of the private sector's ingenuity and responsibility, economic cooperation has been efficient and effective at expanding trade, especially exports, and in securing important raw materials.

This being the case, it goes without saying that the government must plan the implementation of appropriate domestic measures to ensure the smooth promotion of private sector–based economic cooperation. [88]

The Start of Yen Loans

In April 1957 Kishi proposed a scheme for the development of Southeast Asia that would give U.S. aid funds to Southeast Asian countries to allow them to develop resource development projects using Japanese-made equipment. To help him promote this idea Kishi set up a Southeast Asia Development Cooperation Fund (Tōnan Ajia Kaihatsu Kyōryoku Kikin) of ¥5 billion ($13.8 million) within the Ex-Im Bank before his June 1957 trip to the United States, but the plan failed to attract U.S. support.

Failing in this initiative, Kishi sought a bilateral scheme for yen loans. The first bilateral yen loan was negotiated in February 1958 when Japan signed a yen credit with India worth $50 million. This initiative originated in talks between Kishi and Nehru in New Delhi during Kishi's first trip in 1957 and was finalized during Nehru's visit to Tokyo in 1958. This three-year yen loan was extended through the Ex-Im Bank to the Indian government and was to pay for Japanese services and plant equipment. The basic objective was to develop iron ore mines in Goa, in return for which Japan gained an assured supply of two million tons of iron ore annually for ten years once production began. To get the money the Indian government would have to make individual project requests that would be reviewed by the Japanese government on the case-by-case basis developed by reparations policy. The novel aspect of the so-called Goa formula in economic cooperation was that in exchange for assured access to important raw materials, Japan would provide the necessary equipment, technical training, and financing. This qualified as ODA because it involved a government-to-government loan agreement for developmental purposes. On the Japanese side the key players were MITI, the Ex-Im Bank, a group of cofinancing commercial banks, a managing commercial bank, and the goods and services exporters. On the recipient side were the finance ministry and the importer. Figure 3.1 is a diagram of the scheme.

With respect to the bureaucratic politics involved in this initiative, the Goa loan was opposed by MOF, which was concerned over Japan's negative

Figure 3.1 Yen Loan Agreement Model

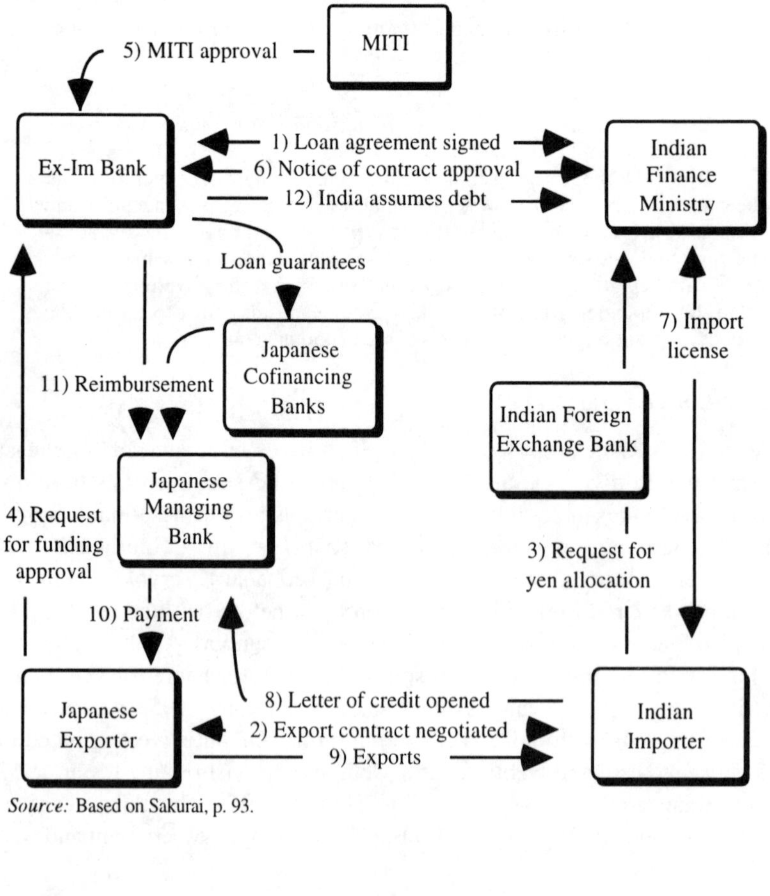

Source: Based on Sakurai, p. 93.

balance-of-payments position, but a MITI official in India expressed the following view: "Extension of loans would result in an increased inflow of our
capital goods and technicians to the country and contribute toward the expansion of the Japanese economic sphere in this part of the world."[89] The
MFA sided with MITI because yen loans would expand the scope of its
diplomacy. The MFA's Asian Economic Cooperation Office began overseeing Japan's yen loans, and in 1959 it was upgraded and renamed the
Economic Cooperation Division.

A second yen credit was extended in April 1958 to India through a
World Bank consortium. This was followed by a third credit in 1959 to
Paraguay to purchase riverboats[90] and a fourth in 1960 to build a hydroelectric power dam in South Vietnam. In the 1961–1964 period there were nine
additional yen loan agreements, four with Pakistan, four with India, and one
with Brazil associated with the Minas Gerais iron development project.

These yen loans were implemented by the Ex-Im Bank in coordination
with the city banks. Early yen loan policy is described as follows: "Unless
tied to natural resources for our country, it cannot be denied that yen credits
were used, as before, as one aspect of an export promotion policy."[91] The de-
nomination of loans in yen, not then a freely convertible currency, preserved
Japan's foreign exchange reserves and tied procurement to Japan.

The Institutional Structure of Economic Cooperation

Despite the start of yen loans, by the late 1950s it was clear to the government and the private sector that a better system was needed. The Ex-Im Bank
was originally designed for short-term export financing. Although its terms
of reference could be modified somewhat, its capitalization and lending
restrictions made it inadequate for financing more than a handful of large-
scale resource development projects. In addition, the Goa formula did not
create Japanese ownership and direct control over developing country
resources—a step that would further ensure stable and secure sources of raw
materials.

Private sector pressure for further government initiatives in economic
cooperation succeeded in mobilizing the LDP. In July 1959 the LDP formed
the Special Committee on Foreign Economic Cooperation (Taigai Keizai
Kyōryoku Tokubetsu Iinkai), and in August it issued a formal policy
statement recommending creation of a ¥20 billion government fund to promote Japanese resource development projects in Southeast Asia. The MFA
and MITI then issued competing proposals for government supervision of the
proposed fund. In November the Keidanren called for the further development of economic cooperation. This gathering consensus produced a Cabinet
order on January 14, 1960, to use the ¥5 billion from the abortive Southeast
Asia Development Cooperation Fund to create a new economic cooperation
agency, to be called the Taigai Keizai Kyōryoku Kikin, otherwise known as
the Overseas Economic Cooperation Fund (OECF). Supervision would be by

the MFA, MOF, MAFF, MITI, and the EPA. Subsequently, bureaucratic infighting led to the elimination of MAFF, and nominal leadership was given to the EPA.

The Cabinet order led to a joint meeting of the Lower House finance, foreign affairs, and commerce and industry committees to authorize the OECF's establishment law. This marked the first occasion where Diet discussions touched on Japan's basic posture toward economic cooperation. The Lower House commerce and industry committee handled the authorizing legislation for this new agency. Because of the disrupted Diet term caused by Kishi's forced passage of the U.S.-Japan Security Treaty, formal establishment of the OECF had to wait until March 1961.[92]

The OECF gave Japan the capacity for officially backed equity participation in overseas resource development projects. The OECF's original terms of reference limited it to investments and yen loans to *Japanese* corporations building projects in the developing world. The intention was not to lend to foreign governments, but to advance Japanese ownership control over the production of vital raw materials in the developing world. In the 1961–1964 period, the OECF scored thirty cases of equity participation or loans relating to overseas development projects, fifteen of which were in mineral development or basic metal production. The OECF did not make a yen loan to a foreign government until 1965.

The development of Japan's economic cooperation did not stop with yen loans and the OECF. In June 1961 the Foreign Economic Cooperation Advisory Council (Taigai Keizai Kyōryoku Shingikai) was formed to review the emerging organization of Japan's economic cooperation. It was chaired by the prime minister and attended by cabinet members as well as prominent private sector leaders. Although it met only three times, it played a key role in rationalizing the system of economic cooperation.

In December 1961 the advisory council agreed that the technical training functions of the Asia Association (along with those of six other semiofficial technical cooperation groups, including the Latin America Association, the International Construction Technology Association, and the Mekong River Development Research Commission) should be incorporated into a new official administrative agency *(tokushū hōjin)* to be called the Overseas Technical Cooperation Agency (OTCA), or Kaigai Gijutsu Kyōryoku Jigyō-dan. MITI and the MFA fought over who should supervise the new organization. The MFA eventually won, but when OTCA was established in June 1962 there was bureaucratic agreement that key posts in OTCA would be reserved for the nominees of other ministries and agencies. As further consolation to MITI, the basic research functions of the Asia Association and the other organizations were transferred to the MITI-supervised IDE, which was then raised from a semiofficial status (zaidan hōjin) to the same "official agency" status of OTCA and OECF, i.e., tokushū hōjin.

Thus, what came out of the deliberations of the prime minister's advisory council was a system based on four implementing agencies: the Ex-Im Bank, which provided trade credits and official yen loans; the OECF, which provided loans and equity capital to Japanese corporations; OTCA, which handled the technical cooperation needed to facilitate the overseas operation of Japanese capital equipment; and the IDE, which oriented Japanese priorities by providing country and regional analyses of developing economies. In the background were a variety of other agencies such as JETRO and the Metals and Mining Agency of Japan (MMAJ) that played more specialized supplementary roles. The yonshōchō deliberated the general questions facing economic cooperation, though virtually all bureaucratic actors were somehow involved in the routine operations of this system as a result of the request-based, case-by-case decisionmaking procedure first established by reparations policy. The private sector could register its preferences with the government through corporatist devices such as the Taigai Keizai Kyōryoku Shingikai, not to mention peak associations like the Keidanren and industry associations such as the Japan Steel Federation or the Japan Plant Exporter's Association. The private sector could also affect the government by lobbying the LDP. The outlines of the system are presented Figure 3.2.

Figure 3.2 The *Keizai Kyōroku* System, 1963

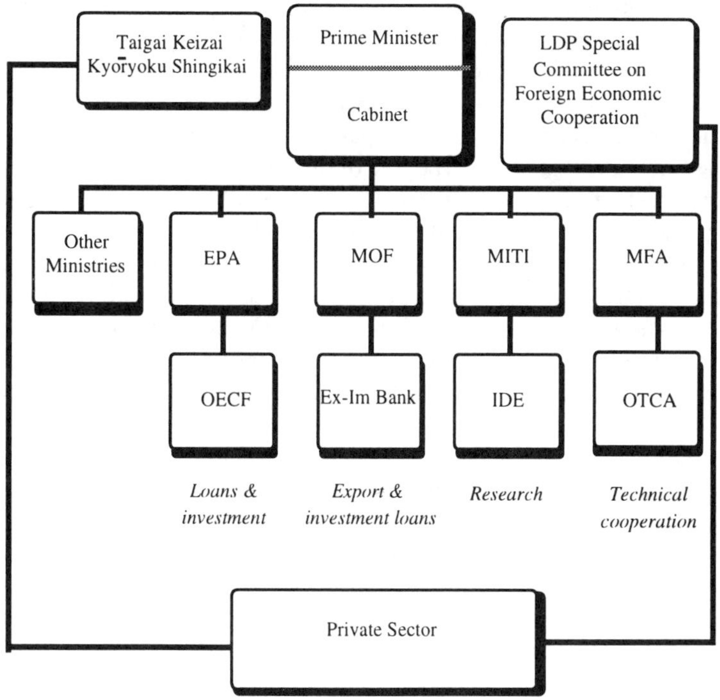

As did the earlier Asian Economic Deliberation Council, which established the basic principles of economic cooperation in 1953, the prime minister's Taigai Keizai Kyōryoku Shingikai provided a mechanism for incorporating private sector views into a policy consensus, authorizing major new initiatives, and brokering bureaucratic conflicts. As a mechanism for reconciling private sector and bureaucratic viewpoints, it was able to register new directions and legitimize changes within the keizai kyōryoku system in ways that the yonshōchō by itself could not. Bureaucratic sectionalism and the need for continuing collaboration with the private sector would not allow the bureaucracy to dictate terms, nor would this have been wise if the Japanese government wanted to develop a competitive private sector.

A similar function was played by the First Provisional Study Committee on Administrative Reform (Rinji Gyōsei Kaikaku Chōsakai), which studied areas of administration where bureaucratic rivalry was a serious problem for the private sector. The problem of keizai kyōryoku was that beyond the frictions within the yonshōchō it involved the private sector and most of the main ministries and agencies in ongoing activities. A 1964 report by this committee stressed the need to unify *(ichigen-ka)* trade, aid, and investment measures. This was one of the first concise formulations of the basic keizai kyōryoku aim of unifying aid, trade, and investment that forms the background to the call for "three-into-one" economic cooperation in the Japanese government's 1992 ODA policy declaration. To facilitate interministerial coordination it recommended ministerial cross-postings among ministries involved in economic cooperation.[93] Cross-posting has since been adopted as a norm within the keizai kyōryoku system.

In drawing lessons from the formation of this system, one should note that it was unnecessary to introduce and pass authorizing legislation defining its outlines and policy mandate. The role of the Diet was narrowly restricted to altering existing agencies or creating new ones after Cabinet orders or *shingikai* recommendations were issued. A relatively small circle of bureaucrats, business executives, and conservative politicians designed the system, and their decisions were legitimated post hoc by Cabinet orders or Cabinet-initiated legislation. Also noteworthy is that the MFA saw economic cooperation as a means of supporting Japan's national interest in economic development and as a vehicle for building bilateral relations with the emerging Third World. Only from the latter half of the 1960s did it begin cautiously to expand beyond this narrow conception.

In addition, in this period balance-of-payments constraints were a serious factor affecting spending volume. Comparing the 1958–1960 period and the 1961–1964 period, one sees that Japan's average annual spending declined from $194 million to $112 million. As Japan entered the Ikeda Cabinet's income-doubling plan period, Japan sucked in large amounts of Western technology and invested heavily in infrastructure. To help finance this Japan borrowed $120 million from the World Bank in 1961 and issued $600 million in overseas bonds in the 1961–1964 period. Because of its fiscal needs and negative balance of payments in this period, Japan cut back new aid commitments, and Japan's share in total ODA through the OECD's Development Assistance Committee (DAC) decreased from 4.1 percent in 1961 to less than 3.5 percent in 1964. In this period of active institutional development but reduced spending, the factors determining the articulation of policies and institutions were almost solely domestic. External factors would force adjustments in Japan's economic cooperation system only from the latter half of the 1960s.

The Increasing Sophistication of Keizai Kyōryoku

To conclude this chapter it is necessary to indicate the actual significance of the growth and development of the keizai kyōryoku system. The increasing geographical reach and sophistication of Japan's economic cooperation allowed by the new array of implementing agencies may be seen in a sequence of aid projects, each admired by contemporaneous Japanese experts as models of economic cooperation. The well-organized division of labor among various Japanese agencies and private sector actors in these projects indicates the degree of interministerial and public-private sector coordination the system could achieve in advancing Japan's interests in keizai kyōryoku. The contrast between these projects and the reparations schemes described earlier illustrates how Japan's more developed institutional capabilities allowed state and private sector actors to improvise increasingly large and complex forms of partnership.

North Sumatra Oil Development Project. In this first-ever project for the OECF Japan provided the equipment and services to develop an Indonesian oil field. Because Indonesian law under Sukarno forbade foreign ownership of strategic resources, a production-sharing agreement was reached in 1959. A Japanese firm was formed to develop the oil field with the Indonesian national oil company, Permina.[94] The Japanese firm, the Northern Sumatra Oil Development Company, would provide $53.34 million in equipment and services to Permina, and in return the Japanese firm would share a part of oil production. Equity for the Japanese firm was provided by the Japanese government, the OECF, and Japanese petroleum firms. Loans to finance its activities were provided jointly by the Ex-Im Bank and the city banks (see Figure 3.3).

The Minas Gerais Iron and Steel Mill in Brazil. This huge project featured direct investment and loans to process Brazilian iron ore to supply Japan's steel makers. This project was first identified by the Japan Steel Federation, which authorized Hachiman Steel Corporation to do a feasibility study in 1955. By 1957 the Japan Steel Federation and the Keidanren negotiated a basic agreement with the Brazilian government. In April 1957 the Japanese

Figure 3.3 Northern Sumatra Oil Development Project Financing

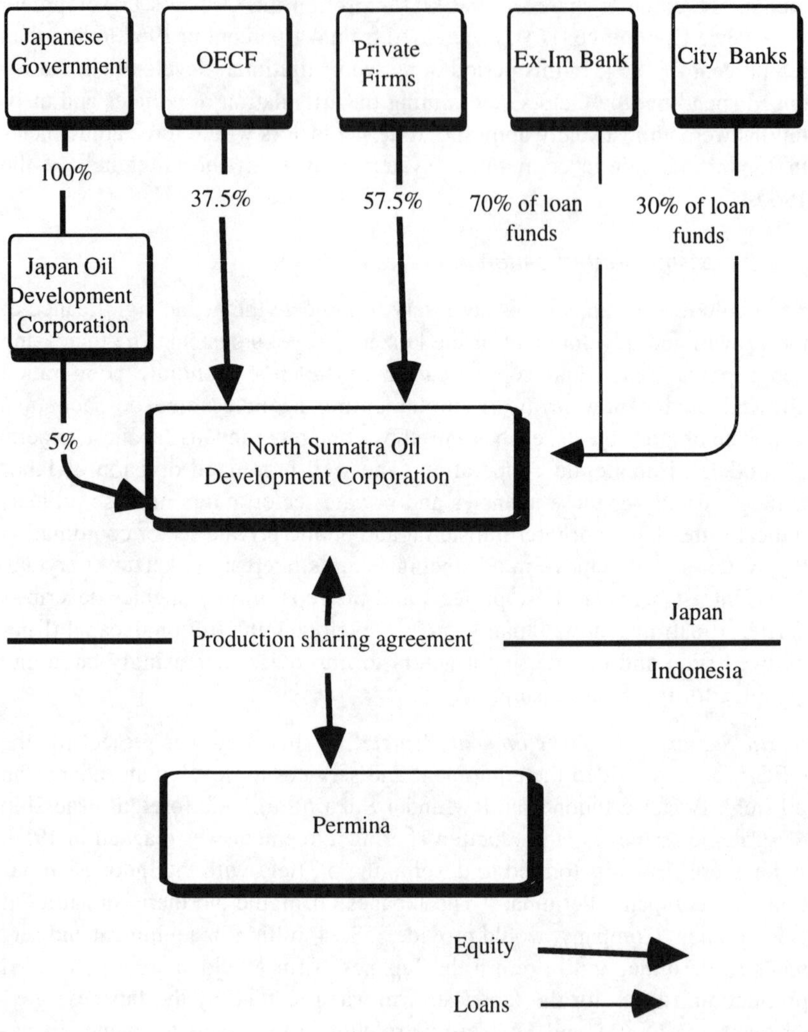

Source: Based on Sakurai, p. 132.

Cabinet approved official financing for the project, and in December 1957 a Japanese investment company called Nihon Usiminas was formed by Japanese steel makers and construction firms in Tokyo. Nihon Usiminas then joined with Brazil's national development bank and national steel company to form a joint venture project management company.

After the OECF was created it injected capital into Nihon Usiminas (24.8 percent ownership share), and Nihon Usiminas continued to obtain working capital loans from the Ex-Im Bank. With this official backing Japanese private firms faced reduced investment costs and risks. Nihon Usiminas' ownership share in the Brazilian project was originally 40 percent, but this was halved to 20.3 percent in 1963 when the Brazilian national development bank bought this share of Japanese ownership to comply with Brazilian laws restricting foreign ownership of Brazilian firms. Interestingly enough, this equity purchase was financed by an unprecedented $17.5 million direct loan from the Ex-Im Bank in 1962. The Ex-Im Bank's terms of reference were amended to authorize this new kind of direct lending activity. After this adjustment, equity was held by the Brazilian government (12.7 percent), private firms (3.1 percent), and the Brazilian Economic Development Bank (63.3 percent). But the fact remained that Japan financed directly or indirectly 84.2 percent of project equity, a fact that facilitated Japanese control over a key supply source for its steel industries (see Figure 3.4).

Besides supplying Japan with iron and iron ore, another important effect of this project was follow-on Japanese investment in Brazil, notably another large iron and steel mill and a large aluminum smelter in the 1970s. Three points set this project apart from the first yen loans. The first is the utilization of the newly established OECF to leverage a Japanese equity position in an overseas resource development project. Second, a huge direct Ex-Im Bank loan was given to a recipient government agency not just for Japanese exports, but also to support direct investment. Finally, a new public-private joint investment formula was devised to create Japanese-controlled natural resource development projects even as developing country restrictions on foreign ownership were being met.

Copper Mining Development in Zaire. This large resource development project addressed the threat of rising resource nationalism in the Third World while successfully penetrating markets previously monopolized by Western countries. For this reason it was viewed in Japan as a major success in Japan's economic cooperation.

Upon achieving independence Zaire declared that all mines would be nationalized by 1966. The Belgian mining firm Union Miniéré refused to negotiate compliance. As a result, in 1967 all of Union Miniéré's assets in Zaire were seized, and it lost its monopoly position inherited from the colonial period. At this moment the Japanese mining firm Nihon Kōgyō stepped in to buy mineral exploration rights in Katanga. Mining geological surveys smuggled out of Zaire during the Katanga rebellion were purchased by a Japanese trading company against just such an opportunity.[95] In 1969 Nihon Kōgyō was joined by the four major Japanese light metal processors and the

Figure 3.4 Minas Gerais Project-Financing Scheme

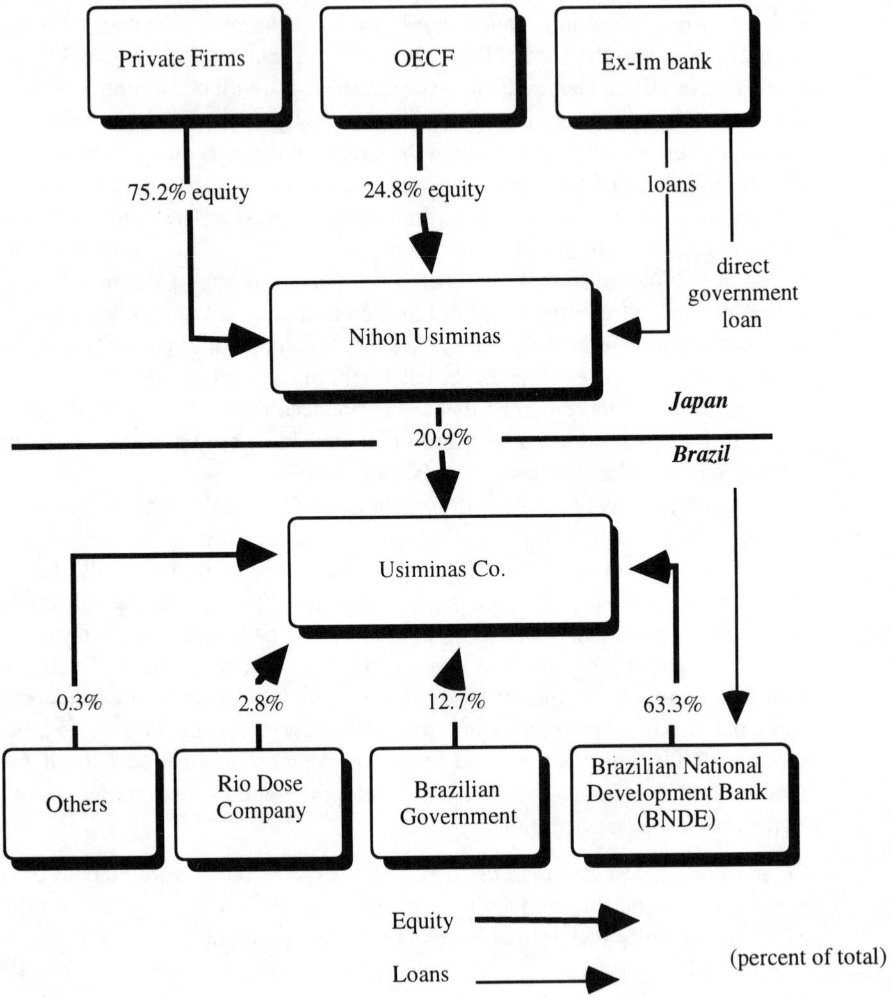

Private Firms

OECF

Ex-Im bank

75.2% equity

24.8% equity

loans

direct government loan

Nihon Usiminas

Japan

20.9%

Brazil

Usiminas Co.

0.3%

2.8%

12.7%

63.3%

Others

Rio Dose Company

Brazilian Government

Brazilian National Development Bank (BNDE)

Equity ——————▶

Loans ——————▶

(percent of total)

Source: Based on Sakurai, p. 125.

Nissho Iwai trading company to form an investment consortium, the Congo Development Mining Company (Codemico) in Tokyo. The OECF and several commercial banks financed its exploration activities.

After finding copper ore deposits Codemico joined with Zairian government to set up the Congo Mining Industry Development Company (Sodemico) in 1969. The Japanese ownership share was 85 percent, and the government held 15 percent, but this government participation was financed by a Japanese capital aid grant, the new type of grant aid made available by OTCA in that year. It was also agreed that Zaire could use Japanese ODA to increase its ownership share to 35 percent within five years of the start of production. The Ex-Im Bank lent funds for mineral development to the Japanese investors in Codemico, as did Japanese commercial banks after receiving repayment guarantees from the Japanese Metals and Mining Agency. Codemico then lent these funds to Sodemico (see Figure 3.5). [96]

Thus, Japan was able to open a new copper ore supply for its light metals industry despite the threat of rising resource nationalism and the entrenched position of Western firms. At the same time, the project satisfied Western demands for more Japanese grant assistance and a broader geographical distribution of Japanese aid. What made this skillful initiative possible was the coordination of the Ex-Im Bank, the OECF, and OTCA with ancillary agencies such as the Metals and Mining Agency and Japanese private banks and firms.

Figure 3.5　Congo Mining Development Project Financing

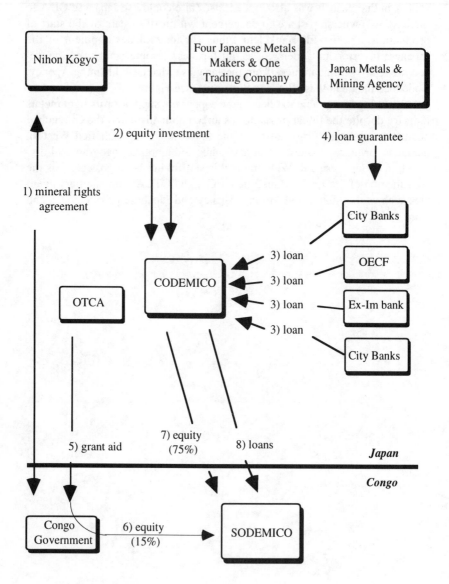

Source: Based on Sakurai, p. 6.

4

ODA Versus
Keizai Kyōryoku

When Japan achieved advanced country status in key international organizations in the mid-1960s, it came under strong foreign pressure to join the Western-organized foreign aid effort. This foreign pressure (gaiatsu) was elicited by Japan's higher political status and economic performance, which obliged it to play appropriate roles in both East-West and North-South dimensions of international relations. Although gaiatsu would have discernible effects on Japan's economic cooperation, fundamental change in the organization of keizai kyōryoku would not occur. Within the system there was not the slightest thought of making Japan's foreign aid noncommercial. Instead, the problem of having to meet Western foreign aid norms became one of altering formal appearances while preserving the substance of the economic cooperation system. The fact that this system was established before gaiatsu intruded into Japanese policymaking matters because a pattern had been established for Japan's economic cooperation with developing countries that would shape Japan's ODA. When Japan assumed the role of an aid donor, the organization and basic policy orientations of its economic cooperation system turned an obligation to assist Third World development into another means of promoting Japan's own economic interests.

THE NORTH-SOUTH DEBATE

At the 1960 UN General Assembly (UNGA) the leaders of the Nonaligned Movement demanded more assistance from the rich nations. The successful Communist revolution in Cuba in 1959, the ongoing crisis in the Belgian Congo, and the start of Communist Chinese foreign aid in 1960 drew Western attention to this demand. This led to the adoption of the United Nations Development Decade program at the 1961 UNGA, in which the rich nations were asked to transfer 1 percent of their GNP to the developing world in the form of grants, loans, and investments, and in which a target annual economic growth rate for the developing world was set at 5 percent.

This new agenda led to the UN Conference on Trade and Development in March 1964 (UNCTAD I), which was convened by the developing countries to discuss their development needs. Japan joined in the deliberations as a member of the rich countries (Group B), thus attaining one of its most important postwar aims, i.e., recognition as one of the advanced industrialized countries. At the same time, the seventy-seven developing countries assembled at UNCTAD (the Group of 77) succeeded in collectively negotiating with the rich nations over issues of global economic management. Aid was a major topic, and during the course of this conference Japan made its first major foreign aid commitment when, as a member of the rich Group B countries, it agreed to transfer resources equivalent to 1.0 percent of its GNP to the Third World.

At the Second UN Conference on Trade and Development (UNCTAD II) held in 1968, the developing world called for a series of measures including commodity agreements, market liberalization, trade preferences for less developed countries (LDCs), special measures for the poorest nations, and at least 1 percent of GNP per annum transferred from the developed nations to the developing world by 1970. The only item gaining general approval was the call for transferring resources equivalent to 1 percent of GNP per year to the developing South, but the significance of this achievement was problematic because there was disagreement as to whether private resource flows at market terms should count.

To identify common ground in the growing North-South debate, two key reports were commissioned in the late 1960s. The first was the Pearson Report published in 1969. This report was commissioned by the World Bank and was drawn up by a seven-member group headed by former Canadian prime minister Lester Pearson; it included representation of Japan by Okita Saburō. This report emphasized the moral aspects of the development issue and called for achievement of the 1 percent of GNP target by 1975, with at least 0.7 percent of GNP given in the form of ODA. The other report was written in 1969 under UN auspices by a committee headed by Jan Tinbergen in preparation for an anticipated UNGA devoted to the theme of a second UN development decade. The approach of the report was to emphasize what was necessary for the developing world to achieve 6–7 percent growth in the 1970s. The emphasis was put on the need for far-reaching policy reforms by recipients and more effective forms of development assistance.

The Pearson and Tinbergen reports formed the basis of the International Development Strategy for the Second UN Development Decade, which was adopted at the twenty-fifth UNGA in the fall of 1970. Among other things this program called for implementation of the Pearson Report's recommendation that 0.7 percent of advanced country GNP be devoted to ODA, and that ODA be untied and more concessional. In the context of this sustained North-South debate, Japan could not escape an obligation to increase its ODA because it now was a rich nation in that debate.

JAPAN IN THE WESTERN ALLIANCE ODA EFFORT

From the beginning of development assistance in Truman's inaugural address, the United States resorted to it as a means of influencing the economic and political development of the Third World. The view that probably best typified the basic policy concept was articulated in a report authored by Max Millikan and W. W. Rostow called "A Proposal: Key to an Effective Foreign Policy."[97] In this view decolonizing Third World societies were fundamentally unstable and easily subverted by communism. To present "a consistent and persuasive alternative" and to promote the "evolution of societies that are stable in the sense that they are capable of rapid change without violence," the United States would help emerging nations through financial as well as technical assistance. The concrete recommendations were (a) the provision of enough capital to meet the absorptive capacity of aid recipients, (b) no tie between economic aid and military pacts, (c) a long and sustained U.S. effort, and (d) the development of new methods for delivering such aid. Thus, to counteract communist influence the United States would have to give a large and steady flow of resources and technical assistance at below market rates to promote Third World economic development.

The United States created the Development Loan Fund (DLF) in 1957 to increase its bilateral aid flows. It also organized a Western aid-giving regime to mobilize the necessary volume of ODA for the long term. The Eisenhower administration created new multilateral mechanisms such as the Inter-American Development Bank, as well as a soft loan facility in the World Bank, the International Development Association (IDA). In January 1960 it reoriented the moribund Organization for European Economic Cooperation (OEEC), the original mandate of which had been to coordinate Europe's receipt of Marshall Plan funds. The United States formed a Development Assistance Group (DAG) within the OEEC, and later in 1960 the OEEC changed its name to the Organization for Economic Cooperation and Development (OECD), for which the new charter mandate was "economic co-operation and consultation designed to facilitate economic development of less-developed countries."[98]

Wishing an even stronger U.S. leadership role, President John F. Kennedy sent a special report on foreign aid to the U.S. Congress in March 1961 stressing the following needs: (1) a long-term U.S. plan for development assistance, (2) the separation of military and economic assistance, (3) the formation of country and regional aid plans, (4) the expansion of joint aid efforts with other advanced countries, and (5) the improvement and consolidation of existing U.S. aid organizations. In the same month Kennedy also announced the Alliance for Progress program, and he requested a total of $4.5 billion from Congress for foreign aid programs. He called for an Agency for International Development (AID) to centralize aid administration, as well as a volunteer technical aid agency, the Peace Corps. These measures were passed in September 1961 in the Foreign Assistance Act.

Under this Kennedy foreign aid initiative, in March 1961 the DAG adopted the Resolution on the Common Aid Effort pledging to (1) increase Western aid, (2) adjust it to recipient country needs, and (3) make it more effective in raising recipient social and economic welfare. The resolution became the charter of the OECD's Development Assistance Committee when it superseded the DAG in October 1961. This committee would play a key role in criticizing Japanese economic cooperation after Japan became a formal OECD member in 1964.

In essence the United States created DAC to help ensure an adequate Western ODA effort. ODA was to have an exclusively developmental purpose, and the more concessional and untied to donor commercial interests, the better would be the quality of aid. DAC established these principles and norms by adopting in 1965 the Recommendation on Financial Terms and Conditions, followed by a supplement in 1969. The supplement defined the concept of "ODA," distinguishing it from "other official flows" (OOF) such as trade credits and from "private flows" such as commercial loans and investments. In addition, the "grant element" formula was introduced whereby the concessionality of ODA could be measured. These principles and concepts would allow DAC to raise and monitor the bilateral ODA of OECD members.

For all its success in organizing and leading a Western aid effort, the United States was unable to sustain its predominant role in bilateral aid giving. As noted by the Clay Commission studying the future of foreign aid, the U.S. burden was disproportionately large, and some of it could be shifted to U.S. allies. In 1965 the share of U.S. ODA in the OECD total was 60 percent; within a decade this figure was halved as the total Western effort increased significantly.

Western Alliance Pressures on Japanese ODA

Sharpening fiscal and monetary travails during the 1960s prompted the United States to shift its foreign aid burden to others, and Japan's growing wealth made it a leading candidate. Japan started the 1960s with the Ikeda Cabinet's National Income-Doubling Plan (Kokumin Shotoku Baizō Keikaku), enacted in November 1960 for the years 1961–1970. The income-doubling target was achieved by 1967, and Japan achieved GNP growth rates of 11.6 percent, per capita personal consumption growth of 9.4 percent, and export growth of 16.8 percent during the decade. Moreover, Japan began to pile up increasingly large trade surpluses, and reserves jumped from $3.5 billion in 1969 to $7.6 billion in June 1971. Japan emerged from the 1960s with internationally competitive steel, auto, machinery, and electronics industrial sectors, a strong surplus balance-of-payments position, and per capita GNP figures comparable to those of Europe.

   With Japan's rapid rise and the development of imbalances in the U.S.
economy, U.S.-Japan relations needed adjustment. By the end of the 1960s
the United States wanted relief from Japanese textile and steel imports, financial liberalization to meet Japan's IMF obligations, and a revaluation of
the yen to cut the Japanese trade surplus. In regional security matters the
United States pressured Japan to do more to support anticommunist forces in
the region, but Japan was unwilling to upgrade security cooperation because
of domestic political considerations. Japan resorted to ODA to signal general
support for Western security aims by participating in the Western consortium
to aid India in 1958, and in other Western aid consortia assisting Pakistan
(1960), Nigeria (1962), Colombia (1963), and Sudan (1963). But these were
largely token gestures designed to improve Japan's image in the West. As the
situation grew more serious in Asia in the mid-1960s, Japan needed to respond to U.S. demands for concrete action. As one concession Japan began
giving significant amounts of aid to South Korea, Taiwan, and Indonesia, and
at the December 1967 Satō-Johnson summit meeting Japan pledged ODA to
"contribute to regional peace and stability."

   In 1964 Japan gained advanced country status in both the GATT and the
IMF, and it achieved membership in the OECD. From this time Japan became
subject to the norms applied to rich donor nations. In 1965 Japan joined other
Western allies in pledging to give 1 percent of GNP to the Third World in the
form of aid and investment and to soften the terms of aid. These pledges were
important because at this time Japan's reparations (which counted as grant
aid) began to decline and its yen loans had a grant element of only about 45
percent.

THE IMPACT OF *GAIATSU* IN THE 1960s

Compared with the 1961–1964 period, the 1965–1970 period saw a threefold
increase in Japan's average ODA level (see Figure 4.1). The overall level increased from $112 million to $361 million per year, with the highest areas of
growth occurring in yen loans (6.3 times) and in contributions to multilateral
organizations (5.7 times). This growth in spending was permitted by the eas-
ing of budget and balance-of-payments constraints, but the impact of gaiatsu
was a critical motivating factor. In this period Japan considered ODA spending "membership dues" *(tsukiai)* owed after joining the OECD and being received as an advanced country.[99]

Diversification of ODA

Reparations payments, which counted as grant aid, began to tail off just as
Japan came under increasing pressure to increase the quantity and quality of
its aid. Japan compensated by changing the OECF's terms of reference to allow it to make yen loans to foreign governments in 1965 and start giving

Figure 4.1 Japanese and DAC ODA, 1961–1970

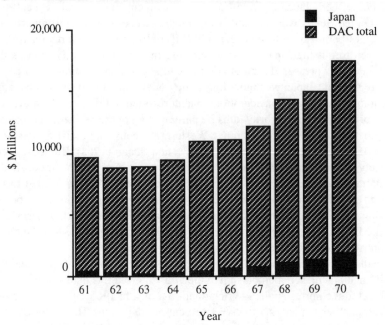

Source: DAC.

nonproject commodity loans in 1966. Commodity loans were meant to help recipients overcome balance-of-payments crises by providing yen to import urgently needed commodities. OTCA's terms of reference were also expanded under international pressures. In 1967 it began administering grant food grain assistance, but it was too little to allow Japan's ODA to meet DAC standards for overall concessionality. Thus, the MFA requested a new program of capital grant assistance as well as a volunteer technical aid program modeled after the Peace Corps. MITI's response was to issue a report stressing the continuing need to develop resources and markets.

By 1969 the conflict was ironed out, and the Japan Overseas Volunteer Corps was put under OTCA supervision, as was the more important capital grant aid program. This program was project oriented and focused on the construction of airports, hydroelectric dams, housing and hospitals for refugees, and the provision of telecommunications equipment and facilities. It was also used to meet U.S. demands for more Japanese burden sharing. In the 1969–1973 period only seven of thirty-five grant aid projects were given to countries other than Laos, Cambodia, Vietnam, and Thailand. In the words of one Japanese analyst, the new program was designed to "kill three birds with one stone" by meeting DAC demands, U.S. demands, and Japan's own export promotion requirements. [100]

As the U.S. ability to give aid declined in the 1960s, a process of shifting the burden to Japan *(katakawari)* got under way. Japan started sizable loan aid programs to South Korea and Indonesia in the mid-1960s as new regimes inaugurated there in 1962 and 1966, respectively, struggled to gain legitimacy. Another step was Japan's active role in establishing a new multilateral development bank, the Asian Development Bank (ADB), in 1965. Also significant was Japan's sponsorship of annual East Asian ministerial meetings on the subject of economic development. These meetings, which were held annually in the 1966–1974 period, focused on Japan's growing role as an aid giver and investor in East Asia, and they produced several Japanese-funded regional projects.

The new matrix of international pressures and opportunities also produced a permanent change in the geographical orientation of Japanese aid. In the 1961–1964 period there were nine yen loan agreements, of which eight were in South Asia. In the 1965–1970 period the number of yen loan projects increased to fifty-two, and the geographical distribution showed considerable change. ODA loans were extended for the first time to Taiwan and South Korea. In addition, precedent-setting loans were given to Iran, Chile, Argentina, Ceylon, Indonesia, Uganda, Yugoslavia, Tanzania, Kenya, Malaysia, Nigeria, Thailand, Afghanistan, Burma, the Philippines, Cambodia, Nepal, and Singapore. Of the total ¥544.6 billion in yen loans, ¥331.6 billion (or 61 percent of the total) was directed to East Asia. Thus, Japan responded to its new international responsibilities by distributing ODA to every developing region in the world, but it moved the weight of aid resources to East Asia, where its own trade and investment activities with developing countries were concentrated (see Figures 4.2 and 4.3).

In terms of the sectoral distribution of ODA loans there was less change. Out of the total of eighty-one yen loan cases, thirty-seven went into hydroelectric dam projects, fifteen to build transportation infrastructure or to procure ships, ten to basic metal production, and eight to telecommunications projects. Besides leaving behind infrastructure assets in recipient countries, this capital-intensive, project-oriented loan program continued the established pattern of subsidizing Japan's engineering consultants, construction firms, and exporters of plant and transportation equipment.

Western Assessments of Japanese ODA

As the OECD began reviewing Japan's ODA, Western analyses of Japan's foreign aid began appearing after 1965. The first was John White's book *Japanese Aid*, which criticizes the hard terms of Japanese aid and argues that narrow economic self-interest motivated Japan's ODA, with some additional consideration given to maintaining relations with the Western nations and to

Figure 4.2 Direct Investment in Developing Countries, 1970

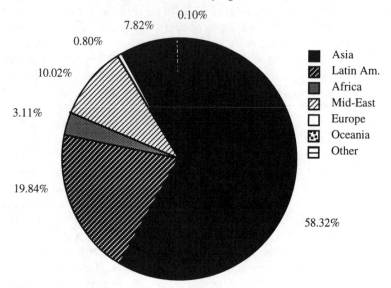

Source: Based on Sakurai, 123.

Figure 4.3 Export Credits to Developing Countries by Region, 1970

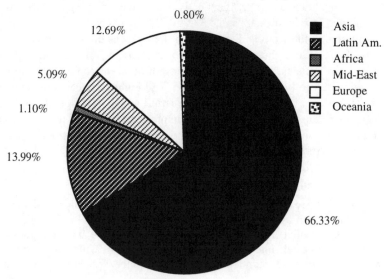

Source: Based on Sakurai, 117.

building international influence.[101] This view was similar to that of Leon Hollerman, who concludes that "clearly, promotion of Japanese exports—especially those of the heavy and chemical industries—is one of its basic objectives." He also notes, "Politically, the objective has been to restore Japan's membership in the club of the 'advanced industrial nations.'"[102]

In the early 1970s one short study suggested that Japan's interest in promoting Asian prosperity and security motivated Japan's ODA,[103] but Hasegawa Sukehiro, a Western-trained Japanese working for the United Nations Development Programme, argues that "while Japanese foreign aid was treated conceptually as a means of assisting its recipient nations in their self-reliance efforts, in reality the aid program was used mostly to realize Japan's potential for her own development and attainment of a proper place in regional and world communities."[104] Other Western analysts of Japan have added their views. In separate works Lawrence Olsen and John Emmerson review Japan's aid program, and they also give greatest weight to the theme of economic self-interest, with some acknowledgment given to Japan's desire to remain a part of the West and to improve regional security.[105] The consensus on Japan's commercial motives implied more than a coincidental relationship between Japan's distribution of ODA and other forms of economic cooperation.

ODA Versus Keizai Kyōryoku

By the end of the 1960s DAC had defined ODA to be noncommercial and recipient needs oriented and had called for more concessional and less tied donor policies. Japan faced a dilemma: the direction of Western norms defining ODA was incompatible with the philosophy inspiring the keizai kyōryoku system. A Japanese expert at this time describes Japan's conception of aid as follows:

> The three pillars of aid *(enjo)* are yen loans, export credits, and private foreign direct investment. They each are directly tied to the expansion of markets and the procurement of resources for Japanese industry. Since loans are in yen they end up paying for imports from our country, but because the money flows to Japanese exporting industries, what goes to recipient countries are Japanese commodities. With export credits, too, the ones who get the money generally are our exporters, and debt goes to the recipient country. It goes without saying that private direct investment is the overseas advance *(shinshutsu)* of Japanese industry.[106]

The place of ODA in keizai kyōryoku is represented in Figure 4.4.

The sharpening contradiction between the evolving OECD conception of noncommercial, untied ODA and Japan's keizai kyōryoku first created a problem in 1967 when, as mentioned earlier, the MFA requested a new grant aid program. MITI insisted that such aid be used to augment keizai kyōryoku. A compromise allowed grant aid to expand Japan's ODA coverage to include

Figure 4.4 The Composition of *Keizai Kyōryoku*

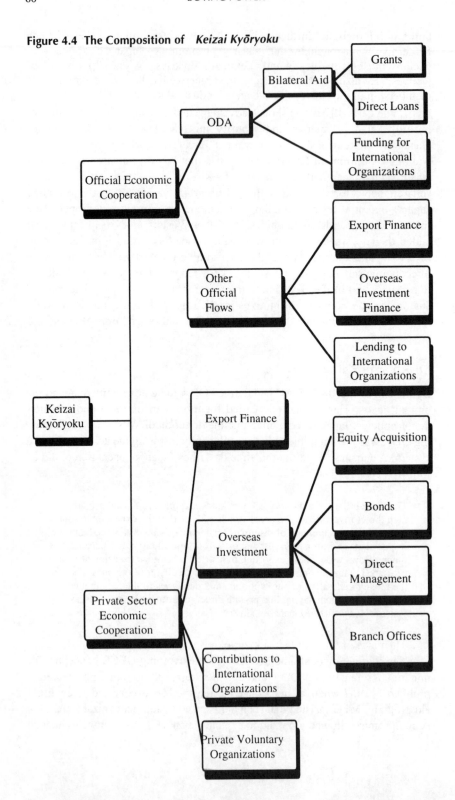

uncreditworthy countries and nonproduction sectors, but it would be fully tied and still associated with capital-intensive projects that subsidized targeted Japanese industries. Thus, instead of giving money or technical assistance directly to governments, Japan would give grants in kind in the form of hospitals, technical training centers, and other nonindustrial projects that involved Japanese trading companies, consulting firms, construction firms, and equipment manufacturers. This incident made clear, nonetheless, that Western ODA norms could interfere with keizai kyōryoku (as they were intended to do) just as Japan turned to shaping policies for its own next stage of development.

Because of its growing trade surpluses and weak domestic consumption, it was clear that Japan would become a capital exporter in the 1970s. The availability of surplus capital coincided with a new Japanese interest in foreign direct investment (FDI). Rising labor and land costs were a threat to the international competitiveness of certain Japanese industries, and industrial pollution threatened domestic health and safety. At the same time, Japan's new status as the world's largest importer of natural resources was a concern in view of the Third World's growing resource nationalism. This would require more numerous and dispersed resource development and offshore processing projects. Thus, it was not surprising that by the late 1960s Japanese experts were urging the promotion of economic cooperation with Asia to exploit economic complementarities and participate in its anticipated growth.[107] In 1969 Japanese finance minister Fukuda Takeo stated that Japan would double its FDI, ODA, and other official trade and investment credits in Southeast Asia within five years.[108] To accommodate FDI growth, in 1970 MOF began automatic approval of FDI projects valued under $1 million.

As Japan stepped up its economic cooperation with Asia, the Keizai Dō yūkai (one of the four major associations representing big business interests in Japan) issued a report in 1968 calling for a new aid ministry or agency that would centralize control and maintain policy coherence. At the same time it called for further private sector utilization in future aid planning. But it was left to officially commissioned policy deliberation councils to create a framework in which keizai kyōryoku could be reconciled with Western ODA norms.

The Taigai Keizai Kyōryoku Shingikai

In order to deliberate the new tasks facing Japan's keizai kyōryoku, in 1969 the Taigai Keizai Kyōryoku Shingikai was reorganized. The group was chaired by the president of the Japan Chamber of Commerce and Industry, but it was actually managed by the vice-chair, Okita Saburo. During its activities in the 1969–1976 period it issued six reports and several opinions at the formal request of the prime minister.

The council was broadly charged by then–Prime Minister Satō Eisaku in March 1970 with the following: "I request the views of this esteemed council on those basic matters that should be considered as, in accordance with our recent economic expansion and rise in international status, we promote economic cooperation in the 1970s." In the elaboration of this request the following three key issues were identified:

> In deliberating the advance of our economic cooperation policy, one item raised that is especially problematic is the nature of aid. In this regard, as DAC and the Pearson Commission report pointed out, there is the problem of aid type, quantity, and conditions.
> Moreover, there is the problem of technical cooperation. It is said that compared with that of other advanced countries, our technical cooperation is still at a low level. Making our excellent technologies useful to the development of the developing countries is an item of importance.
> Finally, there is the question of how to combine trade, private investment, and aid in a skillful manner. This will become a key point in future economic cooperation policy. [109]

On the first main issue, in May 1970 the council recommended fulfilling an existing pledge to increase "aid" (i.e., the sum of ODA, other official flows, and private investment flows) to one percent of GNP by 1975, but it did not recommend any ODA target. It did, however, generally favor a quantitative increase and an improvement in concessionality. Then in September 1970 it was asked for guidance on how to meet demands for aid untying on the eve of a DAC ministerial meeting. An IDE aid expert put the problem as follows:

> For example, if a contract bid on a project funded by our aid money was won by West Germany, this would amount to nothing more than us assuming the burden of financing plant exports by West Germany. Our 'national consensus' would certainly be lost. [110]

The council's response was that Japan should agree to untied aid in principle "in order not to lose international trust and faith in our country," but that concrete measures should be put off to the future. Steps were needed to ensure that Japanese contractors would win bids on Japanese-funded aid projects even after financing became formally untied. The council's recommendations featured the nurturing of engineering consulting firms, involvement in recipient country development planning through technical cooperation, promotion of plant exports, and support of private sector identification of aid projects. In 1972 Japan agreed to allow developing country firms to bid for Japanese aid contracts (LDC-untied), but this had little practical effect on untying Japanese aid because Japanese firms were more competitive. In 1978 the government endorsed the principle that aid should be fully untied, but as of 1994 it has not yet attained this goal.

With regard to technical cooperation, in July 1970 the council responded by noting that Japan's technical cooperation was only 1.2 percent of its ODA (compared with the DAC average of 21.0 percent). It recommended that Japan broaden technical cooperation beyond its project implementation to include recipient government development planning as well as educational and research training. It was hoped this would "make possible an image change in our economic cooperation."[111]

On the more effective coordination of ODA, trade, and private investment, in December 1970 the council urged that Japan's project consulting firms be nurtured and strengthened to enable them to win bids when contract bidding became untied and competitive. This was important because Japanese-designed projects would have specifications favoring bids by Japanese contractors. The council also recommended that the OECF and the Ex-Im Bank eliminate overlapping activities. Thus, DAC pressures to untie loans would affect only the OECF and not the Ex-Im Bank. Finally, the council called for an aid minister to preside over a centralized aid agency or ministry in order to have better speed and coordination in decisionmaking.

The longer-term issue of coordinating trade, investment, and ODA in the face of DAC pressures was complex. A larger report on this topic was issued in September 1971 that has the following rationale for economic cooperation:

> Trade and investment can be expected to promote economic development in developing countries, and . . . our country can acquire necessary resources or goods from developing countries that are cheaper than domestically produced ones. Also, there is the benefit of expanding our export markets. With investment we can develop necessary natural resources, and with respect to our increasingly serious shortages of labor and factory sites, we have the benefit of asking for better conditions for setting up production.[112]

The report advocates adjusting the mix of ODA, trade, and investment to increase the effectiveness of keizai kyōryoku. An example of what is meant is a rough scheme of keizai kyōryoku strategies for different types of developing countries devised by the Ex-Im Bank at this time:

- High growth/low debt (e.g., Malaysia, Thailand): Rely on FDI and export credits supplemented by less concessional loans.
- High growth/high debt (Korea): Jointly use FDI and somewhat concessional ODA. ODA to be targeted at projects strengthening foreign exchange–earning sectors.
- Low growth/low debt (Burma): Somewhat concessional ODA targeted at technical aid or infrastructure.
- Low growth/high debt (India, Indonesia): Concessional ODA targeted at resource development projects that pay for themselves.[113]

Greater effectiveness also meant orienting ODA toward the construction of infrastructure projects to support more Japanese private sector direct investment and trade activities:

> To raise effectiveness it is essential to plan the efficient linkage of private

economic activity and official aid in projects. For example, in cases of private direct investment, use "ODA" to build railways, roads, etc., to transport raw materials and manufactured goods, and to carry out regional development cooperation to nurture local enterprises that will raise local living standards and diversify surrounding industries based on resource development. With regard to trade, build ports and roads in the relevant areas to promote commodity imports. Finally, one must consider projects identified by private firm initiative when providing "ODA."[114]

MITI's Industrial Structure Council

If the managers of the keizai kyōryoku system represented in the Taigai Keizai Kyōryoku Shingikai agreed that ODA should remain integral to keizai kyōryoku, what would orient keizai kyōryoku? The Industrial Structure Council organized by MITI and composed of bureaucratic and private sector representatives recognized the importance of keizai kyōryoku to the development of Japan's trade and industry. At the start of the 1970s Japanese FDI was projected to increase to $3.5 billion by 1980, with over half of it directed to the developing world. The Industrial Structure Council recommended that the ODA component of economic cooperation be used to guide FDI into natural resource processing, joint ventures, technical training, and the cultivation of goodwill.[115] The Subcommittee on the International Economy of the Industrial Structure Council (Sangyō Kōzō Shingikai Kokusai Keizai Bukai) published a report in 1972 that was focused on the use of economic cooperation to upgrade Japan's industrial structure.[116] The report recommends that Japan's growing current account surplus should be used to finance outward direct investment that would improve the competitiveness of Japan's industrial firms and enhance Japan's economic security and influence.

Japan's position in the international division of labor was expressed as follows:

1. The division of labor with developing countries
     In relations with the developing countries, it is not only necessary to have a vertical division of labor with a simple exchange of industrial goods for primary products. It is also necessary to plan an upgraded international division of labor by allowing the step-by-step transfer of simple labor-intensive industries, the local processing of natural resources, and the expansion of finished and semifinished imports; while expanding the provision from our country of advanced industrial goods, plants, technology, capital, and so on.
2. The division of labor with advanced countries
     Meanwhile, among the advanced countries of the same degree of industrialization, because of the increase and diversity of domestic demand caused by the move toward a mass consumption industrialized society, and despite the production of similar kinds of goods, we must expand horizontal relations based on commodities that are distinguished by such features as design, efficiency, type, and so on.[117]

In essence the report concluded that Japan should use economic cooperation to move Japanese industries to developing countries in order to upgrade
Japan's industrial structure. The efficacy of keizai kyōryoku in this process is
described as follows:

> Realizing a rational international division of labor
> Keizai kyōryoku can really make this come about; in order for developing
> countries to continue their economic growth it is necessary for appropriate
> industries to take root there. Thus it goes without saying that we should
> promote every type of keizai kyōryoku and import expansion policy.
> Furthermore, while actively cooperating to nurture those industries needed
> and appropriate for developing countries, and by planning as smooth as
> possible a domestic industrial adjustment, a strongly desired rational in-
> ternational division of labor system and good complementary industrial
> structures can be formed. [118]

Japanese Commentary on Keizai Kyōryoku Policy

At this turning point in Japan's external policies, several volumes in Japanese
dealing explicitly with the future of keizai kyōryoku appeared offering
similar appraisals of existing policy, but different prescriptions. One Japanese
analyst concludes, "One can say that there have been successive changes:
first were reparations as 'expiation' *(shokuzai)* for the war; next were
'membership dues' *(tsukiai)* owed after joining the OECD and being received
as an advanced country; and most recently there is the self-generated and
positive 'drive overseas'*(shinshutsu)*." [119] Writing in 1971 as the new policy
consensus was being articulated, he suggests that ODA should be used to
promote FDI in the following new ways:

- FDI to create Japanese-owned export platforms in developing coun-
  tries;
- FDI to lower labor costs for Japanese firms;
- FDI to remove polluting industries from Japan. [120]

In a 1973 volume, Shishido Toshio, a former EPA research bureau director, notes that by 1980 Japan was expected to supply 40 percent of Southeast
Asia's imports, absorb over 25 percent of its exports, and provide 50 percent
of its ODA. By 1983 Japan was expected to surpass the United States in annual FDI flows to this region. Thus, the issue for Japan was how best to shape
these growing intra-Asian flows for maximum mutual benefit. He notes that
in the 1970s Southeast Asian industrial labor supply would increase rapidly
because of rising agricultural productivity and population growth, and so
employment expansion would be a critical task. Meanwhile, Japan would experience the following: rapid GNP growth, a growing land and labor shortage, growth in the service sector, and worsening industrial pollution. To
shape a rational regional division of labor ensuring mutual benefit, Japan's
economic cooperation policies should ensure that its capital outflow be used

to move labor-intensive production and polluting industries to Southeast Asia, taking care to provide pollution control equipment and improved technology transfer opportunities. [121]

In contrast to the bureaucratic policy thinking exemplified above, other knowledgeable Japanese called for a fundamental change in policy orientation. For example, the Asia research group of the conservative *Sankei Shimbun* wrote a detailed volume condemning Japan's aid efforts in Southeast Asia as nothing more than an alliance of the Japanese government and private sector in a battle against Western corporations for the control of markets and resources there. In the conclusion a Japanese trading company man is quoted declaring, "What Japan is doing is not aid. It is business." [122] The main concern expressed in this volume is that Japan's reparations and ODA were so out of touch with any effort to improve living standards in Southeast Asia that anti-Japanese sentiment was growing. In this sense it foretold the hostile reception Prime Minister Tanaka Kakuei would receive when he toured Southeast Asia in 1974.

A career journalist retired from the *Japan Times* also published a book critical of Japanese diplomacy toward Asia because Japan "could attach importance to [Asia] only as a market supporting the Japanese economy." With regard to the broader North-South issue, he criticizes Japan for thinking only in terms of "aid either as export promotion or as a membership fee to the club of advanced countries." Japan was unable to think in larger terms because of the voraciousness of a private sector likened to "a hyena that would eat its own siblings" and a bureaucracy unable to see beyond petty organizational interests. He describes bureaucratic relations as follows:

> The MFA wants to present a good face to other advanced countries or else wishes to buy a leadership position in Asia with money. MITI uses [ODA] as an export expansion weapon. MOF cautiously checks the international payments and fiscal burden, using suppliers credits and private money to fill gaps as much as possible. Now that the surplus balance of payments has become a problem it will use aid as an expedient to reduce the surplus (but because increased aid merely increases exports this will not cut the surplus). [123]

Although he correctly saw that Japan had an opportunity to broaden its foreign policy in the 1970s, he forlornly concluded in 1973 that "instead of the slogan 'export or die' the new slogan 'resources or die' defines the national interest." [124]

In sum, foreign pressure and criticism of Japan's ODA in the latter half of the 1960s did elicit change. Japan increased ODA volume and concessionality and broadened the type and distribution of ODA. But external pressure on Japan to conform to Western ODA standards could not destroy or circumvent the institutional and ideological basis of Japan's keizai kyōryoku. This policymaking system would differentiate ODA from other categories of keizai kyōryoku as required by DAC, but it would not cease to coordinate

ODA with other keizai kyōryoku elements to achieve Japan's own developmental objectives.

To avoid misunderstanding here two points should be emphasized. First, Japan's ODA was not intended solely for Japan's benefit, but the nature of the keizai kyōryoku system that administered Japan's ODA ensured that it would at least contribute to Japan's own developmental interests. Second, Japan's aims in economic cooperation were not fixed and unchanging. In fact, they were affected by changing internal and external circumstances—as when Japan began promoting FDI in manufacturing and services from the end of the 1960s. The implementation of ODA by the keizai kyōryoku system did, however, involve an inherent conflict between appearance and reality that was managed by keeping policy deliberations within the system from public view.

5

Keizai Kyōryoku in the 1970s

By the end of the 1970s the MFA could point to ODA spending figures that indicated significant progress toward meeting DAC ODA norms. Nevertheless, these superficial indicators of change masked underlying institutional continuities that did not change the character of Japan's ODA so much as refine existing modes of implementation. Japan's ODA in the 1970s developed better coordination with Japan's trade and investment needs along the general lines advocated by the Taigai Keizai Kyōryoku Shingikai and the Industrial Structure Council. If anything the unanticipated first oil shock only pressed Japan harder to find innovative ways of using ODA for its own structural adjustment and economic security needs.

MEETING WESTERN ODA NORMS

At the start of the decade it was clear that Japan would have to deal with an image problem. Aside from the perception of having selfish motives in aid giving, Japan also fell below objective DAC standards for ODA. The 1969 OECD recommendations on improving the quality of Western bilateral aid stipulated that 70 percent of total ODA commitments be grants, that 85 percent of ODA be greater than 61 percent concessionality, or that the softest 85 percent of ODA be 85 percent concessional. By 1972 only 33 percent of Japan's bilateral ODA was in the form of grants, only 40 percent was over 61 percent concessional, and only the softest 67 percent was above 85 percent concessional. Among DAC members Japan joined only Portugal and Italy in failing to meet these standards.

Japan's image was significantly improved by the first ODA-doubling plan *(enjo baizō keikaku)* implemented 1978–1980. Although Japan's ODA still did not meet the DAC average in any key dimension by 1980, the rapid pace of improvement mollified foreign critics. Japan's ODA grew from a figure of $511 million in 1971 to $3.3 billion in 1980. Up to 1978 Japan's ODA/GNP ratio held steady at about 0.23 percent, but the aid-doubling plan brought the ratio to 0.32 percent by 1980 (compared with the 1980 DAC average of 0.37), and its share of total DAC ODA grew from 6 percent in 1976 to 13 percent in 1980 (see Figure 5.1).

Figure 5.1 Japan's ODA as Percent of GNP and Percent of DAC ODA, 1970–1980

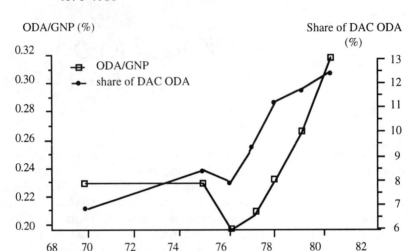

Grant aid increased markedly to compensate for the ending of reparations in 1977. It retained a focus on Indochina as well as a focus on projects such as schools, hospitals, and technical training centers, but it expanded its geographic range. Japan's grant aid increased to 40 percent of its bilateral ODA (still below the DAC average of 75.6 percent). In technical assistance, spending grew from $27.7 million to $277.8 million. This raised its share in bilateral ODA from 5.4 percent to 8.4 percent, but this was still well below the DAC average of 20.4 percent in 1980.

Japan also struggled to improve the quality of its ODA. In 1972 DAC raised the minimum standard for concessionality to 84 percent, and this was raised again in 1978 to 86 percent. By 1980 Japan's ODA concessionality improved to 74.3 percent. The concessionality of Japan's bilateral loan program improved from a 1966–1971 average of 33.53 percent to an average of 48.74 percent in the 1971–1975 period. By 1980 loan concessionality had reached 56.1 percent, but this was still significantly below the DAC average of 74.3 percent. Japan made modest progress toward untying its bilateral ODA when it gave its first LDC-untied loan to Burma in 1971 and promised to give more LDC-untied loans from 1972. By 1978 Japan agreed that full untying of aid loans was desirable and promised to move in this direction. By 1980 less than half remained fully tied.

The geographic orientation of Japanese ODA widened beyond Asia to achieve a global profile. In 1970, 98.3 percent of new commitments were in Asia, but by 1980 this share was reduced to 70.6 percent. In terms of sectoral orientation it remained as before in capital-intensive project construction, mainly in mineral and energy development, metal production, transportation infrastructure, hydroelectric dams, and telecommunications. Japan responded to the rise of the basic human needs (BHN) aid philosophy, which made poverty alleviation a priority, by raising the amount and concessionality of its ODA to the least less developed countries (LLDCs). In 1980 concessionality reached 80 percent, compared with the DAC average of 96.7 percent.

INSTITUTIONAL DEVELOPMENT

The image of Japan's ODA in the 1970s changes somewhat if one turns attention from financial categories to the development of institutional structures. What did *not* happen here is significant. There was no reorganization of the policymaking and implementation system to segregate ODA from private sector trade and investment activity as required by DAC norms, nor was there a streamlining of the system as demanded by certain domestic actors. Instead of major structural reforms, change mainly occurred at the level of implementing agencies, which extended the system's established functions and principles. In other words, the keizai kyōryoku system had become so entrenched as to permit only minor incremental changes.

The Pattern of Incremental Change

In the 1970s it was not only external pressures to change the character of economic cooperation that were resisted. There were internal pressures as well. The idea of creating an "aid ministry" or "aid agency" was first initiated by the private sector and then supported by the Taigai Keizai Ky ōryoku Shingikai. However, sectional rivalry among the yonshōchō would not allow them to formulate a plan to implement the policy recommendation. The status quo was challenged in 1972 when MAFF formulated a budget request to start up its own technical cooperation agency outside of OTCA (which was under MFA supervision). The MFA successfully resisted the original proposal but failed to kill the idea because MAFF, with the support of agricultural constituencies, succeeded in gaining MOF approval for funding to study the idea.

In the 1973 budget request MAFF renewed its proposal, and this time MITI followed MAFF's example and requested funding for its own technical cooperation agency, too. Private sector interest groups related to MITI and MAFF gave strong support because more benefits would flow toward them if they had exclusive control over technical cooperation in their respective areas.

Debate over the proposals arose within the LDP, and the MFA, which lacks numerous supporters among the LDP Diet members, placed the debate in a more favorable forum by registering its strong opposition in the Cabinet through then–Foreign Minister Masayoshi Ohira, who tended to be strongly supportive of the MFA.

At about this time the North-South debate sharpened and the oil shock occurred, giving rise to worries about resource nationalism in the developing world. Then in January 1974 Prime Minister Tanaka Kakuei went on his historic visit to Southeast Asia, where in Indonesia and Thailand rioting students endangered the safety of his entourage. Faced with the need to strengthen Japan's aid effort, Tanaka sought to transcend the bureaucratic wrangling by pushing for the creation of a Cabinet-level aid agency. This idea was successfully vetoed by MOF, which guarded jealously its control over the Ex-Im Bank and OECF.

Thus, the focus of the problem returned to the dispute between the MFA, MITI, and MAFF in the area of technical cooperation. Because these bureaucracies each had the ability to obstruct agreement, a face-saving compromise was the only feasible solution. It was decided to retain the idea of a new umbrella organization but to scale it down to a subsidiary agency (tokushū hōjin) status to include both grant and technical aid. The merit of this proposal was that each ministry could be given jurisdictions inside the new agency, but problems arose over the "scrap-and-build" policy enforced by the Administrative Management Agency and the issue of official jurisdiction over the new agency. The "scrap-and-build" policy meant that before a new agency could be authorized, two already extant agencies would have to be abolished or absorbed by the new bureaucracy. At the same time, the MFA was determined to retain its formal control over the nonloan area of Japan's ODA, but the price would be high.

The solution to this wrangle was worked out within the Cabinet. The MFA agreed to scrap two of its own existing ODA-funded agencies, OTCA and JEMIS (the Japan Emigration Service, an agency that sent "homeless" Japanese repatriated from former colonial possessions to new homes overseas, mostly in Latin America), to allow the creation of the new agency, the Japan International Cooperation Agency (JICA). In addition, the MFA would have to yield actual control over agricultural and industrial technical cooperation activities to MAFF and MITI, respectively, and would have to allow other ministries to share in the implementation of ODA in their respective areas of jurisdiction. This accounts for the present distribution of *amakudari* and *shukko* posts within JICA among the various ministries (see Chapter 7). In return for these sacrifices, the MFA would retain official jurisdiction over OTCA's successor and would gain a small loan program to be administered through JICA.

The compromise that produced JICA addressed the substantive concerns of each ministry, but compared with the initial proposals by MAFF and MITI or the subsequent radical proposal for a central aid ministry made by Prime Minister Tanaka, the end result saw only a relatively modest change in the structure of the system. JICA was similar to OTCA in that the MFA, MITI, and MAFF shared control over implementation (e.g., in OTCA, the MFA had the post of senior executive director, whereas MITI and MAFF each named one executive director), but it differed in that other ministries were more strongly represented. [125] Thus, despite the efforts of two powerful ministries and a prime minister to reform the system, the net result was relatively minor. The existing balance of interests represented by the system and the resulting inertia of institutionalized policies and procedures allowed only incremental change that reinforced the old principle of decentralized interministerial co-ordination. [126] This modest outcome also reflects the fact that the policy de-bate took place outside of the Diet, thereby excluding the opposition parties and citizen's groups that might have favored radical change.

If change against the grain of institutionally included interests was im-possible, change in the direction of the system's existing mandate did occur. At the level of implementing agencies several new specialized agencies were created, including the Kokusai Kaihatsu Sentaa (International Development Center, or IDC) established in 1971. This center was under the guidance of six ministries (i.e., MFA, MITI, MAFF, MOC, MOT, and MPT) to help cen-tralize and coordinate ODA-funded technical training and country-specific policy research programs. Another new agency was the Kokusai Kōryū Kikin (Japan Foundation) established in 1972 under the supervision of the MFA and MEd. An important part of this agency's mission was to promote cultural diplomacy and educational exchange under the ODA budget. Table 5.1 is a list of significant ODA-funded implementing agencies and government-su-pervised nonprofit groups established in the 1970s. Based on the premise that institutional innovation reflects the direction of actual policy, this list indi-cates the trend toward greater technical cooperation and policy research, with the MFA, MITI, and MAFF being the most assertive.

ADJUSTING TO THE FIRST OIL SHOCK

Before turning to specific examples of how Japan used ODA to enhance its economic competitiveness and security after the oil shock, we should briefly review the mechanism for introducing and authorizing new policy directions. In August 1975 the Taigai Keizai Kyōryoku Shingikai confirmed new policy priorities in the wake of the first oil shock. As a general principle its report states:

> As the need arises development cooperation should be comprehensively promoted via the planned integration and linkage of technology and finance, and ODA and private sector activities. Greater attention should be paid to increasing the leveraging effect of every type of cooperation. [127]

It then makes five specific recommendations. First, Japan should raise its ODA/GNP ratio to the DAC average (0.33 percent in 1974). Second, Japan should fit economic cooperation to the characteristics of the recipient. Third, Japan should emphasize large-scale industrial projects where infrastructure,

Table 5.1 New Implementing Organizations Established in the 1970s

Name	Function	Supervisor	Year
Japan Overseas Development Corporation (JODC)	Small and medium-sized industry FDI promotion	MITI	1970
International Development Center (IDC)	Technical cooperation	MOC, MAFF, MOT, MPT, MFA, MITI	1971
Japan Foundation	Cultural and educational exchange	MFA, MEd	1972
Japan Cooperation Center for the Middle East	Energy policy research	MITI	1973
Japan Transport Consultants Association	Technical cooperation	MOT	1973
Japan Overseas Fishery Cooperation Foundation	Technical cooperation	MAFF	1973
Japan Institute of Middle Eastern Economies	Economic policy research	MITI	1974
JICA [a]	Grant and technical cooperation	MFA	1974
Association for Promotion of International Cooperation (APIC)	Foreign policy research	MFA	1975
Agricultural Development Consultants Association	Technical cooperation	MAFF	1977

Source: OECF.
Note: a. Not a net gain for the MFA because JICA replaced OTCA and JEMIS—both of which were under MFA supervision.

plant equipment, and technical cooperation complement each other. The report notes, "In these types of projects, there is great need for the linkage of official cooperation and private sector activities, as well as government financial backing of the private sector, but there are many areas that need improvement in the decisionmaking and implementation systems."[128] This priority reflected an effort to move larger volumes of ODA and FDI in project packages that would have a positive impact on Japan's industrial structure. In the 1965–1970 period there were 68 large-scale project loans (¥8.3 billion average per case); in the 1971–1976 period the number more than doubled to 172 with an average size of ¥10.4 billion.[129] By the 1979–1984 period there were 226 big projects at an average loan amount of ¥15.1 billion. The Asahan project described later in this chapter is a model of success from the Japanese viewpoint.

Fourth, Japan should use ODA to subsidize the international activities of Japan's project design consultants to improve their ability to compete against Western firms in open bidding. Finally, Japanese government officials should take every opportunity to include Japanese private sector personnel in talks with recipient country officials and business executives. These findings signaled Japan's intention to respond to external pressures by pledging ODA increases. At the same time, the Shingikai was unwilling to disengage ODA from keizai kyōryoku.

If the Shingikai registered a new policy consensus among the structurally included elements in the keizai kyōryoku system, the Cabinet's function was to enact the necessary legal authorizations. The first Cabinet council on economic cooperation was the ad hoc Taigai Keizai Kyōryoku Kakuryō Kondankai (External Economic Cooperation Cabinet Deliberation Council) formed in May 1969.[130] It was reorganized in 1973, and in July 1975 the ad hoc Taigai Keizai Kyōryoku Kakuryō Kyōgikai (External Economic Cooperation Cabinet Council) began meeting to approve various ODA-related initiatives. On it sat the chief Cabinet secretary, the chief of the prime minister's office, and the ministers of the EPA, MFA, MOF, MAFF, and MITI. Others were included as needed. In its first action it authorized a revision of the OECF and the Ex-Im Bank activities, making the OECF solely responsible for ODA loans. Another ad hoc Cabinet-level council was formed in 1977 to deal with foreign criticism of Japan's trade surpluses. This council, the Keizai Taisaku Kakuryō Kaigi (the Economic Countermeasures Cabinet Council), approved in December 1977 the general principle of using ODA pledges to meet criticism of Japan's trade surpluses. One should note that in all this there was no substantive role played by the Diet in policy formulation. Its role was limited to legal measures to alter or establish new terms of reference for implementing agencies.

ODA and Energy Security

The 1973 oil shock presented the challenge of improving Japan's stable access to petroleum and petroleum products. As is evident in its economic diplomacy toward China and the Arab world in the 1970s, Japan successfully used its ODA to secure energy from these sources—even as this effort also met Japan's pledges to increase its ODA.

Japan paid special attention to improving its access to Arab oil. Immediately following the oil shock Japan sent a barrage of high-level emissaries to Middle Eastern and Northern African countries to improve Japan's image and economic presence. Between December 1973 and February 1974 Deputy Prime Minister Miki Takeo, MITI minister Nakasone Yasuhiro, and Special Ambassador Kosaka Zentaro toured the Middle East and Northern Africa to make ODA commitments directly or indirectly related to petroleum access. This effort increased the share of Japanese ODA going to the Middle East and Africa from 2.7 percent in 1973 to a peak of 29.0 percent in 1978. The commitments to various countries made during these three trips are summarized below:

Iran: Bandar Khomeini Petrochemical Complex (a total Japanese investment of ¥100 billion, of which the OECF provides ¥36.2 billion in equity and an additional ¥28.8 billion in loans).

Iraq: Agreement on a ¥298 billion ODA loan package to finance six plant projects including liquefied petroleum gas (LPG), fertilizer, and cement plants.
                     A technical training agreement to support plant projects.
                     A ten-year agreement to supply Japan with 90 million tons of crude oil and 1.2 million tons of LPG and petroleum products annually.

Saudi Arabia: Agreement to train 400 Saudi experts and students.
                     Expansion of a vocational training center.

Algeria: Telecommunications project (financed by a ¥12 billion ODA loan).

Morocco: A ¥3.0 million yen ODA loan agreement.

Egypt: ¥38 billion yen ODA loan for Suez Canal improvements.
                     Promise to give a ¥15 billion commodity loan and a ¥15 billion project loan within two years.

Sudan: ¥3.0 billion ODA loan agreement.

Jordan: Telecommunications project (¥3.0 billion ODA loan).

Syria: ¥27 billion oil refinery project financed by ODA and commercial loans.

Bolstered by an official visit to Saudi Arabia by Prime Minister Fukuda in 1978, Japan began planning two more large-scale projects. One was the ¥330 billion Al Jubail petrochemical complex, in which Japan's ownership share was ¥48 billion, of which the OECF would contribute 45 percent. The other was a $255 million methanol plant, of which Japan's ownership share was $77 million. The OECF would contribute 30 percent of the Japanese share.

Economic Cooperation with China

Starting with normalization in 1972, Japan sought to create a stable basis for economic relations, but China wanted favorable terms and a political price from Japan. In 1978 Japan signed a ten-year long-term trade agreement featuring Chinese oil and coal in exchange for Japanese plants and equipment, and Chinese orders were placed for petrochemical plants with four Japanese firms. Also in 1978 a peace and friendship treaty was signed with China that contained an "antihegemony clause" implicitly directed against the Soviet Union. Within a year informal agreement was reached on a list of ODA infrastructure projects that would facilitate China's export of energy to Japan and the import of Japanese plants and equipment.

In December 1979, on the occasion of Prime Minister Ohira's visit to China, Japan pledged to assist with the following six projects: (1) Shijiusuo port construction, (2) railway construction between Yangzhou and Shijiusuo, (3) railway construction between Beijing and Qinhuangdao, (4) Qinhuangdao port construction, (5) railway construction between Hengyang and Guangzhou, and (6) construction of a hydroelectric power station at Wuqiang. Japan would extend loans for these projects annually at bilateral working-level meetings. For the first year (FY 1979) Japan extended an untied ODA loan of ¥50 billion. In December 1980 at the bilateral Cabinet-level meeting in Beijing, the second ODA loan commitment of ¥56 billion was signed. This custom of signing yearly loan agreements to finance ongoing projects has continued to the present and has sustained regular high-level contacts between Japan and China.

As anticipated by the general ODA policy guidelines set at the start of the 1970s, this infrastructure-oriented ODA has provided a foundation for Japan's *shinshutsu* into the growing Chinese market in the 1980s and 1990s. For example, in the first ODA loan pledge, signed when Japanese prime minister Ohira and China's leader, Hua Guofeng, met in Beijing in 1979, two of the six economic infrastructure projects related to the port of Shijiusuo on the Shandong Peninsula, where Japanese firms built a port and a railway link to the city of Yangzhou financed by OECF loans. In 1988, taking advantage of the new infrastructure and a new joint venture law giving more rights to foreign investors, the Japanese government and five Japanese steel makers announced plans to construct a ¥600 billion ($4.5 billion) steel plant in Shijiusuo with an annual output capacity of 3.5 million tons. A substantial part of the construction funding is to be provided on a concessional basis by the OECF and the Ex-Im Bank, without which the joint venture would be commercially unfeasible.

In 1988 the Chinese steel market was projected to grow to 100 million tons by the year 2000. A proposal earlier in 1988 for a South Korean–Chinese

joint venture in steel production near Shandong Province speeded up
Japanese plans for local production. A manager of one of the Japanese steel
firms noted, "We would like to keep Japan's influence there through local
production even if we have to cut exports."[131] The joint venture was capitalized at ¥60 billion, of which 10 percent was to be owned by China, and half
of the 90 percent Japanese share was to be taken equally by the five Japanese
steel makers with the balance provided by banks, trading companies, construction firms, and plant manufacturers. The project was timed to coincide
with the tenth anniversary of the signing of the Sino-Japanese Peace and
Friendship Treaty, and as the largest foreign joint venture in China at that
time it was to be a symbol of Sino-Japanese economic cooperation.

Adjusting Industrial Structure

Besides the issue of securing energy, there was the issue of industrial restructuring. Industrial policy guidelines for the 1970s emphasized the relocation of
Japan's industries that were labor-intensive, polluting, or engaged in natural
resource processing. Japan's capital surplus made it possible to use FDI to
move Japanese firms in these sectors overseas, free domestic resources for
higher-technology industries, increase exports of advanced plant and equipment, and improve Japan's quality of life. This agenda was altered somewhat
by the oil shock, which made the restructuring of Japan's energy-intensive
industrial sectors a high priority.

The sectors most affected by higher oil prices—among them chemical
fertilizers, shipbuilding, low-grade steel, and synthetic fabrics—were aided
by the Special Structurally Depressed Industries' Stabilization Law (Tokutei
Fukyō Sangyō Antei Rinji Sochi Hō) passed by the Diet in May 1978. By
March 1979 ODA-financed orders for the depressed shipbuilding industry
were created by yen loan agreements to provide electric power plant barges to
Thailand, the Philippines, and Bangladesh. Later in the early 1980s Jamaica
and Egypt would be given these plant barges using ODA loans. When the
idea to give plant barges as ODA was hit upon by MITI and the shipbuilding
and plant exporters associations in 1977, the MFA promised the United States
it would place some equipment orders with U.S. firms as a means of reducing
the bilateral trade deficit. Then–MITI minister Kōmoto Toshio commented
about this scheme: "Aid to depressed industries, ODA, and a measure to reduce dollar holdings—an idea that kills three birds with one stone."[132]

In the case of the depressed chemical fertilizer industry, the Industrial
Structure Council's Subcommittee on Chemical Industries, chaired by
Arisawa Hirōmi, recommended that "it is desirable to strengthen the use of
agricultural materials such as fertilizers in grant and loan types of economic
cooperation."[133] This policy recommendation and the 1978 Special Measures
Law merely legitimated post hoc special measures already being implemented. In 1977 a new category of grant aid was created called "aid for increased food production," which subsidized the fertilizer and pesticide indus-

tries by purchasing their products at inflated prices. Although Japan was generous with this aid, recipients sometimes complained that it was not what they
most wanted or needed. Perhaps not coincidentally, the only Association of
South East Asian Nations (ASEAN) joint industrial projects promised by
Fukuda in 1977 that actually materialized turned out to be two Japanese-built
chemical fertilizer plants.

The clearest single example of the flexible use of ODA to aid a domestic
industry facing extinction after the oil shock is the Asahan aluminum project.
It was the first of five large overseas aluminum projects jointly operated by
Japan's aluminum makers (one plant for each of the major Japanese smelting
companies). It illustrates the innovative use of ODA in the 1970s to achieve a
wider range of goals. Though the project evokes Japan's traditional preoccu-
pation with resource security, it is not a resource development project per se.
The project really represents a new direction for a fully industrialized, capital-
exporting Japan. The Asahan project and other so-called *dai-kibō purojekuto*
(large-scale projects) [134] showed how ODA could be used to export certain
declining or undesired Japanese industries to the developing countries, where
the benefits of lower production costs were available and whence Japan could
import the newly transferred production. The 1979 MITI White Paper on
Economic Cooperation describes the large-scale project as follows:

> a large-scale joint venture, mainly in mining and industry, driven primarily
> by the private sector and facilitated by the incorporation of government-
> based economic cooperation. . . . aiming at a large-scale or total transfer of
> funds and technology to stimulate [Japanese] private sector initiative and to
> have a large impact on the economic development of developing countries
> . . . In the middle to long term, these projects have an important role in
> forming a foundation for development in the recipient countries, and in
> promoting continued intimate relations between our nation and the recipi-
> ent. [135]

THE ASAHAN PROJECT

The Asahan project is the largest single aid project ever completed by Japan,
and it is a symbol of Indonesia's modernization. One of its hydroelectric
dams is featured on the 100-rupiah note. Not only has the project helped establish Japan's reputation as an aid giver, but it also helps Japan's economic
competitiveness. This one project supplied nearly one-fifth of Japan's imports
of virgin aluminum by the mid-1980s. If the MFA portrayed the Asahan project as a monument to a new postwar relationship between Japan and
Indonesia, others in Japan saw it as a triumph of keizai kyōryoku and a contribution to the economic security of Japan. Yet in 1988, only four years
after full operations began, Indonesia imposed a temporary embargo on the
project's aluminum exports to Japan in retaliation against Japanese aid
policies.

Project Description

The key components of the Asahan project are the hydroelectric power plants at Sigura-gura Falls and Tangga Falls along the Asahan River, the aluminum smelter at Kuala Tanjung on the Strait of Malacca, and related infrastructure. The hydroelectric power for the project is provided by a system of three dams, with two power stations (each with four generators) and a power transmission system. The peak capacity of the project is 513 megawatts, and the power transmission system consists of a 120-kilometer transmission line and a microwave communications system between the smelter site and the power stations. Ten percent of the electricity (about 50 megawatts) produced by the project is sold to the local power authority at cost (about ¥2.5 per kilowatt). The remaining 90 percent is used by the smelter around the clock.

The aluminum smelter is an electric reduction furnace–type plant with a production capacity of 225,000 tons of high-grade aluminum per year. (By formal agreement, at least two-thirds of the production is exported to Japan.) The technology was sold to the project by the Japanese aluminum makers. Joined with this plant are a gas cleaning system, a carbon anode production facility, an ingot-casting shop, an electric power conversion facility, maintenance shops, and raw material storage facilities. Finally, there is a special materials handling port consisting of a 2.5-kilometer jetty with three berths, equipment, and access roads.

To produce 1 ton of aluminum, the smelter requires the following inputs: 15,000 kilowatts of electricity, 1.9 tons of alumina (imported by Japanese trading companies from Australia), 0.42 tons of coke (imported from the United States), 0.11 tons of pitch (imported from Japan), and 0.020 tons of aluminum fluoride (imported from Surabaya). As of late 1987, when this author inspected the project, the break-even selling price of aluminum for the project was $1,300/ton. Roughly two-thirds of this is due to operating costs, and the remaining one-third is due to capital costs, i.e., depreciation and loan payments.

An attractive complex at the power stations in the midst of steep jungle terrain—including a scarcely used golf course—for the 100 or so workers in the power stations is also provided. A small town of 1,340 houses and seven dormitories was built for the 2,000 workers at the smelter site, with guest housing, schools, a church and mosque, a health clinic, modern sports facilities, a town hall, a post office, shops, and a supermarket built alongside the housing. JICA's role in the project was to finance this "social infrastructure" at the smelter site and power stations, even though the facilities are only for the operation of this industrial project.

The cost of the project at completion was ¥411 billion, with the spending breakdown roughly as follows: the construction cost of the hydroelectric plant, the aluminum smelter, and related infrastructure were ¥90 billion, ¥160 billion, and ¥30 billion, respectively. Start-up costs and operating capital

amounted to ¥40 billion, and the remaining ¥91 billion went in interest payments and fees. [136] Paid-in capital accounts for 32 percent of the cost, and the
balance is provided through loans.

The project is managed by P. T. Inalum, a joint venture between the
Japanese investment consortium called Nihon Asahan Aluminum Co. Ltd.
and the Indonesian government. From the first day of operation in November
1983, an agreement came into force whereby P. T. Inalum owns and operates
the project for thirty years (i.e., the life of the aluminum plant), after which
Indonesia may take over the project.

Background to the Asahan Project

Lake Toba is the largest lake in Indonesia and is located in the center of
northern Sumatra. A product of volcanic action, the lake collects runoff from
an area of over 4,000 square kilometers. The lake has a surface area of 1,100
square kilometers at an elevation of 905 meters above sea level, and a volume
of 2,860 million tons. The average annual rainfall in the area is high at 2,000
millimeters per year, and as a result the outflow from the lake via the Asahan
River averages 110 tons per second. As the river begins its descent through
the jungle it quickly falls some 650 meters through a steep course of rapids
and waterfalls within a distance of only 15.5 kilometers, thus making its hydroelectric potential obvious. Ultimately, the Asahan River empties into the
Strait of Malacca after traversing a total of 125 kilometers. The Asahan
River's potential electric-generating capacity is estimated to be over 1 million
kilowatts.

The Asahan River's potential for generating electricity was recognized
by the Dutch colonial authorities in 1908, but because of the intervention of
World War I the Dutch did not conduct a feasibility study until 1919. A purpose for hydroelectricity was not apparent until a Dutch firm (N. V. Biliton
Maatschappij) discovered bauxite deposits in the nearby island of Biliton.
Because aluminum production requires a great amount of electricity (1 ton
requires 15,000 kilowatt-hours using modern methods) this firm decided in
1941 to construct a hydroelectric dam at Sigura-gura Falls.

At this juncture World War II intervened, and the Japanese displaced the
Dutch in early 1942. After the Japanese takeover Yutaka Kubota—who had
overseen the hydroelectric development of the Yalu River in Korea as presi-
dent of Chōsen Dengyō—was dispatched to Japan's new possession to survey
its energy and natural resources. As a recently commissioned naval officer,
Kubota arrived in Indonesia after having completed aerial surveys of Hainan
Island and Indochina. From the seat of a warplane Kubota surveyed the
Asahan River and identified its potential for generating hydroelectric power.
The Japanese actually began efforts to build the dam the Dutch had planned
at Sigura-gura Falls, but they were cut short by defeat in 1945. What ensued
was a four-year struggle against the return of Dutch colonial rule led by
Achmed Sukarno and Mohammed Hatta.

After the United States of Indonesia was recognized in 1949 at the Round Table Conference in The Hague, the new government under President Sukarno and Prime Minister Hatta set out to build a nation out of a disparate collection of 500-odd tribal groups populating some 13,000 islands. Hatta (b. 1902) was aware of the Dutch and Japanese efforts to harness the hydropower potential of the Asahan River, and after visiting the site in 1952 he made it a personal priority to build the project as a symbol of national achievement and economic development.

In 1953 a French team of consultants was asked to do a feasibility study, and they recommended phased construction of a hydroelectric project and regional industrial development centered on energy-intensive industries such as aluminum smelting and chemical fertilizers. The Indonesian government then asked Japan to build the dam as a reparations project but was turned down.[137] No further concrete developments occurred until 1962, when Indonesia requested Soviet aid in building the project. Work on the project had only begun when a communist-led coup against the military and a military counter-coup in 1965 cut short further progress.

Indonesia charted a new course under General Suharto, who had led the successful countercoup and had saved the country from a downward spiral into chaos. The legacy inherited by Suharto's New Order government was troubled: domestically, the military had to recover from fratricidal splits, and the civilian sector had to heal wounds inflicted by massacres of suspected communists and ethnic Chinese. Moreover, after the years of political drama under Sukarno, there was little material improvement to show for his rule, and there was an immediate postcoup economic crisis to overcome.

The New Order agenda was therefore the consolidation of political order and rapid economic recovery and development. Suharto reversed Sukarno's policies of confrontation with Indonesia's neighbors and the West, and he sought to establish friendly ties with them by rejoining the UN in 1966 and by helping to create ASEAN in 1967. Suharto's New Order Government also welcomed Western political and economic assistance and drafted a new foreign investment law soon after taking power. This brought a large infusion of Western economic assistance.

At this juncture the engineering consulting firm Nihon Kōei (a postwar reincarnation of Chōsen Dengyō), whose president was the same Yutaka Kubota who had originally identified the Asahan project for the Japanese in 1942, offered to conduct a preliminary survey for the project free of charge. The realization of this project had become a personal goal of Yutaka Kubota, who in the postwar period had visited Indonesia in 1954 and 1959 seeking to promote the project. It may be recalled that by this method Kubota had won the contract to build the first Japanese reparations project, the hydroelectric dam at Balu Chaung in Burma. The new government accepted Nihon Kōei's offer, and survey teams were sent from Japan in January 1967 and 1968 to outline plans for a hydroelectric power project with an associated aluminum smelter. In July 1969 Kubota traveled to Indonesia to present the completed survey report to President Suharto personally and discussed ways to realize the project.[138]

By this time the efforts to realize the Asahan project had reached mythic proportions to the Indonesian elite, kept alive by, among others, the elder statesman Mohammed Hatta. If the New Order government could successfully build the project, it would win a great symbolic victory in overcoming the failures of the Sukarno era and could generate optimism regarding Indonesia's destiny under the new regime.

Spurred by Kubota's report and the desire to score a symbolic developmental achievement in a backward and inaccessible area of northern Sumatra, the Indonesian government formed a special Asahan committee headed by the minister of mines to handle implementation procedures. In view of Kubota's proposal to build hydroelectric dams using OECF loans to supply an aluminum smelter with cheap power, in March 1969 the Kaiser Aluminum Co., Alcoa, and three Japanese aluminum makers began studying the possibility of investing in an aluminum smelter.[139] Following this, other Japanese aluminum makers along with Tokyo Electric Power Co. began a private feasibility study in February 1970.

The Indonesian government then declared the Asahan project a top national priority and officially requested an OECF loan for engineering services in May 1970 to pay Nihon Kōei for a detailed study. The loan was approved, but afterwards the two governments could not agree on a project-financing formula. Indonesia then merged the hydroelectric dams and the aluminum smelter into one package and gave notice in January 1972 it would accept offers from foreign investors to construct the package on a commercial basis. Because the anticipated cost would be $700–800 million, by the end of the bidding period in July 1972 no offers were submitted.[140]

The Impact of the First Oil Shock

To salvage the project after this miscalculation, in August 1972 Suharto sent a special emissary to Japan to request the Japanese government to provide special financing to the five Japanese aluminum makers, even as these five firms began a feasibility study (F/S) of the project package and requested special financing from MITI. The Japanese government delayed action, but the first oil shock in the autumn of 1973 drastically changed the situation. The quadrupling of oil prices meant that Japanese aluminum makers, who were 70 percent dependent on fossil fuel–generated electricity, were at one stroke rendered uncompetitive with U.S. and Canadian firms, whose plants were supplied with cheap hydroelectric power.

MITI responded with countermeasures in consultation with the five large Japanese aluminum makers through their designated representative, Sumitomo Chemical Co. To survive these firms had to move production overseas where cheap electricity was available, and so they requested MITI's help. MITI quickly agreed because Japan must import in one form or another all its aluminum, and if Japanese light metals makers went out of business, Japan would become totally dependent on foreign suppliers, thus becoming more vulnerable to supply and price uncertainties. In addition, the export of this energy-intensive industry would reduce Japan's reliance on oil imports and would result in a restructuring of Japan's economy in an energy-saving direction. From this time Japan planned to import half of its aluminum from overseas projects.[141]

Asahan was the first of several overseas aluminum projects identified by MITI and the five major Japanese aluminum makers.[142] With extraordinary speed MITI pledged full government support to the five firms. These firms then signed a basic agreement with the Indonesian government on January 8, 1974, to build the Asahan aluminum smelter. The following week, Prime Minister Tanaka Kakuei and President Suharto met in Jakarta and agreed that all efforts would be made to implement the project.

Preliminary Measures

MITI faced the problem of helping the five Japanese firms raise the ¥250 billion ($800 million) needed to complete the project. Such a sum could not be raised on commercial terms for this project, and official funding on this scale would require agreement within the government and the Diet. In order to start the process of consensus formation within Japan, in October 1974 MITI requested the aluminum subcommittee of the Industrial Structure Council to consider recommending emergency measures for the industry and to designate the Asahan project a "national project." By August 1975 this influential body issued an interim report that states that aluminum production was now a "structurally depressed industry" and that the "development import" (kaihatsu yunyū) policy approach first developed in the early 1950s should be applied as a countermeasure. This authorized special efforts to develop (kaihatsu) an overseas resource (in this case energy) and import (yunyū) its production to fulfill a strategic need in the Japanese economy. But it is worth noting that in July 1975, a month *before* the report of the Industrial Structure Council was issued, the Cabinet approved the special arrangements needed to finance the Asahan project, calling it a "national project."[143]

As MITI was busy preparing these and other matters at home, negotiations between Japan and Indonesia were begun in order to flesh out the agreement in principle reached between Tanaka and Suharto. In July 1975, after the go-ahead was given by the Japanese Cabinet, a master agreement was signed between the Indonesian government and a consortium of Japanese firms formed three months earlier under MITI guidance. This consortium subsequently incorporated itself in Japan as the Nihon Asahan Aluminum Co., Ltd. on November 25, 1975. Under MITI guidance seven large Japanese general trading companies were brought into the consortium, with each assuming a 2.5 percent ownership share in Nihon Asahan, thus sharing the investment risk and cost to the five aluminum makers (see Table 5.2). The general trading companies were promised profitable business in project construction, and as part owners they monopolized the selling of raw material inputs to the project and the marketing of the aluminum ingots.

**Table 5.2 Ownership Shares of Nihon Asahan Aluminum Co., Ltd.
(capitalized at ¥68,375 million)**

OECF	50.0%
Sumitomo Aluminum	7.5%
Nihon Light Metals	2.5%
Showa Light Metals	7.5%
Mitsubishi Light Metals	7.5%
Mitsui Aluminum	7.5%
Sumitomo Trading Co.	2.5%
C. Itoh	2.5%
Nissho Iwai	2.5%
Nichimen Trading Co.	2.5%
Marubeni Trading Co.	2.5%
Mitsubishi Shoji	2.5%
Mitsui Bussan	2.5%

Source: MITI.

In January 1976 Nihon Asahan joined with the Indonesian government to form the joint venture P. T. Inalum, the managing company that legally owns and operates the project. Financial arrangements began falling into place by August 1976, when Indonesia signed the first project-related loan agreement for ¥26.25 billion. Construction began the following month.

After gaining official guarantees from the Japanese and Indonesian governments, and after starting construction, cost overruns increased the estimated cost of the project from ¥250 billion to ¥411 billion. The revision of financial arrangements was overseen by MITI and given official approval by then–MITI minister Kōmoto Toshio in talks with Suharto during a visit to Indonesia in May 1978.[144] It was on this occasion that Indonesia increased its capital share in P. T. Inalum to 25 percent (see Figures 5.2 and 5.3). From this time to project completion in October 1984, construction proceeded as scheduled. On November 6, 1984, fifteen years after his meeting with Kubota in 1969, President Suharto attended the completion ceremony.

The Role of ODA

This project is not just an ODA project. Although it has an ODA component, it cannot be disentangled from the other components of keizai kyōryoku

Figure 5.2 Ownership in P. T. Inalum

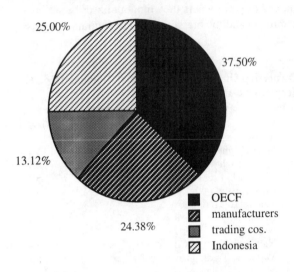

Figure 5.3 Loan and Equity Shares in Asahan Project Cost

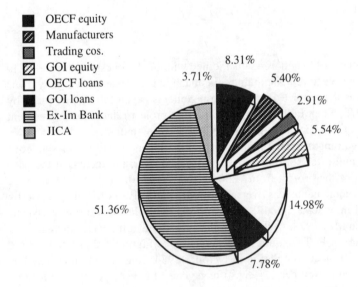

utilized to orchestrate the creation of the aluminum smelter managed by P. T. Inalum but controlled by Nihon Asahan. According to the original agreement, the Indonesian government would hold 10 percent of P. T. Inalum equity; later, at the Indonesian government's insistence, this was increased to 25 percent when financing was rearranged in 1978. This share was increased to 41 percent in 1987. Nonetheless, because the OECF seems to leave management decisions to the private investors in Nihon Asahan, the Japanese trading companies and aluminum makers together control P. T. Inalum with only 29.5 percent of ownership, whereas the Indonesian government, with 41 percent of equity, cannot gain a major voice in management.

The equity purchase in Nihon Asahan by the five aluminum makers and the seven trading companies—totaling ¥34.16 billion—was financed entirely through government-sponsored loans (see Figure 5.4). The Ex-Im Bank loaned the twelve firms 70 percent of the amount, and the rest was cofinanced by the city banks under MOF guidance.[145] The debt carried by P. T. Inalum also tells a similar story. Of the ¥319.9 billion borrowed by P. T. Inalum, 10 percent came from the Indonesian government, and 19.2 percent came directly from the OECF. The rest came from Nihon Asahan, but this amount was supplied to Nihon Asahan by the Ex-Im Bank together with city banks and JICA.[146]

Project Operation

Although the project is a remarkable engineering achievement, in many other respects it has not lived up to expectation. From a financial viewpoint, the project has been somewhat of a disappointment. On the revenue side, the international price of aluminum rose only above break-even point in 1987. Moreover, it is claimed by Indonesian officials that the aluminum, which is of the highest grade of purity, is often sold to the Japanese trading companies at lower grade prices, allowing them to resell it for a profit at its fair price.

On the cost side, the situation is equally troubled, but more complex: In the first place, it must be recalled that P.T. Inalum carries yen-denominated debt, but earns dollar revenues. This has meant that as the yen appreciated 50 percent in the 1985–1987 period, in dollar terms P. T. Inalum's capital cost doubled to roughly $400 per ton, raising the project's break-even point to $1,300 per ton as of late 1987. The situation with regard to production costs is also troubled. According to the Japanese director managing the project, the production cost is in the neighborhood of $900 per ton. A little arithmetic shows that the cost of electricity is roughly $140 per ton, and because the project employs only 2,100 low-wage workers to produce 225,000 tons per year, labor costs are only in the neighborhood of $50 per ton. This means that raw materials and spare parts account for about $700 per ton.

Indonesian officials interviewed at the project site in November 1987 claimed that operating costs have been inflated because all procurement of parts and raw materials must be made through the Japanese firms in the Nihon Asahan consortium, and these firms charge P. T. Inalum exorbitant prices.[147] For example, it was alleged by these officials that from the start of operations, without their knowledge, the major raw material input, alumina,

Figure 5.4 Financing Scheme Behind the Asahan Project's Master Agreement

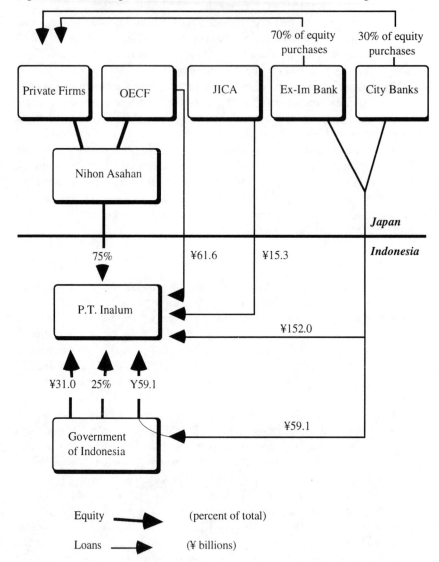

was being sold by the trading companies to P. T. Inalum at $320 per ton—three to four times above the procurement price in that period.

Another allegation was that the purchase of over $40 million in spare equipment and parts from the Japanese firms—a conspicuous item on P. T. Inalum's balance sheet and equal to five years supply just sitting in inventory—was decided by the Japanese directors just to generate sales for recession-struck Japanese firms at the expense of P. T. Inalum. In these and other ways Indonesians claim that P. T. Inalum has been losing money. Since the start of operations in 1982, P. T. Inalum's annual losses climbed from 899 million rupiahs to 51,000 million rupiahs in 1985.[148] If these charges are true, then transfer pricing is being used to shift profit out of the Indonesian project and into Japanese firms, leaving Indonesia with only debt and losses on its investment. The deficits run up by P. T. Inalum forced a capital increase in 1987, which Indonesia used as an opportunity to increase its ownership of capital from 25 percent to 41 percent in an effort to gain more control in project management. This arrangement was finalized during talks between Suharto and MITI Minister Tamura during the latter's visit to Jakarta in January 1987. It was at this time that Nihon Asahan increased its share by ¥24 billion and the Indonesian government increased its share by ¥32 billion.[149]

There are other issues such as technology transfer, employment creation, and regional development related to this project. Upon personal observation of the smelter and power project sites, it is apparent that the transfer of know-how and operational control is not proceeding smoothly. The Japanese sent to the project site are full-time employees of the Japanese equipment suppliers on rotating temporary assignment. They lack the incentive and language ability needed to transfer managerial and technical skills. The result is that there is a high turnover of Indonesian skilled labor who leave the project, and those who stay, including the Indonesian project director and managers, complain of being ignored by the Japanese directors, managers, and technicians, who go about their business without teaching them the most critical aspects of project operations. The Japanese retain numerous management personnel in the project to ensure an uninterrupted flow of aluminum to Japan.

The project's macroeconomic contributions to the Indonesian economy have also been a source of disappointment. In terms of employment creation, the investment of over $2 billion resulted in only 2,100 jobs in the smelter and power stations. The effect these jobs have on the rural regional economy is too small to be noticeable, especially because many of the local technicians have to be brought from Java. As for the new electric power generating capacity, 90 percent is devoted to the smelter, and not all the remainder can be used by the regional power authority because nothing besides the smelter was planned. Thus, the impact on incomes and living conditions in Sumatra has been small.

The downstream effect on the regional economy of the aluminum production is nonexistent because the aluminum retained by Indonesia is shipped to Java to be processed. The development of bauxite deposits in Kalimantan or Billiton to supply the Asahan project as originally envisaged has not materialized because the Japanese trading companies have ready access to alumina from Australia. The effects on the national budget and foreign exchange reserves have been negative because of the Indonesian government's purchase of capital in Inalum, the operating deficits run by the project, and the cost of the project's yen financing.

It is not surprising, therefore, that there is chronic friction over project management. For Indonesians the dilemma is that although they have grievances over Japanese management of the project, they still need Japanese cooperation to maintain the project, and they cannot afford a break in relations with their largest aid donor. Furthermore, Indonesians are loathe to air their grievances publicly because to do so would embarrass Suharto and the New Order government, who have declared the project a success. For the Japanese government the paradox is that the project is supposed to help Indonesia, but the government is unwilling to yield control over such an important source of aluminum for Japan; and the Japanese private sector is demanding profits in exchange for its cooperation.

These tensions led to an open break in relations during annual negotiations over project management between the two sides in April 1988. As reported by the Japanese press, the negotiations centered on the Indonesians' demand that the previous profit-sharing formula of 25 percent to Indonesia and 75 percent to Japan, which was set in 1978, be changed to 41 and 59 percent to reflect the new ownership ratio in P. T. Inalum. This would be in accordance with the original basic agreement, which stipulates that profit shares be determined by capital shares. The Japanese resisted because they did not want a diminished share of profits. In addition, there was disagreement over the marketing price of the aluminum. According to the basic agreement, this was to be determined by the spot price on the London Metals Exchange (LME). The Japanese wanted a lower price in 1988 by basing the purchase price in part on the aluminum futures market of the LME, which had lower prices than the spot market as of mid-1988. In fact, the most crucial issue was not reported. The Indonesian government wished to sell the aluminum on the open market, whereas Japan obviously wished to retain its monopsony power.

Because of Japanese intransigence on these issues, the Indonesians imposed an embargo on aluminum exports. The president of Inalum stated, "Someday we will have over 51 percent of the Asahan project's stock, and management will transfer to the Indonesian side." Nonetheless, the Japanese felt that the Indonesian government could be split on the handling of the issue and that patience would win in the end.[150]

If there is a lesson to be drawn from 1970s-style economic cooperation, it is that after altering and enhancing OECF and JICA activities to fit DAC methods of computing ODA effort, the Japanese government still coordinated ODA within the keizai kyōryoku framework. By incrementally extending the capabilities of the system instead of radically revising it, Japan entrenched its traditional orientation in economic cooperation. As ever, the system was guided by administrative mechanisms rather than Diet debate and initiative.

As Japan developed into a capital and technology exporter, it turned to larger-scale project cooperation to adjust its own industrial structure and secure access to energy resources.

The Asahan project shows how unprecedented amounts of ODA were used with other elements of economic cooperation to adjust Japan's aluminum sector to higher oil prices. The successful deployment of over $2 billion of Japanese capital in the project proved that Japan could use its growing ODA obligations and capital surplus to reshape industrial sectors at home and abroad to build what was termed a more harmonious division of labor with the developing world. Another lesson of the Asahan project is that the bilateral aid relationship is not an equal one. Aid recipients come to depend on donors and cannot afford to choose between them; they have to negotiate the best terms they can with each one. Finally, this project suggests that monumental projects intended as political symbols have no necessary relationship to effective economic development. Showcases of modern technology are expensive, laborsaving, difficult to maintain and operate, and difficult to integrate into the existing economy. Rather than fostering independence, such projects may enhance external dependence if handled incorrectly.

6

ODA Policy, 1980–1992

By the start of the 1980s pressures on Japan exerted by the North-South dialogue eased, but sharp economic and security frictions with its Western allies made Japan continue to resort to ODA. Nonetheless, it would be a serious mistake to view ODA policy in the 1980s merely as reactions to external pressure. There were internally generated agendas that drove Japan's ODA growth as well. The first half of this chapter looks at Japanese ODA in Thailand in the first half of the decade. This case shows how preparations were begun then for inflows of Japanese FDI later in the decade. It also lets one see how Japanese ODA was perceived by Thai officials, journalists, and academics, who are among the most well-trained and experienced of Japan's ODA recipients. The second half of this chapter turns to the question of how Japan's ODA was quickly and thoroughly reoriented toward the urgent new needs of the Japanese economy after the yen appreciation *(endaka)*.

JAPAN'S ODA IN THAILAND, 1980–1987

Japan's ODA policy toward Thailand in this period provides an integrated view of how Japan's ODA impacts an aid recipient that is important to Japan in different ways. Thailand was an important prospective economic partner for Japan in the 1980s. MITI minister Tanaka Rokusuke made two official trips to Southeast Asia in 1980, and on both he spelled out four emphases in Japan's economic cooperation with Southeast Asia: (1) energy development, (2) the promotion of smaller-scale enterprises, (3) cooperation to develop export-oriented manufacturing, and (4) technical training to support these ends. These forays were followed by Prime Minister Suzuki Zenko's tour of ASEAN in 1981, his first official overseas trip, in which he committed ODA to this agenda as well as to MAFF's desire to cultivate food production in Asia tailored to Japan's needs. At the same time, the MFA promised the West increased ODA to states such as Thailand facing communist expansionism. It also pledged to strengthen the basic human needs orientation in its ODA. Finally, it wished to cultivate better bilateral political relations with its neighbors in East Asia.

Japan's importance to Thailand as an ODA donor is indicated by the fact that Japan became Thailand's largest ODA donor in 1975, and in 1985 Japan supplied 68.5 percent of Thailand's bilateral ODA receipts. An IDC report characterizes Japan's ODA in Thailand up to the 1980s as follows:

> Loan cooperation, which makes up the bulk of economic cooperation, is directed toward economic infrastructure, mainly electric power and energy, and roads and transportation. In contrast, grant aid cooperation, although small in amount, is directed toward social infrastructure such as health and sanitation, and education. Most of our loan cooperation items take the form of project finance. [151]

Another report on Japan's ODA in Thailand, commissioned by MITI and carried out by the IDE, notes the same pattern:

> Compared with international organizations or other bilateral donors, the low share of social infrastructure [in loan cooperation] is one distinguishing feature. Nonetheless, in the case of our country, one must bear in mind that this is covered to some extent by our grant aid cooperation. [152]

Thai Analyses of Japanese Aid Policy

In 1981 Japan's exports to Thailand were as follows: machinery and equipment, 55 percent; metal products, 21 percent; chemicals, 12 percent; other, 12 percent. Thailand's exports to Japan were as follows: raw materials, 42 percent; foodstuffs, 36 percent; textiles, 4 percent; other, 18 percent. This was a vertical division of labor in which Japan exported expensive industrial goods to Thailand and imported cheap food and raw materials. This economic relationship informed Thai research into Japan's aid policy in the mid-1980s. Professors Prasartset and Sonteperkswong of Chulalongkorn University summarize Japan's aid policy thus:

> During the 1960 to 1970 [period], Japan launched a "Yen Loan" as a part of economic assistance to developing countries. This tied loan, allocated to Thailand, during 1968 to 1978, totaled 160 billion yen, which obligated Thailand to purchase goods from Japan. This loan has accounted for 85 percent of the total assistance provided by the Japanese government. . . . This loan has an important role as it generated new markets for Japanese exports.
> A consequence of the Japanese assistance is to bring about a perpetual trade surplus with Thailand, since most of them [sic] are provided by tied-loan. Packing [associated] credit as well as foreign investment of Japan also help promote exports to Thailand by making Thailand a locked-in market for Japanese goods and services. Moreover, technical cooperation from Japan introduced Japanese working style [and] technology, especially in the advanced sectors namely telecommunication, medicine, etc., which expedite Japanese exports to receiving countries. Other assistance in the form of expertise, technical as well as cultural cooperation, are also beneficial as it facilitates Japanese trade and investment, especially in the field of agriculture, fishery, automobile industry, textile, etc. [153]

That these views were widely shared among the Thai is indicated by the results of an opinion poll on Thai-Japanese relations conducted in the mid-1970s.[154] As Table 6.1 indicates, Japan's aid practices produced a perception that Japan disregarded Thai interests and sensibilities and that in the overall economic relationship Japan's own interests are better served than Thailand's.

Table 6.1 Thai Opinion Survey

What is your opinion of Japanese trade and investment in Thailand?

Responses (%)

	General Public	Elite
Japan takes unfair advantage of Thailand	41.6	63.3
Japan has been fair to Thailand	10.3	3.9
Japan has been too generous to Thailand	1.0	0.0
Japan is the same as other nations trading and investing in Thailand	20.3	32.0
No opinion	26.8	0.8
Total	100.0	100.0

What is the primary Japanese motive in having given so many loans to Thailand?

Responses (%)

	General Public	Elite
Primarily to help Thailand	8.4	2.3
Primarily for Japan's own interests	45.7	68.0
Primarily for mutual benefit	20.7	25.8
No opinion	25.2	3.9
Total	100.0	100.0

The reasons for this situation were explored in a conference on Thai-Japanese relations held at Thammasat University in 1983. The views expressed by the Thai participants are summarized by Professor Likhit Dhiravegin, dean of the Faculty of Political Science at Thammasat, as follows:

1. The recipient . . . does not have a specific plan for aid given by Japan.
    . . .
2. [Japan] does not pay much attention to technological transfer. . . .
3. Japan does not show any trust in the aid recipient. . . . More important, Japan initiates aid projects rather than responding to proposals of the recipient.

4. [Thailand] does not take the aid given with utmost care because it is a handout. Thus it is not highly valued.

5. Certain aid programs are not in line with local need or appropriate for Thai society, e.g., certain instruments are technologically too advanced. It is difficult and costly to maintain.

6. There are problems of co-operation from the government agencies in the Thai side.

7. Certain negative impacts of aid on Thai societies should be noted:
    a) It worsens the economic imbalance between the urban and rural sector.
    b) The poor usually do not benefit from Japanese aid.
    c) Japan does not pay any attention to non-governmental organizations. [155]

In response to these views, H. Shigeta, counselor at the Japanese embassy in Bangkok, gives the following defense of Japanese aid policy:

> Our aim in extending economic cooperation to Thailand is to help Thailand in her efforts for economic and social development, to promote peace and stability (through the stabilization of the people's life) in Thailand, which is a front-line state facing communist influence in Southeast Asia and to develop further existing friendly relations between two countries. . . .
>
> We are alleged to have other aims, such as promotion of our own selfish economic interests. Some argued that Japanese companies are making profit out of Japanese aid projects using Japanese concessional yen loans and therefore Japan's assistance is benefiting the Japanese companies. In this regard, it must be pointed out that yen loans . . . are generally untied and companies of any country are entitled to participate in the tenders for the projects financed by yen loans. Furthermore, award of contract is made not by Japan, but by the Thai side. The Sathorn Bridge financed by yen loan is, for example, built by Ital-Thai Company. . . . The Government of Japan cares not so much about which company makes profit, but cares about the contribution the project is making to the social and economic development of Thailand.
>
> As a policy, we extend our economic cooperation to Thailand on the basis of requests submitted to us by the Thai government. . . . Strategy for the economic development of Thailand is decided by the Thai Government. . . . However, in considering annual aid projects, Japan feels strongly that the balanced development of industry and agriculture is most desirable in Thailand. For example, Japan is ready to assist Thai government with respect to industrial development in the Eastern Seaboard, which has high priority in Thai five year programme, and has extended yen loans to number of projects including Gas Separation Plant. [156]

Presented with the same list of complaints at a Thai-Japanese conference two years later, the first secretary of the political division of the Japanese embassy in Bangkok, Komatsu Ichirō, gives the same general response: "Japan is providing aid according to the priorities identified by the economic and social development programme of Thailand, and specific aid projects are determined in response to the request from the Thai government." On helping the rural and poor sectors, he states that Japanese financing of Thailand's Bank for Agriculture and Agricultural Cooperatives (BAAC) loans and the Village Electrification Project demonstrated Japanese concern, and that Japan did not give much ODA to nongovernmental organizations (NGOs) because this might "be regarded as a sort of 'intervention in internal affairs.'"[157]

To rebut MFA denials Thai academics cite cases where private sector Japanese consultants accompanied official Japanese missions to negotiate aid project design,[158] or cases where construction of a facility that should have cost 7,000 baht (B7,000) per square meter ended up costing B20,000 per square meter because of tied aid funds.[159] In the end most Thais felt that Japanese ODA "served two important objectives. Firstly it is a political device. Secondly, it serves to expand Japanese business in the receiving countries."[160] In the mid-1980s virtually no informed Thai believed that Japanese aid was noncommercial.

If one wonders why the Thai could not do a better job in controlling the aid agenda, the answer offered by a study of Japan's grant and technical cooperation completed in 1987 by a team of researchers led by Surichai Wankaeo of Chulalongkorn University is:

> It is worth noticing that all administrators mentioned that the grant aid [creates] economic dependency. Japan as the donor has more bargaining power; therefore, Thai can hardly have any choice. In some cases, the lack of knowledge or experience about the particular project on the Thai side makes it more difficult to be independent in the decision making process. . . . Japanese aid in comparison to [that of] others, requires the receiving country to practice according to her restrictions. As a consequence, Japan plays a more important role in the final step of decision making. Thailand as the receiving country is then being influenced. Self-reliance can hardly be achieved if the initiative of aid is indicated by the donor.[161]

Loan Aid in Thailand

In the first six years of ODA loans to Thailand (1970–1975), out of a total of fifteen projects, twelve were for electric power generation or distribution. In the succeeding 1976–1986 period, another ten loan projects were for electrification aiming to deliver electricity even to the rural village level. These loans were counted as BHN-oriented assistance. The question raised by this pattern was why Japan stressed electrification and telecommunications projects in its ODA. Thai academics Prasartset and Sonteperkswong argue that "Japanese assistance which has directly benefited her own trade are electric power projects, radio and television station projects, etc. These activities have encouraged increasing demand for household electric appliances."[162] Another Thai academic notes that "nobody can deny the [beneficial] influence of cheap Japanese radio and television sets and other electrical appliances which are found even in remote corners of the Thai countryside. . . . On the negative side, the availability of the mass-produced gadgets could cause rising expectations of consumers. . . . Hence increased Japanese imports and consequent huge trade deficits with Japan! We cannot simply ignore this aspect."[163] Besides Japan's emphasis on electrification, Professor Khien Theeravit of Chulalongkorn University calls attention to overreliance on Japan's ODA loans:

> It is morally wrong for a government to extend electricity to the poor villages where priority should be given to other commodities rather than electricity to upgrade the villagers' quality of life. . . . Now about 20% of our annual budget goes to debt payment and yet our government still cannot see the negative impact caused by the foreign debt.[164]

After the completion of Japanese ODA-financed electrification projects, Thai imports of Japanese-made electrical consumer appliances in the five-year 1980–1984 period increased 260 percent from B1.68 billion to B4.40 billion. (The next-largest supplier, the United States, exported only B0.40 billion in 1984—one-tenth of the Japanese amount.[165])

In practice Japan's project loans favored Japanese contractors even if they were formally untied. For example, in the mid-1980s the OECF made it a practice to recommend Japanese consultants to Thailand for design work. As a result design specifications for loan projects were written to Japanese standards. These specifications, along with short bidding periods (sometimes less than two months), did not allow others to bid on an equal footing with Japanese firms. It was alleged by observers in Thailand that insider collaboration in "open" bidding through *dango* (the rigging of bids within Japanese industry groups) often determined the outcome, and that Thai line agencies often knew the winning contractor even before the bidding took place. The system was so effective that U.S. and other foreign contractors in Thailand became discouraged from bidding on Japanese-funded aid projects.[166]

The flowback to Japan of officially untied project loans was difficult to determine because the results of bids were kept confidential. Some light was shed by a careful study of the impact of Japanese ODA on the Thai construction industry done by Professor Prasert Chittiwatanapong of Thammasat University. Up to September 1987 the share of OECF construction project loans won by "Thai nationals" was 47.3 percent; Japanese nationals, 45.0 percent; and other nationals, 7.8 percent. But the "Thai nationals" category included "pseudo-Thai" local Japanese joint ventures. The advance of Japanese firms into the booming Thai construction market was conspicuous at this time, with the number of Japanese affiliates increasing from four in 1980 to twenty-three by 1988, with each firm on average employing 200–400 Thai workers under an average-sized group of twenty Japanese managers.[167] Prasert points out: "We do not know what would be the percentage of the Japanese nationals if we include, as we should, the so-called pseudo-Thai firms in the definition. It may go as high as 80–85 percent leaving only a small portion to the pure Thai contractors."[168]

An often overlooked aspect of Japan's heavy reliance on loan aid was the creation of leverage over recipient governments. The Thai government traditionally avoided heavy reliance on foreign borrowing, but from the start of the 1980s the Thai government modified this policy under Japanese encouragement, notably in the case of the costly Eastern Seaboard Development Program. A report on Japanese aid policy in Thailand done by the IDE in 1984 mentions that Japan's loan aid, given at 3 percent interest payable over thirty years, was "super soft" compared with more expensive World Bank or ADB loans.[169] According to Thai finance ministry officials interviewed in 1987, the OECF was "crowding out" World Bank and ADB loans. The IDE report notes that OECF loans increased from ¥46 billion in 1979 to over ¥83 billion in 1982 and goes on to state: "Bearing in mind the pressure of future debt repayment, it is believed that the role of our country, which supplies great quantities of super soft aid loans, will be given an even more important position in the future dynamic development of the Thai economy."[170]

Grant and Technical Aid in Thailand

In the 1971–1976 period, Japan awarded only one grant aid project per year. This increased to an average of two per year in the 1977–1980 period, then to a peak of thirteen in 1983. In terms of value grant aid increased from ¥1.0 billion in 1975 to ¥13.4 billion in 1985, increasing its share in Japan's bilateral ODA to Thailand from 10 percent to 15 percent. The MFA pushed grant aid growth in the 1980s to promote better political relations, notably the ¥1.15 billion Japanese Studies Center at Thammasat University, cultural projects such as the Social Education and Culture Center in Bangkok, and pet projects of the king (including a showcase computer system for the king's principal private secretary). This was part of the MFA's attempt to use ODA in new ways to soften the critical views of Thai academics and government officials. But because the MFA was unable or unwilling to turn its back on Japanese commercial interests, the MFA's efforts were initially unsuccessful. For example, on the one hundredth anniversary of Thai-Japanese relations an official visit by Japanese prime minister Nakasone in September 1987 was disrupted when a ground-breaking ceremony for the B170 million Historical Studies Center in Ayutthaya had to be canceled because of demonstrations. The object of protest was Japanese aid policy which, provided neither Thai input into the center's design nor work to Thai construction firms. A *Bangkok Post* commentary states: "While Thais in general admire the commercial, economic, and industrial capabilities of the Japanese, they see that deep down the Japanese are simply a cold and calculating people. This perception that whatever Japan gives, it will, in the end, always gain, is unhealthy for both sides."[171] When questioned by Thai reporters about the historical center project, the Japanese ambassador, Akitane Kiuchi, stated that Japanese design consultants were needed to ensure that "money from Japanese taxpayers is used effectively," and that Japan's policy was that "the initiative should come from Japanese consultants and Japanese contractors." This prompted a Thai commentator to assert, "Here arises a similarity between Japan and the Soviet Union. Both are one-dimension powers that do not make concessions on what makes them powerful." [172]

This controversy must be seen in relation to an earlier grant aid project, i.e., the Thai Culture Center. The most expensive Japanese grant aid project ever built at that time, the Social Education and Cultural Center (commonly called the Thai Culture Center) cost roughly ¥10 billion and had been completed shortly before the above-mentioned Historical Studies Center. The idea was to give the king a world-class culture center in Bangkok on his sixtieth birthday as a gesture of friendship and as a demonstration of Japanese architectural and construction ability. Interviewed Japanese aid officials indicate that the proposal originated in the Japanese embassy in Bangkok. According to an interviewed Thai government official familiar with this project's request, what the Thais had originally requested was an international convention center, but the MFA suggested a culture center instead. When the original Thai requesting agency rejected this idea, the Thai Ministry of Education was persuaded to request the project. The result was a culture center designed by Japanese architects in an international style reminiscent of Lincoln Center. The lack of Thai design elements offended Thai traditionalists—not to mention Thai architects and construction firms, who were excluded from this landmark building project. It was well known that Japan's grant aid was fully tied, but what mobilized the Thai construction industry at this time was the fact that only local Japanese affiliates seemed able to win OECF loan project contracts. The rapid penetration of the booming Thai market by Japanese construction firms led to a considerable amount of friction that boiled over in the cultural grant aid projects in question. Finally, the culture center incorporated expensive equipment that was difficult to operate and maintain. Equipment repair and replacement parts, even including light bulbs, required placing expensive special orders with Japanese trading companies. The Thai education ministry was expected to have a difficult time obtaining the extra budget for staff and maintenance for this white elephant. The upshot was that upon completion the Thai Culture Center was not officially dedicated on the king's sixtieth birthday as originally planned by the MFA. In short, the Historical Studies Center and the Thai Culture Center fell short of the MFA's political objectives because they crystallized resentment against Japan's rapid penetration of the Thai economy in the mid-1980s. Japan's ODA, which required linkage to the needs of the Japanese private sector, was becoming an inappropriate political tool.

Similar problems plagued technical cooperation. Japanese technical cooperation traditionally focused on training developing country personnel to run Japanese-made plant and equipment, and it relied on Japanese private sector personnel to transfer these skills. As Japanese projects turned to nonproduction areas such as education and culture, Thai officials and scholars began to note the paucity of English-language documentation and the inability of Japanese technical aid personnel to communicate in English.

Agricultural Aid Policy

In the name of BHN Japan increased its ODA to Thailand's agricultural sec-tor, but Thai academics remained skeptical. After reviewing the growing number of Japan's rural ODA projects in Thailand, Professors Suthy Prasartset and Kongsak Sonteperkswong perceive the following:

> Another obvious target of the Japanese assistance is to develop and di-versify the supplying [sic] resources of food, raw material, as well as energy for Japan. In the case of Thailand, the following examples seem to support this argument.
> Due to the oil crisis, the production of synthetic rubber has been ex-pensive and unstable since 1973. Therefore, the Japanese government has assisted in "the Rubber Products Development Program" in 1976. This is also because Japan has used a lot of rubber. Similarly, Japan intend to diver-sify [sic], has helped Thailand in the development of soy bean as well as maize cultivation. Shrimp Culture Development Project and the National Institute of Coastal Aquaculture also get a lot of cooperation from Japan, as shrimp and other fishery products are in great demand in Japan.[173]

The BAAC rural lending program also deserves comment because its funding by the OECF was a departure from Japan's traditional type of project, or "hardware" oriented loan cooperation. This funding was portrayed as a BHN-oriented program. The OECF started extending loans to the BAAC in 1976, and it was the first time Japan used the two-step loan formula whereby the OECF lends funds to a recipient lending institution that can then make small subloans for developmental purposes. The purpose was to give rural small holders short-term cash loans at below market rates. Only peasant farmers who could pledge real assets as collateral were eligible. The Japanese government required the BAAC to compile data on how the loans were spent. The BAAC reported that for the fifth OECF loan (disbursed in the 1981–1982 period), the 1,662 loan recipients used their loans as follows:[174]

Category	Percentage of households
Home improvement	70.0
Radios	68.1
Televisions	46.6
Motorcycles	28.4
Automobiles	4.3

Purchases of farm machines among these households increased as follows:

Type	Numerical increase
Small tractors	33 to 232
Hand tillers	232 to 1,213
Water pumps	582 to 1,229

The increased purchasing power of relatively well-off farmers was directed to consumer and capital goods in which Japanese firms and their local affiliates tended to be most competitive. These loans increased the consumption of creditworthy small holders, but the loans were not given to poor landless cultivators. Instead they widened the income gap between landowning peasants and landless rural labor. A briefing by a BAAC official and a visit to a rural village hosted by OECF and BAAC officials to meet some of the loan recipients seemed to confirm these points. The BAAC loan recipients were all relatively well-off small holders who had savings from farming and from renting land to tenants. In contrast, a tenant farmer interviewed stated that he was unable to save and was occasionally forced to go to moneylenders. Borrowing from local moneylenders entailed 30–40 percent annual interest rates, compared with the BAAC rate of 12 percent repayable over three to twelve years. The fortunate BAAC loan recipients used a portion of their subsidized credit to buy consumer goods and farm machinery—all of which were observed to be Japanese brands.

In this rural village Japan's ODA had helped to supply the electricity, the television and radio broadcast signals, and even the consumer financing to buy imported or locally made Japanese radios, televisions, and farm equipment. One old farmer used his loan to buy a Japanese stereo and a multipurpose Mitsubishi minitractor. When asked what other minitractor brands he had considered buying, he replied there were two others: one was made in Japan and the other in Thailand by a Japanese-Thai joint venture. He was not sure where the money he borrowed came from, but when told he laughed and said that in the past it was the United States and the Soviet Union fighting for the top position in the world—but now Japan had beat them both to become number one.

The Eastern Seaboard Project

The Eastern Seaboard (ESB) Development Program was a manifestation of MITI minister Tanaka's 1981 Bangkok initiative which clearly stated Japan's intent to move Japanese export-oriented manufacturing firms to Southeast Asia. These firms would export back to Japan or to other assembly locations lower-cost components that would enhance the competitiveness of Japan's advanced goods. The point behind Japan's strong backing of the ESB program was that MITI was no longer exclusively focused on opening Thailand to Japanese exports; MITI now was interested in developing locations for Japanese FDI in export-oriented manufacturing.

In 1979 the Industrial Estate Authority of Thailand was set up under the Thai Ministry of Industry to promote Thailand's industrialization by inducing more inward FDI. The idea was to create industrial estates and relevant infrastructure—roads, rail links, an airport or seaport (where appropriate), drainage and flood control, wastewater treatment facilities, electricity, water supply, communications, worker housing, commercial centers, recreational facilities, schools—to attract more investment. The Industrial Estate Authority first approached the World Bank and the ADB to finance a program to industrialize Thailand's Eastern Seaboard, but these agencies refused, citing the project's high cost, Thailand's public sector debt and deficits, uncertain offshore gas revenue prospects, and the low regional development impact behind the basic concept.

The Japanese, however, were eager to back this idea because it could be an ideal location for small and medium-sized manufacturing firms facing high labor and land costs in Japan and for Japanese firms in declining sectors such as petrochemicals and fertilizers. The Asian NIEs no longer served as a low-wage production base, and China, Indonesia, and the Philippines still lacked a hospitable policy environment in the early 1980s. According to JETRO, Thailand was an attractive location for FDI because of: "i) political stability; ii) steady economic development policy and attractive economic performance; iii) abundance of labor force of high quality and low cost; iv) comfort for Japanese people living in [a] Buddhist country."[175]

The feasibility study and basic design of the Eastern Seaboard project was done by Japanese consultants financed by JICA and the OECF. The basic design scheme centered around two industrial estates, one at Laem Chabang intended to promote light industries and exports, and the other at Map Ta Phut designed to accommodate heavy and chemical industries, with each served by a port facility. The Laem Chabang site was located 10 kilometers north of Pattaya, one of the main tourist attractions in Thailand at that time. Plans called for a deep-sea port to handle ships of up to 120,000 tons, an industrial estate of 225 hectares, an export-processing zone of 110 hectares, and related social infrastructure (housing, schools, hospitals, parks, etc.) and economic infrastructure (roads, railways, water supplies, electricity, and telecommunications) linking the site with the hinterland and with Bangkok. The design was to accommodate consumer goods production, basic materials processing, and the assembly of manufactures.

The Map Ta Phut complex was intended to establish gas-related and heavy industries at the point where Thailand's undersea natural gas pipeline came onshore. The core projects were a gas separation plant, a large petrochemical complex, and a large fertilizer complex. A waterfront industrial zone (for shipyards, seafood processing, etc.), an inland heavy industrial zone (for petrochemicals, chemicals, etc.), and a medium and light industrial zone (for agricultural processing, livestock processing, pharmaceuticals, etc.) were planned. Related economic and social infrastructure was also envisioned, with a small airport and a seaport with berths designed to handle a variety of oceangoing vessels, including a special berth for vessels carrying hazardous and toxic chemicals.

Japanese ODA funding for the import cost of the program began in July 1982 with a ¥15.0 billion loan for the gas separation plant at Map Ta Phut and a ¥6.6 billion loan to build a water supply pipeline to the project sites. By September 1987 the OECF had extended fourteen project loans totaling ¥104 billion related to construction of the ESB project with the whole program still less than half finished. The importance attached by the Japanese to this project was indicated by the fact that the ESB program accounted for 29 percent of the OECF's lending to Thailand in this period. Even at this pace, however, the Japanese expressed dissatisfaction that Thai borrowing for the ESB was not more active.

Faced with rapidly growing external debt, government debt, and trade deficit figures toward the end of the fifth plan period (1981–1986), the Thai government made an effort to cut back on the ESB project under advice from the World Bank. A 1984 World Bank study of Thailand's financial difficulties recommends

> continued careful assessment of large industrial ventures requiring Government support of any kind. This last point applies especially to the Eastern Seaboard Program. . . . A recent in-depth assessment of an earlier ambitious program design indicated that it is essential that each major project should be assessed on its own economic merits, and in terms of its feasibility and appropriate timing, given overall public and private finance constraints.[176]

Using unusually blunt language, the study states: "In the transport subsector the major projects which should be dropped or substantially phased back beyond the Fifth Plan period are railway network expansion, Laem Chabang port construction, a new international airport, and the Bangkok rapid rail transit project."[177]

When the Thai government announced it would freeze implementation of the fertilizer project at Map Ta Phut and otherwise slow up implementation of the ESB project because of budget deficits and external debt problems, the Japanese ambassador urged the Thai government to reverse its position.[178] Subsequently, environmental problems arose as the anticipated ship traffic and industrial pollution threatened to damage the important tourist industry centered in Pattaya, located between Laem Chabang and Map Ta Phut. Nonetheless, active Japanese ODA financing preserved all the major components of the ESB program against the advice of the World Bank (by then a relatively minor lender to Thailand) and in spite of Thai technocratic sentiment to cut back.

A National Economic and Social Development Board (NESDB) official interviewed in Thailand in 1987 cited the ESB as an example of poor project preparation by Japanese consultants who did not do a careful financial analysis of the program. To be fair, however, he added that the Thai side was at fault, too, for not having done an independent feasibility study.[179] The Thai ESB program had an estimated total cost of over $2 billion, and at mid-decade it seemed to be an uneconomic project. But what the World Bank did not foresee was the wave of Japanese FDI in the latter half of the 1980s that the ESB helped to accommodate, and with this inflow came more jobs, tax revenue, and export earnings for Thailand.

The main point here is that the ESB project manifested Japan's policy shift in the early 1980s toward preparing Southeast Asia, and Thailand in particular, for Japanese manufacturing firms that would need to relocate to find cheaper labor and land costs to preserve their competitiveness. The ESB also showed how Japan could push its own agenda onto a recipient government against the advice of its own technocrats and the World Bank. What the latter could not know was that Japanese direct investment would accelerate sharply, increasing from B2.7 billion in 1982 to B19.2 billion in just the first half of 1987.[180] What gave Japan the confidence to push ambitious infrastructure construction in Thailand was the knowledge that Japanese government and corporate policy would make Thailand a target of Japanese FDI. The yen appreciation of 1985–1986 only accelerated the underlying need for which Japan was preparing in the early 1980s.

The Penetration of Thai Decisionmaking

Thailand has one of the best aid administration structures in the developing world, first established on the advice of a 1959 World Bank mission. The first five-year development plan was inaugurated in 1961, and the Thai government has since stuck to planned development. The NESDB, which is directly under the prime minister, is responsible for drafting the five-year plans. It ensures that ODA projects match the current five-year plan, and it also handles ODA loan projects. The Department of Technical and Economic Cooperation (DTEC) is responsible for foreign grant and technical cooperation projects. Line agencies are responsible for proposing needed development projects.

There are several other agencies with regular roles in aid planning and administration. The Bureau of the Budget (BOB) must authorize local financing of aid projects. The Bank of Thailand (BOT) can veto projects if they hurt the balance of payments or add unduly to the official debt burden. The Thai Ministry of Finance (TMOF) also reviews the assumption of official debt and signs ODA loan agreements. Finally, the Civil Service Commission must approve the additional staffing requirements in aid projects. The prime minister and several cabinet ministers who make up the Economic Policy Board are responsible for overall coordination of the system.

After the second oil shock the Thai government instituted several policy and administrative reforms under the advice of the World Bank. The Economic Policy Board (under NESDB leadership) began drawing up a list of priority project requests that is revised annually, and a three-year rolling

plan system with annual updates was added. Guidance by the BOB and a special foreign debt service committee limits the number of new projects initiated every year. Finally, in order to bring Thai private sector investment plans
more into line with national plan targets, the Public-Private Consultative
Committee was also formed.

These reforms were analyzed in an IDE report entitled "Economic
Development Planning in the ASEAN Countries and the Nature of Our
Nation's Economic Cooperation."[181] The policy recommendation for Japan
is: "We should consider our economic cooperation after knowing the
likelihood of implementation of those programs and projects given priority by
NESDB, then carry it out."[182] To keep track of Thai government priorities,
Japan began placing "JICA experts," i.e., Japanese government or private
sector personnel funded by JICA, in Thai government agencies. For example,
in 1987 there was a JICA expert in the telecommunications ministry helping
to write frequency specifications, and JICA experts in the Thai agriculture
ministry were guiding Thai production toward commodities of strategic or
commercial importance to Japan. A JICA expert was posted in the NESDB
itself, as well as in TMOF, the Board of Investment, and the Thai Development Research Institute. Whether they sat in line or planning agencies, the
JICA experts were able to gather inside information, affect Thai policy
thinking, and predict Thai decisionmaking. As a result of this technical
cooperation strategy, it is no exaggeration to claim that JETRO now has
better information on the Thai economy than does the Thai government. This
use of ODA is almost invisible to anyone outside the Thai or Japanese
governments, and it is more effective in influencing official decisionmaking
than episodic treaty negotiations.

It must not be forgotten that the NESDB and DTEC review aid requests
from line agencies. Every program and project must be designed, proposed,
and implemented by a line agency, and at this level the Japanese private sector can inject proposals in ways described in later chapters. In addition, aid
requests must be approved by the Thai Cabinet, and this regular involvement
of high-level Thai politicians means that they can, and do, push pet projects
over the objections of NESDB or DTEC technocrats, sometimes at the urging
of Japanese officials or business executives. Thus, Japan has channels of access below, above, and within the Thai economic planning agencies. Japan
can thus shape the Thai position in yearly loan and grant aid negotiations with
Japan *before* the Thai approach the negotiating table. This aspect of Japan's
ODA is noted by Professor Prasert Chittiwatanapong of Thammasat University in assessing Japan's political strength in Asia: "Recently, each year JICA
[has] sent about 200–300 experts to Thailand, stationing [them] at virtually
all government agencies except the military ones. Their access to information
and policy-makers, and intimacy with their Thai colleagues are too valuable
an asset to describe."[183]

By the early 1980s the MFA and MITI agreed on the importance of

ODA, but they differed in their focus of concern. The MFA needed ODA to demonstrate compliance with Western demands for strategic- and BHN-oriented ODA, as well as to cultivate better bilateral relations with governments in Asia. MITI emphasized the need to enhance Japan's economic security and competitiveness by using ODA to restructure Japan's FDI and trade relations with Southeast Asia; MAFF began to use ODA to cultivate food resources for Japan. The implementation of these agendas can be observed in Thailand because of that country's geopolitical and economic characteristics. What conditioned these agendas was the linkage of state and private sector activities in economic cooperation.

CHALLENGE AND RESPONSE
IN JAPANESE ODA POLICY, 1985–1992

By the second half of the 1980s Japan's ODA had grown large enough to attract growing commentary. Frictions with the West over trade and security tended to elicit Japanese pledges of more ODA, and this generally satisfied Western foreign policy experts, who tended to gloss over the economic agenda in Japan's ODA. For example, regarding Japan's ODA William Brooks and Robert Orr conclude: "There is still a commercial component in some current aid programs, but such examples are now the exception rather than the rule."[184] An unwillingness to acknowledge the obvious continued through 1991, when in the conclusion of a Council on Foreign Relations volume on Japan's ODA, Shafiqul Islam called criticism of Japan's mercantilist practices in aid "misguided" and explained:

> It is not so much the case that the government of Japan has been using foreign aid to promote exports; rather, the private sector has been the key factor in developing economic relationships with neighboring countries, by first establishing trade with them and then moving on to finance and direct investment. Foreign aid has often served as a "harmonizer" of these overall bilateral relationships.[185]

In evaluating Japan's ODA Western aid professionals focused on Japan's ODA effort in comparison with other donors. Perhaps the most impartial and cautious appraisal of Japan's ODA at the start of this period was done by the DAC secretariat in preparation for an official biennial review of Japan's aid policies.[186] The general issues the review raises are the low level of budgetary effort, the failure to meet DAC standards for concessionality, a limited ability to meet the needs of the poorest and least developed countries, and poor prospects for developing ODA that would benefit the poorest and least empowered populations in the developing world. It also points out that "the combination of geographic and sectoral distribution and terms has contributed to giving an advantage to procurement in Japan." Suggested changes include a greater ODA/GNP effort; more reliance on grants; a shift of aid toward African LDCs and South Asia, where material resources as well as functional administrative and managerial bases were in shortest supply; a reduced emphasis on aid tying and procurement from Japan; and the creation of a centralized aid agency or ministry to implement a shift in aid priorities. [187]

Individual assessments by Western aid experts could be more pointed. A researcher from the German Development Institute sent to Tokyo to study Japan's ODA policy orientation concludes:

> Competition with the USA and Western Europe has dominated Japan's development cooperation from the outset: until the mid-1970s development cooperation was chiefly a means of promoting exports and safeguarding supplies of raw materials . . . its concentration on Asian countries enabled Japan to regain the advantages it had lost in the region as a result of its defeat in the Second World War.
>
> Now that Japan has risen to become a leading economic power, more is expected of it both internally and externally. . . . Internally, the two oil price shocks emphasized the need for development cooperation to be geared to longer term objectives. Cooperation with East and South-East Asian countries became an integral part of the structural adjustment of Japanese industry (e.g., through off-shore investment), and elements of development cooperation were used to strengthen Japan's commercial contacts with resource-rich developing countries throughout the world. [188]

The second set of Japanese ODA critics were recipients who objected when Japanese ODA seemed intended primarily to benefit Japanese commercial and economic interests. A Western-trained Thai aid official in charge of grant and technical aid has this to say about Japan as a donor:

> Her day-to-day execution of aid very well testify [sic] to her ulterior motives. Being the only country that generously provides grants-in-aid in the form of buildings and facilities, the Japanese government is making a business out of her ODA money and in turn strengthens her private sector role in Japan's foreign aid programme. . . . To a larger extent, other donors and recipients alike have regarded the Japanese aid program as a thinly disguised flow of export subsidies. [189]

Other aid administrators interviewed in Thailand, Indonesia, and the Philippines had similar views. Representative of these views is a 1988 briefing paper drafted by the Philippines National Economic Development Agency (NEDA) on Japanese ODA. The agency's board of directors concludes:

> Japanese assistance is very much "tied" although there have been moves to improve the quality of ODA. . . . For loan assisted projects involving civil works and equipment procurement, the amount that flows back to Japan ranges from $0.75–$0.95 [on the dollar] which is higher than that of the US. A study on the latter shows $0.27 amount of flowback for loans and $0.33 for grants. [190]

Japanese officials in both JICA and the OECF admitted in private inter-views—not for attribution—that these views and criticisms were valid. In fact, several were helpful in explaining the various informal mechanisms employed to manipulate official procedures to benefit the Japanese private sector. The problem is that because these officials do not set basic policy, they can do nothing to change the situation.

A third set of critics were domestic interests outside the institutions affil-iated with the keizai kyōryoku system. The media, academics, grassroots or-ganizations, and opposition parties focused on the waste and corruption in Japan's ODA. Favorite targets were the behind-the-scenes machinations of LDP politicians and private firms to influence project selection; overpriced and inappropriate projects that benefited only Japanese trading companies and exporters; and a systematic bias toward promoting the overseas advance of Japanese commerce. Many of these critics had leftist leanings, but an in-creasing number emphasizing environmental and human rights concerns did not, and some became linked to transnational nongovernmental organizations. These critics wanted a noncommercial, effective, social welfare–oriented ODA program.

The mainstream media played a crucial role in this period in raising popular concern over ODA policy. Japan's ODA first received serious treat-ment by journalists in the early 1970s.[191] A *Sankei Shimbun* investigative group surveying Japan's economic cooperation in Southeast Asia found that reparations and aid were an integral part of "another war" *(mō hitotsu no sensō)* for Japanese commercial predominance in Asia with little relationship to helping the poor. Yamamoto Mitsuru, a *Japan Times* journalist writing a book on Japan's economic diplomacy, finds that "almost all the beneficiaries of 'economic cooperation' are Japanese firms rather than recipient countries, and this is how the commercial principle *(shōbai hon'i)* in Japan's aid policy took shape."[192]

In the key 1985–1992 period, Japan's journalistic community again re-viewed Japan's ODA and reached largely the same results. Ad hoc investiga-tive groups established by *Asahi Shimbun* and *Mainichi Shimbun* each did their own surveys of contemporary Japanese ODA policy. The 1985 *Asahi Shimbun* volume entitled *Enjo tojōkoku Nippon* (Japan: the developing coun-try in aid) was published to alert the Japanese public to the realities of Japan's rapidly growing ODA spending. It offers many examples and case studies of the intimate relationship of Japanese ODA with Japanese private sector busi-ness activity, and it raises concerns about the official secrecy and corrupt practices surrounding ODA decisionmaking. It quotes an LDP member with Cabinet experience saying:

> Aid money is like spy money. The Diet doesn't decide how much goes to which country, and the people are not told how it is being used. Moreover, it keeps growing and growing. As far as being the goose that lays the golden egg in financing political payoffs, it is super high grade.[193]

Although the book failed to galvanize public attention, the 1986 scandal over the corruption in Japanese aid to the Philippines did, and the basic message of the book gained weight. In the wake of the scandal ODA coverage in the print and electronic media jumped, and ODA exposés and scandals became a fairly regular feature of news coverage. Even the normally staid government-owned NHK Broadcasting Corporation aired a scathing documentary report in late 1986 on fraud, mismanagement, and corruption in Japan's ODA projects in the Philippines—for which it was vigorously reprimanded by the MFA and ordered to present further programs on ODA to the MFA for previews and comments. But the level of public interest in ODA was now so high, and the evidence of systemic problems so widespread, that ODA reform became a regular theme in newspaper editorials. In one striking instance, five major dailies (*Asahi, Tokyo, Yomiuri, Mainichi,* and *Nihon Keizai*) ran nearly simultaneous editorials July 12–13, 1988, calling for serious ODA reform on in response to a report on ODA by the Management and Coordination Agency (Sōmuchō). Even weekly mens' magazines began featuring ODA scandals. The popular *Shūkan Posto* went so far as to feature a series of lurid articles on ODA corruption that eventually numbered fourteen over the 1988–1990 period.

Finally, critics within the keizai kyōryoku establishment tended to emphasize the need to improve coordination, effectiveness, and efficiency in promoting existing organizational goals. They tended to advocate several points. First, there was a need to clarify procedures and assume responsibility for overall policy formation. Second, synoptic overall coordination was preferable to interministerial battles over policy priority. Third, fiscal control could be improved by multiple-year budget cycles and a more centralized system for review of budget requests. Fourth, the implementing agencies needed to be better staffed, more independent in evaluating projects, and better able to coordinate activities with each other.

Immediately after the yen appreciation (endaka) in 1985, bureaucratic and producer interests quickly redefined Japan's ODA priorities. In this period there is no doubt that policy responded more quickly and thoroughly to Japan's own economic security and competitiveness strategies than to the concerns of organizationally excluded foreign and domestic critics. This view challenges those who argue that Japanese ODA policy is a traditional diplomatic instrument, is fundamentally driven by Western criticism, or is unaffiliated with Japan's industrial or trade policies. As we compare the success that internal and external stakeholders in ODA had in demanding change in this period, what becomes apparent is that the power to influence policy was a function of organizational position. External stakeholders had the least influence; structurally included actors had significant influence; and the occupants of positions of formal authority and decisionmaking had the most scope for initiative.

FOREIGN DEMANDS ON JAPAN'S ODA

The Plaza Accord of September 1985 marked Japan's political arrival among the great powers when the five main advanced economic powers (the United States, Japan, Germany, France, and the United Kingdom, collectively called the G-5) agreed to address their trade imbalances and wildly fluctuating exchange rates. Japan's agreement to help manage a decline in the dollar exchange rate was indispensable to effective action. Although this caused a larger and faster drop in the value of the dollar than anticipated, in the end the net effect only magnified Japan's impact in the dollar-based global economy. The Western response to the economic rise of Japan was schizophrenic. Resentment of Japan's disproportionate benefits from Western economic and security regimes fed demands for policy changes by Japan. The United States threatened the Japanese government with unilateral trade sanctions using the so-called Super 301 clause added to the 1988 Omnibus Trade Act. But U.S. foreign policy experts still valued conservative rule in Japan because it provided the cornerstone of Western military and political influence in Asia. Moreover, the West needed Japan's capital and technology during the decisive endgame of the Cold War.

Western resentment occasionally spilled over from trade into other areas such as defense. But a Japanese economic colossus rearmed was not really needed and could be destabilizing. This left Western governments at a loss over how to deal with a mercantilist Japan. As happened since 1971, Japan shifted attention from its trade surpluses to its ODA efforts. When Prime Minister Nakasone visited Washington in 1987 to defuse trade tensions, he pledged, in addition to some import liberalization and extra fiscal stimulation, to increase Japan's ODA spending and private capital flows to the developing world as a contribution to the Western alliance. And as it had done repeatedly in the past, the West accepted this as the only realistic modus vivendi with Japan.

Looking back from the early 1990s, the most obvious change was in Japan's ODA volume, but the level of effort relative to GNP remained relatively modest (see Figure 6.1). Nevertheless, this was enough to ease Japan's international dilemmas considerably. ODA spending successfully substituted for politically difficult changes in Japanese market access or security policies, and it created a symbol of political commitment to the present international system. It was not a particularly painful effort because Japan had the ability to pay (determined by healthy numbers in per capita GNP, government budgets, and international balance-of-payments positions).

But as was the case in the past, increased ODA spending also served Japan's own interests because of its economic security rationale, and because in coordination with trade and investment measures ODA could play a role in restructuring Japan's industrial profile and raising its position in the international division of labor.

Figure 6.1 ODA/GNP Ratio for Japan and DAC Average, 1977–1991

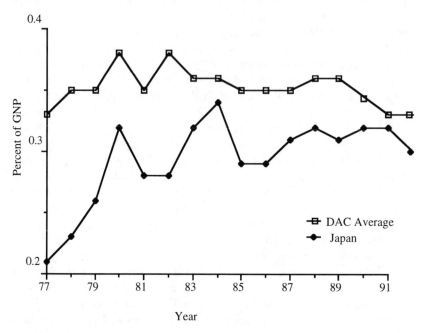

Source: OECD.

Transnational NGOs

Japan's rising international significance as an ODA donor had ripple effects, and NGOs working on global issues began noting Japanese ODA projects that lacked sensitivity to environmental and human rights issues. For example, in March 1987 international attention was drawn to the issue of rain forest destruction when environmental and human rights groups led by the Tropical Rainforest Action Network closed a logging road in Sarawak, Malaysia, to conserve the rain forest and preserve the rights of forest-dwelling indigenous peoples. The Japanese trading company C. Itoh was managing this particular project, and even more damaging was the fact that some ¥200 million in JICA funds had been used to finance the construction of the logging road. This alerted environmentalists to Japan's role in rain forest destruction, an image that was only reinforced by the Barnett Report commissioned in 1987 by the government of Papua New Guinea to review the logging industry. It singled out Japanese firms as the market leaders in various kinds of fraud and overlogging.[194]

Japanese ODA financing of the Indian government's Narmada River development project also drew the attention of Western NGOs. This project, which involved the planned construction of some 30 major dams, 135 middle-sized dams, and over 3,000 smaller dams over the next forty to fifty years, would submerge some 550,000 square hectares of forest and farmland and displace over one million villagers. In September 1985 the OECF announced it would add ¥2.85 billion yen in cofinancing to World Bank funds. By 1987 affected villagers along the Narmada River began organizing protests, and they won the active support of Western environmentalists and human rights groups, who started an international campaign to stop the project.

As part of this campaign European NGOs organized three large international conferences (The International Citizen's Conference on the World Bank; The International Counter-Congress, and The Permanent People's Tribunal) in 1988. Japanese ODA was singled out for criticism, and transnational NGO networks then began to pressure Japan. One manifestation of this was an April 1990 demonstration in San Francisco outside the headquarters of Sumitomo Bank organized by the International Rivers Network and the Rainforest Action Network. Demonstrators carried a giant inflated Godzilla as well as placards denouncing Japanese ODA for the Narmada Project and for its alleged promotion of tropical rain forest destruction. Coinciding with this demonstration, the Japanese chapter of the Friends of the Earth organized a symposium in Tokyo on the Narmada project, attended by 500 activists, that was well covered by the Japanese media. The mobilization of transnational NGOs induced the Japanese government to announce that it would offer no further ODA financing to the Narmada project, which then elicited praise for Japan from international environmental groups.

The more basic point, however, is that in the 1985–1992 period it was clear that Japan would have to make some policy concessions to improve its image in the West. After Japan's importance as an anticommunist bulwark disappeared, Western NGOs critical of Japan could begin to get a more sympathetic ear from Western publics and governments. For this reason Japanese policymakers began to devote ODA spending on such areas as the provision of antipollution equipment where environmental concerns overlapped with private sector needs for new product and new market development subsidies.

DOMESTIC PRESSURES FOR ODA REFORM

What is more remarkable about the 1985–1992 period is the upwelling of domestic criticism of Japan's ODA. In this period domestic criticisms previously touted mainly by the radical left in earlier years[195] emerged in the mainstream media and NGO sectors of Japanese society. More important, calls for reform also emanated from the corporate sector as well as from within the Japanese government itself.

By 1986 the rapidly growing ODA budget began to attract serious public attention because the government was calling for fiscal austerity and a new consumption tax. Just at this moment the so-called Marcos scandal (*Marukosu giwaku*) revealed the corrupt inner workings of the Japanese aid system in the Philippines under President Ferdinand Marcos. This sparked public outrage and demands for meaningful ODA reform.

The uproar started when the personal papers Marcos brought with him when he fled to the United States were seized by the U.S. government and made available to the House Foreign Affairs Subcommittee on East Asia and the Pacific. The papers were made public on March 21, 1986, and they re-vealed that since at least the early 1970s 10–15 percent of OECF loan aid was systematically kicked back to Marcos and his cronies by more than fifty Japanese aid contractors through a system of bid rigging, contract fraud, and illegal payments. These documents, as well as a special investigative com-mission established by the new Aquino government and headed by Senator Salonga in the Philippines, left no room for doubt about this fact. The Japanese media and public were left to ask the obvious questions. First, the amounts were so large and the practice so institutionalized that the Japanese government could not have been unaware of this misappropriation and waste of funds. Why didn't it put a stop to this practice? What many suspected was that a percentage of this aid money was finding its way back to the LDP. Second, the Japanese public now knew their taxes and postal savings were ending up in the wrong hands, but they now wanted to know if anything at all was reaching the poor people of the Third World.

Diet Calls for ODA Reform

Within days of the release of the Marcos papers in mid-March, both Prime Minister Nakasone and Foreign Minister Abe Shintaro pledged to make a full accounting, and the Diet's Upper House Industry and Commerce Committee as well as the Budget Committee began hearings on the revelations. These hearings proved to be highly embarrassing to the government as it stone-walled while the U.S. and Philippine governments were releasing thousands of official documents revealing the questionable policies and practices of Japanese ODA. By April 11 the opposition parties created a special Diet committee to investigate aid to the Philippines (Tai-Hi Keizai Enjo Chōsa Tokubetsu Iinkai), and delegations of opposition Diet members and journal-ists began traveling to the Philippines to gather information denied them by the Japanese bureaucracy.

What the opposition parties and the Japanese media discovered in Manila was that Japanese aid projects were filtered through a selection system that was rigged to benefit Japanese businesses and a corrupt domestic elite, and that too many projects were inappropriate and poorly executed. This fed a stream of reports in the daily papers and weekly magazines, with *Asahi Shimbun* concluding: "Through the Marcos Scandal the aspect of economic aid of Japan, by Japan, and for Japan floats up to the surface."[196] But as the opposition parties searched for more damning evidence of bureaucratic and LDP collusion to use in a crucial upcoming election for both houses of the Diet, the LDP began pressuring the new Aquino government to stanch the hemorrhage of information. At this time a badly needed $316 million package of OECF loans for the new Philippine government was under discussion. When Philippine finance minister Jaime Ongpin visited Tokyo in mid-April to discuss matters, after meeting with Prime Minister Nakasone Yasuhiro, Finance Minister Takeshita Noboru, and Foreign Minister Abe Shintaro, Ongpin said at a Tokyo press conference, "The rebate scandal will become an impediment to the future implementation of yen loans." The rumor reported in the press was that Ongpin called Salonga from Tokyo and asked him to stop the leaks.[197] What ensued was a blackout of further revelations from Manila, and Ongpin was invited back to Tokyo in May to sign the package of OECF loans.[198] As a result Diet action was stalled as opposition demands for information disclosure were turned back by the government's position that unless the Philippine government disclosed the information, Japan could not breach the rights of a recipient government to confidentiality.

The next key case where the opposition demanded Diet access to official ODA documentation was the previously mentioned JICA-funded logging road. The opposition members in the Upper House Foreign Affairs Committee asked JICA officials to present the project's preliminary survey and completion reports, but were refused with the following explanation: "These are surveys relating to disbursement of funds containing information about recipient firms, and because it is not good to make this public, we have decided to make financing-related reports secret, and so cannot make them public."[199]

Even with the backing of an aroused public opinion, the opposition parties in the Diet could do no better than to embarrass the government by repeatedly demonstrating that it had too many things to hide. The opposition and media have used a steady stream of revelations of fraud, waste, and corruption in Japanese ODA to call for reform, but bureaucratic privilege protected by LDP rule blocked Diet debate and passage of ODA policy legislation. The overall impact of regular media and opposition calls for ODA reform on the government was to spur modest incremental measures to increase public confidence.

After the Marcos scandal the government promised to disclose bidding documents for all aid projects by 1988, but in that year it reneged. In the face of continuing official secretiveness regarding ODA, the social affairs bureau of *Mainichi Shimbun* organized its own ODA investigative group to look into how the Japanese taxpayers' money was actually being spent. It produced a book in 1990 entitled *Kokusai enjo bijinesu—ODA wa doo tsukawarete iru ka* (The international aid business—how is ODA being used?) This volume exposed the promotion of Japanese commercial interests and corrupt practices in a wide variety of ODA projects in unprecedented vividness and detail. It concluded that ODA was still being used primarily to supplement the competitiveness of Japanese trading companies and manufacturers and was not helping poor people effectively. The flavor of the book is contained in the opening pages, where a trading company executive gives an account of how he got a grant aid contract:

> First, we worked on important officials and health-related people in the recipient country. We occasionally brought them to Japan for sightseeing in Kyoto and the like. Then we decided that the project would be ODA. So we called the powerful LDP Diet members who were in the health *"zoku"* (i.e., they had influence in the Ministry of Health and Welfare). From some seven companies, with effort we were able to get the contract for the medical equipment. That's all we had to do.[200]

The book so enraged the MFA that it summoned the editors supervising this project to hear its objections. *Mainichi Shimbun* subsequently disbanded this group and put the individuals concerned to other tasks. One member of this group interviewed by this author communicated bitter resentment over the attitude and manner of the government's response.

Grassroots Organizations

The Marcos scandal prompted a number of citizens' groups to agitate for reform of Japanese ODA. Perhaps the most significant effort to develop an alternative "people-to-people" model for development assistance was that of the Japan Negros Campaign Committee (Nihon Negurosu Kyampeen Iinkai), organized by Waseda University professor Nishikawa Jun, with nine regional offices spread throughout Japan. This self-financing group was formed during the Marcos scandal to get private Japanese citizens directly involved in helping improve the living conditions of the poor inhabitants of the Philippines' Negros Island. Although Nishikawa rarely criticized the Japanese government directly, he told the Philippine press that his motivation was to redress the imbalance in Japanese ODA, and he noted that the only Japanese ODA project on impoverished Negros was a power generation plant built for a copper mine and smelter, the output of which was controlled by the Marubeni Corporation. He commented, "No direct assistance is actually extended to the people."[201] This group eventually put out an edited volume in Japanese in 1991 containing the results of their experience in promoting poverty relief and self-reliance through private people-to-people efforts.[202] This alternative approach to development assistance soon gained the endorsement of a wide range of other domestic activists in the area of women's rights, human rights, health care, labor, and academics who were critical of ODA.[203]

The effort to mobilize political opposition to the ODA system in this period centered on Sophia University Professor Murai Yoshinori, the most outspoken domestic critic of Japanese ODA. Murai became acquainted with

Japan's ODA during two years of fieldwork in Indonesia studying rural village society. Capitalizing on the public outrage over the Marcos scandal, in the run-up to the June 1986 Upper and Lower House elections Murai organized an anti-LDP campaign effort based on the theme of ODA reform. The election was lost, but to consolidate the theme of ODA reform, volunteer activists formed a citizen's group called REAL (Reconsider Aid Citizen's League) in September 1986, the first grassroots organization in Japan dedicated exclusively to the cause of changing Japan's ODA policy orientation. The group attracted participants and sympathizers from official as well as opposition and student backgrounds. Its immediate task was to collect and disseminate information on Japan's opaque ODA policy making and implementation systems. The ultimate objective was to gain a Diet-passed law *(ODA Kihon-hō)* defining new ODA policies and procedures.[204] The nature of the obstacles presented by bureaucratic power and long-term LDP rule in Japan will be examined later.

Murai and REAL were active in several ways. First, Murai himself appeared repeatedly in the media exposing cases of ODA failure and corruption, debating government officials, and calling for ODA reform. Second, Murai and REAL shaped Japan Socialist Party, Social Democratic League (Shaminren), and Kōmeitō policy on ODA reform, and they fed the opposition Diet members ammunition with which to attack the government over ODA waste and fraud. Third, they sponsored public meetings and symposia. Fourth, they have informal ties to transnational NGOs, thus inducing external pressure on official policy.

Finally, they have been active publishing books and monographs criticizing Japan's ODA. In 1989 Murai and fellow REAL members put out a slim volume critiquing the commercial orientation and rigged project selection system endemic in Japanese ODA.[205] Murai also coauthored with Japan Socialist Party (JSP, subsequently the Democratic Socialist Party of Japan) chair Doi Takako and REAL representative Yoshimura Keiichi a 1990 volume that contrasts the powerlessness of the Diet to determine ODA policy with the experience of Western legislatures and that holds up Canada's ODA system as a model for a reformed Japanese system.[206] The overall impact of Murai's activities has been to promote domestic and international awareness of Japan's ODA failings in the areas of BHN, the environment, and human rights (including women's rights).

After the impact of the Marcos scandal and the efforts of early activists such as Nishikawa and Murai spread public awareness of certain problems in Japan's growing ODA programs, a broader range of private individuals and NGOs began to look into these matters. A group of students, office workers, and educators (including Murai) frustrated by the lack of change in the wake of the Marcos scandal formed the ODA Chōsa Kenkyūkai (ODA Investigation Study Group) in 1988 to study how Japanese ODA affected poor, local communities in the Asia Pacific region. The result was a 1992 volume containing testimonials by on-the-ground observers of Japanese ODA projects, who invariably found that Japanese business interests benefited but the welfare of surrounding communities was neglected. [207]

Widening interest in ODA also spurred an investigation into Japanese ODA to Indonesia organized by the Federation of Japanese Bar Associations (Nichibenren), which sent an investigative committee there in 1989 to look into the Asahan project. The head of this group reported that "Japan's ODA is not helping local people." [208] By March 1991 the group's Committee on Pollution and Environmental Protection issued a report of a year-long investigation into Japan's ODA to the Philippines, Thailand, Indonesia, and Malaysia. Entitled *Japan's Export of Pollution and Environmental Destruction*, the report emphasizes Japanese ODA's role in promoting rain forest destruction, pollution, and the violation of the rights of local communities and indigenous peoples.

The mechanism by which Japanese branches of transnational environmental groups got involved in pressing ODA reform may be illustrated by the experience of an NGO calling itself the ODA Kenkyūkai (ODA Study Group), formed in 1988 at the initiative of members of the Japanese branches of the Friends of the Earth and the Tropical Rainforest Action Network. JICA had formed an ODA policy study group on the environment and invited environmental NGOs to attend the inaugural party of the JICA group. But NGO participation in the JICA group's deliberations was not allowed. They subsequently offered to meet with JICA to discuss ODA policy but were rebuffed. So the NGOs formed the ODA Kenkyūkai to draft an alternative policy recommendation that was handed to the Japanese government a year later—but this elicited no official response. The effect on the orientation of the ODA Kenkyūkai was described as follows:

> The lesson gained from this experience was that if one pressed the government in general and abstract terms the gate will not open. So we reached the conclusion that there was no alternative to establishing in fact whether or not Japan's ODA was really helping people than to focus on concrete cases. [209]

After several failures to establish direct institutionalized access to information and decisionmaking inside the government, the strategy shifted to one of information gathering through NGO networks and criticism of present policies. The result of this new orientation by the ODA Kenkyūkai was the publication in 1992 of a small primer on Japanese ODA that reaches much the same conclusions as had Nishikawa and Murai; this primer calls for a basic ODA law, a centralized aid agency, and stronger environmental and social concerns. [210]

Since the government denied grassroots organizations direct access to policymaking deliberations, and because these groups had no effective recourse through the courts or the Diet (for reasons discussed in the next chapters), their criticisms of current policy and suggestions for reform turned outward to the media, general public, and overseas NGOs. The activities of the above-mentioned NGOs have been significant in terms of spreading awareness of Japan's ODA shortcomings, but they have been unsuccessful in doing more than eliciting government pledges to improve its policies.

Internally Driven Reform

Within the Japanese government there were several studies commissioned by individual ministries and agencies involved in ODA, but the only ones that attempted to critique the entire administrative system were done by the Management and Coordination Agency (Sō mucho) and the Board of Audit (Kaikeikensa-in). Although they could not be expected to call for radical reform, they did make public enough cases of wasteful and ineffective projects to keep up the pressure for change.

The administrative inspection *(gyōsei kansatsu)* of the aid system by the Management and Coordination Agency (MCA) was ordered following the Marcos scandal. The first of two reports *(kankoku)* was released in July 1988 and focuses on grant and technical assistance. It is based on a review conducted in April–September 1987, and it suggests five areas for reform. First, project follow-up support was needed because it was found in one flagrant case of failure that some thirty-five buses provided by grant aid were inoperative because of a lack of spare parts. Second, grant aid for small projects and emergency relief should not be subject to the slow-moving Cabinet approval process; otherwise, embarrassing cases of late-arriving disaster relief would recur. Third, grant aid paperwork should be moved from the MFA to JICA, as should the grant aid budget allocation. Fourth, technical training provided by Japan needed to be reoriented to the needs of developing countries. Finally, to speed implementation Japan should begin offering prepackaged aid projects. [211]

The proposed reforms were an effort merely to tinker with the existing system. Nonetheless, it symbolized an effort by the government to tackle ODA reform. Then–Prime Minister Takeshita delayed its release by several months so it would follow his appearance at the Toronto Summit, where he pledged to increase ODA spending and to send extra aid to sub-Saharan Africa.

The second MCA administrative inspection, carried out in April–September 1988, concerned the larger loan aid program. Reform proposals were grouped in three areas: project implementation, OECF administration, and policy coordination among the yonshōchō. In the latter two areas reform proposals were minor. But in the area of project implementation, proposals with structural implications were made, including clarification of the respective roles, standards, and procedures of the MFA, MITI, MOF, and EPA in decisionmaking; cosponsorship between MITI and the MFA of project finding missions; agreements between them on what individual recipients' needs are; and the complete untying of construction loans and of (still wholly tied) engineering services loans.

The MCA's inspections found much evidence that Japan's ODA was not improving the welfare of recipient countries, but its recommendations were limited to modifications of existing procedures. It did not evaluate Japan's ODA according to any theory of how ODA can best contribute to the social and economic development of the developing world. And because its reports were premised on maintaining the existing basic administrative structure, the MCA could not consider whether the division of ODA responsibilities among sixteen ministries and agencies had anything to do with the observed ineffectiveness or inefficiency of Japan's ODA. Writing as an individual in an administrative science journal, one of the authors of the official reports acknowledges these problems by stating what could not be included in the official recommendations: "I believe that it is necessary in the future to clarify and make concrete the concept and principles of economic cooperation."[212]

The impact of these reports on the ODA system was modest. Although certain recommendations on improving office efficiency were carried out, others with more substantive ramifications were ignored. The only official action the yonshōchō and other ministries were required to take was to respond in writing to each point raised by the MCA. The responses were vague and stuck to the formulas developed in response to criticisms of foreign governments and the domestic groups.[213] Because there was no objective and legally enforceable standard by which to evaluate the substance or procedures of administrative actions in ODA, the MCA could not establish administrative failure or malfeasance.

As in the case of the MCA inspections, the audits of ODA projects and programs conducted by the Board of Audit, a neutral watchdog commission appointed by the prime minister, were intended to address the problems revealed by the Marcos scandal. The first two audits reported in December 1989 and 1991 acknowledge a significant number of failed and ineffective projects, but because of MFA pressure, normal auditing procedures and full disclosure of results were not allowed, for which the Board of Audit was criticized, especially because ODA now cost over ¥10,000 per capita in taxes. In December 1992 the full contents of another audit were disclosed for the first time. Out of sixty-seven projects in five countries inspected, ten involving a total of over ¥63 billion in ODA spending were found to be serious failures, reportedly mainly because of a lack of coordination between various actors in project activity. Domestic critics of ODA pointed out that the Board of Audit still underreported waste and ineffectiveness because it needed the prior permission and on-site guidance of recipient governments and MFA officials to inspect projects. The board would not draw general conclusions about the ODA system because "as an issue of national policy, this is outside the jurisdiction of the Board of Audit."[214]

Private Sector Calls for Reform

Although the Japanese private sector favored the traditional principle of private sector–led, request-based assistance, it always harbored discontent with the ODA system. There were three main reasons. First, the system generated contradictory sets of administrative guidance from ministries with different mandates. Second, it made the project approval process lengthy, arbitrary, and expensive for those firms wishing to ensure approval of a particular project. Finally, whether mistakenly or not, the private sector believed that Japan's ODA could be cleaned up without damaging keizai kyōryoku. From the private sector viewpoint, a streamlined policymaking and implementation system could be devised that guided Japanese private sector resources to meet developing country needs. The dream of the business sector was to create a centralized aid agency that could serve as a single, authoritative setter of policy priorities and approver of project requests. Failing that, it wanted all the ministries and agencies involved in ODA to establish a single set of objective standards and procedures that would bind all actors.

The Keizai Dōyūkai, like the administrative reform councils discussed below, has been a relatively forward-looking articulator of business viewpoints that registers the general direction of business sentiment rather than the considered weight of corporate sector interests. It has taken an interest in economic cooperation issues since the early 1960s, and in 1968 it called for a centralized aid agency and a unified aid budget—even as it pressed for greater inclusion of private sector viewpoints. In the 1985–1992 period the underlying concerns of the Keizai Dōyūkai were still the same. For example, the Keizai Dōyūkai put out a report in June 1987 entitled *In Search of a New Direction in International Cooperation Policy*, in which it calls for a Cabinet minister for international cooperation to preside over an advisory council that would rein in the various ministries and agencies, and supervise a consolidated economic cooperation budget. Again, it stresses the need for private sector inclusion—while adding the need for greater openness:

> The present closed system centered mainly on government agencies should aim for an open-style cooperation (comprehensive cooperation) incorporating the activities of private sector enterprises and citizens from every strata.
> By this means the scope and quantity of cooperation would markedly increase, enabling the expansion of direct cooperation between the private sectors of Japan and the developing countries, contributing greatly to the vitalization of private sector activities in developing countries.[215]

Besides the Keizai Dōyūkai, ad hoc official commissions composed of business leaders charged with setting an agenda for administrative reform addressed the keizai kyōryoku system. The first such commission, the Provisional Commission for Administrative Reform (Rinji Gyōsei Kaikaku Chōsakai) investigated this system in 1964 as an outstanding example of poor interministerial coordination. In one of its last policy recommendations it called for the creation of a single economic cooperation agency to overcome the lack of coordination within the government. [216] This idea was pushed by Prime Minister Tanaka Kakuei in the mid-1970s, but it was defeated decisively by bureaucratic resistance. After this failure only politically naïve foreign and domestic elements (such as DAC, the opposition parties, and the media) continued to call for a centralized aid agency.

The administrative reform process was revived in 1981 by Prime Minister Nakasone, who created the Second Provisional Commission for Administrative Reform (Dai-niji Rinji Gyōsei Kaikaku Chōsakai, otherwise known as Rinchō). As before, it was a venue for private sector critique of bureaucratic structures, and in its July 1982 report the section on economic cooperation is unusually blunt. It points out that keizai kyōryoku policy planning and implementation were "not adequate," and that too many aid projects were "inappropriate" or "ineffective." Not surprisingly it lays the blame solely on the bureaucracy. The key reform proposal is for a basic policy statement *(kihon hōshin)* to be honored by the sixteen ministries and agencies in the economic cooperation system. At the same time, however, it calls for strengthened government–private sector cooperation: "Based on an appropriate division of labor between ODA and the private sector in keizai kyōryoku, the harmony and complementarity between both sides should multiply the effect of a comprehensive style of economic cooperation." [217]

In October 1990 a new Provisional Administrative Reform Council (Rinji Gyōsei Kaikaku Suishin Shingikai, or Gyōkakushin) was created to propose ways of improving Japan's domestic quality of life and international relations. In its first report issued in July 1991 it again calls for one official statement of basic ODA policy principles to harmonize the government's fractious internal workings, but in response to events like the Gulf crisis there are a number of newer emphases. It discusses ODA as a strategic foreign policy instrument to influence recipient military spending and democratic development. To meet growing cynicism regarding Japan's ODA, it advocates full untying of both loan and grant aid, as well as greater government openness and information disclosure. It also emphasizes the need to pay attention to environmental concerns and to involve more NGOs in aid activity. [218]

The best barometer of big business' serious priorities in ODA, however, is the Keidanren because of its stature and its deep involvement in keizai kyōryoku through its Standing Committee on Economic Cooperation. In the first half of this period the Keidanren cautiously focused on technical issues relating to the use of ODA to move Japanese direct investment into the developing world. A 1987 report dwells on the need to coordinate ODA, tax incentives, and trade and investment insurance schemes, as well as new regulations, to govern the Ex-Im Bank and commercial banks. At this time the Keidanren featured its proposal to create an "international cooperation project promotion system" (eventually resulting in a semipublic corporation called the Japan Industrial Development Organization, Ltd., or JAIDO) as a demonstration of the Japanese private sector's approach to developing poor countries under even the most adverse conditions. The Keidanren did mention the need for a "dramatic improvement in the quality of the Japanese government's bilateral ODA," but this meant mainly greater accommodation of private sector needs and speedier and more efficient operation of the existing system.[219]

But by the end of the decade, having helped define the private sector role in an FDI-oriented economic cooperation policy, the Keidanren began to move cautiously on the issue of ODA reform. Action was needed because continued revelations of Japanese business involvement in questionable aid practices and priorities, as well as inefficient and inoperative aid projects, were coming to the attention of Japanese taxpayers and foreign publics from a wide range of sources, including the Japanese government's own watchdogs of administrative efficiency. Moreover, the Keidanren began to emphasize the need for economic deregulation, for example, by stating in one resolution: "We advocate minimum government intervention, even in industrial policy. . . . While the business community must move away from overdependence on government and become accountable for their behavior and destiny, these efforts must coincide with further administrative reform and deregulation."[220]

This new spirit of independent assertiveness was reflected in a Keidanren report on economic cooperation that depicts a mismanaged ODA system that was damaging to Japan's effort to build a new international role and image. Although the Keidanren report reiterates the importance of the private sector role in ODA, it states that the decentralized system was too slow and was inadequate at ensuring quality aid projects. It recommends that the government draft an ODA charter to explain to taxpayers and foreign observers what Japan's ODA was about. But the Keidanren did not call for Diet action, nor did it call for a more centralized system of administrative or budgetary control. Instead it modestly called for a Cabinet order to ratify policy discussions in the Taigai Keizai Kyōryoku Shingikai.[221]

The Keidanren report reflects a private sector consensus that could not be ignored by the bureaucracy. The private sector as a whole wanted greater openness and full aid untying because it no longer needed aid tying to win project construction bids, and its scale of business in the developing world now dwarfed the size of most ODA projects. Beyond this, the private sector was tiring of dealing with the bureaucratic red tape and political payoffs that confidential tied aid procedures had bred.

The ODA Taikō

The dismal response of the Japanese government to the Gulf crisis of 1990–1991 spurred Gyōkakushin to focus on the conduct of Japanese diplomacy and ODA. In taking up ODA, what Gyōkakushin discovered was that the policy agenda was widening so quickly that it was becoming untenable. On the one hand, foreign policy needs led the MFA to pledge ODA policy measures to address security concerns, democratization and human rights, and environmental protection, as well as other issues such as BHN and women's issues. Meanwhile, other functional ministries and agencies had their own individual agendas in international cooperation and were pushing harder to claim more of the expanding ODA budget. Thus, each ministry— and the bureaucracy as a whole—had little interest in reforms that would take away its discretionary control over growing ODA budgetary resources. To arrest these centrifugual tendencies the second report of Gyōkakushin, issued December 12, 1991, called for an official ODA Policy Outline (ODA Taik ō) that would provide a shared standard for policy performance. The report was handed to Prime Minister Miyazawa, and it led to a Cabinet order approved in December 1991 detailing specific measures to be enacted in 1992. Among these items was the ODA Taikō.

Not only did this remind the government of the Keidanren proposal of the previous year, but it also coincided with oblique criticism from DAC. Japan underwent a biennial DAC review in 1991, and the report of the DAC secretariat bluntly asks Japan to answer this question: "What is the basic rationale of Japan's aid programme and what are its objectives?"[222] That such a fundamental question needed to be asked after twenty-seven years of DAC membership was significant.

The task of drafting the Taikō was given to the External Affairs Office of the Office of the Prime Minister, which was staffed by bureaucrats seconded from the ministries. This ensured that each ministry and agency would be given the opportunity to include their priorities and pet concerns. Meanwhile the Keidanren quickly worked up a report that was issued in March 1992 entitled "How to Make International Contributions Through ODA," which stresses the importance of private sector partnership:

> Among the Asian countries where Japan has placed the emphasis of its economic cooperation, the construction of ODA-financed infrastructure has introduced private sector trade and investment, and this has vitalized the economies of those countries receiving this three-into-one style aid [*san mi-ittai to natte enjo*]. In this way ODA and private sector activities are as two wheels on a cart in the economic development of developing countries, and a system for creating better relations between government activities and private sector activities needs to be prepared.[223]

The Taigai Keizai Kyōryoku Shingikai, chaired by Okita Sabur ō, then called for the speedy drafting of the Taikō and preservation of trinity–style ODA.[224] As part of the informal political process leading to a Cabinet decision, the four-page draft document was submitted to the Special Committee on Foreign Economic Cooperation of the LDP's Policy Affairs Research

Council where it was quickly rubber-stamped on June 26, 1992; within four days it was approved as a Cabinet order *(naikaku kettei)*. The substantive points are outlined below.

Outline of the ODA Taikō

I. Basic rationale
   a) Humanitarianism
   b) Interdependence
   c) Environmental protection
   d) Peace
   e) Self-help aided through provision of training, infrastructure, and basic facilities
II. Principles
   Premised on the sovereign equality of recipients, recipient initiative in requests for aid, socioeconomic conditions, and the overall state of bilateral relations, ODA would seek to:
   a) Balance environmental and development needs
   b) Avoid military applications
   c) Discourage recipient military spending and the development or transfer of weapons
   d) Encourage democracy, market economics, and human rights
III. Items for emphasis
   a) Asian regional emphasis (especially East Asia)
   b) Global issues (e.g., environment), BHN, research and training, infrastructure, structural adjustment
IV. Ways to ensure effective implementation
   a) Better policy dialogue
   b) Better tie-up between loan, grant, and technical aid
   c) Broader cooperation with multilateral and bilateral aid donors
   d) Utilization of the lessons of East Asian development experience
   e) Application of environmental technology to growth needs
   f) Provision of appropriate technologies
   g) Support for private sector technological cooperation
   h) Strengthening of ties to regional cooperation groups
   i) Coordination of ODA, FDI, and trade policy measures to promote private sector cooperation
   j) Promotion of relevant policy research
   k) Consideration for the role of women in development
   l) Consideration for the plight of children, disabled, and elderly
   m) Consideration for the problem of income inequality
   n) Avoidance of unethical or corrupt practices in ODA
V. Measures to gain domestic and international support
   a) Promotion of access to information
   b) More public relations and educational efforts

VI. Implementation system
   a) Develop more and better aid experts and consulting firms
   b) Establish some kind of system for better interministerial contact
   c) Adopt measures to protect the safety of overseas aid workers

Policy Change or Continuity?

There is no doubt that the government believed that the Taik ō was an adequate and meaningful response to the rising chorus of foreign and domestic criticism in the 1985–1992 period, but did it substantially change Japan's ODA policy? The answer is it did not.

The Taikō reads like a laundry list of concerns—which it is. It is a collection of vague aspirations that is uncontroversial, but it is not the result of anything that could be called a public debate over ODA policy, nor did it define specific procedures for effective policy implementation and review. It did not touch the structure of administration or budgeting. As in the past, ODA policy was handled outside the Diet with direct access to government decisionmaking given only to representatives of the private sector. Although in form *(tatemae)* the ODA Taikō honors the Gyōkakushin call for a policy document, it ignores the substantive issue *(honne)* behind this demand, i.e., the need to restructure an administrative system that is badly in need of reform.

Following the promulgation of the ODA Taik ō, the MFA claimed that with Cabinet approval of the Taik ō the comprehensiveness of Japan's ODA was now "unmatched by other advanced countries."[225] As far as the bureaucracy was concerned, the Taikō was the maximum concession to all demands for reform, and further debate was closed. That the Taikō left the basic problem unsolved was indicated by a June 1993 editorial in the *Nihon Keizai Shimbun,* a probusiness newspaper, that explicitly sympathizes with continued opposition efforts to reform ODA and calls on the government to open up and regularize its decisionmaking in order to facilitate public support for further ODA growth.[226]

If substantive change in policy orientation is measured in such terms as new policy legislation, revised decisionmaking structures, reorganized systems of policy implementation, or a new pattern of policy outcomes, then Japan's ODA changed only marginally at best. Thus, in the 1985–1990 period an insulated, bureaucratically dominated ODA policy making system was able to preserve itself against rising external pressures. As explained in other chapters, the ability to resist pressures for change rests on a much broader and deeper domestic structure.

The Japanese government's successful effort to stave off unprecedented pressures for change in ODA is only half the story of the 1985–1992 period. The other half relates to the process of "normal" policy adjustment as ODA shifted its emphasis from enlarging Japanese exports to enlarging Japanese FDI. The ability to meet new challenges to Japan's international economic competitiveness remained an essential characteristic of Japan's ODA in the 1985–1992 period.

DEFINING JAPAN'S ROLE IN A
RESTRUCTURED GLOBAL ECONOMY

The impact of the yen appreciation after the 1985 Plaza Accord on Japan cut two ways. On one hand, it made capital-surplus Japan an economic super-power in the dollar-based global economy. On the other hand, there was the burden of higher domestic costs of production and the new political and eco-nomic obligations that went along with economic superpower status. Japan needed new policies to address the new problems and opportunities.

In 1985 the share of direct investment in Japan's gross capital outflow was only 8 percent, down from 59 percent a decade earlier. Moreover, by mid-decade Japanese manufacturing had only about 4 percent of its produc-tion offshore, compared to about 18 percent for the United States. The appre-ciation of the yen made certain Japanese manufacturing sectors uncompeti-tive, but it also allowed Japan to move this manufacturing overseas and allow imports of the new offshore production. Southeast Asia was a logical location for low–land cost and low–wage cost production in the second half of the 1980s. The problem after 1985 was not lack of exportable capital or poor FDI options; the real issue was how to guide Japan's surplus capital to exploit this opportunity.

A conception that addressed this issue was first offered in a report issued in 1986 by an obscure UN group headed by Okita Saburō. The report calls on Japan to channel $125 billion in capital to the developing world by the end of the decade in what was called a "Japanese Marshall Aid Plan." This plan suggests that Japan should become the world's leading provider of capital and technology for Third World development. Although Japan would run struc-tural trade surpluses, Japan would "recycle" them to the developing world in the form of aid and direct investment. FDI would transfer capital, technology, and management and labor skills to developing countries without creating further debt. Thus, Japan's ODA, trade surpluses, and FDI became interde-pendent aspects of Japan's new leadership "burden." This vision defined the outlines of Japan's post-endaka economic cooperation priorities.

Capital Recycling

MOF was the first to announce the new Japanese leadership initiative, proba-bly because Japan could not ignore pleas to help manage the ongoing interna-tional debt crisis when Japan emerged as the world's single largest source of capital and was earning such huge trade surpluses. The immediate concern of the United States and Western Europe was their exposure to Latin American debt, but beyond this was a larger structural issue of declining net capital flows to the developing world. Japan had to prove that it would use its increased financial leverage in a responsible manner. These pressures led in September 1986 to Finance Minister Miyazawa Kiichi's announcement that Japan would "recycle" $10 billion in public and private capital to the developing world over the next three years. There were four components to the plan: the creation of a special ¥60 billion Japan Fund in the World Bank, a $2.6 billion contribution to the World Bank's soft loan facility, a $1.3 billion contribution to the Asian Development Bank's soft loan facility, and a $3.6 billion government loan to the IMF.

This plan was followed by a second $20 billion recycling pledge that Prime Minister Nakasone brought to Washington, D.C., in May 1987. It was a notably hasty effort to produce an *omiage*, or "gift," for the United States before visiting to discuss the bilateral trade imbalance. Japan pledged to give $8 billion in official contributions and private capital lending to set up special funds in multilateral development banks; $9 billion in policy-based loans through the OECF, Ex-Im Bank, and Japanese commercial banks in coordination with the World Bank and IMF; and $3 billion in untied loans by the Ex-Im Bank and commercial banks. The Ex-Im Bank was cast in a new lending role because export finance was no longer a priority. The recycling proposals eased trade friction by linking Japan's trade surpluses to a total of $30 billion in new Japanese capital for the developing world—something wanted by Japan, the West, and the Third World, but for their own reasons. (The $30 billion commitment was folded into in a new pledge in 1989 to recycle $65 billion in the 1987–1992 period.) MOF was willing to guide Japanese capital to the indebted countries using the Ex-Im Bank and OECF in parallel with World Bank or IMF conditional lending programs. In fact, Japan increased its balance of medium- and long-term bank lending to Latin America by $15 billion in the 1986–1988 period—even as the United States and Europe reduced their totals. [227]

MITI was close on the heels of MOF in offering a new initiative in economic cooperation called the New Asian Industrial Development (AID) Plan. Announced in January 1987 in Bangkok by MITI minister Tamura Hajime, it committed Japan to help develop export-oriented manufacturing in Asia, but this pledge lacked a detailed outline until later in the year. Because of the New AID Plan's complexity and geographical focus, it will be discussed below in the context of Japan's emphasis on restructuring relations with Asia.

The MFA responded to endaka by formulating new ODA pledges for Prime Minister Nakasone to announce at the 1987 Western economic summit. One pledge was to meet Japan's 1992 ODA dollar spending target by 1990, and another was a pledge to give an extra $500 million of ODA to sub-Saharan Africa within three years. The yen appreciation made more dollar spending possible with no extra Japanese budgetary effort, but if anyone noticed they were too polite to mention it. Japan followed this up at the Western summit in 1988, when Nakasone announced the Fourth ODA Plan which promised $50 billion in ODA over the 1988–1992 period—something that helped to draw attention, but it still did not raise Japan's effort as a proportion of GNP. Realizing that the United States would cut its ODA in a new period of budgetary troubles, the MFA aimed to become the world's largest ODA donor, and the theme of Japan as an ODA superpower began to develop in Japanese diplomacy.

BUILDING ASIAN LEADERSHIP

Another central element of Japan's new global leadership role was regional leadership. After endaka Japan began to use its increased economic leverage to restructure political and economic relations with Asia in fundamental ways. The role of Japan's ODA in this effort was critical. As mentioned above, the New AID Plan was focused on Asia, but unlike MOF- and MFA-sponsored pledges, it did not set a spending target; it merely stated MITI would help develop export-oriented manufacturing in Asia, and it linked this to the larger issue of restructuring Japanese and Asian industrial structures toward greater interdependence.

MITI's New AID Plan

The core of the New AID Plan was an effort to relocate Japanese manufacturing rendered uncompetitive by the yen appreciation to new low-cost sites in Asia. At the outset it is worth noting that this plan dovetailed with the plans of Japan's manufacturers that wanted to internationalize production. For example, after the yen appreciation NEC Corp. began diversifying its production overseas according to a concept it called "mesh globalization." This called for the movement of production of low-end finished goods and parts to Asia, whence they could be exported to advanced country markets. An international purchasing office to coordinate Asian parts production and shipment to the rest of the world was planned. NEC would keep R&D functions and production of advanced products in Japan. Those products mostly serving the U.S. market would be made or assembled in the United States.[228] Besides giant firms like NEC, small and medium-sized manufacturers were also interested in moving overseas as a result of the yen appreciation. According to a November 1986 survey by the Ministry of Labor, 26 percent of Japanese manufacturing firms with over 1,000 workers had already started to expand overseas production, and another 26 percent were considering overseas production.[229]

The New AID Plan promised to help Japanese firms realize their plans, and so MITI could count on their cooperation. With ODA to accelerate and guide natural market forces, MITI could then pledge to Asia's developing economies Japanese joint-venture investment in export-oriented manufacturing in Asia that would give them capital, jobs, technology, tax revenue, and

foreign exchange earnings. This effort would put Japan firmly at the core of
the dynamic Asian economies. These objectives are indicated by Okabe
Takenao, the division director of MITI's economic cooperation department,
who was in charge of compiling the plan:

> In the background was our decision to cooperate actively, from a com-
> prehensive national point of view, in resolving the economic problems con-
> fronting the developing countries arising out of accumulated debt and low
> primary product prices. And then Japan also has to change its economy to an
> internationally cooperative style because of the difficult present economic
> environment. In other words, it is necessary to plan a change in the indus-
> trial structure and change from an export-oriented style to a domestic de-
> mand–led style, but in this it has become necessary to plan the promotion of
> overseas investment and technology transfer by our nation's enterprises.
> Accordingly, it is necessary to emphasize cooperation with Asia Pacific,
> with which we have the deepest historical and geographic ties, and which
> promises potential development in the future.
>
> Actually, in spite of the fact that Japan has deep historical and geo-
> graphic ties with Asia, looking at economic relations, where, for example, in
> the case of ASEAN, trade is only 10 percent and investment is 20 percent, at
> present the weight is relatively low. I think one factor that may explain this
> is that up to now in trade a vertical division of labor has existed wherein we
> import primary goods and export manufactured goods. Moreover, in in-
> vestment, firms recently are wanting to invest as a way of dealing with the
> stronger yen, but it is mainly toward the United States and Europe, whereas
> toward the developing countries the growth rate is low.
>
> And so it is necessary to step up trade and investment with the develop-
> ing countries. That is why as Minister Tamura stated, a "creative division of
> labor" should be set up, i.e., a multidimensional, substantial economic coop-
> eration constructed not only to raise the trade share of industrial goods, but
> also to promote capital and technology flows, thereby forming a horizontal
> division of labor. This is the basic idea.[230]

As in the 1981 MITI initiative toward ASEAN, this plan envisaged the
creation of export-oriented manufacturing and agro-industries in Asia using
economic cooperation measures, but it is distinctive in three ways.

1. *Scope of Implementation*. The scope of this planning framework extended
beyond the ASEAN countries to include China and South Asia. The operational crux of this initiative was the formation of bilateral Japanese-recipient
steering committees to plan successive phases of industrial cooperation. A
MITI official explains his ministry's economic cooperation agenda in the following way:

> First, we carefully analyze such things as the status of the target country's
> economic development and its development potential, and select those in-
> dustries that show promise as future exporting industries. Next, in order to
> nurture the selected industries we construct a concrete strategic plan together
> with the recipient country. Then we inject in a concentrated manner all the

technical cooperation schemes implemented by the various organizations included in the New Aid Plan related to economic cooperation such as JETRO, JICA, AOTS, and JODC, and package this together with the capabilities of those private sector firms that are thinking of offering capital or technology.[231]

By 1988 the ASEAN Four (Thailand, Malaysia, the Philippines, and Indonesia) and China were incorporated into this framework; by 1992 Pakistan, Sri Lanka, and Bangladesh were added, and China came to be considered sui generis.

2. *More effective ODA*. From the start of the 1980s MITI was particularly interested in using Japan's ODA to increase Japan's trade and investment in Asia more effectively. The Japanese government's own studies of ODA effectiveness consistently stressed the need to link individual projects to an overarching goal. One representative study of aid effectiveness in Thailand concludes:

> The different kinds of grant aid each give rise to their own special forms of economic cooperation and are achieving success, but between them, aside from the mutually reinforcing use of general grant cooperation and project-style technical cooperation, they are not always closely related. In particular, there is a need to have a comprehensive and consistent aid program linking loan cooperation with technical and grant cooperation in order to raise their mutually reinforcing effectiveness.[232]

MITI addressed this problem by defining how grant, loan, and technical cooperation would be used in each country in relation to the general aims of the New AID Plan. Project selection would be coordinated by a more careful process of country-specific planning (see chart). The country planning process was intended to match types of Japanese investment to the emerging comparative advantage of each recipient country. Planning was to proceed according to the three phases outlined below.

The first phase identified target sectors for Japanese investment and technology transfer in each recipient country. This involves the drawing up of a "master plan for comprehensive cooperation" *(sōgō kyōryoku masutaa puran)* in which industrial sectors that are attractive are selected for penetration by Japanese direct investment, and existing recipient policy and resource barriers are identified. In particular, the target country's industrial policy, foreign investment policy, industrial estate construction plans, and degree of infrastructure development are given attention. To facilitate cooperation Japanese JICA experts are placed in recipient planning agencies. For example, in 1987 Japan had two JICA experts in Thailand's Department of Industrial Promotion and one expert in the Malaysian Industrial Development Agency coordinating New AID Plan procedures, and Japan had started three-year comprehensive industrial surveys of both countries.

After sufficient study official memorandums of understanding between

Implementation Phases of Japan's New AID Plan

Phase One: Infrastructure for export industries

A. *Cooperation (yen loans) to prepare an infrastructure base, i.e., industrial estates, ports, airports, railways, roads, telecommunications, etc.*
B. *Cooperation (project-style technical cooperation) in preparation of related facilities such as trade training centers, export inspection centers, and product and technical development centers.*

Phase Two: Technical cooperation to develop export industries

A. *Dispatch of experts and receipt of trainees in production technology, management, product development, etc.*
    1. Trade and industry promotion through Japan External Trade Organization (JETRO)
    2. Dispatch of experts: Japan Overseas Development Corporation (JODC)[a]
        Japan International Cooperation Agency (JICA)
        ASEAN Trade & Tourism Centers
    3. Receipt of trainees: Association for Overseas Technical Scholarships (AOTS)[b]
        ASEAN Centers, etc.
    4. Development surveys: JICA
        Engineering Consultants Firms Association (ECFA)[c]
        Japan Plant Exporters Association[d]
    5. Project-type technical cooperation: JICA

B. *Marketing cooperation such as market surveys, marketing promotion, distribution improvements.*
    1. Developing country trade and industry promotion center activities (JETRO)
    2. ASEAN Center activities
    3. Japan-China Trade Expansion Council

Phase Three: Financing of export industries

A. *Targeted credit schemes such as two-step loans or two-step investment for targeted industrial sectors (via OECF and others)*
B. *Organization of Japan-host country joint ventures, technology tie-ups*
    1. Asian Industrialization Project (JETRO)
    2. Small and mid-sized enterprise overseas investment promotion activities (Japan Chamber of Commerce and Industry)[e]
    3. Overseas investment advising (Small and Mid-sized Enterprise Agency)[f]
    4. PAC Consulting (JICA)
    5. ASEAN Center activities
C. *Special investment financing (Ex-Im Bank, JODC)*

a. JODC is a quasi-public corporation under MITI guidance that subsidizes foreign direct investments (FDI) by Japanese manufacturers
b. AOTS is a quasi-public corporation under MITI guidance that aids Japan's FDI in developing countries by training developing country personnel at the investing firm in Japan.
c. ECFA is an industry association whose ODA project-identification activities are subsidized by MITI.
d. Also known as the Japan Consulting Institute (JCI), this association of whole plant exporters engages in activities similar to those of ECFA.
e. The JCCI is active in pushing FDI by Japan's smaller subcontracting industries.
f. This agency is administered by MITI and works with JCCI, JETRO, and the Ex-Im Bank to promote FDI by the smaller industrial firms threatened by the yen appreciation.
See *Kokusai Kaihatsu Jânaru* No. 379 (July 1988), pp. 55–56.

Japan and recipient governments are drafted singling out the sectors targeted for Japan's keizai kyōryoku. As of 1988 Thailand and Malaysia had already selected their target sectors, which were metalwork, toys, chemical fibers, ce-ramics, and furniture in the case of Thailand; and auto parts, electronics, ce-ramics, and rubber products in the case of Malaysia.[233] As for how agreement is reached on such matters, a MITI official explains that "the agencies are doing their work, but Japanese experts enter and give advice on the basis of the recipient side's request. Since their side is making industrial policy, one cannot say that Japan is pushing ideas on them. Japan is offering experience, and the other side makes the choices."[234]

The second phase was to draw up "industrial sector development strategy guidelines" *(sangyō sekutaa ikusei senryaku gaidorain)*. These guidelines use ODA-funded design studies to specify needed infrastructure such as industrial estates, technical training centers and programs to support the targeted indus-tries, and specific changes in recipient government policies to attract Japanese direct investment. A MITI official explains:

> Some firms want to go [to Bangkok], but because the infrastructure is lack-ing, they are saying that they cannot make the move. So the Thai govern-ment is building the Laem Chabang industrial estate to attract labor inten-sive industries. . . . Compared with other industrial estates such as Masan in Korea or Kaohsiung in Taiwan, what incentives can Laem Chabang offer to attract firms? If it is not more attractive than other industrial estates, Japanese firms will not move in. We can make suggestions on this kind of "soft" know-how and have the Thais accept whatever they find accept-able.[235]

The third phase was the actual implementation of plans. In accordance with the master plan and the sector guidelines, key projects and programs are implemented, and the desired export industries are established through in-flows of Japanese FDI.

3. *An Asian Division of Labor.* The focus on Asia also involved the concept of an Asian division of labor in which Japan would inject appropriate tech-nology and capital into the sectors of emerging comparative advantage among the Asian economies. This would develop an interdependent, com-plementary division of labor in Asia influenced by flows of Japanese goods, capital, and ODA. The *1986 MITI Economic Cooperation Yearbook* con-cludes its chapter on this topic with the following:

> The "international division of labor strategy" of our country's enterprises is progressing quickly in the developing areas of Asia. From a macro-view-point, production and investment in Asia's developing countries will in-crease, and from a micro-viewpoint, parts procurement and manufactured exports from existing locations will be reorganized and new bases will be set up. We can expect a dynamic development of overseas activities and a deepening of the international division of labor. . . . Horizontal economic

ties of trade, capital, and technology flows among the Asian developing countries will be formed, and this will work toward the important task of building a dynamically developing "creative international division of labor."[236]

What was envisioned was already evident in Japan's trade with the Asian NIEs. Compared with the previous year, in 1987 Japanese imports from the Asian NIEs of televisions increased 559 percent; electrical fans, 218 percent; and electronic calculators, 140 percent. It is estimated that 90 percent of the televisions, 50 percent of the fans, and 70 percent of the calculators were produced in Japanese factories.[237] Japan increased its imports of manufactures from the NIEs quickly in electronics and machinery, but this mainly represented access for overseas Japanese production. The same thing was happening with ASEAN. JETRO reported that in 1986 Japanese subsidiaries or joint ventures produced one-third of Japan's manufactured imports from Thailand. In the same year, Japanese firms accounted for 13 percent of Malaysia's total exports of manufactured goods, and exports to Japan were growing rapidly as large Japanese corporations moved production there to supply the Japanese market.[238] Thus, Japan was attempting to use FDI and import liberalization measures to manage both the restructuring of its own economy as well as the pattern of Asian industrialization and trade flows (see Figure 6.2). MITI called this coordinating effort the construction of a horizontal division of labor with Asia, and three-into-one economic cooperation was the key policy tool.

The ASEAN-Japan Development Fund

To advance Japan's regional leadership, in his September 1987 visit to Thailand then–Prime Minister Nakasone announced that Japan would set aside $2 billion from his $20 billion recycling pledge to promote the development of the private sector in ASEAN, but no further details were given because the MFA had to work out the implementation details with MITI and MOF. An outline of the ASEAN-Japan Development Fund (AJDF) initiative was provided by Prime Minister Takeshita when he attended the last day of the ASEAN summit meeting in December 1987. It consisted of three programs.

The first program was a $200 million program to build regional industrial projects funded by the OECF and the Ex-Im Bank. OECF lending would be at 3 percent and Ex-Im Bank lending at 0.5 percent below Japan's prime rate. The firms would be joint ventures with at least two ASEAN partners and one non-ASEAN (primarily Japanese) partner. The second program was a $1.6 billion fund to finance joint ventures on a country-by-country basis. Two-thirds of this fund would be provided by the OECF and the other third by the Ex-Im Bank. The third program involved the creation of an innovative $200 million investment firm to support export-oriented Japanese joint

**Figure 6.2 Japanese FDI in Manufacturing to Asia, 1980–1988
(by selected sectors)**

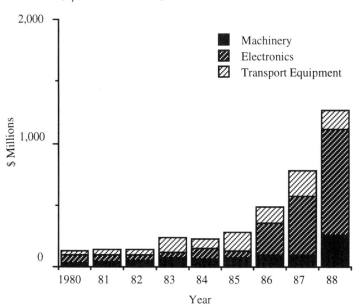

Source: MITI, 1990.

venture firms in the ASEAN countries by buying the equities they issued on local capital markets. The vehicle, called JAIC (explained later in this chapter), featured OECF participation to reduce private investor risk.

With the endorsement of ASEAN or of an ASEAN member government, Japanese joint ventures would be eligible for AJDF funds and Japanese ODA-funded technical assistance. The sectoral targets would be agrobased industries, manufacturing industries, industrial infrastructure, and rehabilitation of plants—not coincidentally, the same as those of MITI's New AID Plan. The basic design of the plan was finalized in April 1988.

The ASEAN countries warmly received this proposal because it addressed their concern to promote export-led industrialization and to crack the Japanese market in manufactured or processed goods. Nonetheless, some expressed concerns that the plan was strictly business oriented and would not address ASEAN's social development needs.[239] Recently stung by the 40 percent appreciation of their already large yen-denominated debt, and wary of the chance of further yen appreciation, the ASEAN negotiators also requested near-zero interest rates and dollar or currency basket loans, but these requests were turned aside.[240]

By its placement within the framework of the $20 billion recycling pledge and its focus on injecting Japanese manufacturing firms into the

ASEAN economies, the AJDF plan is a combination of previously announced keizai kyōryoku concepts that the MFA repackaged for ASEAN. The ASEAN heads of state were pleased that Japan would send its prime minister bearing gifts to court their favor, and Takeshita left the ASEAN summit with authorization to speak for ASEAN at the next Western economic summit.

PRIVATE SECTOR POLICY INPUT

The reason the new pledges were short on specifics at the time of their announcement was that although a ministry like MOF, MITI, or the MFA could commit Japan to certain goals, nothing concrete could be accomplished before implementation through the private sector could be arranged. This process of consultation and consensus formation was decentralized, ad hoc, and composed of many groups with overlapping representation. Nonetheless, what anchored this process were organizations embedded in the keizai kyōryoku system, and the boundaries of deliberation were set by the structure of the keizai kyōryoku system. Illustrations of how this amorphous process developed and shaped policy follow. Generally speaking, the keynote for this process was provided by the Taigai Keizai Kyōryoku Shingikai, which issued a report on May 15, 1987, that called for a comprehensive reorientation of Japan's ODA to alter Japan's industrial structure to cope with the yen appreciation.[241]

The Vision Study Group

One of the earliest and most interesting efforts to devise implementation strategies for Japan's new ODA and recycling pledges was the Kokusai Kyōryoku Bijiyon Kenkyūkai (International Cooperation Vision Study Group), chaired by Okita Saburō and hosted by the International Development Center (IDC). This was an ad hoc study group consisting of distinguished experts and representatives of key institutional actors in Japan's keizai kyōryoku system, together with a strata of junior bureaucrats and researchers involved in Japan's ODA. The study group would hold meetings in IDC's offices in Toranomon at which senior government officials were invited to present policy issues, after which a general discussion would take place.[242] The group's recommendations were read widely and helped to shape the general consensus regarding how Japan would guide its growing ODA and promote the recycling concept in line with Japan's own restructuring needs.

The first report, issued in July 1987, contains four main policy proposals offered in connection with the recycling plan. The first is expansion of Japan's trade insurance system along with a revision of the tax system to give the private sector incentives to increase trade and direct investment in the developing countries. The second is the creation of a joint public-private sector "project-finding fund" to help identify ODA/investment project opportunities.

This is the concept that ultimately produced the JAIDO and JAIC initiatives detailed later in this chapter. The third proposal is to increase ODA loans for local cost financing, which would speed up infrastructure project construction and move Japanese capital exports more quickly. The fourth proposal is for planned country-specific cooperation strategies facilitated by an increase in the quality and quantity of Japanese experts in recipient countries.

The Vision Study Group followed up in February 1988 with another report on how to make the investment project selection process plan-rational, and at the same time keep the Japanese private sector happy. The answer had to do with nurturing and deploying more able technical personnel. The report recommends more JICA project design contracts for Japanese consultants, more private Japanese design consultants serving in government agencies, and more development experts in recipient countries. These personnel would constitute an "information network" linking the public and private sectors that would be better able to identify projects that meet the criteria of both. They would "construct an information network based on numerous and deep relationships between organizations in the developing countries, the [Japanese] government's ministries and agencies, implementing agencies such as JICA, OECF, and JETRO, research bodies such as IDC and IDE, and private firms."[243] Finally, the Vision Study Group advised the government to send more personnel to institutions like UNDP or the World Bank in order to acquire expertise and widen access to information.[244]

What distinguished the Vision Study Group's activities was its focus on moving from a passive to an active principle of project selection. Under the leadership of Okita (who simultaneously served as chair of the Taigai Keizai Kyōryoku Shingikai from January 1988), the Vision Study Group was heavily oriented toward the public policy aspects of keizai kyōryoku, and the recommendations of the Study Group helped to articulate the new direction in Japan's economic cooperation after endaka.

The Keidanren Response to Recycling

The manner in which public-private sector coordination is achieved through peak business associations is illustrated well by a policy study group formed by the Keidanren. After Nakasone unveiled the $20 billion pledge in May 1987, the Keidanren's Standing Economic Cooperation Committee (headed by Haruna Kazuo, the chairman of the general trading company Marubeni, Ltd.) organized the Surplus Recycling Problem Deliberation Council (Kuroji Kanryū Mondai Kondankai). The Keidanren wanted to ensure that the government had realistic ideas about how to increase FDI in the indebted developing countries.[245]

The deliberation council focused on the issues of trade insurance and project identification identified by the Vision Study Group. The Keidanren made it clear that without Japanese government guarantees and incentive schemes, the private sector would not do the government's bidding. In order to gather background information the Keidanren sent study missions to UNDP, World Bank, the International Finance Corporation (IFC), and other international development finance institutions. The deliberation council then issued a report at the end of 1987 with conditions and proposals that MITI accepted in principle.[246]

This led to the formation in January 1988 of the Special Subcommittee to Promote Project Formation by the Keidanren's Economic Cooperation Committee. The focus was on identifying direct investment projects that would not add much to developing country debt and would earn both profits and foreign exchange.[247] By May the Keidanren and the Japanese government agreed to set up an equally owned joint stockholding company, with half of the capital to be owned by the OECF and the other half to be put up by Keidanren members.[248] Initially called the International Cooperation Project Promotion Company (ICPPC), half of its capital was provided by the OECF and the other half by fifty Keidanren member firms led by ten large banks, six trading companies, and six construction firms. The idea was to target Japanese joint venture projects in Asia and Latin America for equity investment and/or project lending. Selected projects would be supported by ODA-financed infrastructure and other government measures where necessary. MITI promised to improve trade and investment insurance systems to cover the investment risks, and MOF also agreed to cooperate by drafting legal amendments in 1988 to allow the Ex-Im Bank to lend directly to private firms overseas, a step that would lock in commercial lending to the targeted joint ventures.

The ICPPC, whose name was later changed to the Japan Industrial Development Organization (JAIDO), was staffed initially by seven workers provided by Marubeni, Mitsubishi Electric, and other firms. Initially, ten projects were selected, each having an annual planned production of roughly $240 million, at least half of which would be for export. After reviewing forty-six projects recommended by Japanese plant makers, banks, and trading companies, ten were selected in 1988; these included copper mines in the Philippines and Chile, a Brazilian paper pulp mill, a Mexican tourist resort, and a computer firm in India.

In reaction to the need of Japanese firms to restructure in the face of depressed domestic demand and a stronger yen, by 1993 JAIDO was putting priority on finding projects in Asia, Latin America, and the former Soviet Union that would allow large Japanese manufacturers to sell off obsolete plant and reduce managerial staff by sending them as technical advisers along with the equipment. A local joint venture would be formed with equity participation by the recipient country government and firms as well as JAIDO and Japanese trading companies and manufacturers. The joint venture would use the imported plant equipment to sell profitably in the local market. Such projects would be supported by investment and trade insurance provided by the Japanese government, and the recipient country's participation would be financed by international development financing including that of Japan.[249]

The creation of JAIDO was an implementation measure arranged between the government and the Keidanren that skillfully blended public and private sector personnel, activities, and objectives. This initiative shows how institutionalized networks of relations between the government and the large-scale private sector facilitated the creation of a new organization and implicated ODA in the broader keizai kyōryoku framework.

The Trading Companies' Response to Recycling

In May 1987 the Taigai Keizai Kyōryoku Shingikai, under Noboru Gotō, chair of the Japan Chamber of Commerce and Industry, issued a report calling for a stronger trade and investment insurance system to promote private sector flows to the developing countries.[250] As mentioned above, the Keidanren's Surplus Recycling Problem Deliberation Council also requested MITI to design appropriate measures, and in May 1988 the same call was made in a report by the ad hoc Committee on Research for Indebted Country Issues and General Trading Companies. This committee was formed in 1987 by the Japan Foreign Trade Council, the association representing the largest Japanese trading companies. These trading companies and affiliated plant exporters were holding at that time ¥1 trillion in commercial claims against developing countries, and without new government support they would not add much to this.[251] Under concerted private sector pressure, by early 1988 MITI formed the Trade Insurance (Bōeki Hoken Shingikai), and by the summer MITI agreed to formulate more generous lending, trade insurance, tax incentives and investment guarantees for firms planning investment in the indebted developing countries.

Keizai Dōyūkai Response to Recycling

The Japan-ASEAN Investment Corporation (JAIC) is also noteworthy because it offers an example of how the financial industries could influence ODA policy. After the announcement of MITI's New AID Plan in January 1987 and the Nakasone recycling plan in May 1987, the Keizai Dōyūkai formed a study committee to promote the flow of Japanese capital into ASEAN stock markets. The prime movers in the Keizai Dōyūkai were the cash-rich banks and securities firms who wished to enter into the booming ASEAN financial markets. By the fall of 1987 the Keizai Dōyūkai issued a report entitled *Nihon-ASEAN kyōryoku no arata na tenkai wo motomete* (Requesting a new opening in Japan-ASEAN cooperation), which it presented directly to Prime Minister Takeshita, who subsequently included the idea in the $2 billion AJDF proposal.[252]

In 1981 Keizai Dōyūkai members had established a ¥1.1 billion investment fund controlled by JAIC to facilitate joint ventures with ASEAN firms.

The JAIC fund remained inactive because JAIC members had other sources of financing available on more attractive terms. In an effort to activate JAIC, Japanese banks and securities firms gained the backing of MOF, which directed the OECF to buy equity in JAIC in 1985.[253] Nonetheless, JAIC remained inactive until it was incorporated into Japan's recycling plan in 1987. Then an additional ¥2.7 billion in capital was added to the company in 1988, half supplied by the OECF, raising its capitalization to ¥3.8 billion. The number of private shareholders increased to 137 large Japanese firms, and a former executive from Nomura Securities Co. who had been serving as president of a Nomura affiliate was named as JAIC's president and chief operating officer. MOF requested the city banks to put up funds for JAIC's first investment fund of ¥7 billion, which was to purchase equities in ASEAN stock markets.

The investment targets of the first fund were Japanese joint venture projects in industrialization, natural resource processing, export promotion, and plant rehabilitation in ASEAN. These ventures were to be staffed chiefly by local citizens, were to be of medium size, and were to have the potential to produce internationally competitive goods for export. It was hoped that ASEAN capital markets would be developed enough within five years so that the purchased securities could be sold (profitably) and the proceeds reinvested. The reason offered by the president of JAIC for not investing in non-Japanese-affiliated local enterprises was that the Japanese side lacked the necessary knowledge of local conditions to make investment decisions.[254] It was more likely JAIC wanted to control risk and assist Japanese firms who wished to relocate to ASEAN.

In order to identify potential investment targets, JAIC relied on personnel supplied by the four big Japanese securities firms and three city banks to gather investment information. At the same time, the other JAIC member firms, as well as the offices of JETRO, Japanese organizations, Japanese firms, and Japanese chambers of commerce located in the ASEAN countries, were expected to suggest candidates for investment. Finally, the investment offices of the ASEAN governments and the many ASEAN financiers affiliated with the original JAIC were expected to respond to requests for detailed information on prospective investments.[255]

Thus, JAIC was a vehicle designed to help Japanese securities firms move into ASEAN capital markets. Equally important was the fact that JAIC encouraged local Japanese joint ventures to utilize ASEAN capital markets.[256] If the organization of JAIC represented an innovative expansion of coordination into financial sectors, the Keizai Dōyūkai's opportunistic response to the government's recycling plans and its ready access to policymakers through existing policy networks explained the quick authorization of this new venture.

As illustrated by the origins of new trade and investment insurance measures, as well as by the formation of JAIDO and JAIC, a number of private sector initiatives were designed in institutionally sponsored study groups or deliberation councils. In these insulated settings bureaucrats and private sec- tor leaders could confer frankly to reorient Japan's ODA away from export promotion and toward the promotion of overseas investment and production.

Three-into-One Economic Cooperation

The process of policy deliberations and consensus formation within the sys- tem described above stayed within the established pattern of keizai kyōryoku. By 1988 two policy concepts were extracted from the diffuse set of delibera- tions stimulated by the endaka and they defined the core of Japan's post-en- daka ODA policy. These concepts were three-into-one economic cooperation *(san mi-ittai)* and the horizontal division of labor in Asia.

The Taigai Keizai Kyōryoku Shingikai's 1987 report is the first to use the slogan san mi-ittai, a term that is used by Japanese Catholics for the doctrine of the Holy Trinity. The term is featured in the *1988 MITI Economic Cooperation Yearbook* and the 1988 MITI White Paper on International Trade. To explain what it means, Nangaku Masaaki, director-general of MITI's Economic Cooperation Department, states: "With regard to how our economic cooperation should be in the future, the White Paper calls for pro- moting a 'holy trinity' type of comprehensive economic cooperation com- posed of aid, direct investment, and imports to promote the industrialization of the developing countries. This is based on the same kind of thinking as the so-called New AID Plan that MITI has been promoting."[257] The 1988 White Paper on International Trade also features this slogan. While noting the trend toward the formation of regional economic blocs, it calls on Japan to open its markets to Asian exports, extend more aid and technical cooperation to Asian neighbors, and make stronger efforts to transfer capital and management re- sources to them.[258]

This san mi-ittai slogan subsequently gained a standard English transla- tion of "three-into-one," and it became the center of the government consen- sus on ODA. In its first official Japanese-language report on ODA, issued in 1987, the MFA grudgingly acknowledges with no further comment that "by means of aid and investment, as well as imports, a *san mi-ittai* kind of coop- eration is expected."[259] Even the MFA-drafted English-language press release announcing the Fourth ODA Plan faithfully, if only briefly, alludes to the agenda of the economic ministries:

> The Government of Japan . . . will strengthen its implementation system in such ways as expansion of personnel, fostering of country experts, deepen- ing of regional studies, strengthening of project finding and formulation, intensification of evaluation activities, and utilization of consultants. Coordination with private-sector activities will also be strengthened.[260]

The EPA's five-year economic plan, entitled *Sekai to tomo ni ikiru Nihon*

(Japan living with the world), sums up the outlines of the new post-endaka keizai kyōryoku orientation. The five-year plan lays out the basic consensus within the Japanese government as to future policies, and the section on economic cooperation states that "comprehensive economic cooperation (Holy Trinity style of economic cooperation) will be promoted linking and integrating assistance, investment, and trade."[261] The views of the Taigai Keizai Kyōryoku Shingikai and the study groups of the Keidanren, the Japan Foreign Trade Council, Keizai Dōyūkai, and the Vision group were incorporated into the basic government policy consensus:

> Greater use will be made of trade insurance and the Ex-Im Bank to promote the provision of new capital from the private sector. An effort will be made to gather, organize, and make available more information on the developing countries' securities to support these countries' efforts to procure capital through the issue of securities. . . . An effort will be made to promote the conclusion of bilateral investment guarantee protocols, to strengthen the identification and definition of promising projects by making more information available on the investment climate within the host country, and to promote improvements in the investment climate with the use of investment insurance, The World Bank's Multilateral Investment Guarantee Agency (MIGA), the Ex-Im Bank's investment guarantees, and other means to encourage capital recycling through direct investment. Efforts will also be made to promote greater use of the investment fund under the ASEAN-Japan Development Fund (AJDF).[262]

The Horizontal Division of Labor in Asia

The general notion of an Asian division of labor, which gained prominence after endaka, goes back to the 1950s when it was formulated by researchers associated with the Ajia Kyōkai (which subsequently was absorbed by the IDE). In a previously cited 1956 foreign ministry report on Japan's economic cooperation with Asia, Okita writes: "If every country would try to pursue the same pattern of industrialization there may arise wasteful use of capital resources, or undesirable contraction in foreign trade or, in some cases, excessive competition in the export market." Today the best-known analyst of the Asian division of labor in this tradition is Watanabe Toshio, who follows the same basic line by advocating that the comparative advantages of Japan, the NIEs, the ASEAN countries, and China be managed in such a way as to promote complementarity among these economies.[263] As already explained above, the New AID Plan strengthens the "horizontal division of labor" and intraregional economic flows. And it also allows the MFA to show that Japan is liberalizing access to its market, although this may be done selectively.

Since 1985 Japan's FDI in Asian manufacturing grew quickly from about $500 million a year to over $3 billion a year. It is difficult to tell how much of this growth is associated with Japan's ODA, but there can be no doubt that through the provision of direct subsidies, infrastructure, technical training, in-

formation, and risk-reduction measures it had an appreciable impact on the
quantity and quality of this investment, especially in such targeted sectors as
electronics and machinery. One way to see the effect of Japanese FDI in
ASEAN on regional trade flows is to note the market orientation of relocated
Japanese electronics firms and their affiliates. These firms needed low-cost
production and assembly to maintain their competitiveness no matter if they
were subcontractors or the most advanced Japanese firms. Note that in 1989
about 69 percent of this production was exported and that over half of this
portion was exported to other countries in Asia, thus accelerating intraregional trade flows (see Figure 6.3).

Figure 6.3 Direction of Sales of Japanese Electrical Manufacturers in ASEAN, 1989

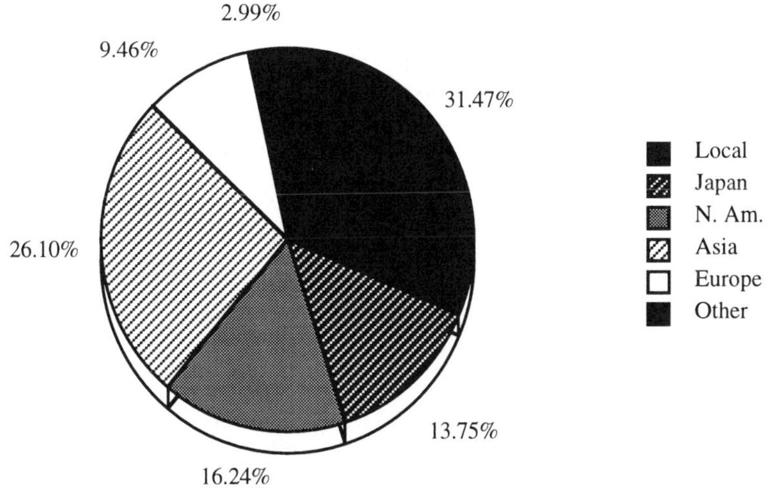

Source: JETRO.

This new emphasis in Japan's ODA policy is welcomed by Japan's
Asian neighbors, who wish technology transfer and export earnings. In giving
a Chinese viewpoint, Lu Zhongwei states: "The implementation of Japan's
economic cooperation with Asia of the *san mi-ittai* type, which ties together
trade, investment, and ODA expansion, is greeted with anticipation."[264]

The Asian Brain Policy Study

An interesting report on how Japan should develop trinity-style economic cooperation to create a new Asian division of labor, was produced for the EPA
in 1987 entitled *Promoting Comprehensive Economic Cooperation in an*

International Economic Environment Undergoing Upheaval: Toward the Construction of an Asian Network.[265] No doubt this report was only one of several confidential ODA policy research efforts commissioned by agencies of the Japanese government, but it offers an interesting insight into how keizai kyōryoku policy experts would like to apply these concepts.

The study was executed by the Japan Research Institute (Nihon Sōgō Kenkyūjo), a private, nonprofit research foundation (zaidan hōjin) that was established in 1970 under the sponsorship of the EPA and MITI.[266] Okita Saburō was on the board of directors, and the institute's director of research, Shiota Nagahide, graduated from Tokyo University's law department in 1961 and worked for Sumitomo Trading Co. for ten years before entering the institute.[267] The report's foreword notes:

> It is becoming increasingly necessary to rearrange economic cooperation in a comprehensive manner. The Taigai Keizai Kyōryoku Shingikai is currently pointing to the need for the *san mi-ittai* comprehensive economic cooperation of ODA, import expansion, and direct investment. For these reasons, this research investigates the kind of impact the changing international economic environment and the development of our nation's comprehensive economic cooperation will have on both the Japanese economy and the Asian economy, as well as the impact on intraregional economic relations. The objective of the report is to offer a concrete policy "package" to promote an economic cooperation of "comprehensivized" *(sōgō-ka shita)* ODA, trade, and direct investment.[268]

The report was compiled by a team of six researchers, led by Shiota, that conducted extensive interviews at home and abroad. Japanese academics, experienced "veterans" in keizai kyōryoku, and specialists were consulted, and six overseas survey missions (to Korea, Hong Kong, Singapore, Indonesia, Malaysia, and Thailand) were sent to interview recipient academics, government officials, and specialists in think tanks and international organizations. The funding for this kind of report is covered by the Japanese ODA budget.

The report states that Japan, the Asian NIEs, and ASEAN were high-, middle-, and low-grade economies that formed a system that could be shaped and regulated by Japan's keizai kyōryoku. It states that a movement of capital and technology from upper-grade states to middle-grade states and from middle-grade to lower-grade states was expected. To smooth this process industrial adjustment efforts by each country would be required.[269] To coordinate this process the report proposes a regional economic planning mechanism called the "Asian Brain" that would influence who produces what within this Asian system. Trade and investment agreements that allocate to each country those industries that best suit its comparative advantage would then be negotiated.[270] The report summarizes the functions of the Asian Brain as follows:

> 1. Control Functions: The vitalization of an Asian Network and control over the appropriate disposition (i.e., direct investment) of industry within

the region. In addition, regulation over carrying out direct investment in certain countries within certain periods in a concentrated manner in order to prevent evil effects.

2. Cooperation Functions: Among ODA projects (especially grant aid) done in joint participation style, there will be allocation of the funding shares among all countries, as well as the role of each so as to provide the best resources (people, material, technology, etc.). [271]

The organization of this Asian economic planning mechanism is unclear, but the central role of Japan is taken for granted: "With a view toward setting up this gigantic economic cooperation with an appropriate role in international society, Japan's exhibition of leadership in creating this 'Asian Brain' would be a great contribution with respect not only to the Asian region, but also to international society as a whole." A diagram from the report is shown in Figure 6.4.

Figure 6.4 The Asian Brain and Three-into-One Economic Cooperation with Asian NICs and ASEAN

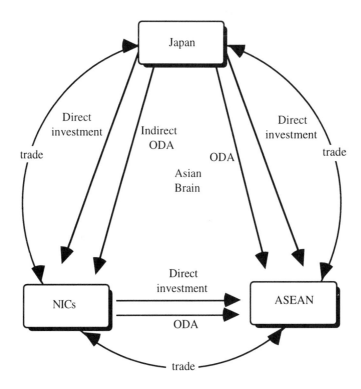

Source: Nihon Sogo Kenkyūjo.

The report develops the idea of indirect, or "linkage," ODA in which Japan coordinates with NIEs to give ODA to the ASEAN countries. The report states: "Within the region composed of Japan, the Asian NICs, and ASEAN, there are three countries either implementing or planning to implement ODA: Japan, Korea, and Taiwan. . . . It would be desirable to consider carrying out projects jointly among mainly these three countries."[272] By 1993 Japan was already implementing cooperative ODA ventures with South Korea and Taiwan and was planning cooperative ODA measures to develop Indochina with Thailand.

The key point about the 1980–1992 period for Japan's ODA policy is that it remained linked to, and coordinated by, an entrenched keizai kyōryoku system. This system would respond to Western criticism of Japan's free-riding with absolute increases in ODA spending, but it would not relinquish its control over how the money would be spent. The system also insulated bureaucratic policy planners from popular demands for an open process of policy formation and implementation, and it gave private sector interests privileged, intimate access to decisionmaking. This allowed Japan's ODA policy to respond quickly and comprehensively to the challenge of the yen appreciation, and this contrasts with the minimal impact media and opposition demands for policy change had in this same period. This is not to suggest that Japan's ODA did not also serve as an increasingly important diplomatic instrument in this period. It did, in ways that will be detailed in a later chapter.

7

The Project Cycle
and the Structure
of Included Interests

Because of its origins and path of institutionalization, it would be surprising if Japanese ODA could be detached from the keizai kyōryoku system. In fact, ODA is still integral to this system today. To understand why there are poor prospects for fundamental change, one should look at the reality of policy implementation rather than at policy declarations. The starting point for this discussion will be the Japanese project cycle. Since its beginning in cases of kaihatsu tōshi, and in its further development in reparations and the activities of the Ex-Im Bank, OECF, and JICA, keizai kyōryoku has focused on capital-intensive projects that promote exports, develop new sources of raw materials imports, or facilitate Japan's FDI. This project orientation has largely determined the existing system of aid implementation.

Project-oriented assistance is organized around the "project cycle." First, a project must be proposed, and then engineers and other experts are needed to do a design proposal. The proposal is evaluated by the donor and recipient to assess its technical, economic, and financial feasibility; social, political, and sometimes environmental impact; harmony with current policy; merit relative to other proposals; etc. If a funding request is made and approved, project design and construction contracts are let, and after completion operation commences; evaluation is subsequently necessary to learn from the experience.

The problem at the start of the project cycle is that developing countries—by definition—suffer from shortages of the funds, skilled experts, and administrators needed to identify and propose capital-intensive projects. Thus, developing countries often cannot by themselves start the project cycle. This is where the aid donor usually steps in to "guide" the recipient toward making sound aid requests according to the donor's "aid philosophy." The World Bank conducts country- and sector-specific economic surveys and offers advice in project selection based on the premise that infrastructure bottlenecks and "irrational" policies must be removed to allow better market-oriented growth. AID takes a roughly similar approach, identifying developmental needs based on economic and sociological studies of the recipient country, and it guides requests accordingly.

PROJECT IDENTIFICATION IN JAPANESE ODA

Japan's official noninvolvement in project identification is where the philoso-phy of the Japanese ODA system is revealed. The documentation required by the Japanese government for project proposals is complex, and recipient gov-ernment agencies sometimes are unable to get past even the initial paperwork. Thus, there is a gap created between what Japan's request-based system re-quires and what developing countries are able to achieve in the way of aid re-quests. This reflects the continuing reliance on the y ōseishugi policy principle first developed in the reparations program. Then, as now, the facade of prin-ciple (tatemae) is respect for the self-expressed needs of the recipient; whereas the true intent (honne) is to give Japanese business the opportunity to "inject" project requests in recipient countries. Other things being equal, the Japanese government then approves only those requests that serve a Japanese public policy aim and that also complement, but do not displace, commer-cially viable trade and investment. This is called the "injection system" *(chū-sha seido)* by keizai kyōryoku insiders.

The Traditional Injection

The role of Japan's general trading companies in generating aid requests is often stressed by Japanese experts. The following example illustrates their catalytic role in the project cycle:

> At the end of the 1960s Mitsubishi Corporation hit upon the idea of building an international airport at Mombasa, Kenya, to exploit promising tourist resources for regional development. A feasibility study begun in 1970 was enthusiastically received by the Kenyan Government which, how-ever, was unable to finance the project. Mitsubishi then lobbied for a special yen loan from the Japanese Government. Though no such loan had ever been offered before to an African country, the Japanese Government, after some hesitation, was finally persuaded to extend it as economic assistance. . . . It took Mitsubishi over three years to secure the necessary funding and another five years to complete the airport. The company used its orga-nizer/coordinator capacity to arrange and supervise all the construction work; it hired builders and procured materials and equipment.
> . . .
> Following the success of the Mombasa project, Mitsubishi Corporation was asked by Malawi, Kenya's southern neighbor, to construct a similar air-port. The Company again secured special loans from both the Japanese Government and the African Development Bank and began construction of an airport in 1978.[273]

As this quote indicates, Japanese private sector firms–trading companies, consulting firms, and trade associations—will often absorb the cost of preliminary design studies that will be given to requesting agencies in the recipient government. Thus, it is not unusual for recipient governments to have several ready-made proposals on hand at any given time. If a line agency decides to request a prepared proposal, it will have the backing of the injecting Japanese private sector actor.[274]

Project-Finding Missions

A variation on this injection system is the so-called *puro-fai* (project-finding) mission. The project-finding mission is usually jointly organized and financed by the Japanese government and ODA-related trade associations such as the Engineering Consulting Firms Association (ECFA) or the Plant Exporters Association of Japan. A high-level delegation representing association membership will visit developing countries and discuss a number of large-scale preliminary project proposals. Project-finding missions are helped by locally posted Japanese officials in the embassy; the staffs of the local JETRO, OECF, and JICA offices; and local Japanese business representatives who set up briefings and appointments with local officials and politicians. The objective is to identify a number of large projects for Japanese aid financing. The recipient government will then request ODA funds from the Japanese government to study the feasibility of identified projects, and these are invariably funded.

JICA Experts

Another way of injecting project proposals involves the so-called JICA expert who is sent from Japan to sit in recipient government planning and line agencies. These experts are sent using technical cooperation funds, but they may come from either the public or private sector. Increasing numbers are being sent shukkō-style (temporary secondment of personnel) to sit in recipient government agencies for one or two years. There they gather information on the local economy, give advice where appropriate, and help to propose aid projects and policy changes in consultation with Japanese and local actors.

This type of technical assistance has been advocated by the Taigai Keizai Kyōryoku Shingikai since the early 1970s and deserves some comment. From observation in Thailand and Indonesia it seems that besides project identification, another aim of this kind of technical cooperation is to integrate Japanese personnel into the planning activities of recipient government agencies. For example, in 1987 it was observed in Thailand that a JETRO economist was posted as a JICA expert in Thailand's Board of Investment (BOI), which is responsible for collecting data on all foreign investment and approving inward foreign direct investment proposals. Another Japanese official was posted in the Thai development planning agency, the National Economic and Social Development Board (NESDB); and a former EPA official was posted in the Thai Development Research Institute (TDRI), Thailand's main semi-public development research organ, to study Thailand's regional industrial development plans. These experts did not have teaching or training responsibilities, nor did they have effective language skills. Their real task was to gain access to information and policy formulation inside the Thai bureaucracy.

Other JICA experts sit in line agencies where they help to draft policies and formulate aid requests. Some are only minimally employed in make-work situations. For example, a visit in 1987 to the Bureau of Inland Transportation in Indonesia, which is responsible for all land and water transportation in a country composed of hundreds of islands stretching over 3,000 miles, revealed that it had a professional staff of ten, and only three had post-graduate degrees. According to the director, the most pressing need was for trained personnel to carry out independent project identification and to upgrade gridlocked urban transportation planning and operations. An aid request to set up a training program for these purposes was denied by the Japanese aid agencies. Instead, a request for technical experts from Japan was encouraged, but what was delivered were four railway engineers—laid-off victims of the privatization of Japanese National Railway Corporation (JNR).[275] The director noted that having four railway engineers was not a cause for complaint, but they did not speak English, and they could not be kept fully occupied. But they were available to design aid projects according to Japanese specifications involving railway construction and rolling stock. He also noted that in Japutapek a railway repair yard was staffed with thirty former JNR technicians financed by Japan's grant ODA.

Request Procedures

Once a project has been identified, Japanese ODA can be requested to study its feasibility, but such requests are far from automatic. Developing countries usually have an economic planning ministry whose task is to formulate a development strategy. This means it reviews aid project requests made by line ministries and agencies and ranks them by how well they fit into the current national development plan. Another recipient government bureaucracy that can veto project requests is the finance ministry. It usually judges the worth of a project according to such criteria as the budgetary impact and whether or not the project will create long-term financial burdens or benefits. It is not unusual for a project to be endorsed by the development planning agency only to be denied positive support by the finance ministry (or vice versa). Finally, it is not uncommon for politicians in recipient countries to push for certain projects despite the objections of their own or of Japanese bureaucratic actors. Thus, the handling of project-oriented aid regularly involves every level of political decisionmaking in the developing country.

Once the recipient government decides to make a formal request, it must be routed through the Japanese administrative system. The economic cooper-

ation staff in Japan's overseas embassies processes official requests. The ambassador signs all official ODA requests, but traditionally the head and staff
of the economic section in overseas embassies *(keizai-han)* have been representatives of such ministries as the MPT, MITI, MAFF, or MOC—and it is
not uncommon for private sector personnel to be seconded to overseas embassies as well. [276] Only in the 1980s has the MFA started to put a diplomat in
charge of the economic section, and even then only at selected embassies.
The staff of the economic section is almost entirely non-MFA because the
MFA has limited authority and technical expertise in keizai kyōryoku.

In practice, embassy staff members promote the policies and interests of
their home ministry, agency, or commercial group. This can mean, for example, that a MAFF representative may discourage an aid project for cassava
production because this could hurt Japanese growers of sweet potatoes; or it
could mean that aid grants of fertilizers and pesticides might be promoted by
the MITI and MAFF representatives to assist these depressed industries in
Japan; or it could mean that a project or program with poor financial controls
would be discouraged by the MOF representative.

In grant aid projects a request for a basic design study normally must be
approved by both the embassy and the local JICA office before being referred
to Tokyo. When the project is to be built with OECF loans, the request for a
JICA-funded prefeasibility study (P/S) or feasibility study (F/S) will have to
be approved by the OECF, JICA, and the local Japanese embassy. Roughly
half of the official requests for preliminary project design assistance are
granted once they are sent back to Tokyo. Figure 7.1 shows the grant aid request procedures.

After the request is reviewed in Tokyo, a team will be sent to discuss the
request with recipient government officials. If talks are successful a subsequent team of private consultants will be sent with instructions to do the actual basic design report (in the case of grant aid) or F/S (in the case of loan
aid; see Figure 7.2). In the case of grant aid, implementation normally follows
completion of the basic design, but in the case of loan aid projects, the JICA-
funded F/S will be handed over to the recipient government, which then must
submit it to the OECF, where it will be reevaluated by the yonshōchō.
Approximately one-third of JICA-funded loan project feasibility studies lead
to implementation by the OECF. [277]

Bilateral Consultations with Major Recipients

The Japanese government has instituted annual consultations with thirteen of
its largest aid recipients to determine project approvals. These consultations
are intended to let recipient governments coordinate their aid requests and to
help the Japanese government ensure that aid funds are used effectively. With
each of the thirteen major recipients, separate consultations are held for loan
requests and for grant requests (which includes technical cooperation). The

Figure 7.1 Grant Aid Request Procedures

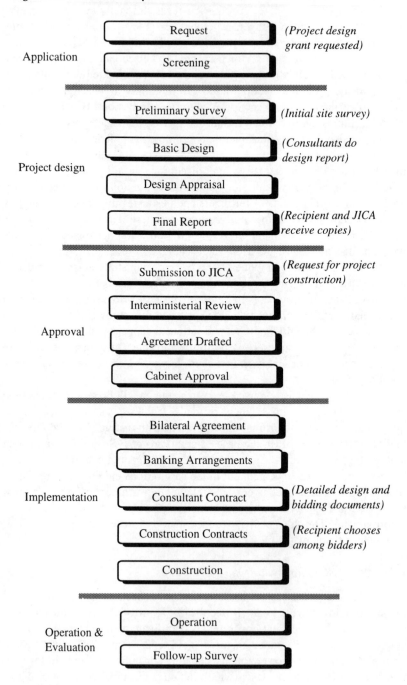

Source: JICA.

Figure 7.2 OECF Loan Procedure

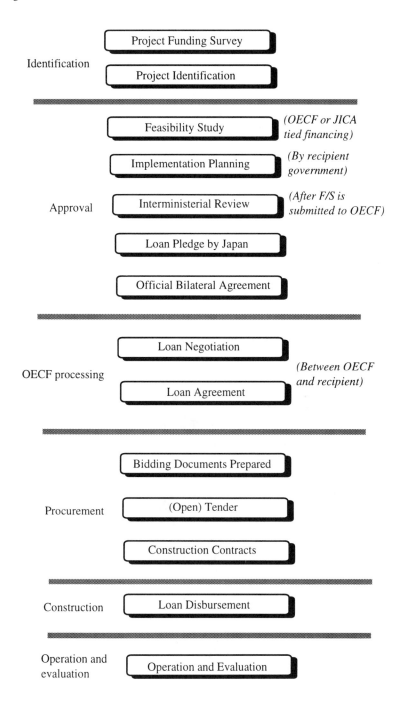

Source: OECF.

leader of the Japanese team at these consultations is usually an MFA official accompanied by OECF or JICA staff. The agenda is to choose projects for funding from a list of proposals. Usually there are a number of projects that both sides agree should be implemented, and others are ruled out by one side or the other. Thus, discussion focuses on the borderline projects.

Recipient countries can expect a certain number of project approvals based upon a funding level set each year by the Japanese government. Grant aid consultations cover projects in different stages of preparation, and they usually identify a number of candidate projects slightly in excess of the number likely to be implemented in order to give room for adjustment later in the approval process. Some grant aid projects that have been adequately studied and prepared are approved for immediate implementation, others are designated for preliminary study and design, and the rest may need further discussion and fine-tuning before a final decision is made, perhaps in the following year's consultation.

Loan aid consultations are similar to grant aid consultations. Each loan project usually already has a P/S or F/S and has been evaluated by the OECF; what remains to be done in the consultation is for both sides to agree on which projects are to be implemented from the following year. As in the case of grant aid, discussion centers on the borderline candidate projects.

Using Formal Procedures in Keizai Kyōryoku

Keizai kyōryoku required the linkage of aid, trade, and investment objectives, but Western pressure required Japan to differentiate its keizai kyōryoku–implementing agencies into ODA and non-ODA components. Thus, JICA and the OECF evolved into ODA-focused agencies, and the Ex-Im Bank withdrew from making ODA yen loans. JICA normally handles social infrastructure or technical services, and the OECF handles economic infrastructure. Should the project be engaged in direct production for profit (e.g., resource-processing plant projects), then near-commercial financing will suffice, and the Ex-Im Bank will contribute loans or equity investment in collaboration with the Japanese private sector. These differences constitute a division of labor in large, complex keizai kyōryoku projects.

A concrete example of this is the Huanzala mine in the Dos de Mayo province of Peru. The mine is operated by the Compania Minera Santa Luisa, which was established in 1968 and is entirely owned by Mitsui Mining & Smelting and Mitsui & Co. in a ratio of 7:3. The mine annually produces approximately 285,000 tons of high-grade silver, lead, and zinc ore, all of which is shipped to Japan for processing. In 1961 a mining engineer from Mitsui Mining & Smelting identified the project, and his firm obtained mining rights with an option to purchase. In 1963 the Ex-Im Bank lent ¥2.466 billion for initial project development, and after commercial feasibility was established Mitsui exercised its option to purchase and formed Santa Luisa S.A. in 1968. In 1971 the OECF lent ¥353 million to Santa Luisa S.A. for expansion of the mine, and in 1973 the Ex-Im Bank lent another ¥782 million for equipment purchases. Also in that year, the Metals and Mining Agency of Japan began giving subsidies amounting to nearly ¥700 million for further mineral exploration, and in 1975 JICA gave a loan of ¥445 million to build a new 58-kilometer road to improve access to the Callao port. JICA funded this road project because the Peruvian government officially requested the project as social infrastructure.[278]

The Focus on Capital-Intensive Projects

The Japanese government traditionally favors projects that directly or indirectly promote its own investment and whole plant exports. ODA is meant for projects, or parts of projects, that are not commercially viable (such as infrastructure). The Japanese private sector and recipient governments are structurally included in the project cycle, and they respond to the Japanese government's criteria to generate matching project requests. In this way the Japanese government guides the Japanese private sector and recipient governments toward capital-intensive requests. The yōseishugi system is efficient in that the Japanese private sector is left to identify those projects that it can accomplish profitably, and the system is also effective in helping the Japanese private sector to develop a detailed knowledge of developing country governments and business practices that will enhance its non-ODA business activities as well (see Figure 7.3).

The main drawback of the system is that the Japanese government is unable to ensure that project requests are high quality or that they make real contributions to a strategic agenda in each country. This request-based system has also made it difficult to apply Japan's ODA to other issues such as appropriate and effective technology transfer; responsiveness to a recipient's full range of priorities; or other key issues such as delivering services to the poorest groups, environmental security, or human rights.

A Hypothetical Project Request

A simple hypothetical project request can present an integrated review of the basic features of the Japanese project cycle. In this hypothetical case a general trading company in a keiretsu group containing a Japanese shipbuilder and a construction firm contacts the head of the recipient's ministry of transportation and introduces a plan for an ocean ferry service with piers and terminals in the expectation of providing the ships, construction materials, equipment, and project managerial services. The project will require the procurement of land, certain legal rights, construction materials, ships, related equipment, technical training, and engineering and consulting services. But first, an F/S would be required before a loan request for implementation could be made. Thus, the first step is to request grant aid for an F/S.

Local Japanese officials will also have to be contacted by the trading

**Figure 7.3 The Effect of the Structure of Included Interests on
            Project Selection**

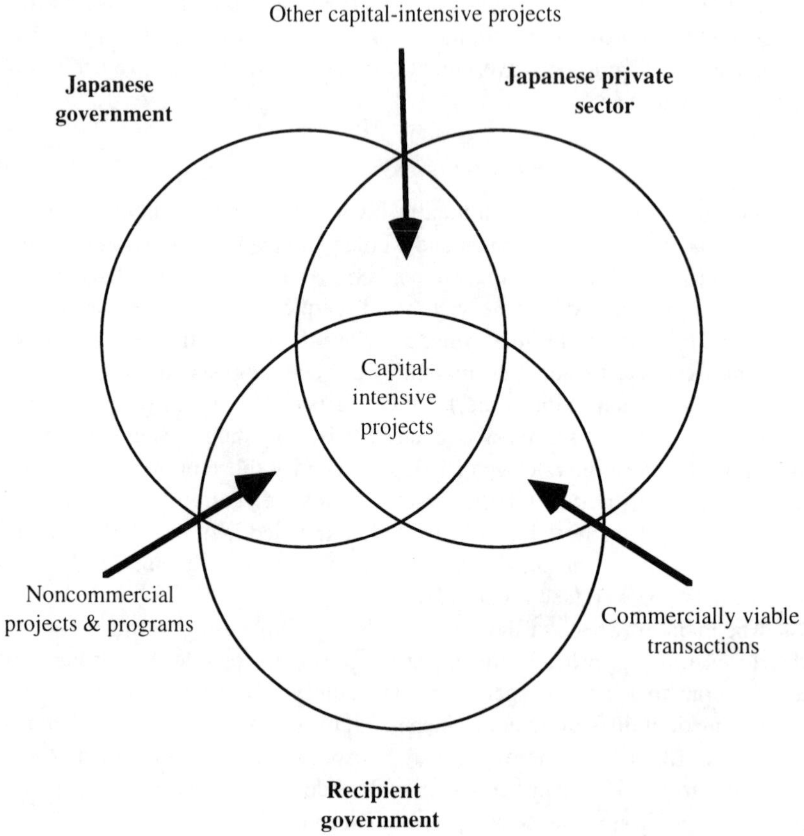

Other capital-intensive projects

Japanese
government

Japanese private
sector

Capital-
intensive
projects

Noncommercial
projects & programs

Commercially viable
transactions

**Recipient
government**

company and the recipient transportation ministry with regard to the request
for the F/S. Aside from the OECF and JICA offices, the economic section
of the Japanese embassy will have to give a favorable opinion if Japanese
ODA funds for the F/S are to be gained. The Japanese MOT officer in the
economic section of the Japanese embassy will be chiefly responsible
for initial appraisal of the idea. (In any case, MOT will be contacted in
Tokyo either directly or via JICA or MFA headquarters.) The MITI embassy
officer may support the project as well because new orders for ocean ferries
would help the depressed shipbuilding industry back home. The MOC
official may be persuaded to support the proposal because he knows that
a Japanese construction firm will be contracted to build the terminal
facilities. If the MFA is persuaded that the project will please important

recipient politicians and will have high visibility, it will have reason to approve.

The recipient government transportation minister may welcome the project because it will redound to his credit and may improve transportation and stimulate the development of the economy. In coordination with local and central government politicians, the transportation ministry will have to secure land for piers and terminals and draft the appropriate legal provisions. In order to do this certain requirements will have to be met. The recipient finance ministry will have to be persuaded to provide budgetary funds to purchase the required land, hire additional staff, and support the local start-up costs associated with the project. The central development planning agency will also have to be convinced of the importance of the project because its approval is needed before the project can be officially requested. In this regard "contributions" by the trading company to recipient politicians could play an important role.

After a supportive consensus is established, the trading company will draw up a preliminary request for an F/S in the name of the recipient transportation ministry. The request will specify the project's developmental rationale, design, procurement needs, and work schedule. If it clears the recipient aid request procedures, it will then be submitted to the Japanese embassy, which will send it back to Tokyo after a preliminary screening. An outline of the project will be drawn up, and a contact mission (composed of an MFA, MOT, and JICA representative, with perhaps a nongovernmental expert as well) will be dispatched to the recipient to verify the project request and to draw up a report including the scope of work (S/W) for the F/S and a rough cost estimate. After the return of the mission to Tokyo the report will be studied by the relevant ministries and agencies. If a favorable finding is issued, a JICA grant will follow to pay for an F/S to establish the technical, financial, and economic feasibility of the project.

Next, several consultants will be invited to bid for the contract to do the F/S. Because official JICA procedure requires the recipient government to supply a list of invited bidders, it is easy for the Japanese trading company to arrange to have itself or a proxy nominated. From an initial group of ten invited bids a short list is chosen, and the recipient government is formally responsible for choosing the winner from this list. In cases where the recipient government has no strong preference, JICA officials can be influential in designating a winner. Even an inexperienced proxy can complete the F/S with the help of the trading company, and when finished the F/S is presented to the recipient transportation ministry.

The next step is to submit a request to the OECF for a loan to finance project construction (because the ferry service is expected to be financially viable with concessional financing). After being processed by the Manila OECF office, the request is sent to Tokyo, and after the concerned ministries and agencies give approval, the OECF's technical appraisal division will send one or two people to evaluate the plan. They will meet with relevant local actors and inspect the project site. Upon their return a report is drawn up, and a recommendation is made to the yonshōcho committee.

The yonshōchō representatives that routinely decide on OECF project approvals meet once a week to discuss a prepared agenda. They are usually noncareer staff who act on instruction from their ministry. With no problems uncovered by the OECF report, the project is placed on the list of projects to be reviewed at the annual loan consultation with the recipient. If both the recipient and Japanese sides agree at the consultation, then the project will be implemented. After the loan agreement is signed, a tied loan to pay for detailed design and preparation of bidding documents will be given. In a bidding procedure essentially the same as the earlier JICA bid, the Japanese trading company will come in as the managing consultant over detailed design, procurement, and construction. An international open tender will be arranged for procuring the ships, related equipment, and construction materials and services. A short list will be drawn up, and the recipient government will then choose the main contractors. Later, another request to JICA for grant technical training for the operation and maintenance of the ships is possible.

In this hypothetical case a routine approval is likely because elements of the Japanese private sector can expect profits; the recipient transportation ministry can expect to gain new and greatly desired facilities; local politicians can expect to gain prestige and other benefits; and key Japanese bureaucratic actors with expertise and concerns relevant to the proposed project are satisfied that their separate aims in ODA are being met. Other bureaucratic actors with nothing at stake, such as MAFF or the MPT, will have little to say in this particular decision. In this example it may be seen how ODA project selection is determined by the structure of the project cycle and the nature of the included interests.

Finally, one should note that this type of request-based, project-oriented ODA system inhibits the use of ODA as a political sanction because Japanese private sector contractors wish to avoid any interruption of project construction. This aspect of Japanese aid contrasts with the policies of other ODA donors such as the United States, who are free to reduce ODA over issues such as human rights violations, stolen elections, or narcotics production.

STRUCTURAL CORRUPTION IN THE ODA PROCESS

Interviewed Japanese aid officials allege that existing formal procedures do not inhibit the injection system because the recipient government can choose an injecting firm to design or supervise a project even in an "open" bid. If the injecting firm is not qualified to bid, it can find a qualified agent. In such cases the selected consultant will submit the lowest bid for the project design contract either because of an expected kickback or because it will get the detailed design from the injecting firm. The design specifications will be tailor-made so that the injecting firm will win the subsequent procurement contracts.

This informal practice is not unknown to Japanese observers. The practice of dangō (bid rigging) is not uncommon in Japan's domestic public works projects, and it operates in the ODA business as well.[279] By Western standards this kind of collusive behavior is considered unfair and corrupt. Among actors structurally included in keizai kyōryoku, however, the "fair" outcome ensures that each insider gets an allocation of business and profits. Another result of this system is that consulting firms sometimes charge inflated design fees and submit bidding documents with exaggerated cost estimates and inappropriate equipment selection in order to benefit the anticipated contractors. Because the Japanese aid agencies and the MFA lack expert staff to evaluate design and bidding documents, high profits can be realized by the private sector.

It is worth noting, however, that Japanese aid contractors often argue that business in the aid field is not lucrative because of the money needed to pay off officials in Japan. For example, cash gifts may be needed to get a firm onto the short list of bidders. It was for precisely this reason that a JICA official was arrested in 1986. Japanese aid agency officials indicate privately that influence peddling for the same purpose by LDP politicians is rife. Cash is also needed to pay off recipient government officials who select the winners of bids. Thus, in the aftermath of the fall of Ferdinand Marcos it was revealed in Philippine government documents made public by the U.S. House Subcommittee on Asian and Pacific Affairs that from 10 to 15 percent of the value of loan aid contracts won by Japanese firms was kicked back to Philippine government officials.[280] In response to criticism of aid procedures in the Diet arising out of this scandal, the LDP and the Japanese bureaucracy responded by noting that what Philippine officials did was beyond Japanese legal jurisdiction and that Japanese private firms were acting in ways dictated by Philippine customs and practices.

The request-based system thus allows the Japanese government to keep at arm's length the unsavory practices of recipient governments and Japanese firms overseas. Though Japanese bureaucrats cannot deny knowledge of these activities, they point out that officially speaking, recipient governments are responsible for aid requests, for awarding contracts, and for monitoring the legality of all procedures within its borders. This position is disingenuous because the system was deliberately designed to operate as it does, as indicated by diagrams of the project cycle in Japanese government publications (see Figure 7.4). Moreover, it is known that JETRO has run a seminar for plant and machinery exporters in which topics studied included "the promotion of bribery" *(wairo no susume)*.[281] It should be noted that in many developing countries, graft and bribery are customary practices among public officials

Figure 7.4 ODA Loan Project Cycle

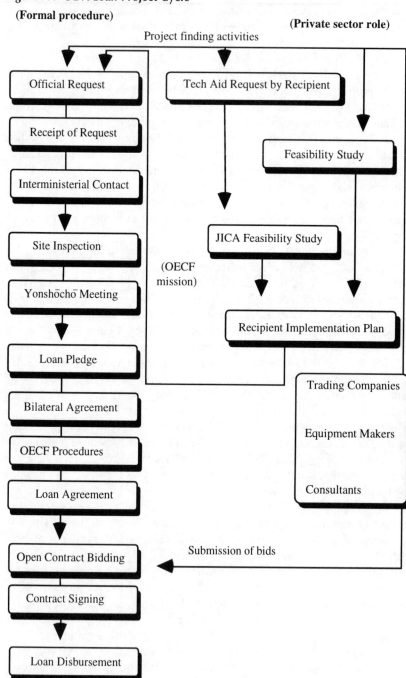

(Formal procedure)

(Private sector role)

Source: MITI Whitepaper on International Cooperation, 1986, p. 327.

who aspire to Western levels of consumption. In this sense the request-based system is well adapted to penetrating developing countries precisely because it allows for graft and corruption while giving the Japanese government deniability. It also has the desirable political effect of creating a pro-Japanese constituency within the recipient government.

THE ISSUE OF ODA UNTYING

Japan has improved in meeting DAC's formal standards for untying its aid by allowing open international bidding on its OECF-financed projects. The realities of the Japanese project cycle suggest, however, that Japan's ODA remains more tied to Japanese contractors than the formally open and competitive bidding procedures would suggest. Aid contracts administered by JICA can be bid upon only by Japanese firms, and because JICA funds the basic design and feasibility studies for aid projects, this means that project design specifications are drafted to Japanese standards. This gives Japanese firms a great advantage even in fully open contract bids. The situation in the OECF is more subtle. Though loans for project *construction* are now untied, OECF loans for *engineering design* needed to draw up construction bidding documents can be tied. This policy nurtures Japanese engineering consultants and benefits the Japanese firms that bid in subsequent tenders. Moreover, recipients have reported that the OECF was still encouraging them to choose the Japanese consultant that drew up the F/S or the detailed design in subsequent stages of bidding, construction supervision, and initial operation.[282] In other words, even as aid is officially untied, Japanese procedures can still encourage the flowback of aid to Japan.

To answer charges that OECF construction loans were still effectively tied, the Japanese government promised in 1987 to make public the results of ODA procurement bidding starting from 1988. In 1988, however, the government changed its mind, allegedly at MFA insistence. It announced the intention to reveal the details of selected large contracts involving untied loans. Because of this secrecy it is impossible for an outside observer to evaluate the real effect of formal untying. The effect in the Philippines was measured in a 1988 report coauthored by the president of the Philippine Institute for Development Studies and the assistant director-general of the National Economic and Development Authority (NEDA) in which they estimate that the flowback of Japanese aid ranged from 75 to 95 percent.[283]

In technical cooperation a new emphasis is project technical aid. Two examples indicate the Japanese interests involved. In 1987 contracts worth a total of ¥4.6 billion ($34 million) were won by NEC, Shimizu Construction Co., and a Japanese trading company to build and equip a television broadcasting station funded by Japanese aid in Thailand; and in 1986 in Indonesia, contracts totaling ¥1.9 billion ($14 million) were won by Tobishima Construction Co. and Sumitomo Shoji to build and outfit an electrical engineering training facility financed by Japanese aid. The effect of such centers will be to establish Japanese technical standards and create follow-on procurements as these nations expand their telecommunications networks and electronics industries.

The Importance of ODA to the Private Sector

The importance of ODA to the overseas advance (shinshutsu) of Japanese firms is apparent from the information revealed by such industry publications as the *1988 Plant Exporters' Yearbook*.[284] In the category of trading companies, for example, from 1986 to 1987 Sumitomo Shoji won twenty-seven main project manager contracts in the developing world. Seven involved Japanese bilateral ODA projects, three involved Ex-Im Bank funding, and three involved World Bank funding. The seven Japanese ODA projects were worth ¥22.3 billion ($165 million), or 25 percent of the total value of the contracts signed in this period. In the case of Marubeni, Ltd., five of twenty-four project-related contracts signed in LDCs were financed by Japanese ODA, accounting for $38 million, or 28 percent of the total value of contracts signed in the developing world.

As for Japanese construction firms, Kajima Construction Co., Japan's largest construction firm, won a total of fifteen major project-related construction contracts in the LDCs in the 1986–1987 period. Of this number, five were directly funded by Japanese ODA, and at least three more contracts were funded indirectly by Japan's ODA through Japanese engineering firms giving subcontracting work to Kajima. Another of Japan's largest construction firms, Shimizu Construction Co., won twelve contracts in LDC project construction. Of these, nine were financed by Japanese ODA and were worth ¥8.7 billion ($64.4 million), or 60 percent of the value of all contracts signed.

As for major Japanese equipment makers, NEC won thirty-two major contracts in LDCs in the year beginning in April 1986 (mostly for telecommunications equipment), and ten were financed by Japan's ODA program. These ten are worth ¥37.8 billion ($280 million), or 30 percent of the value of all contracts signed in the developing world. Fujitsu won nine contracts worth ¥41.8 billion ($309 million) in the same period, and four were awarded through Japan's ODA programs, accounting for 52 percent of the total value.

Whole plant exporters are also subsidized by Japan's ODA. Mitsubishi Heavy Industries signed export contracts for thirteen whole plants, five of which were directly financed by Japan's bilateral ODA. These five projects were (1) a thermal power plant in Egypt in cooperation with Toshiba Electric Co. and Mitsubishi Shoji worth ¥25 billion ($185 million); (2) a gas turbine electric power plant in Bangladesh in cooperation with Mitsubishi Electric Co., Shimizu Construction Co., and Nissho Iwai worth ¥8 billion ($59 million); (3) a hydroelectric power plant in Burma in cooperation with Mitsubishi Electric Co., Sakai Steel Works, and Kajima Construction Co. worth ¥12.6 billion ($93 million); (4) a ship container crane in North Yemen in cooperation with Mitsubishi Shōji worth ¥1.4 billion ($10 million); and (5) a thermal power plant in Syria in cooperation with Mitsubishi Electric Co. and Tōmen Trading Co. worth ¥30 billion ($222 million).

Finally, the nurturing of engineering consulting firms has always been a priority in Japan's ODA because they play a key role in penetrating new markets for Japan's plant and capital equipment exports through their control over project design and specifications. Japan's largest engineering consulting firm, Nihon Kōei, won nineteen major consulting contracts for overseas projects in the year from April 1986, and all but one were commissioned through Japan's bilateral ODA program. The work, valued at over ¥12 billion ($89 million), consists mainly in performing F/Ss, master plans (M/Ps), detailed project design (D/D), and construction supervision for such projects as irrigation and hydroelectric dams.

Japan's second-largest consulting firm, Pacific Consultants International, won twenty-one major contracts in the same period, of which eighteen, valued at ¥6.2 billion ($46 million), are directly funded through Japan's bilateral ODA. Projects to be designed or supervised include airports, road systems, the development of China's Hainan Island, railways, and ports. It may be recalled that Nihon Kō ei and Pacific Consultants International are direct descendants of Japan's colonial administrations in Korea and Manchuria, respectively, and have always been nurtured by government policy.

In sum, an understanding of how Japan implements the project cycle is critical to assessing the aims and effects of Japan's project-oriented bilateral ODA. The details of implementation indicate how the Japanese state can nurture large-scale Japanese industrial and commercial interests using agencies and procedures that appear to be following the official norms of noncommercial ODA.

8

The System of ODA Administration

One characteristic of a decisionmaking system is that it filters information and reduces a wide range of theoretical options to a narrower range of policy outcomes. In the absence of external compulsion the range of outputs usually reflects the balance of organizationally included interests, and in the case of ODA the inclusion of economic and other functional ministries with their private sector clients explains much about the thrust of Japan's ODA. The structure of relations between government and private sector organizations is worth a more detailed examination to understand the nature of state-societal relations in this area and to explain why the system resists structural change in the face of domestic and foreign pressures for reform.

The outstanding characteristics of the central bureaucracy are its autonomous power in conjunction with strong sectionalism, and these are evident in the ODA policy making process. Yet it should be of interest to ask how policy irrelevance to societal interests on one extreme and policy gridlock due to bureaucratic wrangling at the other extreme are avoided; either extreme could be the logical outcome of the previously mentioned characteristics. The answer suggested by Japan's management of economic cooperation is that barriers between state and society and those between government ministries have been lowered or penetrated to construct relations of interest coordination and reciprocities that put bureaucratic politics into a larger institutionalized context.

A bureaucratic politics paradigm is too limited for explaining Japan's ODA. First, with intrabureaucratic rivalry as the main independent variable, societal interests become exogenous and relatively unimportant factors in policy analysis. Yet it is the linkage of societal interests to the bureaucracy that explains the continuing responsiveness of policy to extrabureaucratic interests and agendas. ODA policy making may have a consistent character, but it avoids gridlock because there are quasi-corporatist mechanisms that work out a general consensus among actors within the system regarding the scope for legitimate action by each actor. These mechanisms may not be broadly representative of societal interests, but they are inclusive of progrowth private sector, bureaucratic, academic, and media viewpoints. At the level of implementation the bureaucratic politics model also does not identify the role of the private sector as an important phenomenon. Yet this aspect of Japan's ODA is the key to understanding how public-private sector coordination is achieved. This allows the private sector to have a degree of license to shape and use government policy to achieve its profit and growth objectives in ways that are consistent with bureaucratically determined public policy goals.

The institutionalist approach used here examines not just horizontal relations within the bureaucracy, but also the vertical relations between state and society, or more specifically the vertical relations between the Japanese bureaucracy and the private sector. Cognizance of this matrix of institutionalized linkages in ODA allows one to appreciate a broader range of "facts" in policymaking. The following section will deal primarily with horizontal relations among the main ministries. The subsequent section will examine the selectively structured vertical relations between state and society. In both discussions intermediary organizations such as *shingikai*, the economic cooperation implementing agencies (tokushū hōjin), and other associations (*shadan hōjin* [non-profit business association] and zaidan h ōjin [nonprofit foundation]) play crucial roles. In these intermediary organizations the practices of amakudari (the placement of a retired government official in a well-paying position within a client organization; discussed later in this chapter) and temporary secondment of personnel (shukko) mark them as vehicles for information exchange and interest coordination among members of the system. Considered as a whole the matrix-like system of relations allows a degree of interministerial and public-private sector collaboration without which keizai kyōryoku would be impossible.

BUREAUCRATIC AUTONOMY

To understand the ODA system a short digression into the nature of autonomous bureaucratic power in Japan's parliamentary democracy is required. In the early 1960s when the United States and other countries passed basic legislation to establish policy principles and administrative systems, Japan merely created implementing agencies under the guidance of one or another of the yonshōchō, leaving the basic principles and objectives of foreign aid undefined in statutory law. Then, as now, the introduction of basic policy legislation in the Diet would risk crippling keizai kyōryoku. Rather than fighting to make the objectives and procedures of this policy area explicit, it has been organized on the basis of discretionary administrative authority.

The Significance of LDP Rule

A key basis for this situation was the fact that the LDP used its control of the Diet to shield the keizai kyōryoku system from public oversight. In 1986 when the Marcos scandal broke, the solid LDP majority blocked an opposition effort to introduce a law establishing Japan's ODA policy, and in August 1988 Prime Minister Takeshita could state in the Diet that his government was giving no consideration to a law to govern Japan's rapidly growing ODA program or otherwise restructure the ODA system through Diet initiative. So long as the LDP held an absolute majority in the Diet, no strong public oversight of ODA was feasible.

When strategic policy initiatives were needed the bureaucracy or the private sector could raise the need in the LDP's Policy Affairs Research Council (PARC) to determine how the LDP would handle the opposition parties and the electorate. Deliberations inside PARC allowed the LDP to use its professional judgment as to when and how legislative action should be taken. Its political expertise is indicated by the high rate of Diet passage of Cabinet-sponsored bills.[285] In the case of ODA the relevant PARC venue for discussion was the Special Committee on Foreign Economic Cooperation (Taigai Keizai Kyōryoku Tokubetsu Iinkai). Because economic cooperation fell between PARC's regular standing committee structure (which had a one-to-one correspondence to bureaucratic structure), a special committee was formed to cover developments in this policy area. In 1993 over eighty LDP members belonged to this special committee, with perhaps fifteen to twenty in regular attendance. Appearances by officials from various ministries and by representatives of the private sector maintained a flow of information exchange. PARC recommendations are reviewed by the LDP's Executive Committee before being approved for Cabinet action. (In a simultaneous and coordinated process the bureaucracy approves the same measure for Cabinet action.)

As a result of this process, the primary information flow from the bureaucracy was to the LDP—not to the Diet. In most cases involving ODA, Diet action was avoided altogether—as when new initiatives such as the ODA-doubling plans were authorized by Cabinet or ministerial order. Through restriction of the role of the Diet, the role of ODA in keizai kyō-ryoku was preserved, and the problem of pluralistic stagnation or ungovernability that might have accompanied full Diet deliberations of ODA policy was avoided.[286]

The Weak Role of Public Opinion

In theory public opinion in a parliamentary democracy can be aroused to demand change. But in everyday affairs the mass media is constrained by the press club system whereby each ministry gives the media access on the understanding that violation of unwritten rules will be punished with expulsion. This helps to explain the blandness of reporting and the poor record of investigative journalism in Japan. It also ensures that administrative actions remain obscure. Cabinet decisions are not automatically disclosed, nor are administrative decisions and deliberations within ministries and agencies. Statutes providing for mandatory public disclosure of information such as the U.S. Freedom of Information Act had little chance of passing the Diet so long as the LDP ruled. ⟩ 167-8

The main institutional conduit through which the public could gain regular access to information regarding administrative matters was the Diet. Through its budgetary and legislative functions, the Diet's intended role is to set policy, keep the public informed, and oversee the bureaucracy. The problem is that the Diet itself has been kept in the dark. To support the LDP the bureaucracy would not keep the opposition parties informed. Only rarely did Diet bodies investigate administrative activities, even in cases of suspected wrongdoing. [287] Discussions in committees or in the full Diet were normally routine explanations of Cabinet bills. Each Diet representative is funded for only two staff aides, so Diet representatives are dependent on the bureaucracy for information and policy research. To serve Diet members' information needs well over 200 bureaucrats are on call to explain the policies of their respective ministries and agencies.

⌈To understand how such an institutional arrangement could remain legitimate, it should be pointed out that despite the liberal political philosophy embodied in Japan's postwar Constitution, the people's right to know in Japan is not a deeply rooted political conviction. This is at least partly attributable to the fact that the prewar attitude of *kanson-minpi* (literally, "revere officials, disdain the people") has continued into the postwar period, sustained by the continuing power and aloofness of the Japanese state.⌋ 168

Weak Judicial Remedies

Another cornerstone of bureaucratic power in Japan is the poor efficacy of appeal to the judiciary when it is claimed that the bureaucracy has either overstepped its authority or failed to carry out its duties. A Western student of the Japanese legal system writes: "The identification of litigation as a threat to the political and social status quo is implicit in all writing on Japanese law and society, and recent scholarship argues persuasively that self-interest has led the Japanese elite to take deliberate steps to discourage litigation."[288]

The most infamous case of official stonewalling of litigation against the government is the twenty-eight-year-long litigation of Professor Ienaga Saburo, who originally sued the government in 1965 for censoring 323 passages of his 1962 manuscript of a Japanese history textbook. Among those censored items were descriptions of Japanese Army behavior during World War II. Ienaga argued this was illegal and asked for ¥1.87 million in compensation. The Tokyo District Court ruled in 1974 that eight censored items were illegal abuses of the Education Ministry's inspection system and ordered the government to pay ¥100,000 in compensation. But in 1993 the Supreme Court overturned this judgment, and in its first ruling ever on the government's textbook screening system, it rejected all of Professor Ienaga's claims. This illustrates how difficult it can be under the present system of statutes and judicial practice to sue the government.

As a matter of general orientation the Japanese courts have tended not to interfere in administrative matters. The prewar judiciary had no jurisdiction over matters of public law, and the so-called administrative courts that handled public law only passed judgment on statutes. In other words, administrative orders and regulations—which in theory emanated from the emperor—could not be litigated, and petition for redress could be made only directly to the bureaucracy. This bias is still detectable in the contemporary system. Under the postwar Constitution the independent judiciary under the Supreme Court is empowered to review all legal disputes, and the Court Organization Law repealed the prewar court system. The 1962 Administrative Litigation Law did allow private individuals to sue the government, but only on restricted grounds as follows.

In cases where an individual argues that his or her own individual rights and interests have been violated, a case must be filed within three months of the disputed administrative action. In cases where an individual argues that an administrative action violates existing law, there is no legal filing period, but he or she must show "grave and manifest" illegality for the courts to agree to rule upon the case. Finally, in cases where there is administrative delay and inaction, a person must prove personal harm. In such cases, however, the most that courts can do is to find "illegality of inaction." In this case courts cannot order an administrative organ to take a specific remedial action. In the view of prevailing Japanese jurisprudence, this imposition of a court's will on an administrative organ would violate the principle of the "separation of powers."[289]

An incomplete statutory framework also makes it difficult to prove in court that an administrative action or inaction is "illegal." In cases where a dispute centers on the substance of an administrative action, a strong defense can be constructed on the basis of the vaguely worded establishment law of the concerned ministry or agency. A passive judiciary that accepts a broad interpretation of a ministry's establishment law permits an enormous range of discretionary action.[290]

An alternative approach would be to build a case on procedural law, i.e., claiming that an administrative action is illegal because it was not taken in accordance with legally established procedure. This strategy is very difficult in Japan because Japan, unlike the United States and the European countries, has no law establishing general administrative procedure.[291] This absence is not coincidental—it facilitates administrative guidance by the bureaucracies by leaving room for arbitrary actions with little scope for judicial appeal by the regulated party. The inability of the Diet to establish a statutory framework for administrative procedures is a consequence of LDP rule, and it is a conspicuous handicap in the effort to realize democratic control of the bureaucracy.

Yet another barrier to using the courts to check the bureaucracy is the fact that it is not unusual for a suit against the government to wait on a court calendar for ten or more years before being heard. The fundamental bottleneck is the lack of judges available to hear cases. Throughout the postwar period only approximately 500 candidates have been allowed to pass the annual national law exam, and only they can become judges, lawyers, or prosecutors. Taking into account the number of annual retirements, the number of judges available is inadequate to serve a nation of some 120 million, making actual litigation in the civil courts a prohibitive alternative.

The above paragraphs show that factors such as a traditional respect for the bureaucracy, lack of transparency in administration, a legislative branch fulfilling only part of its intended functions, a collusive relationship between the LDP and the bureaucracy, and a passive judiciary help to support bureaucratic autonomy and to leave the power of policymaking in the hands of the bureaucracy. The lack of effective external oversight means that the bureaucracy as a whole can work out new policies and implementation procedures relatively free of legislative and judicial intervention. The relevance of the foregoing to ODA is that policymaking and implementation are accomplished in an opaque process of decisionmaking that cannot be changed or restructured by litigation or legislation.

The Legal Basis of Administration

The legal framework for national administration gives the bureaucracy great discretionary power, but it has certain provisions that have facilitated the structured inclusion of the private sector and the participation of most of the main ministries and agencies in ODA.

The Constitution of Japan creates the parliamentary Cabinet, but the system of administration is defined by statutes. The organization of the central bureaucracy is defined by the National Government Organization Law. It articulates an ideal of jurisdictional autonomy and organic interministerial coordination:

> [The bureaucracy] shall, under the control and jurisdiction of the Cabinet, be made up of a system of administrative organs having a well-defined scope of authority and responsibility and specific functions.
> The national administrative organs shall, under the control and jurisdiction of the Cabinet, maintain liaison with one another so that they may consummate their administrative functions as an organic whole. [292]

This law goes on to authorize creation of ministries *(shō)*, agencies *(chō)*, offices *(fu)*, and commissions *(iinkai)*. It does not specify their number, but it does define a model of internal organization. The *shō* and *chō* are the building blocks of the central administrative bureaucracy, otherwise known as the main ministries and agencies, or *kanchō*. Of great relevance to the organization of keizai kyōryoku is the fact that the National Government Organization Law also allows national administrative organs to establish, on their own authority, policy councils (shingikai), subsidiary agencies, local or overseas branch offices, and other bodies in the course of carrying out their responsibilities. This provision gives the prime minister the authority to establish the Taigai Keizai Kyōryoku Shingikai; MITI the authority to establish the Industrial Structure Council; and the EPA the authority to establish the Economic Deliberation Council (Keizai Kondankai). These mechanisms have played a key role in authorizing new priorities for Japan's ODA. This law also allows the licensing of subsidiary organizations such as the Association for the Promotion of International Cooperation (APIC) or the Engineering Consulting Firms Association (ECFA), which have important roles in ODA policy implementation.

The actual number of main ministries and agencies, and their respective jurisdictions, are not set except by their respective establishment laws. A ministry's establishment law defines its jurisdiction in broad terms, and this gives it great flexibility in regulating societal activity through ordinances and administrative guidance. The establishment law also specifies the responsibilities of its constituent bureaus *(kyoku)* and departments *(bu)*.

To ensure interministerial consultation and coordination, the National Government Organization Law specifies that the number and responsibilities of bureaus and departments cannot be expanded without amending the establishment law. Moreover, the number and jurisdictions of divisions *(ka)* and offices *(shitsu)*, although not defined by the establishment law, must be authorized by a Cabinet order. In either case there will be a need for Cabinet action, and this means all the main ministries and agencies must review the measure. The norms and principles of this system have two key implications for ODA.

First, every main ministry and agency whose jurisdiction in national administration is broached by ODA activity (there are sixteen) must be involved in that portion. Accordingly, each gets budget and personnel for this purpose. Their scope of involvement may vary in practice, but in principle they must be involved to ensure that the bureaucracy "may consummate their administrative functions as an organic whole."

Second, any effort to change the bureaucratically determined keizai kyōryoku system is practically impossible. For example, to establish a centralized main aid ministry or agency means that the jurisdictions, personnel, and budgets of virtually all of the other main ministries and agencies would have to be pruned back. The difficulty of doing this explains why proposals to create an aid ministry since the 1960s have gone nowhere. Even a small effort by one ministry to expand its jurisdiction unilaterally in this area could easily fail. Any proposal to add an ODA-relevant office and function is reviewed by a meeting of all of the administrative vice-ministers prior to submission to the Cabinet.[293] This procedure makes it difficult for any one ministry or agency to expand the scope of its jurisdiction at the expense of others.

MANAGING CHANGE

There is no authoritative central decisionmaker in the ODA policy making system, nor is there a clear-cut procedure for expediting change. Instead, the system depends on a high degree of institutionalized coordination among various ministries, agencies, and private sector actors for effective implementation, and it is held together by a broadly based consensus articulated periodically through peak deliberation councils as to the means and ends of Japan's ODA. Because the policymaking system maintains a closed set of interests that regulates itself through a set of norms that are largely informal and consensual, rather than legislated, policy change tends to be slow and incremental.

The most common type of policy change is adjustment in the amount or allocation of ODA funds, minor alterations in the mix of ODA programming, or the introduction of new types of ODA activity in reaction to emerging needs. Because of the need for consensus among structurally included actors, a joint perception of a problem, the nature of its cause, and the range of possible solutions must be built up. A procedure to accomplish this goal must involve all actors and result in some concrete expression of the new underlying consensus.

Because neither the courts nor the Diet could create effective domestic pressure for change in ODA policies, and because individual members of the ODA policy community are loathe to upset the network of compromises and the balance of interests that allow the system to operate relatively smoothly, the main source of change is the international environment. Foreign and Japanese observers alike recognize that deliberate pressure from other countries is often the only way to impel change inside Japan, and the term invented to describe this phenomenon is gaiatsu, literally meaning "outside pressure." Consequently, gaiatsu is a powerful force for change that is viewed with ambivalence: If controlled by Japanese interests it can be a convenient and positive force for change; if uncontrolled it can be a destructive force threatening to overturn the balance of interests supporting Japan's "domestic harmony" and developmental imperative.

External pressures can induce members of the system to call for change, but such calls must conform to existing principles and norms if there is to be any hope of success. Then it must gain bureaucratic approval of any new administrative arrangements. A draft proposal will have to be circulated among affected main ministries and agencies and their comments solicited. This can invite bureaucratic obstruction and the intervention of private sector actors and allied LDP politicians. If there is not a preexisting consensus on the action to be taken, the process can be derailed here. To manage change, therefore, intermediary bodies such as shingikai and *kenky ūkai,* which allow a full range of included bureaucratic and private sector interests to define problems and their solutions jointly, play a critical role. As policy proposals are advanced and reformulated through various overlapping policy discussions, a general consensus supportive of change can emerge.

When a major change is on the agenda, deliberations will be held within the LDP's PARC bringing in bureaucratic and private sector representatives. Within the private sector, the Keidanren, the Japanese Chamber of Congress and Industry (JCCI), the Keizai Dōyūkai, and other organizations will intensify their study activities. Within the government each concerned main ministry and agency will set up formal and informal internal study groups (kenky ūkai) to set policy proposals, and activate shingikai bringing in retired bureaucrats *(yūshikisha),* representatives of the business world *(keizaijin),* and other prestigious nongovernmental opinion leaders in order to incorporate social interests and legitimate the concerned ministry's policy preference.

At the same time, interministerial talks will be held in an effort to map out the general lines of a consolidated bureaucratic position. When strong bureaucratic actors disagree, this inevitably creates wide-ranging conflicts that can endanger the consensus and coordination needed to implement ODA. Rather than endanger the stability of the entire enterprise with stubborn demands for radical change, the major actors in the ODA system will settle for changes of a piecemeal nature.

After the desired result is agreed upon by included actors, the LDP is informed of the new initiative. In order for the LDP to play its role in representing Japan abroad, adjusting domestic interests, brokering bureaucratic conflicts, and passing any needed legislation, LDP politicians must know the interests and issues at stake. In addition to the party executives, there are certain senior Diet members who have influence in ODA-related issues, and they must be consulted on all important changes in ODA policy. In terms of formal procedure an LDP position must be approved by the relevant committees in PARC and then by the Executive Council before it can be referred to the Cabinet for consideration. LDP involvement allows favors to be traded and previously ignored private sector interests to be addressed. After this the Cabinet issues the necessary implementing orders or legislative proposals. ODA policy changes are implemented without alteration by the opposition parties in the Diet.

THE ORGANIZATION OF ODA ADMINISTRATION

It can be difficult for foreign observers to pin down exactly how the system is legitimated, why it has its present structure, or where one can go for a

definitive and unified expression of ODA policy. It can be tempting to
believe that the MFA has final authority because it explains ODA policy. The
MFA's jurisdiction over external diplomacy means it serves as the main
window through which the Japanese government passes information to the
outside world. To achieve the diplomatic ends of ODA, the MFA has an
interest in convincing others that it is not economically self-interested.
Instead, the MFA's interest has been to stress Japan's humanitarian concerns
and desire to contribute to the Western alliance. But this window function
does not mean that the MFA can or should control economic cooperation
policy.

Overall System Coordination

Domestically oriented national policy deliberation councils, or shingikai, play
a crucial role in the overall management of the ODA system. They are not a
creative or innovative force, but they register the views of major actors and
are needed as authoritative pronouncers of a policy consensus that guides
activity within the system. The membership and agenda of shingikai can be
controlled by the bureaucracy because councils are usually formed under
administrative initiative. They are needed to coordinate vertical relations
when the strategies of the state and the private sector need to be discussed
and adjusted. They also can be important in managing horizontal relations
between main ministries and agencies when bureaucratic routines need to be
transcended and reorganized, and when extrabureaucratic parties can help
broker new agreements. As such, shingikai help coordinate a matrix of
horizontal and vertical relations in policymaking. The Taigai Keizai Kyōryoku Shingikai played this role when it recommended the creation of OTCA
and the OECF at the start of the 1960s, when it responded to Western
criticism and the oil shocks in the 1970s, and yet again after 1985 when ODA
had to be turned to the promotion of a new division of labor in Asia. In these
cases the core elements of Japan's postwar political economy worked in
deliberation councils such as the Taigai Keizai Kyōryoku Shingikai to define
their common interests.

Taigai Keizai Kyōryoku Shingikai membership (August 1993)

Name	Affiliation*
Ishikawa Rokuro (Chair)	Japan Chamber of Commerce and Industry
Ito Tadashi	Japan Foreign Trade Council
Imai Keiko	Sophia University
Uchida Shigeo	Nihon Keizai Shimbun
Ohba Tomomitsu	International Finance Information Center
Kakudo Ken'ichi	Central Agricultural Bank of Japan

Satomi Yasuo	Overseas Construction Association of Japan
Shimao Tadao	Association for Tubercular Prevention
Tagaki Tsuku	Bank of Tokyo
Tanaka Ryoichi	Japan Labor Union Federation
Nishigaki Akira	OECF
Fujiwara Ichiro	Electrical Power Development Corp.
Hoshino Masako	International Volunteer Center of Japan
Maruyama Yasuo	International Labour Organisation
Monden Hideo	International Development Center
Yanagiya Kensuke	JICA
Yamaguchi Mitsuhide	Export-Import Bank
Yoshino Bunroku	IDE
Yonekura Isao	Keidanren
Toyoshima Tooru	JETRO

* Several members are former bureaucrats in amakudari positions with these organizations.

Coordination in Policy Implementation

Perhaps the most accurately nuanced description of the administrative system in ODA was given by Matsui Ken, a career Bank of Japan official with extensive experience in economic cooperation. He wrote in 1983:

> In our national administration of economic cooperation, the MFA is the window facing outward, but internally the official principle *(tatemae)* is that it is carried out through deliberations among the relevant ministries and agencies, who each have their own jurisdictions. But in normal practice those who confer intimately over economic cooperation issues are the MFA, MOF, MITI, and the EPA. These four stand at the core of the economic cooperation administrative system.[294]

The status of the implementing agencies in keizai kyōryoku is difficult to understand based on appearances. Matsui notes that "because the administration of economic cooperation is conducted through interministerial consultation, supervision of implementing agencies is not simply by the supervising ministry alone."[295] What he means is that actual supervision over JICA is divided among several ministries. The same is true of the OECF, but MOF exercises the most influence there.

What follows is a description of Japan's main ODA implementing organizations (see Figure 8.1). It illustrates how JICA and the OECF act as intermediaries in interministerial coordination as well as in public-private sector collaboration in this complex policy area. Their organizational structure gives concrete expression to the principle of keizai kyōryoku, and it

Figure 8.1 Outline of the Administration of ODA, 1992

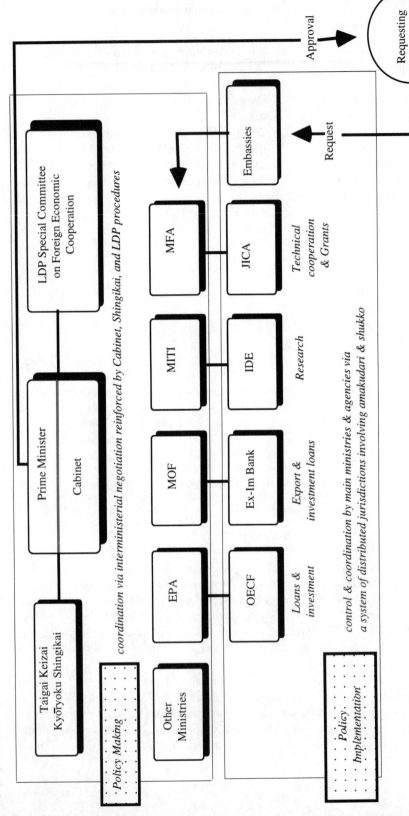

illustrates how core structures in Japan's political economy have institution-alized their relations.

As already mentioned the National Government Organization Law authorizes main ministries and agencies to supervise subordinate foundations, public corporations, agencies, and other entities if deemed necessary for effective administration. Such subsidiary agencies (tokushū hōjin) are empowered to implement government policies, but they have separate legal status. This is a convenient way for main government ministries and agencies to set up activity in areas where highly technical expertise is needed, where special financial arrangements are wanted, or where flexible coordination between different ministries and private sector interests is required in policy implementation. In the area of ODA all three conditions have to be met.

Another consideration favoring creation of implementing agencies is the fact that their staff members are hired as private employees *(shokuin)* and not as state civil servants *(kokka kōmuin)*. Japan has made efforts since the 1968 Personnel Reduction Plan, reinvigorated in 1983 by the recommendations of the Second Provisional Commission for Administrative Reform, to reduce the number of civil servants. For the past twenty years the absolute number of national government personnel has been reduced every year. Japan has less than 2 percent of the population working in the national government, by far the lowest percentage among the major OECD countries.[296] Because the staffs of implementing agencies are not counted by the law limiting national government personnel, main ministries and agencies can use them to gain new staff resources.

To avoid confusion it should be noted here that different legal entities are often called "agencies" in English. The nine agencies under the jurisdiction of the office of the prime minister are all chō, and with one exception all are headed by an official with ministerial rank. Other legal entities may also be called "agencies" in English translation, but in Japanese they have such names as *jigyōdan* or *kōdan* that signify a secondary status in Japanese government administration.

Tokushū Hōjin

One of the principal types of subsidiary organizations is the public corporation, or tokushū hōjin. According to the MFA, in keizai kyōryoku there are eight main ones aside from JICA and the OECF (see Table 8.1). In reaction to Western pressure to meet ODA standards, the main aspects of keizai kyōryoku that qualify as ODA have been put under the OECF and JICA. Each tokushū hōjin is established by Diet legislation or Cabinet order and is supervised by the government through one or more main ministries and agencies. The government is able exert operational control through its financial support and by its right to appoint officers, issue orders, collect reports, and make on-the-spot inspections.

Table 8.1 The Ten Main *Tokushū Hōjin* in *Keizai Kyōryoku*

Name	Function	Supervising Ministry	Year of establish-ment
Ex-Im Bank (Nihon Yushutsunyū Ginkō)	Trade and investment finance; structural adjustment lending	MOF	1950
Japan External Trade Organization (Nihon Bōeki Shinkōkai)	Trade promotion	MITI	1958
Institute of Developing Economies (Ajia Keizai Kenkyūjo)	Economic and political research to expand economic cooperation	MITI	1960
Employment Promotion Projects Corporation (Koyō Sokushin Jigyōdan)	Technical training	MOL	1961
OECF (Kaigai Keizai Kyōryoku Kikin)	Official equity and loan cooperation	EPA	1961
OTCA (Taigai Gijutsu Kyōryoku Jigyōdan)	Official technical assistance	MFA	1962
Metals and Mining Agency of Japan (Kinzoku Kōgyo Jigyōdan)	Metal ore finding and development	MITI	1963
Japan National Oil Corporation (Sekiyū Kōdan)	Oil and gas development	MITI	1967
The Japan Foundation (Kokusai Kōryū Kikin)	Cultural exchange	MFA	1972
Agricultural Land Development Agency (Nōyōchi Kaihatsu Kōdan)	Agriculture development	MAFF	1974

Source: MFA, *Kokusai kyōryoku handobukku* [International Cooperation Handbook], (Tokyo: MFA, 1983).

Among the advantages of tokushū hōjin are freedom in employing staff; flexibility in contracting with foreign and domestic entities; the ability to generate revenue, issue bonds, or accept private sector equity participation; and legal "distance" from the government. Because of their government backing via personnel, financing, and regulatory arrangements, tokushū hōjin are able to operate in areas where the private sector cannot be freely induced to provide resources and services, or where a fair and impartial standpoint is required. These characteristics are useful in areas that cross the jurisdictional boundaries of government ministries or in activities that have a quasi-public, quasi-private nature.[297]

The history of tokushū hōjin goes back to the early Meiji period, when the government set up state-owned industries in textiles, steel, and shipping. In the postwar period tokushū hōjin such as Nippon Telephone and Telegraph (NTT), the Japanese National Railways (JNR), and the Japan Tobacco and

Salt Monopoly were set up to take over assets and activities previously ad-ministered directly by the government. Others such as Japan Air Lines Co., Ltd. (JAL), the Japan Development Bank (JDB), and Kokusai Denshin Denwa Co. (KDD) were set up in new areas of initiative. As new areas of regulation proliferated in the postwar period, the number of tokushū hōjin increased from 21 in 1946 to 104 by 1965. Today several of these tokushū hōjin (such as the JNR, JAL, and NTT) have been successfully privatized to wean them from public subsidies.

INTEREST COORDINATION IN JICA AND OECF

JICA and the OECF serve as organizational nexuses where horizontal and vertical relations are managed at the level of policy implementation. Without these intermediary organizations the main ministries and agencies could not jointly administer Japan's ODA, nor could ODA be coordinated with the activities of other agencies and private sector firms in keizai kyōryoku. It is well known that JICA and the OECF each have a permanent staff under the official guidance of the MFA and EPA, respectively, but the roles of other main ministries and agencies and those of the private sector are neither widely known nor understood. Figure 8.2 shows how the organization of ODA administration formally appears.

The System of Distributed Jurisdiction

The distribution of jurisdictions within implementing agencies was the answer to the dilemma posed by the need to respect the jurisdictional claims

Figure 8.2 The Formal Appearance of ODA Administration

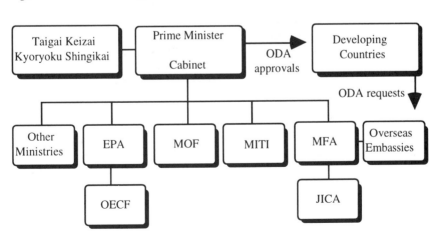

of sixteen main ministries and agencies over ODA, while at the same time making economic cooperation an effective instrument to raise Japan's status in international political and economic hierarchies. By using case-by-case decisionmaking the system determines which ministries set policy and evaluate projects. Jurisdiction is distributed based on the type of project requested and the Japanese contractors involved. For example, if there is a request for an irrigation dam, the project must be referred to MAFF for study; if it is a hydroelectric dam, it must go to MITI. If it is a drinking water supply project, it must be sent to the MHW; but if it is a sewage project, it must go to MOC. This principle of determining proper jurisdiction based on the nature of the project request is complemented by another principle that allocates positions within implementing agencies to main ministries and their private sector clients according to the type of activity conducted. This staffing principle ensures that jurisdictional rules in case-by-case decisionmaking are being honored. The system of distributed jurisdictions allows many main ministries and agencies access to ODA on terms they have agreed upon and institutionalized.

The system is most evident in the structure of JICA and the OECF. As tokushū hōjin, OECF and JICA are formally under the jurisdictions of the EPA and MFA, respectively. In reality, the EPA and MFA do not exercise "control" over their subordinate agencies in the normal sense of the word, i.e., by controlling the hiring and firing of personnel and autonomously setting policy guidelines governing agency activity. Instead, they "preside" over organizations that include all ministries with jurisdictional claims and that coordinate public policy with private investment and trade activity.

If one digs into JICA and the OECF, one sees that the MFA and EPA have only limited interest in and control over actual policy implementation. Actual staffing arrangements are the key to understanding how these agencies successfully coordinate policy implementation among such a wide range of actors. At any given time roughly a third of each agency's permanent staff is exported to other government or private sector organizations, and they are replaced by personnel imported from other actors in the keizai kyōryoku system. What facilitates this surprising degree of personnel exchange and cross-posting are the practices of secondment (shukko) and the placement of retiring bureaucrats in client organizations through amakudari.

The Cross-Posting of Personnel

The practice of amakudari is well known, but shukko may require a word of explanation. Shukko means that one organization loans an individual to a host organization for such reasons as technical training, interorganizational liaison, or managerial and staff support. In JICA and the OECF it often involves a two-way transfer with outside organizations. Shukko is different from amakudari in that active career personnel are transferred to other organizations, usually for only a year or two. In JICA and the OECF the person imported by shukko is listed as holding an official position, though he or she continues to receive a paycheck from the real employer. The host organization expects this person to bring not just individual skills, but also those of the home organization. The home organization wants its employee to study the host organization and to promote home organization interests. The person on secondment embodies an ongoing interorganizational relationship of mutual cooperation and influence. As a result of his or her experience, this person will promote the relationship between both organizations for the rest of his or her career. Thus, shukko creates relations of interdependence, shared experience, and close coordination among the wide range of actors in Japanese ODA. It penetrates the barriers between ministries, as well as the divide between public and private sectors.

When it occurs between organizations of different rank and prestige, shukko often embodies an authority relationship. Staff sent from superior agencies dominate key decisionmaking posts in the subordinate agency, whereas staff from subordinate agencies sent to superior agencies are largely restricted to staff support. By this technique even detailed decisions on individual projects can be coordinated between organizations. This is the model for shukko between main ministries and the private sector, with implementing agencies providing the venue for contact and coordination. This practice allows the private sector insight and input into government policies, and it gives government a better awareness of the problems of business, thus enhancing policy effectiveness.

A clear example of this in ODA is provided by the MFA's Economic Cooperation Bureau. This bureau has two main tasks in bilateral ODA. One is processing the official requests for grant and loan aid collected through its overseas embassies. Much of this work merely involves referring paperwork to the relevant ministries and agencies. The other main task is explaining Japan's ODA to foreign and domestic audiences. The MFA's priority is on the latter, as may be seen in the fact that the highest concentration of MFA officers is at the minister *(shingikan)* and councilor *(sanjikan)* levels. These ranks specialize in policymaking and diplomatic representation. In contrast, at the working level of the division director *(kacho)* and below, the MFA makes only a minimal commitment of career officers to the processing of ODA requests.

To handle paperwork the MFA relies heavily on personnel on shukko from other ministries, agencies, and private sector firms. The MFA may have two or three career officers in the loan, technical, and grant aid divisions (usually the director, deputy director, and task coordinator), but the rest of the staff of each division are so-called noncareer MFA employees or outsiders. In 1987 there were 117 full-time MFA staff of all descriptions working in the bureau and 170 temporary staff from outside, of which 50 were employees from other ministries and agencies. (The same reliance on private sector personnel exists in the ODA staffing of other members of the yonshōchō.

MITI, MOF, and the EPA each have one or more sections managing ODA and related activities, and their total full-time staff numbered forty-one, thirty-seven, and nineteen, respectively.)[298] The one glaring omission among ministries sending staff to the MFA is MITI, a result of the chronic conflict between these two ministries. But the MFA will exchange officers with MOF, and other ministries and agencies send staff on a regular basis. Private sector financial institutions and consultants also place personnel in the MFA on a regular basis.

There are three important reasons for this heavy reliance on non-MFA personnel. The first has to do with the MFA's lack of technical expertise in ODA issues. This shortcoming is partially overcome by bringing in public or private sector personnel who either can do the work themselves or can find advice in their home organizations regarding implementation issues.

The second reason has to do with the basic consensus underlying the ODA system. The MFA cannot decide policy by itself, nor can it exclude other bureaucratic actors from overseeing those areas of ODA that fall within their jurisdictions. The nature of a project request determines who the MFA must consult over its final disposition in accordance with the established bureaucratic norms governing ODA administration. Having personnel from key public and private sector actors ensures that everyone in the ODA system stays informed of requests and ongoing negotiations. This also allows the MFA to coordinate views with important domestic interests even at the project level, and it improves the MFA's sensitivity to domestic interests in its diplomatic activities.

The third reason has to do with the MFA's organizational interests. The MFA is perennially short of human resources, so staff borrowed on shukko are welcomed. Private firms are invited to rotate their staff through the MFA, thus giving their staff valuable experience, information, and contacts; and in return these firms supply the MFA with free personnel. These workers are officially listed as MFA staff, but some are outside the personnel ceiling set for the MFA, and their salaries are paid by their home companies. Such workers are called *tebento*, literally meaning that they "bring their own lunch." Currently, the financial industry is favored for acceptance into the MFA because of the Japanese financial industry's critical need to develop internationally minded and informed staff. In return for access to the MFA, these firms will accept retiring MFA bureaucrats as highly paid advisors.

It may be observed that where horizontal (i.e., interministerial) coordination is critical, amakudari and shukko are common. For example, in the case of the EPA—which must consult with the entire Japanese government in drafting the five-year plans that lay out the government's basic policy stance toward social and economic affairs—the top three administrative posts (administrative deputy director-general, councilor, and Bank of Japan policy board member) were in 1988 filled by officials originally from MOC and MITI. Two officials from MOF and one each from

MOL, the EPA, and the Procurement Agency occupy five of the six *buchō-*level positions, and up to a third of the councilors and division directors in the EPA are on loan from other ministries and agencies.[299]

Shukko, as well as the ability to tap the personnel resources of other organizations inside the keizai kyōryoku system, may also explain how the OECF's and JICA's combined staff of only 1,300 could administer a bilateral ODA program with net annual disbursements of $3.85 billion in 1986; or how, for example, the OECF and JICA could oversee a program disbursing $152 million dollars in 1986 in Pakistan with no locally stationed personnel, though the U.S. AID program needed well over 200 officers in five different offices implementing a program of roughly the same funding level. In 1989 Japan was able to manage a program disbursing $1,145 million in Indonesia with Japanese and local professional staff of thirty-six, whereas the United States managed a program of only $31 million with ninety-four professional staff (forty expatriates and fifty-four local professionals).[300] The ability to borrow personnel and otherwise draw on the resources of other networked organizations explains how the OECF's full-time ODA staff of 280 and JICA's staff of 951, the overwhelming majority of whom are nontechnical generalists, could administer $7.8 billion in aid commitments in 1989.

The Distribution of Posts in JICA

As explained earlier, under its charter as a tokushū hōjin, JICA is under the formal authority of the MFA. Presidents of JICA are always retired MFA administrative vice-ministers who play mostly a ceremonial role. They are not chosen because of their interest or expertise in ODA issues, but because they have achieved the highest bureaucratic post in the MFA, that of administrative vice-minister, and after retirement they are expected to represent the official relationship between the MFA and JICA. They may on occasion intervene in particular decisions, but usually they restrict themselves to a ceremonial role and have little direct contact with ongoing policy implementation. As of 1988 the two vice-presidents were retired MITI and MAFF officials placed through amakudari, and they served the same functions as the president. Six of the eight senior directors *(riji)* were placed in JICA by outside ministries through amakudari. The senior directors are formally responsible for overseeing the activities of certain departments, and in practice they are concerned with exerting influence in accordance with the interests of their home ministries.

If we look at the staffing of the posts critical to operational decisionmaking at JICA (see Figure 8.3) we discover that many are serving at JICA on shukko from other ministries, and that through shukko other ministries are able to control those areas of JICA activity of particular concern to them. For example, MOF has direct control over the Finance and Accounting Department. This means that MOF formulates JICA's annual budget requests and oversees all current financial operations. Through

Figure 8.3 Amakudari and Secondment to JICA from Other Ministries and Agencies (as of early 1988)

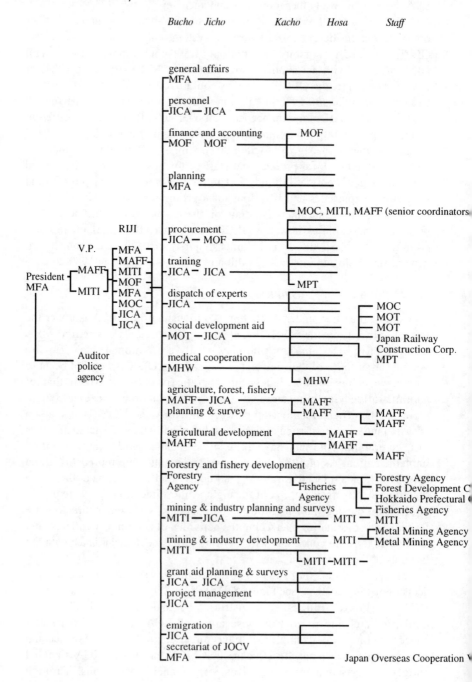

budgetary control it is not an exaggeration to say that all JICA activities are subject to MOF's direct scrutiny.

A look at Figure 8.3 also shows that the yonshōchō and other ministries administer the functional areas of grant aid and technical cooperation of particular interest to them. Nothing of importance leaves those departments without the knowledge of the relevant ministry. This ensures that ODA policies are implemented in ways that accord with the interests of these ministries. It is interesting to note that the MFA controls only three departments through shukko and that two of them are not engaged in technical implementation activities. The more important of the two, the planning department, has senior coordinators from MOC, MITI, and MAFF to ensure that their interests are included when future strategies are mapped out. The placement of executive directors, vice-presidents, and the president are also carefully distributed among outside ministries to ensure that JICA continues to respond to their interests. The individuals who fill these posts are important because they must agree to any changes in the policies governing JICA.

In sum, each case of shukko and amakudari between JICA and the main ministries and agencies represents a power relationship and reflects the right of each ministry and agency to regulate activities that normally would fall under its jurisdiction. Ministries and agencies "own" certain posts in JICA and rotate their personnel through these JICA posts on an ongoing basis. Ownership of these posts has been determined through interministerial negotiation and allegedly is certified by a Cabinet agreement that, however, is not available for public inspection. Recognition of these facts puts the question of the MFA's role in JICA in a more problematic light. As Figure 8.3 indicates, the MFA's commitment of personnel is minimal, and it must share control over ODA implementation with other powerful ministries such as MITI, MAFF, MOC, and MOF.

In practical terms, the MFA has neither the personnel nor the expertise to handle ODA implementation. More important, based on the principles expressed in the National Government Organization Law, the other ministries do not recognize the MFA's right to decide policy in such fields as industry, agriculture, transportation, or construction. This is why sixteen main ministries and agencies are brought into ODA policy making and implementation on a case-by-case basis by JICA and the OECF, and are funded through the ODA budget. The MFA's implementation role is limited to coordinating and adjusting relations between Japan and foreign actors, receiving the official requests through its overseas embassies, and explaining these relations to the Japanese public. Thus, it manages inputs into the system, and it takes the lead in explaining ODA both internationally and domestically even though it lacks the power to freely determine the form and content of ODA activities.

As a result of these considerations, in reality JICA is an agency cut up into separate jurisdictions. Thus, it would be more correct to say that the Japanese "government" controls JICA and that the MFA presides over JICA in the name of the "government."

The Distribution of Posts in the OECF

The difference between formal appearance and underlying reality also holds true for the OECF. Although the OECF is formally under the EPA, in reality it is MOF that has strongest control. From MOF's point of view, as an official lending institution using public funds, the OECF most properly falls under MOF control. In view of MOF's power over the budget, the other main ministries and agencies are not willing to contest this argument.

MOF's control is evidenced by its control of key posts within the OECF (see Figure 8.4). MOF names the president *(sōsai)* and the senior director (riji) in charge of general affairs through amakudari. At the operational level, control over the general affairs department is important because the head of this department clears the annual budget requests, controls personnel appointments, chairs the weekly meeting of department heads, handles special problems that arise, and coordinates OECF activities with the government. MOF's appointees occupy the complete chain of command leading to the head of this department and down into the detailed work of the budgeting division and the accounting division. The general affairs department is the only one where the director-general is non-OECF career staff, and MOF appears determined to retain control over this post. In 1987, when the director-general (from MOF) was to be rotated out of the OECF, before vacating his post he sent all OECF career staff qualified to succeed him overseas to head OECF representative offices, allowing MOF to nominate a replacement candidate with no opposition.

In view of the importance of the general affairs department, MITI and the MFA used to post one person each through shukko in the posts of deputy director-general. Because the MFA was either uninterested or unable to utilize this post, in the early 1980s it stopped seconding a person, and today only one deputy director-general remains, the MITI representative. From the foregoing it should be clear that MOF—and not the nominally responsible EPA—is the dominant actor within the OECF.

The OECF is similar to JICA in that representatives of main ministries and private sector firms are brought into the organization on shukko to participate in implementation activities. Unlike JICA, which is responsible for supplying feasibility studies and technical training, the OECF's need for hardware expertise is relatively modest and is mostly limited to appraising project loan proposals. Nonetheless, in some key functional areas outsiders dominate the OECF. For example, in the three technical appraisal departments, which are responsible for screening loan projects, nineteen out of a total of twenty-one staff members are on secondment either from other government agencies or the private sector, and four out of the five *kacho*-

level personnel are on secondment from MITI, MAFF, MOT, and the EPA. (See chart in Figure 8.5.)

In the loan departments, which assess the financial feasibility of projects and administer loan disbursement and collection, there is heavy reliance on staff who are on shukko from public and private financial institutions. This is because private sector loan officers have the skills to do financial analyses and to administer reliably the complicated financial procedures in disbursing and collecting OECF loans. The private sector financial institutions have an incentive to provide these personnel because the institutions handle the ODA and related trade and investment financing. In addition, as Japan's financial industry internationalizes, it is in great need of staff with experience in dealing with foreign project financing, official borrowing, and coordination with international financial institutions such as the World Bank.

The greatest concentration of OECF career staff is in the overseas representative offices, where they explain OECF procedures, inspect ongoing project construction, and greet visitors. Yet at any given time, a third or more of the OECF's career staff is absent on shukko to other government ministries and agencies, or to private sector firms in engineering services, construction, finance, or commerce.

The Division of Labor Between JICA and OECF

As implementing agencies, JICA and the OECF are made to complement each other. JICA finances social infrastructure such as housing, schools, training centers, and hospitals on a grant basis, whereas the OECF finances industrial projects and economic infrastructure construction through long-term concessional loans. JICA also complements the OECF by financing fully tied technical design studies of the sort required in OECF loan applications, and after project construction JICA is able to provide the technical cooperation to support project operation. According to official information, about one-third of the OECF's projects originate from JICA-financed feasibility studies; in 40 percent of the cases the borrower government somehow produces the project request, and 6 percent are the result of Japanese project-finding missions.

Yet JICA and the OECF have certain similar characteristics. In the first place their career staffs have a general educational background and are not made up of professional economists, accountants, engineers, trained development planners, or development administrators. In other words, their permanent staff do not provide project or program design services to aid recipients. This staffing policy is explained by the fact that these agencies look for the kind of talent needed to coordinate the broad range of actors and activities in ODA. When special technical expertise is needed, it is borrowed or contracted from the private sector, even if what results may not best meet the needs of aid recipients. What is important is that aid project identification, design, and construction end up in the hands of Japanese firms. In reality,

Figure 8.4 Amakudari and Shukko in the OECF (as of late 1987)

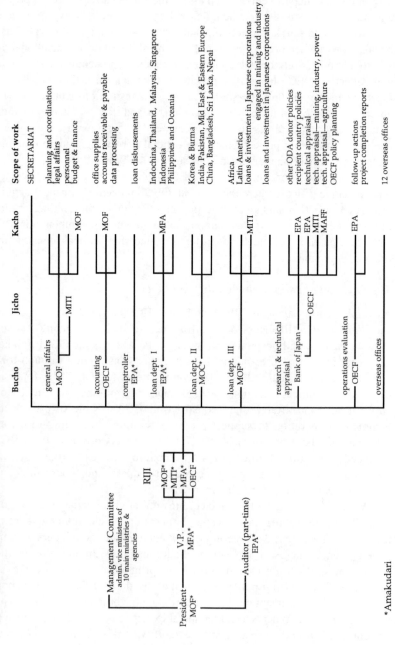

Bucho	Jicho	Kacho	Scope of work
			SECRETARIAT
general affairs			planning and coordination
MOF	MITI		legal affairs
			personnel
		MOF	budget & finance
accounting			office supplies
OECF		MOF	accounts receivable & payable
			data processing
comptroller			
EPA*			loan disbursements
loan dept. I			Indochina, Thailand, Malaysia, Singapore
EPA*		MFA	Indonesia
			Philippines and Oceania
loan dept. II			Korea & Burma
MOC*			India, Pakistan, Mid East & Eastern Europe
			China, Bangladesh, Sri Lanka, Nepal
loan dept. III			Africa
MOF*		MITI	Latin America
			loans & investment in Japanese corporations
			engaged in mining and industry
research & technical			loans and investment in Japanese corporations
appraisal			
Bank of Japan	OECF		other ODA donor policies
		EPA	recipient country policies
		EPA	technical appraisal
		MITI	tech. appraisal—mining, industry, power
		MAFF	tech. appraisal—agriculture
operations evaluation			OECF policy planning
OECF		EPA	follow-up actions
			project completion reports
overseas offices			12 overseas offices

RIJI
MOF*
MITI*
MFA*
OECF

Management Committee
admin. vice ministers of
10 main ministries &
agencies

V.P.
MFA*

President
MOF*

Auditor (part-time)
EPA*

*Amakudari

Staffing

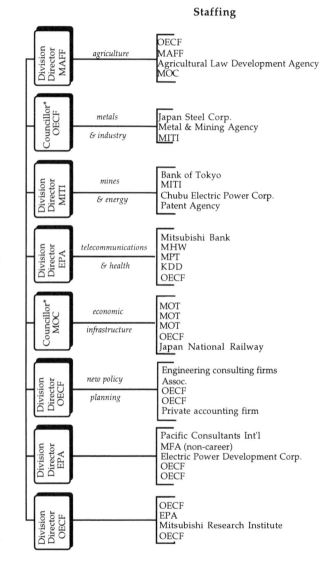

Figure 8.5 Staffing of the OECF Research and Technical Appraisal Department

* Functionally equivalent to Division Director.

then, the OECF and JICA are primarily ODA implementation coordinators and channels of financing. Their career staff members are not engaged in ODA policy decisionmaking, nor do they have detailed experience or expertise in disciplines relating to Third World development. In view of Japan's philosophy of keizai kyōryoku, that kind of staff is neither needed nor desired.

In terms of morale and benefits, however, there are differences between the OECF and JICA. The OECF is an agency under the supervision of four ministries, but it enjoys the favor of MOF. In addition, the OECF is not nearly as penetrated by amakudari and shukko as JICA because technical and basic policy issues relating to selection and design of OECF projects usually have been resolved prior to their submission to the OECF. Constant friction among the yonshōcho and generous funding by MOF create more room for initiative by the OECF, and opportunities for promotion and training for its staff produce good morale. In contrast, JICA is funded less generously through the MFA, and because main ministries and agencies have strong jurisdictional claims at the stage when projects are selected for technical evaluation, key posts in JICA are dominated by government officers through shukko. As a result the JICA career staff have fewer opportunities for training and promotion and poor prospects for amakudari. This leads to wry jokes that JICA is a "colonized" agency and contributes to poor morale among the JICA career staff.

The system of distributed jurisdictions and cross-posting of personnel in JICA and the OECF does not make full sense until one sees the many shadan hōjin and zaidan hōjin involved in ODA. According to the normal pattern of vertical administration *(tatewari gyōsei)* in Japan, a ministry will have a number of client organizations under its supervision. Thus, when a main ministry or agency moves into a new policy area it can move existing client organizations to this area, or create new ones. The problem this poses for ODA is that when main ministries share jurisdiction, they must accommodate their different, or only partially overlapping, families of clients in policy implementation. Vertical relations between the state and private sector are thus an additional feature of JICA and the OECF, and numerous personnel from private sector clients of the most heavily involved ministries may be found inside JICA or the OECF at any given time. So not only are JICA and OECF coordinating horizontal relations between ministries and acting in concert with other tokushū hōjin such as the Ex-Im Bank, but they are also linking the private sector to ODA administration.

Zaidan Hōjin *and* Shadan Hōjin *in ODA*

Some distinctive features of regulation in Japan are the trade and industrial associations that both organize competition as well as promote policy dialogue at the sectoral level with the relevant government ministries. Many are descendants of wartime control associations established by the government, and are today licensed by one or more supervising ministries whom they assist in formulating and implementing policy.[301] Because of the trade- and industry-promoting orientation of Japan's ODA, as well as its central role in administering Japan's industry and commerce, MITI has the most devel- oped network of affiliated trade associations in ODA implementation, as will be detailed below.

Generally speaking, the Japanese bureaucracy uses private, nonprofit associations to implement policy for reasons similar to those cited for the use of tokushū hōjin. There are two main types of associations: the private foundation (zaidan hōjin) and the private association (shadan hōjin). The initiative to form such organizations often comes from the government when the aim is to extend bureaucratic control over, and to implement government policies via, the private sector. In the case of the zaidan hōjin an endowment is set up, with the help of a ministry, that may be supplemented by private membership fees and income from contracted work. This is common when the activity is not directly related to profit-making activity, and a ministry can exert very strong control if it funds most or all of the endowment of the zaidan hōjin. In contrast, shadan hōjin lack an endowment and rely on government subsidies, private membership fees, and contracted work. It may be said that in general, the private sector orientation is stronger in shadan hō- jin than in zaidan hōjin, but both make available technical expertise and staff resources, and both promote orderly relations between the private sector and the government. They also play key roles as channels for policy dialogue with the government, and there can be close information and personnel exchanges through amakudari and shukko.

As indicated earlier, private sector integration into the ODA system is managed through zaidan hōjin and shadan hōjin, which have a vertical, patron-client relationship with one or more ODA supervising ministries. These links make members of these associations eligible for ODA-related work. In the case of zaidan hōjin, often a major portion of the association's endowment and operating budget comes from a government ministry, and so the patron-client relationship is fairly clear and strong. In the case of shadan hōjin, where there is no endowment, government ministries may still exert influence if the association itself or the association's membership is dependent on government-controlled subsidies and contracts. A small sample of private associations involved in Japan's ODA is described below.

The Federation of Economic Organizations or the Keidanren, is a shadan hōjin established in 1961 under the supervision of MITI. Nevertheless, it maintains close contact with the MFA, MOF, and other ministries as well. Its basic objective is to present the government and the public with proposals and views of corporate Japan on the whole range of national issues confronting Japan at any time. Organizations like the Keidanren can help big business close ranks to press demands and set conditions vis-à-vis the government. For example, in 1987 the Keidanren called for ODA measures to reduce the risk of investing in developing countries and to have public financing of ODA project identification.[302] These concerns were reflected in the new social and economic plan released in spring 1988, and MITI picked up specific elements of the Keidanren's proposals.

Aside from committees specializing in bilateral economic ties with Japan's main developing country trade partners, the Keidanren has a standing committee on keizai kyōryoku that undertakes ongoing policy-oriented studies on Japan's ODA. It has been particularly active in advancing ODA policy proposals through the mass media via consultation with the LDP's Policy Affairs Research Council and through consultation with the Japanese bureaucracies chiefly responsible for administering ODA.

Another key association is the Japan Chamber of Commerce and Industry (JCCI). Although it is formally a tokushū hōjin, it acts more like a business association in the sense that it emphasizes private sector interest aggregation rather than administrative function. The JCCI gained official status in 1914 and falls under the formal supervision of MITI. It was created to represent the major Japanese municipal chambers of commerce in their dealings with the Japanese government or foreign chambers of commerce. An important function of JCCI has been to advise the government and LDP on how keizai kyōryoku should be implemented, especially in advancing the interests of its many small and medium-sized business members. The president of JCCI, Noboru Goto, was the chairman of the prime minister's Taigai Keizai Kyōryoku Shingikai in the 1970s and early 1980s. Since the yen's appreciation in 1985–1987, the greatest priority at JCCI in terms of economic cooperation has been moving the production of Japan's small and medium-sized firms overseas. JCCI is able to help by organizing ODA project-finding missions or arranging for the dispatch of experts via the Japan Overseas Development Corporation (JODC).

The Japan Foreign Trade Council is active in representing the concerns of trading companies in Japan's ODA policies. The Nihon Bōeki Kai, otherwise known as the Japan Foreign Trade Council, was established in 1947 as a shadan hōjin under the supervision of MITI, incorporating all of Japan's major general trading companies and some of the specialized trading companies. The role of Japan's trading companies in exporting plants and supervising overseas project construction is very important. They specialize in identifying projects, and they generate income by coordinating project design, procurement, construction, and financing. An example of the council's activity in ODA is the report it issued in May 1988 calling on the Japanese government to help the trading companies play a stronger role in ODA project identification and design. As background information the report states that Japan's plant exports had fallen from a peak of $17.5 billion in 1981 to only $7.5 billion in 1986, and that a major factor in this decline is the increased risk of investing in the developing world and the lack of project finance, especially in the debt-ridden nations. For planning aid to these countries, the report calls on the Japanese government to provide the general trading companies with better trade insurance, tax incentives, and subsidies for project identification activities in the developing countries suffering from debt problems.[303]

The largest window association of engineering consultants is the Engineering Consulting Firms Association (ECFA). It is a shadan hōjin established in 1964 under the guidance of MITI. The purpose of ECFA is to promote the activities of Japanese engineering consultants in the developing countries. Its member firms specialize in designing economic infrastructure and plant construction. ECFA is regularly requested by MITI to form and dispatch survey teams to developing countries to do preliminary work on project identification. Fifty percent of the cost of these surveys is paid by the government. In the early 1980s roughly 200 such teams were sent abroad each year, and this number has since certainly increased dramatically.[304]

Other engineering consultants associations have similar relations with other ministries, such as the Japan Transport Consultants Association (under MOT), a shadan hōjin established in 1973; the International Engineering Consultants Association of Japan (under MOC), a shadan hōjin established in 1956; or the Japan Telecommunications Engineering & Consulting Service (under the MPT and MITI), a zaidan hōjin established in 1978.

The Overseas Construction Association of Japan (Kaigai Kensetsu Kyō-kai) is the largest window association between the government and the construction industry in the area of ODA. It is a shadan hōjin established in 1955 under the guidance of MOC to promote the Japanese construction industry's expansion overseas. Its members include 57 of the largest construction firms in Japan, as well as eight smaller construction industry associations. It studies overseas business conditions; organizes overseas project-finding missions; responds to business inquiries; and coordinates construction industry activities with the government, potential clients, and other private associations.

The Nihon Puranto Yushutsu Kyōkai, or the Japan Consulting Institute (JCI), is a major window association for Japan's plant exporters. Originally (and more accurately) translated as the Plant Exporters Association of Japan, it is a shadan hōjin established in 1955 under the guidance of MITI. Its members consist of the thirty-one largest industrial firms specializing in whole plant exports, and its purpose is to dispatch consultants to do feasibility studies, identify projects, give advisory services in the construction and operation of plants in developing countries, and promote overseas investment. MITI subsidizes 75 percent of its overseas activities through the ODA budget. In 1987 this amounted to at least ¥224 million.[305] In a similar vein is the Japan Machinery Exporters Association (JMEA), a zaidan hōjin established in 1947 by MITI to promote machinery exports. It has 550 member firms representing the entire range of capital goods makers in Japan. In the area of ODA it conducts feasibility studies, promotes technical cooperation, and coordinates with other associations and government agencies involved in economic cooperation.

The above-mentioned industry associations are used as tools in ODA implementation by the Japanese government, but they also are effective in pushing their own interests through direct dialogue or through LDP politicians.

The MFA's Network of Client Associations

The creation of client organizations is not easy for any ministry because the extra budget needed must be approved by MOF. For this reason one rough indicator of a ministry's involvement in ODA implementation is the number of its client organizations using the ODA budget to fund its activities. By this measure the MFA and MITI are the two most involved ministries in ODA.

Because the MFA does not have a large domestic clientele, and because its activities are by nature noncommercial, it has the largest network of ODA-related zaidan hōjin in policy research and technical cooperation. Three examples of zaidan hōjin under MFA guidance are the Association for the Promotion of International Cooperation (APIC), the Japan Institute of International Affairs (JIIA), and the Japan Foundation. APIC was established in 1975 to collect information, promote conferences and academic exchanges, and publish an annual report in English on Japan's ODA. JIIA was established in 1960 to conduct foreign policy research, organize conferences, and publish journals and monographs. It has been increasingly involved in ODA-related conferences, academic exchanges, and policy research. The Japan Foundation was established in 1972 and is playing a growing role in ODA-funded cultural diplomacy through expanded academic exchange and overseas Japanese-language training programs. Another example of a technical cooperation–oriented zaidan hōjin is the Japan Organization for International Family Planning, set up in 1968 under the joint supervision of the MFA and MHW to implement family planning projects. The character of the MFA's network of associations may be seen in Table 8.2, a list compiled by the MFA. All but two are zaidan hōjin, reflecting the weakness of the MFA's base of private sector clients.

In areas with broader policy relevance, a technical cooperation organization may have several supervising ministries. One example is the Kokusai Kaihatsu Sentaa, or International Development Center of Japan (IDC). This zaidan hōjin was set up in 1971 to be of broad service in ODA, and it reports to the MFA, MITI, MOC, EPA, MAFF, and MOT. It trains public and private sector personnel in ODA project appraisal, holds seminars and symposia on development issues, and conducts sector- or country-level development studies of developing countries. Based on these reports the Japanese government can narrow the range of projects it will consider in a particular country and pass this information on to its clients. As the only significant research body employing several researchers oriented toward

Table 8.2 MFA-Supervised Private Associations

Name	Function	Jointly supervised with
Foundation for the Welfare and Education of the Asian People	Aid to orphans, widows, and refugees	—
Africa Society of Japan	Economic and cultural cooperation	—
Industrial Development Cooperation Association	Industrial development	MAFF, MITI, MOL
Japan Organization for International Family Planning	Family planning	MHW
Interchange Association	Bilateral relations with Taiwan	MITI
International Development Center	Development planning and training	MITI, MOT, MAFF, MOC, EPA
The International Nursing Foundation	Nursing exchange and cooperation	MHW
International Cooperation Association	Political and cultural relations	—
Association for the Promotion of International Cooperation	Information dissemination	—
Association for International Technical Promotion	Provision of educational materials	—
Association for International Cooperation in Agriculture and Forestry (shadan hōjin)	Food production research and cooperation	MAFF
International Management Association (shadan hōjin)	Membership in the World Council of Management	—
International Medical Foundation	Medical cooperation	MHW
Japan Institute of International Affairs	Policy research	—
Japan Association for UNICEF	UNICEF support	—
National Federation of UNESCO Associations in Japan	UNESCO support	MEd
Foreign Press Center of Japan	Information dissemination	—
Latin America Association	Foreign policy research and outreach	—

Source: MFA, *Kokusai Kyōryoku handobukku* [International Cooperation Handbook], 1983.

issues of social development, the IDC is more "progressive" than other components of the ODA system.

There are scores of other private associations funded wholly or in good part through the ODA budget. In the long run, in return for cooperating with bureaucratic policies and interests, the private sector members of an association can expect to influence government policy and will enjoy the protection and patronage of bureaucratic regulation. This relationship benefits a ministry by leveraging its administrative control, and it also gives officials the opportunity for amakudari into member firms. Finally, a ministry can count on strong support by its organized client membership and by related *zoku* LDP Diet members when jurisdictional battles with other ministries arise.

Although there may be as many as a hundred shadan hōjin and zaidan hōjin involved in the study and implementation of Japan's ODA, it is difficult to compile an authoritative list. The longest single list may have been published in 1983 by the MFA. It listed fifty-eight main private associations in ODA that play key roles in aggregating and incorporating the private sector in ODA policy making and implementation. Not surprisingly, the ministry with the most listed clients was the MFA with eighteen (already listed above); MITI had fifteen; MOT had thirteen; MAFF had nine; MEd had seven; MOC had four; MOL had three, as did the MHW; the EPA had two; and the MPT, MOF, and the Science and Technology Agency each had one. (Because some client associations have more than one supervising ministry, there is double counting in the above numbers.)

The important points to note here are that ministries very active in ODA tend to have a larger number of client policy-implementing organizations in this area, and that these associations or research organizations do not gain access to JICA and the OECF without the sponsorship of a main ministry or agency.

MITI's Client Network

MITI has the most powerful and diverse set of private sector affiliations in the area of ODA, and this implementation network is at the core of Japan's project-oriented ODA. Although nonproject assistance (such as structural adjustment lending or two-step loan schemes), as well as nonindustrial project aid (such as Japanese studies centers), is gradually increasing, the political strength of the MITI network explains why these other forms of ODA are still pulled toward Japan's industrial and commercial interests. MITI's representation of its ODA implementation network is indicated in Figure 8.6.

In Figure 8.6, the administrative core is MITI's commercial policy bureau. The first concentric ring contains ODA-oriented tokushū hōjin, and the outer two rings contain zaidan hōjin and shadan hōjin. As one moves toward the periphery, the private sector nature of the organization appears to increase. It is worth noting that MITI includes the OECF and JICA in its domain even though they are under the formal supervision of the EPA and MFA, respectively. The reason is that the system of distributed jurisdictions gives MITI influence in those organizations. Another point about the MITI diagram is the extensive inclusion and utilization of the private sector. The sheer size of this network means that MITI cannot centrally command this system. But the regular transaction of business and the cross-posting of personnel through shukko and amakudari among member organizations helps

Figure 8.6 MITI and MITI Affiliates in ODA

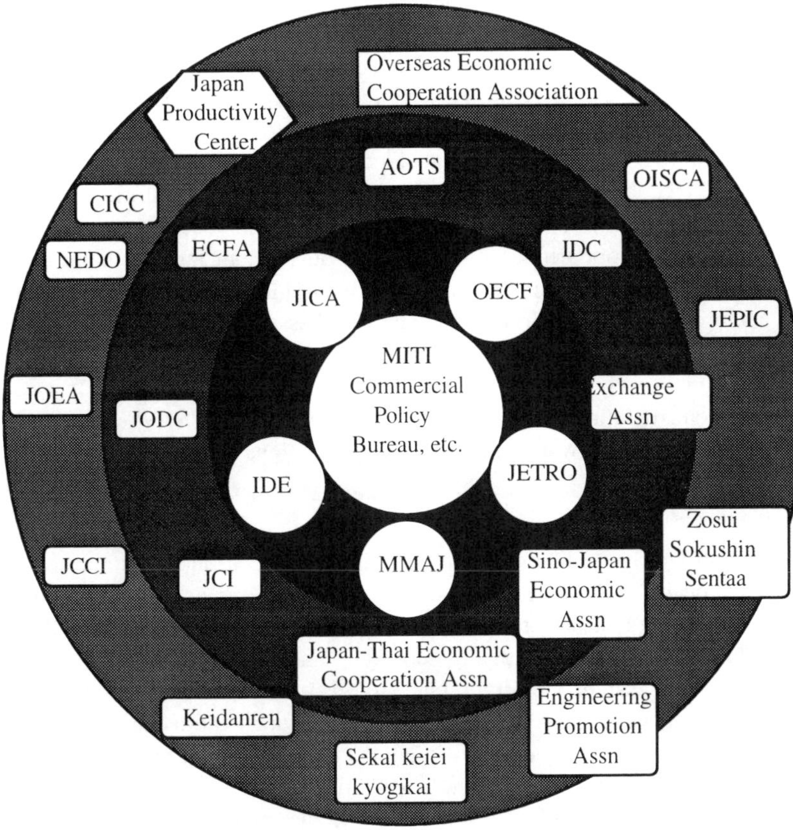

Source: *Kokusai Kaihatsu Janaru,* no. 379 (July 1988): 86.

to achieve the density of linkages and the level of transparency needed to maintain the general stability of the system without explicit directions from MITI. Thus, for example, when a plant exporter wishes to arrange for ODA financing for technical training of local personnel, it will make the right connections in JETRO, JICA, JODC, and the Association for Overseas Technical Scholarship (AOTS) without having to go to MITI until approval of final arrangements is needed. A few MITI affiliates in ODA are described later in this chapter.

Japan External Trade Organization

JETRO became a tokushū hōjin in 1958, and it falls under the supervision of MITI, which provides most of its funding. In the late 1980s about 30 percent of its budget was classified as ODA, and such activities as the promotion of imports from the developing world and the promotion of developing country industrialization through Japanese private direct investment would fall in this category. JETRO's importance in ODA is expected to increase because it is to play a major role in MITI's plan to use ODA to promote Japanese direct investment in ASEAN, as well as agroindustrial production for export to Japan. Rather than direct financing, JETRO's role is to identify joint venture opportunities and to provide related technical and advisory services.

JETRO has been most active in gathering economic information through a large network of overseas offices, and it monitors local business conditions and identifies opportunities for Japanese business in Japan's major overseas markets through seventy-eight overseas JETRO offices. The information gathered is provided in both raw and processed form to other government agencies and to the more than 6,000 private firms that are JETRO members. High-quality, country-specific economic analyses are maintained by a JETRO research affiliate, the World Economic Information Service (WEIS), and JETRO puts out a wide range of trade publications and reports.

Metals and Mining Agency of Japan

The MMAJ was established in 1963 and is under the supervision of MITI. Its mandate is to promote the discovery and development of new nonferrous metal ore deposits around the world and to secure stable supplies for Japanese industry. As a nation critically dependent on overseas sources of metals and ores, Japan assigns vital importance to this task. The MMAJ is authorized to conduct surveys and research and to provide funds and technical expertise to achieve this aim. It specializes in conducting mineral surveys for developing countries in the ODA program. In 1982 the MMAJ initiated thirteen surveys, with an average duration of three years. In the same year it spent ¥2.2 billion in such survey activities (funded out of the ODA budget). It has played an important role in identifying metal ore development and processing projects, and its staff sit in JICA and the OECF through shukko.

MITI-Affiliated Zaidan Hōjin

The Association for Overseas Technical Scholarship is a zaidan hōjin set up in 1959 under the supervision of MITI to bring developing country private sector personnel to Japan for technical training. In 1985 AOTS trained 2,420 persons from developing countries, compared with 5,549 trained by JICA. MITI provides 75 percent of the cost through its ODA budget. In 1987 this amounted to ¥4.5 billion. More recently AOTS has started overseas training courses. Normally, after a general orientation course, trainees are placed in a Japanese company. The need for training developing country personnel arises out of Japanese exports of plant and equipment, and training usually takes place in the exporting firm.

The Japan Overseas Development Corporation (JODC) is a zaidan hōjin established by MITI in 1970 with several purposes in mind. One is the promotion of investment in developing countries by Japanese small and medium-sized firms through interest-free loans. Another is the development of primary commodity production in LDCs through low-interest financing to local private sector projects. Finally, JODC engages in technical cooperation by sending experts and advisers from Japanese firms to help operate developing country private enterprises. These activities are funded by Japan's ODA. In actual practice the Japan Chamber of Commerce and Industry often arranges the sending of JODC experts to overseas Japanese joint ventures. In 1985 JODC dispatched ninety-one experts to developing countries. MITI provided 75 percent of the expenses for this activity. In 1987 MITI ODA subsidies to JODC amounted to ¥1.2 billion. MITI has delegated to JETRO the task of keeping track of AOTS and JODC activities.

One finds that public-private sector relations can be close, but bureaucratic sectionalism tends to compartmentalize them into vertical ties between a main ministry and its subsidiary agencies and private associations. But this tendency is mitigated by intermediary agencies like JICA and the OECF that not only mesh the jurisdictional claims of rival ministries, but also accommodate the various clients of these ministries. In this way bureaucratic sectionalism and public-private sector differences are routinely managed, and a freer exchange of information, personnel, and economic resources is facilitated. Thus, a system of horizontal and vertical coordination is achieved that allows ODA to respond to a variety of agendas, but the most central ones are those of its most central actors, i.e., the yonshōchō.

ODA Financing

It should be noted that the financing of Japan's ODA has certain implications for policy. MOF requires that most of Japan's ODA be loan assistance. This makes the share of grants in Japan's ODA the lowest in DAC (see Figure 8.7), and so overall concessionality is also among the lowest in DAC. MOF dislikes grant aid because it is financed entirely out of the revenue-financed general account budget, whereas ODA loans through the OECF rely mostly on borrowing from the Fiscal Investment and Loan Program (FILP), which is funded by the post office savings system and national pension systems. Government purchases of OECF equity, direct subsidies from the general account budget, and repayments and earnings from past loans cover the spread between the OECF's cost of borrowing these funds and the earnings it gets from its ODA loans.

The general account budget is used for bilateral grant and technical cooperation, as well as for contributions to UN functional agencies such as the UN Development Programme. By far the two largest recipients of general account funds classified as ODA are the MFA and MOF, but there are now sixteen other main ministries and agencies that receive such funds. The

Figure 8.7 Grant Element of Total ODA

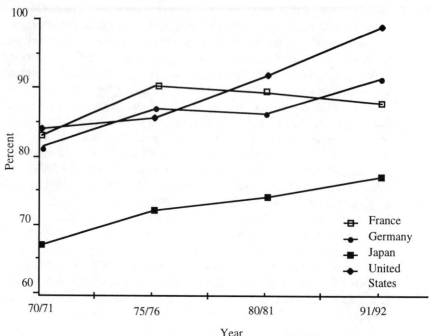

Sources: OECD.

amount received by the MFA is allocated mainly for operating JICA, financing grant aid, and making contributions to the UN specialized agencies. The MOF allocation is mainly for subsidizing the OECF, paying for special types of ODA such as debt relief and aid for food production, and contributing loans and capital to international financial institutions. The other ministries, which together account for only about 15 percent of the general account budget, are funded to carry out their own international cooperation activities with developing countries in their respective areas of jurisdiction. The modest claim on the general account budget by these ministries can be misleading. The policymaking system distributes power over JICA and the OECF first of all to the yonsh ōchō, and then to the rest of the main ministries and agencies through the system of distributed jurisdiction. This means that although the funding of JICA and the OECF may flow through the MFA and MOF, this does not mean that they control these funds exclusively. [306]

Japan's ODA administration may be insulated from public scrutiny and pressure, but it has its strengths. Ever since the contemporary system matured in the early 1960s, its coordination structures have maintained its integrity. A system of distributed jurisdictions within key implementing agencies creates a system of vertical and horizontal interest coordination that allows a wide range of bureaucratic and private sector structures to advance their agendas in ODA. Shingikai and implementing agencies play crucial intermediary roles breaking down bureaucratic sectionalism and public-private sector differences to achieve a broad direction for policy and close collaboration in implementation.

9

ODA as Foreign Policy: Buying Power in the International System

Mounting foreign criticism of Japan in the 1980s gave the MFA leverage over other domestic actors in the keizai kyōryoku system because it demonstrated the MFA's need for more resources to manage foreign perceptions. The MFA was then able to push new agendas in ODA to make it into a pillar of its diplomacy in the 1980s. Nevertheless, Japan's ODA in the 1980s could still be linked to economic agendas through policy concepts such as the New AID Plan, the ASEAN-Japan Development Fund, and three-into-one economic cooperation.

To better understand the significance of ODA in Japan's foreign policy one must understand that the high politics/low politics distinction that informs Western thinking about foreign policy can be misleading and irrelevant. The dimension of high politics (that is, the threat and use of force and other coercive instruments) remained mostly beyond the scope of postwar Japanese diplomacy. As a result of the Yoshida Doctrine, Japan's postwar foreign policy initiatives were restricted to areas of low politics involving Japan's economic interests. This meant that Japanese diplomacy was intimately related to the use of economic instruments to raise Japan's international standing. Japan's ODA fit this low-politics agenda well because it was organized to facilitate Japan's economic rise as well as to advance its prestige. So it was that the economic and political roles of Japan's ODA were not so much on different planes as they were complementary.

THE FOREIGN POLICY ASPECT OF ODA

To understand ODA's role in Japan's external relations, one needs to examine Japan's changing position in international structures. Viewed from this perspective Japan is no exception to the rule that states adapt their strategies to the incentives and constraints imposed on them by the international system. [307] To guide this discussion it is useful to borrow Robert Gilpin's distinction between the international hierarchy of political prestige and influence, and the international hierarchy of capabilities that is indicated by relative economic power rankings. Gilpin notes that following hegemonic wars international political hierarchies are created that reflect the hierarchy of state capabilities at the close of conflict. During ensuing periods of peace, however, uneven rates of economic growth among states change the relative rankings of states in the hierarchy of capabilities, but the political hierarchy remains static. This dis-synchronization produces international tension as states rising in economic power want to see corresponding changes in political arrangements. Hegemonic war is the expected result when another state gains a credible capability to challenge the state that is predominant in the international political hierarchy.

Leaving aside the issue of whether today the cycle of hegemonic war must continue, the relationship between distinct international economic and political hierarchies in this paradigm is useful for conceptualizing Japan's postwar strategy in the international system. Defeat in World War II did not substantially change the orientation of the modern Japanese state; it merely altered its strategy. From the Meiji period the Japanese state was oriented toward raising its status in the Western-dominated international system. The same can be said of the postwar Japanese state. But what set postwar Japan apart from the prewar Japanese state or "normal" postwar states was its choice of strategy. Whereas a state might be expected to more or less automatically translate economic capabilities into military capabilities in order to strengthen its diplomacy, in the strategy devised by Prime Minister Yoshida Shigeru postwar Japan would restrict itself to economic means. This was an unconventional choice but quite rational. Because of the global security commitments of the United States, Japan could free ride on a U.S. security guarantee—a classic case of the weak exploiting the stronger security partner.[308] This allowed Japan to climb the international economic hierarchy all the faster. Nevertheless, in Yoshida's diplomatically trained mind, economic growth was not an end in itself. He stated at the outset, "The day will come when our livelihood recovers. It may sound devious, but let the Americans handle [our security] until then."[309]

This structural approach provides us with a concept for bridging the divide between economic policy and foreign policy. If there is any law in international politics, it is that states will apply their economic capabilities to raise their political position. One can view Japan's economic and commercial agendas in ODA not as antithetical to Japan's political agenda, but as complementary and basically similar in overall objective. As Japan raises its position in the international division of labor, it supports its efforts to rise in political hierarchies. This interdependence of economic and political strategy is implicit in the yonshōchō's role in coordinating Japan's ODA. Though its members may disagree over discrete decisions, they do not question the value and legitimacy of the institutional arrangement that supports the overall national strategy. What brought these bureaucratic actors together to coordinate a densely organized system of intrabureaucratic distributed jurisdictions and public-private sector relations was early postwar agreement to raise the position of the Japanese state in the international system by relying almost exclusively on the cultivation of economic bases of power. To flesh out this framework we will indicate how ODA was used to aid Japan's rise to economic superpower status. Then the discussion will turn to Japan's use of ODA as a diplomatic instrument. Here it will be clear that while ODA moved to a central role in Japan's diplomacy in the 1980s, it continued to play a key role in Japan's international economic strategy.

Climbing the Economic Hierarchy

One can see the relationship between Japan's position in the international division of labor and its economic cooperation policy by noting how the economic objectives of ODA changed over the postwar decades. In the 1950s Japan exported cheap consumer goods to the United States to pay for imports of capital goods and technology. At the same time, Japan exported durable goods to Asia to purchase Asian raw materials. Japan's strategy to raise itself from this intermediate position between the advanced U.S. economy and the developing areas of Asia was to import U.S. technology and build its own heavy and chemical industries within a protected domestic market. To give these infant industries economies of scale and exposure to international competition, and to secure cheap, stable supplies of raw material inputs to nurture these industries, the government used reparations and yen loans to promote their exports to the developing world.

In the 1960s the more completely institutionalized keizai kyōryoku system expanded this basic approach in order to establish the international competitiveness of Japan's heavy and chemical industries by the end of the decade. At the same time Japan was focused on moving its current account from deficits to surpluses. To this end it retained extensive trade and capital controls, used an undervalued yen to promote exports, channeled foreign exchange toward technology imports, and developed larger and more comprehensive keizai kyōryoku techniques. The chief indicators of success were the emergence of a trade surplus from the mid-1960s; an export structure characterized by capital- and technology-intensive goods such as steel, autos, cameras, and electronics; and a balance-of-payments surplus by the end of the decade. By 1970 Japan's position in the international division of labor became comparable to that of the United States, and Japan experienced increasing trade friction with the West while it established the groundwork for economic predominance in Asia.

In the 1970s Japan augmented its vertical relationship with Asia with greater exports of mostly advanced goods and services, more imports of mostly energy and raw materials, and growing amounts of direct investment in areas other than resource extraction—a development financed by Japan's growing trade and savings surpluses. Japan's relationship with the United

States in the international division of labor became more competitive, with an export structure that challenged U.S. manufacturing in its home market and in third-country markets. As Japan made inroads against U.S. manufacturing sectors, bilateral trade became unbalanced enough to affect political relations.

The end of foreign exchange and balance-of-payments constraints in the 1970s allowed Japan to increase ODA volume dramatically in the 1970s, which it did for various reasons. Western criticism of Japan's trade surpluses prompted Japan to offer more ODA as a way of reducing Japan's current account surpluses, and the first oil shock prompted Japan to use ODA to secure access to energy supplies in the Middle East and China. But there was also a new element in Japan's strategic economic agenda. The 1970s saw the end of cheap domestic labor and a new domestic concern over industrial pollution. This elicited a new policy orientation toward upgrading Japan's industrial structure.

MITI began calling for an advance by Japanese industry into higher-value-added, knowledge-intensive production. The need to upgrade Japan's industrial structure under conditions of full employment and rising wage costs prompted keizai kyōryoku policy makers to begin reconsidering how relations with the developing world should be managed. It was recognized that Japan's emerging capital surplus in the form of more FDI and ODA could promote Japan's economic competitiveness—not only by resource development, but also by moving offshore to Asia those labor-intensive and polluting industries in which Japan was losing competitiveness. This led to expanded concepts of "comprehensive economic cooperation" that could help restructure Japan's economy as well as its external trade and investment relations in ways that would enhance its competitiveness and economic security. The 1970s version of comprehensive economic cooperation was the large-scale project, and the best example of this expanded conception of keizai kyōryoku was the Asahan project, which helped to save Japan's aluminum industry after the first oil shock.

The 1980s witnessed a continued successful advance into high-technology industrial sectors as well as a growing trade and capital surplus. The increasingly urgent need to move labor- and land-intensive manufacturing offshore via FDI in the 1980s explains why Japan began to use ODA to build industrial parks such as the Eastern Seaboard project in Thailand even though the World Bank and ADB could not justify the project according to market measures of efficient resource allocation at that time. This project signaled a more systematic effort by Japan to restructure its economic relationship with Asia into one that would be more "horizontal," i.e., characterized by significant Japanese imports of manufactured goods, many made by Japanese affiliates in Asia. This emphasis became predominant after 1985 when Japan turned into the world's largest capital exporter but was faced with the problem of declining international competitiveness in sectors critically affected by the yen's appreciation. Japan then decided to abandon its "full set" industrial structure and move lower-value-added industrial production overseas while retaining high-value-added sectors at home. The coordination of ODA, FDI, and trade to achieve this restructuring became the 1980s template for comprehensive economic cooperation. Figure 9.1 shows how direct investment increased relative to ODA during the 1980s.

Figure 9.1 Japanese Direct Investment in Developing Countries and ODA, 1978/79–1989

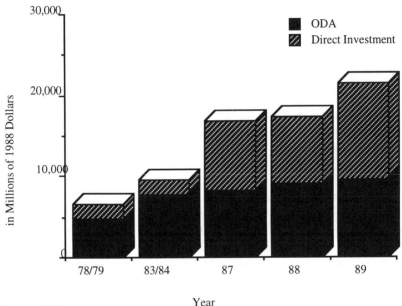

Source: MITI.

This new orientation had three aspects. It meant continued export promotion in higher-value-added areas such as construction services, capital goods, and financial services. It also meant the speedy and effective relocation of lower-value-added Japanese manufacturing through FDI, which would free production factors for higher-value-added activities. Finally, it entailed import liberalization to allow "reverse-imports" *(gyaku yunyū)*, that is, the importation of finished goods as well as industrial parts and components produced overseas by Japanese firms. Procurement of these cheaper parts would make Japanese industry more competitive. This explains the emergence of the three-into-one ODA policy and its central role in keizai kyōryoku policy from the mid-1980s. Although this new policy aimed to integrate the Asian economies into a networked production zone managed by Tokyo, the Japanese would call this a horizontal division of labor because for the first time Japan would be importing significant amounts of manufactured goods from Asia, even though much of it would be made by Japanese subsidiaries and affiliates.

Restructuring the international division of labor in this way was beyond the scope of Japan's economic cooperation—until the mid-1980s. That was when Japan's enormous capital surplus and the yen's increased international buying power gave Japan the ability to influence the restructuring of the Asian economies. The turning point in policymaking was marked by MITI's New AID Plan, the ASEAN-Japan Development Fund, and the articulation of the new san mi-ittai keizai kyōryoku concept. From this point the central concern of the economic ministries and the private sector was to use ODA in coordination with trade and investment promotion measures to turn the East Asian economies into an integrated production base supporting Japan's new role as a main pillar in a regionalized tripolar world order.

A new regional division of labor would have developed through the logic of unmanaged market relations, but Japanese ODA policy would be to speed the relocation of declining Japanese industries to lower-cost Asian developing economies, and to see that complementary production and trade patterns rather than competitive ones would predominate in intra-Asian economic relations. This would organize what Okita calls a "flying geese" pattern of regional interdependence led by Japan. Using its capital surplus in ambitious ODA and FDI schemes, Japan would organize bilateral discussions with recipients on the transfer of new technologies, jobs, and export earnings if the latter would help Japanese firms gain the best growth opportunities. This may be one reason that Japan increased the share of bilateral ODA from two-thirds to three-quarters of total commitments.

In sum, Japan routinely used ODA to promote the development of its own trade and industrial structure; and as the scale of Japanese industrial, financial, and technological resources has grown, so have the ambitions behind ODA. Table 9.1 summarizes these points.

Climbing Political Hierarchies

The Yoshida strategy's priority on rebuilding Japan's economic power explains why the MFA made Japan's early postwar economic reconstruction and development a top aim of its diplomacy, and why it linked the process of diplomatic normalization in Asia to the start of keizai kyōryoku in the early 1950s. The initial task of the Japanese state was to rebuild a dynamic economy, for without this it would have no means of raising its international status. This explains why MITI, MOF, and the EPA came to be responsible for shaping the substantive aspects of keizai kyōryoku during the 1950s and why the MFA was satisfied with the role of diplomatic facilitator. In the mid-1960s, when Japan's high-speed growth mechanism was in gear and Japan began to develop surplus wealth, however, the MFA began to apply economic resources toward winning greater international prestige and influence. From

Table 9.1 Japan's Evolving *Keizai Ky ōryoku* Priorities, 1960–1990

	60–70	70–80	80–90
Industrial & trade policy theme	• create competitive heavy & chemical industries • export-led growth	• create competitive knowledge-intensive industries • export-led growth • adjustment to higher energy prices	• abandon "full-set" industrial structure • internationalize Japanese manufacturing production • horizontal division of labor in Asia
ODA policy themes	• export promotion • resource development	• resource development • export promotion • industrial relocation	• FDI promotion • import promotion • export promotion • resource development • "Three-into-one" ODA

this point the MFA began to rely on ODA to meet U.S. demands for greater security contributions in Asia, to demonstrate Japan's commitment to North-South reconciliation, and to otherwise establish its worthiness for graduation to higher rankings in international political structures. This reliance on ODA reached a peak in the 1980s, but by the early 1990s there were indications that the heyday of ODA diplomacy had passed.

By any realist standard the Yoshida strategy and ODA diplomacy have to be viewed as an imaginative and brilliant success. In structures such as GATT, the IMF, UNCTAD, and the OECD, Japan achieved advanced country status in the mid-1960s. In the 1970s its economic stature made it a charter member in the Western economic summit meetings. In the 1980s Japan's ODA contributions won it greater recognition in international financial institutions and the UN, as well as at Western economic summits. In Asian regional structures such as ASEAN and Asian Pacific Economic Cooperation (APEC), Japan became an acknowledged leader. By the 1990s Japan began a credible campaign for a seat on the UN Security Council based almost solely on what some derisively called "checkbook diplomacy." To get a clearer picture of the political uses of ODA, we will turn to the development of ODA diplomacy.

MANAGING POLITICAL FRICTIONS

The 1970s saw a number of occasions when Japan was pressured to announce new commitments to resolving North-South problems. In April 1972 at an UNCTAD general meeting Japan pledged to increase its ODA to 0.7 percent of GNP. Encouraged by OPEC's success in challenging the North, the developing countries called for a special UNGA meeting in April 1974, at which a resolution was passed calling for a New International Economic Order (NIEO). The direct North-South negotiations demanded in the NIEO materialized in December 1975 when the Council on International Economic Cooperation (CIEC) was convened under UN auspices. At the CIEC's second general meeting Japan offered a vague pledge to double its economic cooperation.

By the mid-1970s the oil-producing developing countries were flourishing; creditworthy middle-income countries were piling up external debt; and the poorest countries and others severely damaged by the oil shock, i.e., the "most seriously affected countries" (MSACs), were left behind in a condition of economic stagnation and absolute poverty. Attention in the North-South debate started shifting from bloc negotiations to the plight of the poorest populations in the Third World, as evidenced by the pledge of oil-rich developing countries and the North to extend debt relief to the LLDCs and MSACs at a March 1978 UNCTAD meeting.

In 1978 the MFA issued a report compiled by the head of its economic cooperation bureau on the need for Japan to address the North-South problem. The first reason cited was Japan's new responsibility as a major economic power in a global economy no longer manageable by U.S. leadership alone. More to the point was the second reason cited, i.e., Japan's high degree of dependence on developing country economies. They supplied over 50 percent of Japan's total imports in 1974 (figures for the United States and the European Community [EC] were 40 percent and 20 percent, respectively), representing 11.9 percent of Japan's GNP in 1974, and they absorbed 46 percent of Japan's exports in 1976 (compared with 35 percent and 20 percent for the United States and the EC, respectively). The prospect was for increased dependence on developing country energy and minerals, and so the report concludes: "Therefore, as we become an economy dependent on the developing countries, taking the long-term view of the North-South problem and making the first move now is extremely important for our economic security." Other reasons cited include the need to meet DAC ODA standards, the need to better regulate Japanese FDI, especially in Southeast Asia, and the need to open the Japanese market to developing country exports.[310]

Efforts in international fora were made to maintain momentum behind the idea of North-South negotiations. In the late 1970s the World Bank commissioned Willy Brandt and others to write a definitive report on North-South issues. The February 1979 Arusha Declaration by the Group of 77 (G-

77) called for reform of the "unjust and inequitable" Bretton Woods system
to be discussed at the May 1979 UNCTAD V meeting, where Japan's prime
minister pledged a more needs-oriented aid policy. The Brandt Commission's
report was released in 1980 (recommending a 0.7 percent ODA/GNP ratio by
1985), and in August 1980 a special UNGA adopted the Third Development
Decade program, at which time Japanese foreign minister Okita Saburō
pledged continued Japanese ODA increases.

Trade Frictions

In 1971 the OECD nations had an overall trade surplus of $7.4 billion, of
which almost 80 percent, or $5.8 billion, belonged to Japan.[311] Under pres-
sure from the United States to cut its trade surplus in 1971, Japan refused a
U.S. demand to revalue its currency but promised in September to take other
steps including: an increase of ODA to meet the DAC ODA/GNP average,
more concessional lending, and better aid administration by separating the activities of the OECF and the Ex-Im Bank. This was the first of many times
Japan would offer increased ODA as a concession to Western criticism of
Japan's trade surpluses. Despite these pledges, in 1972 the U.S. trade deficit
hit $6.5 billion, and 60 percent was attributable to Japan.

By 1976 the OECD nations as a whole recovered from the 1973 oil
shock and enjoyed a real growth rate of 5.2 percent, a slightly higher rate than
their average in the decade before the oil shock. At this point the issue of
post–Bretton Woods international financial stability became a question of
managing trade and capital flows among the major advanced Western countries.

The problem among the OECD nations, however, was that recovery
lacked synchronization, resulting in large economic imbalances and currency
instability. The United States enacted a fiscal stimulus before the 1976 election, but others, including Japan, would not match this and instead chose to
rely on external demand to fuel domestic growth. Its industries accordingly
mounted an export drive on the U.S. market. This started a Japanese recovery,
but it also caused another round of serious trade friction (see Figure 9.2). The
United States demanded a reduced Japanese trade surplus in talks between
U.S. trade representative Robert Strauss and Special Economic Cooperation
Minister Ushiba Nobuhiko in January 1978 and at the Bonn Summit in June
1978. In both instances Japan pledged to double ODA in five years, improve
ODA quality, and move toward full untying of its ODA loans to assuage
trade friction.

Although in theory ODA would reduce Japan's current account surplus
and dollar reserves, it would not reduce the trade surplus because ODA is
recorded as an outflow in the capital account. One should recall that in the
early 1970s the Industrial Structure Council advocated balancing an anticipated structural trade surplus with a capital outflow guided by ODA to further
upgrade Japan's economic security and international competitiveness. This

Figure 9.2 Japan's Trade Surpluses, 1970–1978

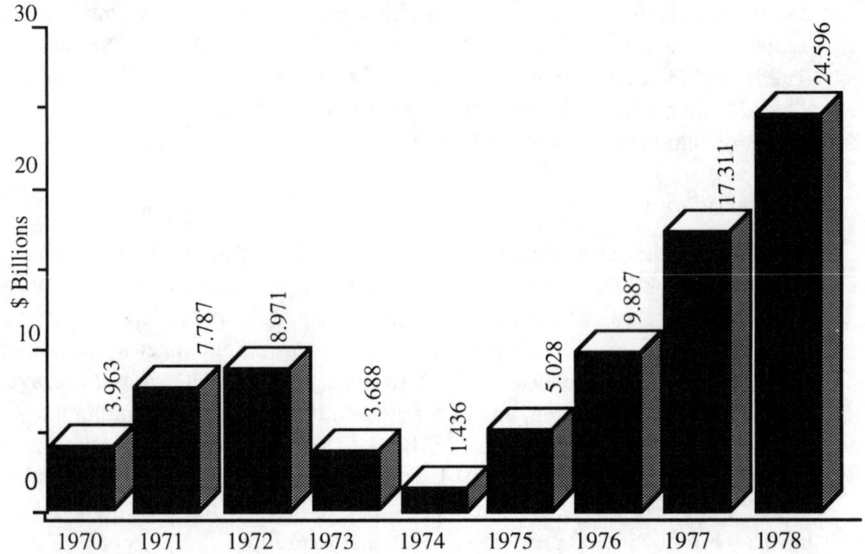

Source: Bank of Japan.

strategic intention may not have been appreciated by the Western allies as they praised the aid-doubling plan announced in 1978. The success of the first aid-doubling plan in meeting foreign criticisms of Japan's trade surplus and weak alliance contributions prompted Japan to announce a second ODA-doubling plan in 1980 to meet continuing criticisms.

Western Security

At the start of this period the United States was cautiously optimistic at the global level as a result of the successful Nixon visit to China in 1972 and the conclusion of the SALT I agreement in 1973, but it was still concerned about preventing a "domino effect" in Southeast Asia in the wake of its withdrawal from Vietnam. Accordingly, it pressured Japan to bolster stability there by increasing aid to Indochina, especially South Vietnam, which Japan agreed to do in the Nixon-Tanaka joint communiqué of July 1973. After the fall of Saigon and the seizure of power by the Khmer Rouge in Cambodia in 1975, the focus of U.S. security concern shifted to the ASEAN states, and Japan accommodated U.S. requests for increased aid, although Japan also had its own reasons for doing so.

The Soviet invasion of Afghanistan in 1979 effectively ended détente and ushered in a new period of superpower competition. The Soviet takeover of Afghanistan was alarming because the fall of the Shah of Iran in early 1979 left Western security interests in the oil-rich Gulf undefended. The United States sought to respond to the buildup of the Soviet Pacific fleet and to preserve Western access to the Gulf under conditions of budgetary stress, and it turned to Japan to increase its alliance contributions in the 1980s.

Japanese Diplomacy in Asia

The urgency for Japan to strengthen its ties and influence in the region was brought about by a weakening U.S. commitment to Asia in the 1970s. The perception caused by the Nixon Doctrine of 1969, the U.S. accommodation of Mainland China in the 1972 Shanghai Communiqué, its pullout from Vietnam in 1973, and the fall of Saigon in 1975 was reinforced by Carter administration plans to remove troops from Korea, implement a "swing strategy" that would transfer U.S. forces out of Asia in a military crisis, and the U.S. derecognition of Taiwan in 1979. This made it more important for Japan to develop an independent set of strong bilateral ties within the region. Thus, Japan used ODA pledges to improve ties with ASEAN and to start relations with the Asian socialist states. The overall goal was to cultivate a pro-development, nonideological, and peace-promoting role in Asia supported by a concept of "omnidirectional diplomacy" *(zenhō'i gaikō)* that the MFA briefly articulated in the mid-1970s.

Japan's first major initiative toward ASEAN was the January 1974 overseas tour of Prime Minister Tanaka. It was, however, a spectacular failure because Tanaka had no new ODA commitment in hand, and large student riots protesting Japan's economic domination disrupted his schedule in Indonesia and Thailand. Japan expected gratitude for its level of economic cooperation, but it was instead rebuffed and reminded of its own increased dependence on overseas sources of food, raw materials, and energy at a time of resource nationalism and discontent in the Third World.

A more successful initiative came in 1977 when Prime Minister Fukuda attended the August 1977 expanded ASEAN Summit Meeting and announced the so-called Fukuda Doctrine. The price for attendance was a $1 billion ODA pledge for five ASEAN joint industrial projects, and in his speech Fukuda committed Japan to a nonmilitarist policy of close consultation ("heart-to-heart diplomacy") and evenhanded brokerage of improved relations between ASEAN and communist Indochina.

Japan also took initiatives toward the Asian socialist states. In an attempt to influence Vietnam, Japan normalized ties in 1973 and started grant aid in 1975 and ODA loans in 1978. It opened relations with Mongolia and toward North Korea when it extended Ex-Im Bank credits and expanded trade. The main target, however, was China, with which Japan succeeded in stabilizing political and economic relations by using promises of ODA, technology transfer, and direct investment. To meet Western and ASEAN concerns, the Japanese government announced the "three principles of economic cooperation with China" (Tai-Chu Keizai Kyōryoku San Gensoku). Japan pledged to: (1) consult Western allies; (2) take into consideration the need to sustain a balance in Japanese ODA between China and the rest of Asia, especially ASEAN; and (3) restrict ODA only to nonmilitary purposes.

Although Japan succeeded in stabilizing economic relations with a re-form-oriented China, its broader attempt to build an "omnidirectional" regional identity failed because the Cold War was not yet over. By the end of 1978 the Soviets had a new naval base in Vietnam, a conspicuous buildup of its Far Eastern forces, and what appeared to be a Vietnamese proxy that had successfully invaded Cambodia. By January 1979 Japan had to side with the United States, China, and ASEAN by cutting economic assistance to Vietnam, and it pledged $50 million to ASEAN in Indochinese refugee assistance.

The Diplomatic Uses of ODA

From the foregoing discussion it is clear that in the 1970s Japan resorted to ODA pledges when it needed to answer a widening variety of external demands and criticisms. Below is a summary of major Japanese ODA commitments in the 1970s:

ODA Pledges to the UN and Other Multilateral Organizations

April 1972	Japan pledges to give at least 0.7 percent of its GNP in ODA before UNCTAD.
November 1972	Japan joins the African Development Fund.
July 1976	Japan joins the Inter-American Development Bank.
June 1977	Japan promises to double "economic cooperation" at the second CIEC meeting.
May 1979	Prime Minister Ohira pledges more ODA targeted at "human development" at UNCTAD V.

G-7 and DAC Pledges

September 1970	Japan pledges to consider aid untying.
October 1972	Japan pledges before DAC to untie more aid and improve quality.
1978	Japan pledges to untie aid fully.
June 1978	At a ministerial OECD meeting Japan promises to double ODA.
July 1978	Prime Minister Fukuda promises ODA doubling at the Bonn Summit.

ODA Pledges to the United States

September 1971	Japan pledges to meet the DAC average ODA/GNP ratio.
July 1973	Prime Minister Tanaka promises President Nixon aid to Indochina.

November 1974	Prime Minister Tanaka promises President Ford an increase in Japanese ODA.
August 1975	Prime Minister Miki promises President Ford more Japanese humanitarian aid in August 1975.
February 1977	Prime Minister Fukuda promises President Carter increased aid to ASEAN.
January 1978	Minister for Economic Cooperation Ushiba promises U.S. trade representative Robert Strauss a doubling of ODA within five years.
May 1978	Prime Minister Fukuda visits Washington and promises ODA doubling.
May 1979	Prime Minister Ohira pledges continued ODA to ASEAN in a visit to Washington.

ODA Pledges and First-time Commitments to Asian Neighbors

February 1971	Japan makes first yen loan to North Korea (¥7.2 million).
April 1972	Japan pledges to untie ODA loans partially at the Asian Ministerial Meeting.
October 1975	Japan makes first grant aid agreement with the Democratic Republic of Vietnam (¥8.5 million).
March 1977	Japan reaches first grant aid agreement with Mongolia (¥5.0 million).
July 1978	Prime Minister Fukuda promises $1.0 billion in ODA for joint ASEAN projects.
July 1978	Japan makes first yen loan agreement with Vietnam (¥10 million).
July 1979	Japan pledges $50 million for Indochinese refugee assistance to ASEAN to be channeled through the UN High Commissioner for Refugees (UNHCR).
December 1979	Prime Minister Ohira pledges $1.5 billion in yen loans over five years to China.

The First ODA-Doubling Plan

Japan's first ODA-doubling plan was a general-purpose vehicle for support-ing Japan's diplomacy with the West, with the South, and in Asia. The initial pledge to double Japan's economic cooperation was made at a UN-sponsored North-South conference in June 1977 to head off anticipated criticism of Japan's laggardly ODA effort. The pledge was to double its economic coop-eration within five years, but Japan was then criticized because it did not specify (1) whether economic cooperation meant ODA or whether private fi-nancial flows were included; (2) what the plan's base currency would be; or (3) whether it was based on the budget, new official commitments, or actual disbursements. From this experience it was clear that ODA was the compo-nent of economic cooperation that had diplomatic value.

A year later the Japanese government clarified the terms of its pledge when it came under heavy Western pressure over its trade surplus. By this time the Cabinet-level Taigai Keizai Taisaku Kyōgikai had been set up to manage trade frictions, and it had endorsed the principle of using ODA as a countermeasure. Japan would double the annual ODA disbursement figure of 1977 by 1980 in dollar terms. In addition, Japan would improve its ODA effectiveness and raise the ODA/GNP ratio. This plan was first promised to the United States in January 1978 during special bilateral economic negotiations. Subsequently it was reiterated by Prime Minister Fukuda in Washington in May 1978, presented again at the OECD high-level meeting in June, and officially pledged at the Bonn Summit in July. In September a meeting of the Japanese Cabinet officially endorsed the plan, and in October a supplementary budget was set up to help fund the plan.

The wide-ranging use of this ODA-doubling plan was successful, and the MFA developed a list of diplomatic uses for increased ODA spending. First, there was the need to promote long-term security by fostering peaceful development. Second, Japan had to avoid criticism in DAC over its lagging ODA efforts. Third, Japan had to promote friendly relations with countries that provided Japan with raw materials and other trade and investment opportunities. Fourth, there was the humanitarian obligation to alleviate suffering. Finally, Japan wished to use ODA to consolidate its relations with the rest of Asia.[312]

Although its ODA still was not up to par, from the first ODA-doubling plan Japan set out on a course of increasing its ODA to preserve and strengthen ties with the natural resource–rich Third World, with its Western allies, and with its Asian neighbors—even as it used ODA to help augment its economic security and competitiveness. Below is a summary of Japan's ODA-doubling pledges up to 1987:

The first medium-term plan (1978–1980)
> This plan set a target of disbursing in 1980 twice the amount disbursed in 1977 in current dollar terms. The target of $2.849 billion was exceeded by 18 percent, with a total of $3.353 billion disbursed in 1980. Under this plan total ODA volume rose $1.5 billion in real terms, and the ODA/GNP ratio increased from 0.21 percent to 0.32 percent.

The second medium-term plan (1981–1985)
> This set a $21.4 billion target for cumulative spending over the 1981–1985 period, an amount twice that of the previous five-year period in current dollar terms. Actual spending under the plan came to $18.1 billion, 16 percent short of the target, largely because of an unanticipated slowdown in loan disbursements.

The third medium-term plan (1986–1992)
> As originally announced in September 1985, this plan set out to achieve three related objectives: (a) improvement of the ODA/GNP ratio (b) spending of over $40 billion over the 1986–1992 period, and (c) disbursement in 1992 of $7.6 billion, an amount double the amount spent in 1985.

The fourth medium-term plan (1988–1992)
    Announced in 1987 after the yen's appreciation, this plan pledged to disburse
    some $50 billion over this period and meet the DAC average for the ODA/GNP
    ratio.

ODA and Alliance Friction in the 1980s

In 1980 the UN General Assembly adopted the New International Development Strategy for the Third Development Decade, and the Brandt Commission report was issued. Both events helped to elicit the second Japanese
pledge to double its ODA, this time over the 1981–1985 period. Soon after-
ward, however, North-South negotiations reached an impasse and fell into
eclipse. Marked differences in developmental performance among Third
World countries showed that the critical factor in development was not
foreign aid. The oil-importing economies that overcame the oil shocks tended
to have a vigorous private sector and to be export oriented. In contrast, oil-
importing economies that relied on import-substituting industrialization
strategies, state-run industries, and heavy foreign borrowing precipitated the
international debt crisis in 1982. As a result the focus shifted from aid to the
policy orientation of developing countries. This became apparent in 1981 at
the Cancún Summit when the recently elected U.S. president Ronald Reagan,
backed by British prime minister Margaret Thatcher, called for developing
country policies to stimulate the private sector. The South was unable to present a coherent response.

Meanwhile, pressure on Japanese defense and trade policies increased
sharply. Japan's growing trade surpluses continued to be a sore point. In
addition Japan was pressed by the United States and Europe to inherit some
of their developing country debt problems. In addition to these economic
issues, there was U.S. criticism of Japan's minimal defense contributions. In
January 1980 Defense Secretary Harold Brown called on Japan to increase
defense spending to 1.0 percent of GNP. Japan responded by offering its
ODA as a Western security contribution, and it pledged to earmark more
ODA for Afghan refugees and for "frontline states" facing communist threats.
It also cut ODA to Soviet-occupied Afghanistan and ceased all but
humanitarian aid to Vietnam. But when the new Reagan administration
snubbed Tokyo by inviting South Korean president Chun Do Hwan to
Washington for important security talks before meeting the newly elected
Japanese prime minister, Tokyo realized that further steps were necessary.
When Prime Minister Suzuki Zenko followed Chun Do Hwan to Washington
in June 1981 he made Japan's first public commitment to the idea of a "sea-
lane" defense stretching 1,600 kilometers from Tokyo, and he spoke in terms
of an "alliance" between the United States and Japan. He also agreed to give
economic aid to South Korea because of its key importance in Northeast

Asian security. Failure to stand by these pledges brought about his downfall, but his successor, Nakasone Yasuhiro, managed to meet U.S. expectations in these matters.

As Japan's diplomatic agenda became one of managing Western criticism, it was clear that Japan's potential military contribution was limited, in terms of both what the LDP could manage in the face of constitutional and political constraints and what Japan's neighbors would tolerate. This brought the focus back to ODA. In 1983 the Commission on Security and Economic Assistance, chaired by Frank Carlucci, recognized ODA as a Western security contribution. This implicitly endorsed Japan's substitution of increased ODA for changes in its defense and trade policies. Japan contributed 79 percent of DAC's growth in the 1980–1985 period and increased its share of DAC ODA spending (see Figure 9.3 and 9.4).

Figure 9.3 Four Major Donor Shares of Total DAC ODA, 1971/72–1991/92

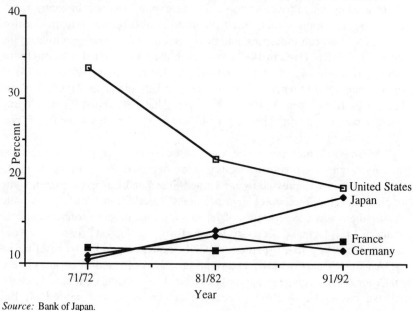

Source: Bank of Japan.

Improvements in ODA Quantity and Quality

Japan fulfilled its promise of more ODA volume, but it suffered other shortcomings as measured by the OECD. For example, in 1985 Japan devoted only 0.29 percent of GNP to ODA, below the DAC average of 0.36 percent,

Figure 9.4 Net ODA Disbursements by Four Major Donors, 1982–1992

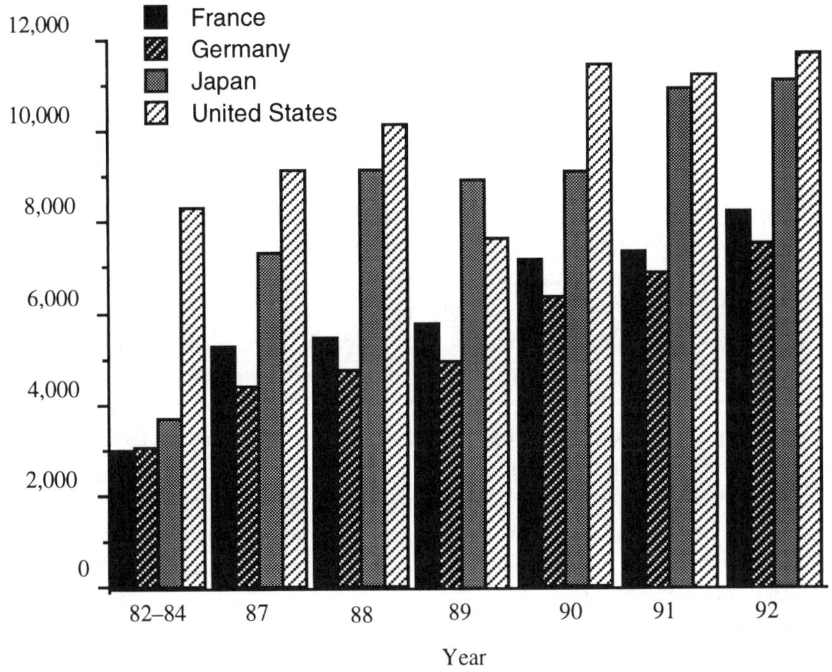

Source: DAC, 1994.

and this figure improved only marginally to 0.31 percent in 1991. And in terms of the percentage of the central government budget devoted to ODA, at mid-decade Japan gave only 1.0 percent, compared with the DAC average of 1.8 percent, but this figure for Japan increased to 1.25 percent by 1991.

Japan also continued to lag in overall concessionality, which was the lowest in DAC at 73.6 percent, compared with the DAC average of 91.4 percent in 1985.[313] Japan's figure dropped to 67.3 percent in 1991. Other indicators of quality also remained problematic. For example, only 13.7 percent of Japan's ODA went to the LLDCs in 1985, compared with the DAC average of 22.5 percent. By 1989 this figure increased marginally to 16.2 percent. In technical aid, which is an indicator of technology transfer effort, Japan also ranked near the bottom of DAC. This accounted for only 11.1 percent of Japan's ODA, compared with the 20.4 percent DAC average in 1985. This figure for Japan increased to 17 percent by the end of the decade, but it was still half the DAC average.

Japan did make some progress in diversifying its ODA by functional sector. Japan increased the proportion of spending on health, education, and sanitation, which is taken to reflect BHN effort, while the share of ODA devoted to industrial production decreased. This does not mean, however, that Japan is no longer targeting trade and industry; its new ODA program lending that emerged in the late 1980s targets mainly industrial sectors, and the Ex-Im Bank's concessional lending has tended to target this area as well. After 1985 the Ex-Im Bank's commitments of untied concessional lending increased from nothing to about $6 billion annually by the end of the 1980s. At the same time, Japan's ODA retains a heavy emphasis on building economic infrastructure.

In the latter half of the 1980s Japan also began to emphasize nonproject ODA for the first time. In grant ODA Japan pledged $500 million over three years in nonproject aid to sub-Saharan Africa at the 1987 Venice Summit, and this pledge was renewed in 1990 for $600 million. This has helped Japan expand its geographical distribution and sustain aid to the least developed countries. In the area of nonproject loans Japan expanded use of commodity loans (which are intended to finance imports of important commodities), and from mid-decade Japan began pushing policy-based lending through cofinancing multilateral development bank structural adjustment loans (SALs) and sector adjustment loans. In addition, Japan introduced sector program loans in Indonesia and the Philippines at the end of the decade to induce change in regulations and resource allocations in dialogue with Japan.

Japan began emphasizing program assistance for several reasons. First, it was noticed in the mid-1980s that OECF loan projects were being delayed because in too many cases local project costs could be covered neither by recipient governments nor by Japanese ODA. In addition, it was noted that project loans are difficult to administer and that simply increasing the size and number of project loans to accommodate Japan's ODA growth targets would not be feasible without a drastic overhaul of the implementing system. Therefore, Japan began approving financing of local project costs through commodity loans to speed up the disbursement of project loans, and to move larger volumes of ODA Japan began looking to cofinance quick-disbursing program loans worked out by the World Bank or other multilateral development banks. More recently, Japan's own sector program loans have provided a vehicle for bilateral policy-based lending.

Japan also made progress in untying its ODA. By 1985, 65.6 percent of Japan's ODA was fully untied (as compared with the DAC average of 46 percent). The percentage remaining fully tied was 18.6 percent, and the remaining 15.8 percent was restricted to Japanese and/or developing country contractors. Roughly 85 percent of partially tied loan project funds were awarded to Japanese firms in 1985. This progress followed Japan's endorsement in 1978 of the principle of full aid untying. Although claims were made that the fully untied funds were still rigged to favor Japanese contractors, the Japanese government would not reveal the results of open bids at mid-decade, citing the recipient countries' need for confidentiality. Under continuing criticism Japan moved quickly to eliminate fully tied project loans by 1989, and in grant aid only project assistance remained fully tied to Japanese firms. Full information disclosure by the Japanese government is still lacking, but according to released information only about 40 percent of loan project funds were awarded to Japanese domestic firms in 1989.

Finally, Japan began more systematic efforts to improve its ODA effectiveness. The strong growth in budgetary outlays for ODA began attracting the attention of taxpayers and MOF, who wished to see these funds well spent. Moreover, the programmed funding growth gave functional ministries an opportunity to pursue a more active overseas policy agenda. The MFA got interested in improving the quality of aid projects because inoperable, unneeded, or inappropriately designed projects hurt the image of Japan's ODA at home and abroad, especially as failed projects became a focus of domestic media attention after the 1986 Marcos scandal. The MFA inaugurated the first project evaluation procedure in 1981 by forming a group to do postcompletion surveys of selected projects, and it began publishing these surveys in 1983. The EPA began a series of studies to improve the macroeconomic and sectoral impact of Japan's ODA on recipients starting with its 1983 report on the four large ASEAN countries. MAFF also began a program of policy research in 1983 and published its first survey of Indonesian and Thai projects in 1986. MITI commissioned the IDE from 1982 to begin studying the impact on ASEAN economies of selected mineral, agricultural, and industrial projects. Thus, in the areas of diplomacy, agriculture, and industry, shortcomings in the technical and political aspects of project identification, selection, construction, and operation were identified and studied, and by the start of the latter half of the decade a general consensus over what needed to be done took shape.

JICA and the OECF began to draft individual country surveys to gain a more comprehensive picture of Japanese ODA agendas in each country, as did other organizations such as the IDE and IDC. In addition, high-level missions began to be sent to countries, led in several cases by Okita Saburō, to confer with recipient governments over the future emphasis of Japanese ODA. More emphasis was put on aligning project identification activities with larger plans using new JICA and OECF funding for project development, as well as bilateral economic cooperation committees of the type created under the New AID Plan. In addition, postcompletion evaluation surveys became a regular feature of JICA and OECF activities by the start of the 1990s, with project maintenance becoming the target of a new OECF funding program.

In line with past practice the MFA used ODA to emphasize Japan's leadership in helping the developing world. As a result of depressed commodity prices and debt problems, private capital and trade credit flows to the developing countries plummeted in the early 1980s, making Japan's growing ODA relatively more important. Nonetheless, despite the high indebtedness

of Latin America and sub-Saharan Africa, the geographic distribution of
Japan's ODA continues to reflect Japan's focus on political and economic relations with Asia (see Figure 9.5).

Figure 9.5 Regional Distribution of Japan's ODA, 1979 and 1989

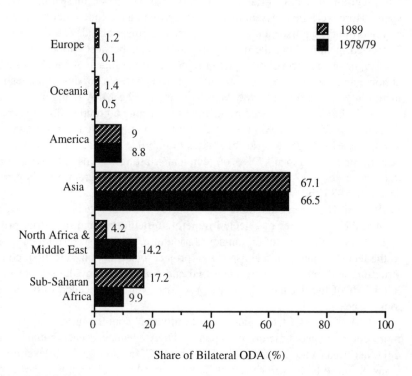

Share of Bilateral ODA (%)

Source: DAC, 1994.

Strategic Aid

Japan's contribution to Western security was to be more ODA to frontline
states facing a Soviet threat. The actual amounts involved were of marginal
significance and did not represent a basic reorientation of Japan's ODA, but
they were so well advertised by the MFA that they created Western perceptions of new Japanese "strategic aid." Table 9.2 indicates Japan's allocation
of ODA to these countries in dollars and as a percentage of total net ODA receipts from DAC members just before and after Japan made its strategic aid
pledge in 1980. In terms of proportional effort Japan significantly increased
its alliance burden only in the cases of Turkey, Jamaica, and Pakistan, but in

these three cases the volume increase over the 1978–1984 period totaled only $65.9 million—less than 3 percent of Japan's bilateral ODA spending in the year 1984. In the case of Egypt, a country of critical importance to stability in the Middle East, Japan's effort actually decreased both in absolute and relative terms. The absolute level of ODA to Thailand rose quickly, but this did not keep pace with overall DAC ODA inflows, and as indicated earlier the type of assistance was more relevant to Japanese private sector concerns than to Western security concerns. Moreover, after the security threat dissipated from the mid-1980s, Japan's ODA continued to grow. The annual flow increased between 1983 and 1989 by 28 percent, indicating that in Thailand a Soviet threat was a coincidental factor in Japan's ODA. The bottom line is that Western security concerns did not recast actual geographical or sectoral distribution patterns in Japan's ODA, but they could account for its diplomatic rhetoric.

Table 9.2 Net Bilateral Japanese ODA to Selected Frontline States
           (in millions of dollars)

	1978		1980		1982		1984	
The Middle East and Northern Africa								
Egypt	118.8	(13.8%)	123.0	(10.4%)	61.6	(5.0%)	81.5	(4.9%)
Turkey	5.1	(3.3%)	5.4	(0.8%)	27.3	(5.2%)	36.9	(19.5%)
Latin America								
Jamaica	0.1	(0.1%)	0.2	(0.2%)	3.4	(2.2%)	14.1	(9.0%)
South Asia								
Pakistan	46.9	(12.4%)	112.4	(33.1%)	95.3	(23.8%)	67.0	(22.1%)
ASEAN								
Thailand	103.8	(69.0%)	189.6	(62.2%)	170.3	(62.7%)	232.0	(65.0%)

Note: Japan's share of net ODA receipts from DAC members in parentheses.

COMPREHENSIVE SECURITY AND ODA

There was a serious security dimension to Japan's ODA, but it had to do with advancing Japan's own international standing, and not that of the United States. By the end of the 1970s shifting international factors challenged the domestic consensus supporting Japan's keizai kyōryoku. Unlike during the 1950s and 1960s, when Japan was still struggling economically, by the 1980s the MFA and academic foreign policy experts no longer believed that eco-

nomic and commercial interests could be Japan's exclusive concern. This led
to a growing divergence of thinking between the MFA and MITI that broke
into the open in 1980. The conceptual differences were significant in their
own right, but they also had implications for ODA policy.

Table 9.3 Key Policy Reports, 1980–1981

Date	Author	Title
March 1980	MITI	Policy vision for the 1980s
July 1980	Comprehensive Security Study Group	Comprehensive security strategy
November 1980	Taigai Keizai Kyōryoku Shingikai	On the future of economic cooperation
November 1980	MFA	The concept of economic cooperation
March 1981	Japan Economic Research Center	The concept of economic cooperation

The impact on MITI of a new awareness of global economic interdependence and a changing security environment changed its definition of "comprehensive economic cooperation" *(sōgō-teki keizai kyōryoku)*. The concept of comprehensive economic cooperation first received prominent treatment in the 1979 MITI yearbook, and it was associated with the large-scale project of the Asahan type:

> Economic cooperation projects in which ODA and private sector economic cooperation are effectively linked are a model for comprehensive economic cooperation, and in order to consider how Japan's economic cooperation ought to be conducted in the future, a case study will be presented.
> The Asahan Aluminum Project in Indonesia is a large-scale project carried through to completion as that country's core project, so to speak. The project has contributed to Indonesia by effectively utilizing natural resources, affecting other industries, promoting employment, transferring technology, nurturing small- and middle-sized industries, and developing a region. As for our nation, not only is it useful as a secure, long-term source of aluminum, but it has significance as a "monument" to Japan-Indonesian economic cooperation.[314]

Thus, the so-called large-scale project was held up as the prime example of comprehensive economic cooperation to achieve a balance of economic and political effects.

But in 1980 MITI introduced a security orientation into its keizai kyōryoku policy statements. In its policy vision for the 1980s the Industrial Structure Council identified four structural factors that had supported Japan's postwar growth: (1) cheap and plentiful oil, (2) the clear predominance and leadership of the United States in politics and economics, (3) the availability of Western advanced technologies, and (4) the extended growth of the postwar global economy. But according to MITI the security problem of the 1980s and beyond was that these structural supports were weakening, and Japan would eventually have to build an independent foundation for growth.[315]

The strategy of the 1980s would be to emphasize three themes: Japan as an economic power, Japan as a resource-poor country, and Japan as a work and leisure society. All three themes involved the use of ODA already tested the 1970s. First, ODA would contribute to Japan's continued growth by relieving economic frictions with the West and building more extensive relations with developing countries. Second, ODA would deal with Japan's dependence on imported energy (89 percent) and food (55 percent) by developing more numerous and geographically dispersed sources of food, energy, and raw materials. Finally, ODA could help achieve an "industrial structure rich in creativity" by moving land- and labor-intensive industries, energy-intensive industries, and polluting industries overseas. This would free domestic resources for higher-technology industries, reduce dependence on energy and raw materials imports, and promote an improved domestic quality of life.

MITI also developed an index of national economic security effort. It is interesting because, as implied by the comprehensive security concept articulated by the Comprehensive Security Study Group, it equates keizai kyōryoku and industrial R&D spending with military spending as an index of national security effort. The report calls for an increase in Japan's economic cooperation indicator to 3.0 percent of GNP by the end of the 1980s.[316] Although Japan did not meet its target, it did become the largest source of ODA and of private capital flows at market terms ($15 billion, or two-thirds of total private flows) to the developing countries by 1989.

The reason economic cooperation was considered equivalent to defense spending was that in an interdependent world economy, the cultivation of technological and financial dependence on Japan would increase Japan's international leverage and thereby enhance its economic security.[317] So in 1980 comprehensive economic cooperation still meant the coordination of ODA, trade, and investment, but MITI now emphasized how keizai kyōryoku could help change Japan's extensive international economic ties from a vulnerability into a source of further growth, security, and an improved quality of life. Figure 9.6 is a MITI illustration of the concept.

Table 9.4 Economic Security Spending as Percent of GNP (1977)

	R&D	Economic Cooperation*	Subtotal	Defense	Total
Japan	1.7	**1.4**	3.1	0.9	**4.0**
United States	2.4	**1.0**	3.4	6.0	**9.4**
Federal Republic of Germany	2.0	**2.2**	4.2	3.4	**7.6**
France	1.8	**1.9**	3.7	3.6	**7.3**
United Kingdom	2.1	**3.8**	5.9	5.0	**10.9**

Source: OECD.
Note: Includes ODA, export credits, and FDI minus commodity imports from developing countries.

Figure 9.6 Comprehensive Economic Cooperation in the 1980s

COMPREHENSIVE *KEIZAI KYŌRYOKU*

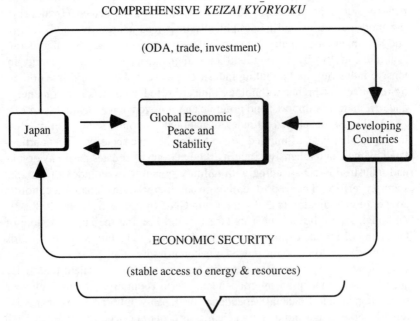

The formation of desired relations of interdependence
(The stable expansion of commercial relations)

Source: Based on Tsusho Sangyo Gyosei Kenkyukai (1983), p.113.

The Study Group on Comprehensive Security

After Masayoshi Ohira became prime minister in 1978, he commissioned a study commission to recommend long-term national policies to the end of the century. A subgroup of the Ohira commission was the Research Group on Comprehensive Security (S ōgō Anzen Hoshō Kenkyū Gurūpu), led by Professor Inoki Masamichi. The Soviet invasion of Afghanistan and the subsequent strong U.S. pressure on Japan to increase its military role in Western security made this group's deliberations timely. The study group's report pointedly introduces the need for a new Japanese security strategy by stating at the outset: "When considering the problem of Japan's peace and security, the most basic change in international affairs occurring in the 1970s was the end of America's clear superiority in both the military and economic areas."[318]

According to this group Japan needed a concept of "comprehensive security" (sōgōanzen hoshō), which was "the protection of the people's livelihood against various threats." According to the study group this vaguely worded concept would require the coordinated application of economic, political, and military policies at three distinct levels: the level of global affairs, the level of selected groupings or alliances, and the level of independent national effort. Some examples of what it wished to promote at each level were: arms control, better North-South relations, and free trade at the global level; good relations with political allies and key economic partners at the intermediate level; and military security as well as economic productivity and export competitiveness at the national self-help level.[319] With the exception of military security, ODA commitments had been used successfully in the 1970s to advance each of these goals, and the report strongly emphasizes the need to use ODA in the new comprehensive security strategy.[320] The group's sponsorship by the prime minister, as well as its largely academic composition, gave its report legitimacy as an impartial assessment of Japan's national interests from a viewpoint that transcended bureaucratic politics.

This report prompted the Taigai Keizai Kyōryoku Shingikai to emphasize the security significance of ODA.[321] It recommended an ODA/GNP effort at the DAC average level to promote the following goals: stable North-South relations; access to energy, food, and raw materials; leadership in improving social welfare in the Third World; and an image as a role model for the non-Western world. This new emphasis did not mean, however, that the old emphasis on ODA coordination with private sector activities was displaced. The group reaffirmed this core principle with a call for further coordination with the trade and investment elements of keizai kyōryoku.

The MFA Effort to Redefine ODA

The MFA responded to this new concern about comprehensive security by forming a study group on economic cooperation within the Economic Cooperation Bureau that issued a report in November 1980 on the reasons for giving official development assistance.[322] The MFA was careful to specify ODA *(seifu kaihatsu enjo)* in the title because it could not directly challenge MITI's jurisdiction over keizai kyōryoku.

The MFA was also careful to draw a distinction between what the OECD and UN agencies thought ODA was about (humanitarianism and global interdependence) and why the MFA thought Japan should give ODA.[323] Japan's "uniqueness" in giving ODA *(dokuji no riyū)* was that it considered ODA "the cost of constructing an international order that secures Japan's comprehensive peace and security."[324] Whatever the expectations of the international community, ODA really was about national security as far as the MFA was concerned. Security was defined with respect to four core agendas:

> ⌈We are a nation desiring peace; a great economic power that continues to develop; a nation with an extremely high degree of external economic dependence; and a modernized non-Western nation that faces special expectations from the developing countries. For the first three reasons we strongly desire law and order in international society and changes in the international environment that will benefit us on the basis of a broad peace and security that will deliver to us military security as well as sources of energy, important raw materials, and food. With respect to the fourth reason, we are in the best position to help improve the international environment, especially in North-South relations. For these purposes one of the most effective measures is ODA.[325] ⌋ 22 8

Thus, the MFA diverged from the traditional keizai kyōryoku conception of ODA favored by MITI on certain key points. Economic and commercial interests, though still important, would have to make room for strategic political considerations in the distribution of ODA. For example, its report mentions that ODA could be used to enhance the security of Japan's sea-lanes by targeting littoral states. In addition, cultivation of political influence in the non-Western world could begin with ODA diplomacy. The key point is that overconcentration on economic and commercial activities benefiting Japan would be politically damaging and hurtful to Japan's broad comprehensive security effort. This stance did not mean an end to the MFA's support of the basic principle of public-private sector coordination in ODA, but the MFA did wish to turn ODA more toward political and security issues. Thus, from the start of the 1980s the MFA began playing a two-level game in ODA policy. In the international realm it fought off Western criticism of Japan's ODA, whereas in domestic interministerial struggles over ODA policy it used foreign criticism to argue for a greater say over the types, amounts, and distribution of Japan's ODA.

As part of its turf struggle, the MFA started introducing semantic distinctions to distinguish ODA from keizai kyōryoku. Whereas in 1978 the MFA was still using the term *seifu-beesu keizai kyōryoku* (government-based economic cooperation) to refer to ODA (a term favored by MITI),[326] this term would vanish from MFA's usage by 1980, to be replaced by seifu kai-hatsu enjo (official development assistance). At the same time, keizai kyō-ryoku was replaced by kaihatsu kyōryoku (development cooperation) in MFA publications wherever possible. By distinguishing ODA from other components of economic cooperation, and by emphasizing its importance as a foreign policy tool, the MFA was attempting to expand its influence over ODA.

It achieved this in certain ways, for example, by issuing annual reviews of ODA performance from 1987 in Japanese and by linking ODA to broader political objectives. In the second half of the 1980s Japan raised the share of Japanese ODA devoted to sub-Saharan Africa to demonstrate greater humani-tarianism and cultivate a new political constituency in the developing world. It also increased cultural grant aid to promote international friendship and the dissemination of Japanese culture, and it raised ODA spending to surpass the United States to become the world's largest donor by the end of the decade. This new ODA superpower status supported the MFA's call for a new "global partnership" in which Japan would support the international security role of the United States and help manage the global economy, and in return it expected equal status with the United States in international decisionmak-ing fora, including the UN Security Council.

In all this it is important to note that MFA objectives did not exclude the economic agenda implicit in the keizai kyōryoku system. The MFA did not want revision of the policymaking system, and it openly touted the ability of Japanese ODA and investment to foster dynamic growth and development in Asia. Because of its economic cooperation efforts, Japan gained the highest positions of influence in formal and informal regional economic cooperation regimes. In this way the MFA could use Japan's economic predominance in Asia to gain predominance in budding regional political structures. Thus, in a very real sense Japan could successfully buy power with its ODA. Through the latter half of the 1980s the MFA continued to control foreign perceptions of Japan's ODA, to push for new kinds of ODA in symbolic measure to win new friends and assuage critics, and to protect the keizai kyōryoku system from outside scrutiny.

The Limits of ODA Diplomacy

The end of the heyday of ODA diplomacy will probably be marked at the early 1990s. Through the 1980s Japan had no concrete reason to believe that the Yoshida strategy had become obsolete, and so it continued to believe that ODA, together with other aspects of Japan's economic strength, could be used to answer Japan's major political problems. But by 1991 Japan's *Diplomatic Blue Book* admitted that "checkbook diplomacy" would henceforth no longer be sufficient to secure Japan's interests.

Several events in the early 1990s forced Japan to confront the need to begin looking for new diplomatic strategies. First there was Operation Desert

Shield/Desert Storm. Despite the $4 billion in aid Japan promised to frontline Gulf countries and the $9 billion Japan gave directly to the United States to subsidize the operation, Japan earned little political credit because it refused direct participation in this UN-sanctioned multilateral collective security action. Moreover, Japan's inability to participate hurt its case for a permanent seat on the UN Security Council. The Japanese public and decisionmaking elite could see that ODA was not enough to support Japan's political aspirations and needs, and Japan passed legislation in 1992 that enlarged the role of the Self-Defense Forces (SDF) to include UN-sponsored peacekeeping operations (PKOs).

Second, there was the new U.S. East Asian Strategy Initiative announced in 1990, which called for a phased drawdown of U.S. forces in the region and a more modest U.S. role as a security balancer in Asia. Japan's answer to the need for measures to dissuade China, North Korea, and other regional states from seeking to exploit the situation was to announce in April 1991 that it would link its ODA to recipient government policies on military spending, weapons production, and weapons exports. Later in 1991 the United States unexpectedly decided to withdraw from its Philippines bases, and this set the stage for renewed Chinese territorial claims to the Senkaku Islands and the Paracel and Spratley Islands in the South China Sea in early 1992. Within the year China was negotiating with Russia to purchase jet fighters and other military technology that would allow it to enforce its expanded maritime claims (and interdict Japan's vital sea-lanes). Also in this year a new U.S. government under President Bill Clinton pledged to rectify Japan's trade practices but otherwise to focus mainly on domestic issues. This direction in bilateral relations indicated that Japan would need more than ODA to manage its regional security interests in the long term, and Japan began putting greater emphasis on institutionalizing a regional security dialogue through ASEAN and other fora.

Third, there was the hydra-headed problem of nuclear proliferation in the post–Cold War world, where rivalries between regional powers were expected to be less regulated by superpower intervention. It surfaced in one form in North Korea's temporary withdrawal from the inspection regime of the International Atomic Energy Agency (IAEA) in 1992 after inspectors found possible diversion of plutonium to unknown uses. In other forms it took the shape of the retention of nuclear weapons by newly independent republics of the former Soviet Union (Ukraine, Kazakhstan, Uzbekistan), as well as possible uncontrolled transfers of nuclear weapons and weapons technology out of the former Soviet Union via the black market. And then there was the problem of unacknowledged nuclear states such as India and Pakistan. As Japan considered the indefinite extension of the Nuclear Nonproliferation Treaty (NPT) in 1995, the issue was whether it would bind itself to permanent nuclear inferiority even as de facto proliferation increased the number of nuclear-capable states. At the 1993 Western economic summit, when Japan was asked to declare its intention to sign the NPT renewal, it caused concern by simply refusing to commit itself. When Foreign Minister Mutō Kabun did pledge to sign the NPT renewal, he followed it with the in-formal comment to the Japanese press: "If it comes down to the crunch, pos-sessing the will that we can build nuclear weapons is important."[327]

Finally, the bursting of the bubble economy in 1991–1992 only under-lined the fact that the upbeat economic and fiscal conditions that supported Japan's checkbook diplomacy would not be permanent. The immediate effect on Japan's 1993 ODA/GNP ratio was to reduce this figure to 0.26 percent—the lowest since the 1970s. Longer-term structural factors such as the rapid aging of the Japanese population mean that in twenty years a national savings surplus could be gone and both fiscal and international balances could be un-der pressure. This implies that continued growth of Japanese ODA would be feasible only through the medium term, with other means needed to support Japan's position in international political hierarchies in the longer term.

As Japan reacts to the fact that its long-term security prospects are in question, it is being forced to move gradually beyond low politics.[328] Japan's domestic debate has moved quickly beyond PKOs to whether Japan should become a "normal" country able to use force as others do in the international system. Structural realist logic dictates that with the eroding credibility of the U.S. security role in Asia and a rapidly growing and politically ambitious China—not to mention the problem of nuclear proliferation on the Korean peninsula just next door—Japan is facing growing incentives to find a new in-ternational strategy. The end of the Yoshida Doctrine means the decline of ODA-centered diplomacy, and initiative in Japan's diplomacy today has turned to the area of security, where it is slowly expanding Japan's security options and capabilities and awaiting future developments.

Although Japan's ODA has been of critical importance to the MFA's diplomacy, it should not be viewed exclusively in those terms. Nor should ODA be viewed exclusively as an instrument of economic policy, although this aspect of ODA has been underappreciated, and for this reason has been the focus of this book. The main point is that one must overcome the concep-tion of foreign policy and economic policy as being dichotomous and unre-lated if one is to appreciate the significance of Japan's ODA. Japan wants its bilateral ODA to raise its position in economic and political international structures, and it has been remarkably successful in doing so. Not only has ODA consistently helped Japan raise its position in the international division of labor, but it has given Japan leadership status in global fora. It also has given the Japanese state a means to begin organizing economic and political hierarchies in Asia. The question for the future, however, is whether ODA can supply adequate security for Japan, and here the prospects are problem-atic.

10

Conclusion

Since its inception keizai kyōryoku has been used to develop strategic re-source supplies for Japanese industry, open developing country markets, help Japanese industries achieve or maintain international competitiveness, sustain domestic industries in cyclical downturns, and ease the adjustment costs of Japanese industries facing declining competitiveness. Japan's ODA has been able to promote these ends because it is incorporated into the keizai kyōryoku policy making system, which is designed to reconcile both state and private sector objectives. This explains how and why Japan's ODA facilitates the steady upgrading of Japan's position in global economic and political hierar-chies. 233

There are two major contexts that give Japan's ODA significance. One is the nature of policymaking in Japan and how the case of Japan's ODA might fit into contemporary thinking about this question. The case of ODA does not fit into the sector-specific "iron triangle" model of policymaking, in which a discrete issue area is governed by one ministry, one group of expert LDP Diet members (zoku), and one kind of interest group. The system of distributed jurisdictions in policy implementation links together the 16 main ministries and agencies and their respective clienteles in civil society. The yonshōchō role in managing this system, which was worked out through interministerial negotiations in the 1950s, means that ODA priorities are in industrial and trade policy, foreign policy, and financial policy. The value of the case of ODA is that, contrary to some opinion, Japanese bureaucratic actors are ca-pable of coordinating their behavior to manage a strategic agenda.

The other context framing Japan's ODA is the international system within which Japan—as any other state—devises strategies to raise its status. What distinguishes the efforts of each state are the choice of strategy and the skill with which it implements its basic designs. Here is where Japan's ODA can help to shed light on what made postwar Japan's international behavior distinctive and successful.

THE RELEVANCE OF ODA TO
THE STUDY OF JAPANESE POLICYMAKING

Some care must be taken in choosing an approach to policymaking that can account for the range of influences acting on Japanese aid policy. Some ap-

proaches tend to reduce causation to one level of analysis, but the task here is
to put policy determinants at the international, state, and societal levels of
analysis in their proper perspective.

In the pluralist approach the polity (i.e., those who have the power to
hold government accountable) is made up of individuals who organize into
groups to advance their interests. Democracy is maintained by competition
among myriad groups, and the result is a neutral role for the state in regulating and registering societal pressures.[329] One problem with this approach is
that it overlooks the autonomy that states enjoy. One recent volume on U.S.
foreign economic policy notes that "the conventional view of a 'weak' state is
inadequate. . . . Government officials play a more active and innovative role
and . . . state structures play a more crucial shaping and constraining role than
the conventional wisdom predicts."[330] In other words, even the sectionalized
and societally penetrated U.S. state can have enough autonomy to use societal
actors as instruments of state agendas.[331] In the case of Japan, Daniel
Okimoto observes, "Liberal pluralism has trouble explaining such features of
Japanese policy making as extensive and informal elite networks, blurred
lines of demarcation between the public and private sectors, the functional
importance of the intermediate zone between the state and private enterprise,
and evidence of political cartelization in certain policy domains."[332] In this
study of ODA we find that Japan's taxpayers, citizen's groups, and opposition parties have had little success in making policy expressive of their values.[333] In contrast, business has benefited greatly from Japan's ODA, but the
role of the bureaucracy in structuring these outcomes cannot be ignored.

Traditional realists tend to ignore domestic interest groups and discuss
statecraft as if the task was to make the one choice among all available alter-
natives that would advance the national interest the farthest.[334] This unitary
rational actor model is justly criticized because it obscures the impact on
policy of domestic structures and because it relies on unrealistic epistemolog-
ical assumptions.[335]

To address these shortcomings the bureaucratic politics approach focuses
on how foreign policy decisions are actually made.[336] An important characteristic of foreign policy is that the state tends to have more autonomy and
initiative than in domestic issues. This explains the key assumption that certain "core" bureaucracies determine policy.[337] Bureaucratic conflict in the decisionmaking process produces policies that are not so much the result of
synoptic, rational calculation as of "pulling and hauling" among bureaucratic
actors with different interests, or of incremental decisionmaking driven by
bureaucratic routine and "satisficing."[338] This approach is adopted by Alan
Rix to study Japanese aid policy, and it usefully clarifies the roles and interests of key bureaucratic actors.[339]

Nevertheless, this model has a few well-known difficulties. First, it is not
well suited to analyzing foreign economic policy where the rationale for autonomy is weaker and where societal factors have strong interests. Second,

the bureaucratic politics model itself does not explain the strategic choices states make that provide the basis for bureaucratic routine. Peter Katzenstein notes: "Models of bureaucratic politics abstract so little from the different strategies of foreign economic policy which need to be explained that they cannot clearly specify either the content of political strategies or the influence of particular intra-bureaucratic factors in the advanced industrial states."[340] To understand the roots of a state's basic policy orientation and how bureaucratic actors have come to administer a particular policy area, different approaches are needed.

A state's basic orientation is influenced by its position in international structure. The competitive international system constrains each state to adopt strategies that are appropriate to its position in international structure. In this way the international system "shapes and shoves" the behavior of states.[341] This approach has been used by David Lake to explain U.S. tariff policy, and he points out that "the constraints and opportunities of the international economic structure are influential and . . . domestic political factors, normally granted analytic autonomy from [international] systemic incentives, are best understood as interacting with these constraints."[342] If this structural approach can explain the general orientation of a state, it cannot, however, explain why similarly situated states choose different courses of action, or why they pursue the same strategies with different results. Although international structure has relevance as a policy determinant, one needs also to accommodate domestic unit-level factors in decisionmaking.

In this regard the decomposition of domestic society into classes or relations of production can be a useful complement to international structural approaches. Barrington Moore, for example, explains the emergence of communist, fascist, or democratic political institutions in terms of which class elements (in a set composed of the nobility, peasants, the bourgeoisie, and workers) combined to form a ruling coalition during the crisis of modernization.[343] This approach has been extended by Peter Gourevitch to the area of foreign economic policy to explain the different tariff policies adopted by late nineteenth-century Germany, France, Britain, and the United States in terms of variation in coalitional structures and particular institutional and leadership factors.[344] Like the pluralist approach, however, the class analysis approach is a societally driven model of political change that can miss the critical importance of state autonomy. Neo-Marxists have been quick to point this out,[345] as have non-Marxists.[346] And the degree of state autonomy could be what differentiates East Asian political economies from Western ones.[347]

Institutionalist Perspectives

As the foregoing discussion indicates, simply reducing policy causation to one level of analysis is unsatisfactory. The problem is to put international, state, bureaucratic, and societal determinants of policy in their proper relationship, while allowing for the fact that no two political systems organize and weigh these influences in exactly the same way. By focusing on the institutionalized linkages between state, society, and the international system, one can address the complexity of policy causation and make the model dynamic by incorporating a theory of institutional origins and change.

The term *institution* refers neither to a behavior itself nor to a particular group or interest. It refers to an established structure of relations and procedures that permit individuals to pursue their interests, but this is patterned in such a way as to achieve a collective result, i.e., an institutional mandate. Politics in such a setting is regulated and channeled by organizational structures and procedures that selectively incorporate actors and define their choices.[348] Power is measured by the ability to determine institutional objectives. Actor self-interest is the motive for action, but the perception of self-interest is strongly conditioned by an actor's organizational position. Status and role determine the type and direction of pressure any particular actor or group can exert on others, and organizational inclusion imposes a set of rules, sanctions, and rewards for various types of behavior. Institutional structures also filter and channel demands from the state, societal, and international levels. It is true that exogenous factors such as charismatic leadership or external shocks can disrupt institutions, but if framework structures remain intact, these exogenous factors act as random variables explaining deviations from the norm, and not the underlying trend line.

The basic architecture of these structural patterns originates in response to crises that force discontinuous change in the underlying relations of state and society. At these junctures the role of new ideas may be critical in restructuring or redirecting institutions in ways discussed below. Even at such times of discontinuous change, however, old structures and ideas can still play a role in shaping new ones by facilitating the formation of some political arrangements and discouraging others.[349] After basic structures have been reorganized under the impact of exogenous shocks, institutional growth and routinized decisionmaking during more settled times create basic policy continuity—at least until another exogenous crisis or event brings structural upheaval. Thus, in periods of political stability, policy becomes a function of institutional structure, and structural change typically only follows the exogenous shock of large historical events such as wars, domestic upheavals, or economic crises. Using this "path dependent" notion of "sticky" change based on explanations of historical sequence and qualitatively different phases of institutional change and development,[350] one is better able to relate the institutional heritage and historical experiences of a particular country to its distinctive political economy and strategic orientation.

With regard to the controversial relationship between state and society, whether a state should be analyzed as a dependent, intervening, or independent variable is not known a priori; the question is a matter for empirical investigation. Peter Katzenstein suggests that greater centralization in state institutions than in societal ones, combined with the density of networks that penetrate the boundary between state and society, helps to explain the degree of state autonomy in formulating foreign economic policy.[351] John Zysman suggests that state-led strategies of industrial adjustment require state structures with the following characteristics: at least partial bureaucratic autonomy from parliament and from interest groups; a range of discretionary administrative and financial instruments in the hands of these bureaucrats; and an ability to generate a view of where the industrial economy should go.[352] Both Katzenstein and Zysman find that Japan is strongly differentiated from the United States and Great Britain in the strength of state initiative and the capacity for strategic planning, but the organization of institutions supplies the comparative framework. Katzenstein has also given explicit attention to the influence of international structure on state institutions by studying small Western European states. These small states responded to the liberal postwar international political economy by using relatively centralized state and societal structures to form democratic corporatist policy networks that allowed these states to pursue flexible adjustment strategies.[353]

To explain economic policy orientation Peter Katzenstein makes an institutionalist argument when he argues that how state and societal actors link up to form stable policy networks could explain the character of a nation's foreign economic policies.[354] In comparing economic policy making in Britain and France, Peter Hall incorporates domestic and international structural factors in the following way:

> The cases of Britain and France suggest that five sets of structural variables will be most important for the course of a nation's economic policy: the organization of labor, the organization of capital, the organization of the state, the organization of the political system, and the structural position of the country within the international economy. Some might like a shorter list of independent variables, especially since each of these varies along several dimensions; but economic policy making is a complex process, and a careful consideration of the French and British experience suggests that any further reduction would fail to capture the full range of factors affecting their policies.[355]

The institutional approach suggests that different patterns of state-societal organization can explain the variation of economic policy and strategy among countries similarly situated in the international division of labor. Thus, one would expect that an economy in which finance and industry are aligned through close institutional linkages will likely communicate to the state different policy preferences than one in which intersectoral relations are limited and ad hoc; or that economic policy determined by legislatures, as opposed to insulated bureaucracies, will have different characteristics and orientations.[356]

Finally, to complement discussion of the institutional approach it would be useful to deal with the role of ideas. One could argue that policies and institutions are the consequences of ideational factors. For example, Adam Smith is credited with undermining the traditional mercantilist approach to trade policy with his powerful free-market argument.[357] Smith's argument may indeed have impelled European governments in the nineteenth century to move toward free trade.[358] The fact is, however, that despite the ideological hegemony of the free trade argument, it may be safely asserted that no sovereign government has ever actually implemented a pure free trade policy in its home market; nor has the GATT trading system done so, since it regards tariff reduction as a process of reciprocal tariff concessions.

More qualified claims about the role of ideas have greater plausibility. As Max Weber argued, through "elective affinity," ideas can unite with interests to determine history.[359] This insight has been applied by Judith Goldstein who has pointed out that when economic crises open the door to new political coalitions, they may fail to gain entry if they lack an adequate ideological justification for desired courses of action.[360] Nonetheless, she hedges this by stipulating: "ideas influence policy only when they are carried by individuals or groups with political clout," and, "structures do constrain the possible options that the new governing coalitions can successfully implement."[361]

Other cognitive factors are also relevant to state-society relations. Japanese institutions have been explained in terms of distinctive cultural and psychological orientations of the Japanese people,[362] or by referring to the persistence of prewar values,[363] or by showing how lessons learned in the prewar period could shape postwar industrial policy.[364] These deeply embedded cognitive factors may explain why Eleanor Hadley observes that with regard to Keynsianism, "both in the high growth era and since the OPEC shocks, it is clear that its impact on [Japan's] public policy has not been strong."[365]

The ideational factor cannot be reduced to institutional structure; it plays at key moments an autonomous role in changing and legitimating institutions, though in other circumstances the direction of causality may be reversed. Nevertheless, institutional factors are the focus in this study because in keizai kyōryoku only those ideas that served powerful material interests have driven meaningful change, whereas others such as Western ODA norms have been deflected. This should not be surprising because once established, institutional structures can be expected to stabilize themselves organizationally and ideologically and then act as anchors resisting efforts to uproot the system.

With regard to Japan, Chalmers Johnson's study of MITI as the "pilot agency" guiding Japan's rapid industrial development is a classic institutionalist study. Johnson argues that Japan's "high-growth system, like the basic priorities of the state, was not so much a matter of choice for Japan as of necessity; it grew out of a series of economic crises that assailed the nation throughout the Shōwa era."[366] Johnson persuasively argues that what MITI is and does precludes one from classifying Japan as a liberal regulatory state. The key political contradiction managed by the modern Japanese state has not been domestic class conflict per se; rather, it has been external and historically rooted in modern Japan's late development and confrontation with the West. Postwar Japan continued to be organized to catch up with the West, and accordingly the state continued its role of cultivating the nation's industrial and financial power. For this reason the state did not displace the market, but learned to use it to serve developmental goals. This orientation gave Japan a different set of policy tools and a different strategic orientation than other advanced Western states. Johnson thus draws a distinction between, on the one hand, the Japanese capitalist developmental state, and on the other, the Western liberal regulatory state.

Another institutionalist approach to Japan's political economy is that of Daniel Okimoto, who argues that Japan is a "societal state" or a "network state." In his view, the Japanese state is

> able to exercise power only in terms of its network of ties with the private sector. The existence of various organizational structures in the Japanese economy gives MITI numerous levers, or points of access, by means of which to intervene in the marketplace. In the same vein, bureaucratic power is also relational in the sense that it emerges from the structure of LDP-bureaucracy-interest group alignments and the political exchanges that take place among them. The secret to the power of the Japanese state is thus embedded in the structure of its relationship to the rest of society. Japan is without question a societal state.[367]

In contrast to Johnson's analysis, which views the Japanese state as an independent variable and societal actors as intervening variables in the policy process, Daniel Okimoto offers an analysis of Japanese industrial policy that seems to view state and society as interdependent and mutually determining variables.

The difference might be glossed over by pointing out that Johnson's analysis covers pre–oil shock Japan, whereas Okimoto's study is less historical and relies on post–oil shock case studies. As T. J. Pempel argues, there could very well be a qualitative difference between these temporally distinct Japans.[368] Nevertheless, Johnson views the Japanese state as having an intrinsic authority. In contrast, Okimoto argues that "the Japanese state derives its legitimacy from its capacity to coordinate industry-specific efforts and national goals." It is not quite a strong state: "The Japanese state has no choice but to rely on consensus, habits of compliance, and voluntary cooperation on the part of private actors to get things done. It simply cannot base its rule on coercion, threats of legal sanctions, or unilateral imposition of its own will on society."[369]

The Case of ODA

The case of ODA shows how the boundary between state and private sector is selectively penetrated in policy deliberation councils (shingikai), public corporations (tokushū hōjin), trade associations (shadan jōjin), nonprofit foundations (zaidan hōjin), and informal policy study groups (kenky ūkai). At the same time, we see Japanese ODA consistently pressured by external actors such as the United States and the OECD. Thus, depending on the case it would be possible to locate causation in the state, society, or the international system. To begin to locate the relative importance of these levels of analysis in determining ODA, one should point out that keizai kyōryoku was first organized by the MFA, a postdefeat refuge for planning bureaucrats from the prewar Greater East Asia Ministry such as Okita Saburo. The postwar state required the success of Japan's industry and trade in order to raise its own international standing. By inviting the leaders of Japanese firms that had heavy Asian interests in the prewar period into the deliberation council that devised the private sector–led, government-supported principle of keizai kyōryoku, the state enlisted the private sector in rebuilding Japan's economic relations with the rest of Asia. In other words, the statist, developmental orientation of the Japanese bureaucracy explains how and why the private sector was invited to help design economic cooperation. Private sector success in the developing world became a shared goal among the main ministries and agencies, i.e., a state priority. To pursue this state priority, however, horizontal coordination between vertically segmented main ministries and agencies had to be organized, and this was done by the yonshōcho and the elaborate system of distributed jurisdictions.

The fact that the foundations of keizai kyōryoku were built in the early 1950s before the LDP existed, and before Western theories of foreign aid were developed, suggests that one should look elsewhere for the initial policy impulse. After the LDP was formed its role was to prevent the Diet from being used to disrupt the policy agenda, and it brokered deals between the bureaucracy and business interests outside of the Diet. This role explains why the LDP avoided substantive policy debate and legislation in the Diet.

Bureaucratically sponsored fora tended to be where public authority interacted with private interests to set economic policy. This allowed the state to structure access to policymaking, and the ability to grant or withhold access gave it leverage over societal interests. The material interests involved are obvious, but the ideological basis for close collaboration between state and private sector was a conservative nationalism that viewed Japan's postwar economic recovery and growth as the path to renewed great-power status.[370] Although it was structurally disadvantaged, the private sector was not passive or powerless. It could at least demand profitability in return for cooperation. This was not a trivial matter. The need to achieve profitable activity led to a myriad of intermediary structures and information exchanges to ensure that policy would lead to market-sustainable outcomes.

In the area of foreign policy, the security treaty with the United States gave Japan strong incentives to rely on economic power in its postwar diplomacy. Until the 1980s Japan's diplomacy was keyed to the reconstruction of Japan's economic power, but when Japan emerged as an economic superpower with global interests and larger political obligations, the MFA looked for ways to use Japan's economic power to achieve purely political objectives. This explains why ODA became such a key part of Japan's answer to trade and defense frictions with the West, and how it came to play a crucial role in building independent networks of bilateral relations with the developing world, especially in Asia.

At base the keizai kyōryoku system was a function of the interdependent and mutually supportive postwar coalition formed between the bureaucracy, the LDP, and the private sector—as well as the international linkage between conservative Japan and the United States. This basic coalition of interests itself has to be explained in terms of international structure, objective economic necessities, historical context, ideological factors, institutional legacies, and political leadership.

U.S. Occupation authorities encouraged conservative predominance and industrial recovery after the United States lost China as its main Asian ally in 1949. This meant that after the Occupation destroyed the power of the prewar military and internal security bureaucracies, the economic bureaucracies were left to set the postwar agenda for the Japanese state. The continuity with the prewar state that these civilian bureaucracies embodied left the postwar state still ideologically oriented toward organizing society to raise Japan's international status, and it resorted to economic nationalism to orient the nation toward rapid capital accumulation. It was aided in this by the bureaucracy's autonomous power to plan and shape public-private sector linkages, as well as by the objective economic needs of early postwar Japan. The "export-or-die" mentality that the state promoted made sense for a war-devastated and import-dependent Japan, and this convinced the population that production should be a national priority. The Korean War boom helped Japan recover, but the post–Korean War recession and trade deficits reminded it of the need to develop industrial export competitiveness. To help answer this need the state organized keizai kyōryoku well before the LDP was formed in 1955.

For its part the United States wanted to prove that capitalist democracy was possible in Asia. This allowed postwar Japan to offer its own economic success as its contribution to U.S. containment strategy in Asia. Along with its acceptance of U.S. military bases, this was enough to win a unilateral security guarantee from the United States. This arrangement with the United States reinforced Japan's state-organized developmental agenda and freed Japan to focus on the cultivation of economic power as a means to raise its international status. Here the key entrepreneurial role played by Yoshida Shigeru, who negotiated the terms of the U.S.-Japan Security Treaty and established developmentally oriented conservatism in postwar Japan, cannot be overlooked.

That institutional linkages determining ODA policy would be most developed between domestic coalition members could be predicted.[371] The underlying stability of Japan's state-managed conservative coalition explains why Japan's ODA grew out of the keizai kyōryoku system and could not be removed from it. When pushed to the wall by foreign and domestic critics in 1992, the state and private sector actors, even with their increasingly divergent agendas, used the well-oiled routines of the keizai kyōryoku system to draft the ODA Taikō and enact it through Cabinet order in 1992. This illustrates how an organized system channels pressures for change along established lines to produce predictable results. Included actors could not redesign a system that yielded them so many benefits even though their respective interests and agendas may be growing apart.

Figure 10.1 illustrates the pattern of ODA linkages between core categories of actors until 1993. The thickest line denotes the earliest and most densely institutionalized relationship between the bureaucracy and the private sector. This relationship involves such structures as the prime minister's Overseas Economic Cooperation Deliberation Council; implementing agencies such as the OECF, JICA, and JETRO; peak business associations such as the Keidanren which maintains a standing committee on economic cooperation; and sectoral business associations of plant exporters, trading companies, engineering consulting firms, construction firms, and the like. The next thickest lines in the diagram denote the regularized informal links of the LDP to the private sector and the bureaucracy. In the area of ODA this role is organized through, for example, the Special Committee on Economic Cooperation in the LDP's Policy Affairs Research Council. This triangular linkage defines the basic interests served by Japan's ODA policy.

Figure 10.1 Main ODA Linkages

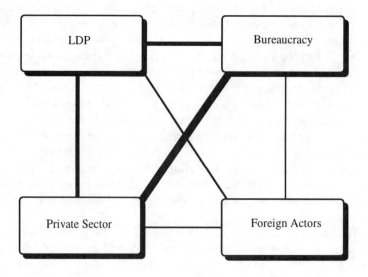

The formal link between this domestic interest triangle and foreign actors consisted of bilateral aid relationships and Japan's membership in multilateral aid regimes. These links tended to be managed by the MFA in its capacity as the representative of the Japanese government to foreign governments, but depending on the functional issue area, other bureaucratic actors had jurisdictional claims that the MFA had to observe. The LDP maintained less formal links with foreign elected officials through bilateral parliamentary leagues, and Japan's ODA could turn these into conduits for influence peddling. Strong LDP politicians with leading positions in bilateral parliamentary leagues, such as Watanabe Michio in the Japan-Indonesia parliamentary league, have been in a position to broker ODA project and program agreements. Finally, the Japanese private sector is brought into regular contact with recipient government bureaucrats, politicians, and firms through their participation in ODA implementing agencies and ODA projects. Japan's ODA also leverages the importance of overseas Japanese chambers of commerce as well as other private sector–based exchanges.

What foreign actors perceive through these different sources of information is a bewildering montage of disjointed images and agendas. The formal request procedures managed by the MFA, OECF, and JICA mask many important realities, and the links recipients may have with the Japanese private sector and with the LDP politicians tended to be used to influence individual ODA requests. Because these links failed to provide comprehensive information and leverage to foreign actors, they are represented by the thinnest lines in Figure 10.1.

Who or What Drives the System?

The case of ODA offers a cautionary example to those who would mechanically apply to Japanese institutional realities certain models of policymaking developed to make sense of U.S. institutions and political processes. The bureaucracy is too strong and partisan, the role of the legislature is too weak, and the linkages between bureaucratic actors and the private sector are too institutionalized and exclusionary to fit the basic premises of pluralist models of policymaking. ODA policy is anything but the product of freely competing, diverse societal interests working through a neutral and politically accountable state.

The rational choice approach as applied by Ramseyer and Rosenbluth to Japanese politics is the most recent variant of this societally centered approach. They start by pointing out that voters acting as "principals" choose legislators as their agents and that legislators then choose bureaucrats and judges who will "mitigate [the voters'] problems." Then they conclude that "the institutions which endure are those that solve the problems of the political players."[372] In their view institutions are changeable "rules of the game," i.e., a dependent variable shaped by individuals acting to maximize their self-

interest. Like the pluralist model, their approach relies on civil society to explain the Japanese state and its policies.

In the case of Japan this basic assumption is too reductionist and ahistor-
ical. In neither prewar nor postwar Japan did Japanese civil society design
and authorize the Japanese state. Under the authoritarian Meiji state, individual Japanese were not citizens. They were subjects, or in rational choice
terms, "agents" of the only "principal" in the Meiji state, i.e., the emperor.
Women could not vote, children were educated by the state to worship the
emperor, and the state defined and punished thought crime. This was not fer-
tile ground for the presumed dynamic of institutions responding to the preferences of individuals acting as principals. It is equally difficult to explain the
postwar Constitution (which was imposed on the Japanese government by
U.S. Occupation authorities) or the postwar bureaucracy (which maintained
continuities of structure, personnel, and ideology with the prewar civilian bureaucracy) as an artifact of rational individual choices made in civil society,
especially because Ramseyer and Rosenbluth's chosen vehicle for transmit-
ting societal preferences, the LDP, did not even exist until a decade after
Japan's reconstruction effort began.

Ramseyer and Rosenbluth argue that younger, back-bench Diet members
of the LDP were served by the party's leadership, thus confirming that
institutions served the best interests of individual members. In fact, the events
of 1993 showed that this was not true, for it was predominantly younger
back-bench members who defected from the LDP and brought about its
downfall. Ramseyer and Rosenbluth also argue that the bureaucracy follows
the directions of elected politicians, but recent events show that the
bureaucracy was still able to push its fiscal stringency and consumption tax
agendas onto new parties in power, even as those parties unsuccessfully tried
to impose bureaucratic reform and consumption-oriented measures after
taking power.

The institutionalist approach of this book envisions individual and organizational actors acting to maximize their material interests within institutionalized settings that structure their choices, but the critical difference is that at
the macro level, institutions are not understood to be simply the product of
rules that individuals can readily change. Actor self-interest is a necessary element in explaining the keizai kyōryoku system, but it is not sufficient. Any
account of policymaking structures has to take account of international factors, episodes of crisis-driven change, ideological factors, and domestic institutional legacies that constrain collective and individual decisionmaking.

The Strong State

In contrast to the societally centered approach to policymaking, the strong
state approach makes the bureaucracy an independent variable in policymaking. The oversimplified view of this argument makes influence a unidirec-
tional flow from the state to other actors. In fact, both the proponents and

critics of this view agree that there is *not* a one-way flow of information and influence. Strong state proponents such as Chalmers Johnson argue that the state has preponderant influence in relations with societal actors, whereas others disagree with this proposition. Michio Muramatsu and Ellis Krauss talk of "patterned pluralism" in which regularized interaction between the LDP, the private sector, and the bureaucracy determines policy. Then there are those such as Daniel Okimoto and Richard Samuels who emphasize sym-biosis or reciprocity over state guidance in Japanese policymaking. Patterned pluralist or reciprocal consent interpretations accommodate public-private sector interdependence and mutual influence. But so can a strong state argument.

In any discussion of a strong state, it might be legitimately objected that no state bureaucracy is monolithic.[373] This is certainly true in the case of Japan.[374] But what distinguishes bureaucrats as a class of political decision-makers is that as tenured salaried government officials, they are preoccupied with issues of hierarchical authority, legally defined jurisdictions, administrative rules and routines, specialization, and technical efficiency. This gives highest priority to organizational proficiency in carrying out assigned functions.[375]

Unlike elected politicians, who weigh policy decisions according to material interest and popularity considerations, bureaucrats are oriented toward effective technical solutions. Problems become narrowly defined and adapted to a complex organizational environment where stability and continuity are valued. The implications of such a class holding an extraordinary degree of power and discretion in decisionmaking raises the question of accountability and democratic responsiveness. If there are weak or underdeveloped bureaucratic oversight mechanisms combined with a bureaucratic propensity to define national agendas, one can then speak of a strong state.

The case of keizai kyōryoku suggests that the Japanese state remains strong in this sense, but that as Japan's progrowth consensus has eroded and as the number and size of external stakeholders in ODA have increased, it has had to become more accommodationist. From the mid-1960s, when Japan gained advanced country membership in the UN and the OECD, and as it assumed a greater role in U.S. containment policy in Asia, a key policy task became how to meet Western and Third World expectations while still allowing keizai kyōryoku policy networks to determine actual policy. These external stakeholders explain the inauguration of Japan's grant aid program (to meet ODA concessionality norms) as well as Japan's nonproject assistance (commodity loans to help the anticommunist New Order regime in Indonesia) in this period. Through the 1970s the Japanese policymaking system appeased pressures from the developing countries and other advanced countries to increase the quantity and quality of its ODA. By the end of the 1970s, when Japan's ODA-doubling plans began, ODA was seen as a means of deflecting criticism of Japan's trade and defense policies.

The growing size and impact of Japan's ODA in the 1980s mobilized nongovernmental external stakeholders. In the mid-1980s the Marcos scandal spurred the domestic media to expose the corrupt and commercial character of Japan's ODA and excited taxpayer outrage. By the end of the 1980s Japanese ODA began to attract the attention of transnational nongovernmental organizations. This caused the Japanese state and private sector to make largely symbolic concessions to these new external stakeholders in the 1992 ODA Taikō.

In sum, the Japanese bureaucracy has been increasingly responsive to the demands of others. The proliferation of external stakeholders and the divergence of agendas among included actors suggests that Japan's ODA system could not be created today if it did not already exist. Therefore, some might reason, the strong state no longer exists. Nevertheless, we must also realize changes are occurring only at the margins and that the most far-reaching policy initiatives today (the New AID Plan and the linkage of ODA to security objectives) still serve the state's basic agenda of raising its international prestige and power. Moreover, institutional inertia allows bureaucratic actors to retain privileged and insulated positions in organizational hierarchies, even if they are subject to increasing demands for accountability. Although the state may have to accommodate the agendas of external stakeholders more than ever, it has not had to include them. The absolute criteria for state strength would be weak, underdeveloped bureaucratic control mechanisms and bureaucratically organized and authorized national agendas. In the case of ODA these criteria are met because despite the fact of mutual influence between the state and private sector, bureaucratic actors hold more leverage over private sector actors than the latter have over the bureaucracy.

Even though routine procedures within keizai kyōryoku structures are collaborative, the more fundamental questions are who established these structures, for what strategic purpose, and under whose authority. The system that developed was defined and authorized by the state to help raise Japan's status in the international system. The private sector may collaborate and benefit from this broad state agenda, but it did not establish it. The private sector is subordinate to and dependent on bureaucratic affiliations, licenses, and approvals to have membership in this system, and it must follow administrative guidance as an organizational norm. The fact that open defiance of bureaucratic power is very rare may not indicate harmony and equal influence so much as reflect the futility of frontally challenging the entrenched authority and wide-ranging powers of the state within this institutional setting.

This is *not* to say that the private sector is powerless. The included private sector's subtle power and influence in ODA are based on organizational inclusion and informal norms. As noted previously, the state's dependence on the private sector to provide information, personnel, and resources requires it to accommodate private sector demands. It also constrains the state's ability to monitor and control all aspects of policymaking and implementation. As a result the private sector has real influence over actual ODA policy and practice. This private sector leverage is based, however, on the occupation of inferior positions in organizational hierarchies, and thus in any important contest with bureaucratic actors over organizational norms and purposes, the private sector must defer.

In sum, the origins and institutional structure of Japan's ODA policy reflect the role of the postwar Japanese state in guiding the private sector toward national developmental goals. Without denying that bureaucracy–private sector relations are marked by reciprocities and mutual influence, it is the state bureaucracy that holds the balance of power. The private sector has been accountable to the state, but the reverse has not been the case up to 1993. This lack of accountability—not the lack of inclusion—is at the root of the private sector's criticism of the ODA system today. As for the LDP, its demise in 1993 removes it as a player, but basic policy continuity confirms that the LDP role was always of secondary importance. The situation in 1994 is indicated by Figure 10.2, which shows relations of mutual influence between included actors but the superiority of the bureaucracy in formal authority structures and informational resources. The public-private sector networks remain stable even though the LDP's loss of Diet control threatens its political brokering function in the system.

Figure 10.2 Bureaucratic Predominance in ODA (post-1993)

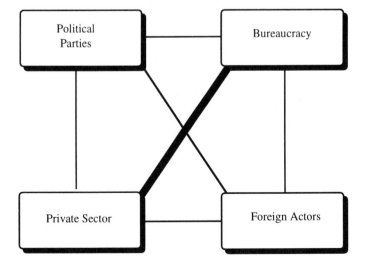

State Strength and Smarter Capitalism

Finally, the case of ODA illustrates how state strength can lead to smarter capitalism. Not all strong states have been smart or effective in achieving developmental goals. This has been amply demonstrated by Latin American authoritarianism and Eastern European communism. These cases have reinforced the firmly held belief in the United States that, as Charles Lindblom puts it, states have strong thumbs but no fingers. That is, states may be strong, but they lack the information, skills, and flexibility to match private sector decisionmakers in reacting to market signals.[376]

The experience of Japan and other East Asian states casts doubt on this proposition. A growing number of empirical studies on the political economy of these states indicate that East Asian states consciously "get prices wrong" and channel resources into areas where comparative advantage does not presently exist but may be built in order to speed the growth and structural development of their economies.[377] This literature indicates that if states are not only strong, but also anticipatory and dexterous, then intervention can speed up economic growth and structural development.

One basis for a positive state contribution to economic performance is the amelioration of market failures. Markets chronically underproduce collective goods; and in practice, information barriers and transaction costs and risks skew allocation to suboptimal ends. Japan has used ODA to compensate for these market failures. For example, Japan has used ODA to induce private sector actors to enhance collective welfare by developing more numerous and diverse overseas sources of energy, food, and raw materials. To overcome information costs that Japanese firms confront when dealing with developing countries, the Japanese government uses ODA to finance the collection, analysis, and dissemination of information about the developing economies via such agencies as JETRO and the IDE, not to mention JICA and the OECF. ODA is also used to lower transaction costs and risks for Japan's private sector by providing tailor-made infrastructure in target economies (such as the Eastern Seaboard complex in Thailand), influencing economic policy in recipient governments, and subsidizing business development activities as well as final sales and investments.

A qualitatively different and more ambitious state role in guiding economic development is the creation of comparative and competitive advantage where none existed before. According to the traditional theory of comparative advantage, what one profitably produces and trades is determined by fixed endowments of production factors. Today, however, it is often argued that the revolution in telecommunications, information processing, and transportation has made capital and technology more mobile, and the knowledge-intensive nature of advanced goods and services makes training and education more important. This means that state policies can change factor endowments to create new areas of comparative and competitive advantage. Developmental states place the highest priority on this policy agenda.

There can be little doubt that Japan's ODA is the product of a developmental state. The example of Japan's New AID Plan illustrates how the Japanese state is using ODA to move manufacturing with declining competitiveness to lower-cost production sites in Asia. This has the effect of upgrading Japan's industrial structure and reducing input costs. Japanese firms with declining competitiveness are moved to offshore locations—where their competitiveness can be retained and where they will give eager recipients comparative advantage in new areas. For recipients the infusions of Japanese capital, technology, technical training, and access to global markets provided by the New AID Plan promise a credible shortcut to export-oriented industries. These recipients know that their own comparative advantage can be changed through inflows of capital and technology from the advanced countries—and this change can be accelerated if they follow Japan's lead.

The intention of Japan to use its ODA to improve its comparative and competitive advantage may be clear enough, but how is Japan able to identify and exploit strategic opportunities? The answer is public-private sector linkages. Chalmers Johnson identifies three types of market-conforming intervention that the Japanese state has experimented with. The first is licensing the private sector to manage the achievement of public goals, but this inevitably raises questions of effectiveness. The second is direct state control of private assets, but this inevitably leads to questions of efficiency. The third type is public-private sector cooperation. This combines acceptable levels of state effectiveness and private sector efficiency, but it is the hardest to maintain. Nevertheless, it allows the state to develop both thumbs and fingers to manage its industrial and trade structures in a global context.

The case of ODA reveals a variety of intermediary institutional mechanisms organizing public-private sector cooperation and information exchange. These intermediary structures allow the state to use the ODA-related agencies and the Japanese private sector as antennae to identify trends and business opportunities. Experienced economic planners are then able to map economic activity at the global, country, and sectoral levels, and they can draw on ODA-funded agencies, business associations, and think tanks for policy recommendations. The private sector is allowed to articulate its own needs and propose new ODA schemes, and the bureaucracy chooses to support only those ideas that contribute to important state goals (e.g., the Keidanren-sponsored JAIDO). The private sector interest is to identify barriers to Japanese trade and investment, draw attention to potential market opportunities, and ensure that the state adjusts policy to actual needs and capabilities. The incorporation of private sector information and analysis through intermediary structures enables the state to be smart, as well as strong.

A good example of smart ODA is the two-step lending scheme first developed with Thailand's BAAC. It was found that a barrier to the relocation of smaller Japanese manufacturers in ASEAN was that existing ODA mechanisms and methods could neither identify local Asian joint venture partners nor finance these smaller and more numerous tie-ups. But by lending ODA funds to recipient industrial development banks, which were then tasked to finance Japanese joint ventures, potential local partners could be identified, and financing could be administered.

Finally, flexible decisionmaking ensures that policy can adjust to chang-ing circumstances. The impact of the first oil shock on the proposed Asahan project is a case in point. Japan's economic planners quickly approved the languishing Asahan proposal as a countermeasure to the heavy impact of the oil shock on the domestic aluminum industry. MITI decided to move Japanese aluminum producers overseas, and with the cooperation of MOF quickly mobilized over $2 billion in ODA and private capital to design, build, and operate the Asahan project.

JAPAN'S ODA AND THE INTERNATIONAL SYSTEM

From a broad international viewpoint Japan's ODA has supported Japan's rising economic power and competitiveness, and it has improved Japan's po-litical standing with the West and the developing world. Based in part on its ODA contributions, Japan has represented ASEAN's views at the Western economic summits since 1988, and since the 1991 Houston Summit Japan has professed to communicate China's views. Japan is now seeking a seat on the UN Security Council, and it claims a "global partnership" role with the United States. 250

But equally important for Japan is the fact that its bilateral ODA has helped to construct a strong set of independent ties to its Asian neighbors. This region has always been the geographical focus of Japanese economic cooperation policy, and here is where it is likely to have the most profound impact on Japan's role in the international system. After the Cold War the East Asian countries and areas are rapidly normalizing political and economic relations with each other. This helps to explain why East Asian dynamism will likely gain still more momentum as China and Indochina are integrated into the region, and this development cannot fail to have profound implica-tions for the rest of the world. The main political question arising out of this trend is whether the region's diverse members will discover a collective East Asian interest strong enough to institutionalize regional groupings. Here is where Japan is playing a decisive role because it has the wealth and influence to be an organizer of regional economic and political deliberations and be-cause it has compelling interests to do so. 250

In its international relations Japan faces a basic problem of balancing its interests in Asia and the West. It is an island nation close enough to fall within the cultural orbit of the Eurasian continent but distant enough to main-tain a feeling of distinctiveness and relative security. Throughout the postwar period it has deepened its economic involvement in Asia while maintaining a close relationship with the United States and the rest of the advanced West. As mentioned in Chapter 9 this basic policy line is being challenged by post–Cold War trends. When it views the West, Japan sees saturated markets and a weakening security guarantee from the United States, and when it views East Asia it sees not only the world's most attractive economic market for the foreseeable future, but also a new need to expand its involvement in Asian political and security affairs. The net effect of these trends has been to turn Japan more toward Asia.

In addressing the West, Japan portrays its ODA in isolation from its commercial activities in deference to Western sensibilities on the subject; but toward Asia, Japan has linked its ODA to its trade and investment in the three-into-one economic cooperation formula since in the mid-1980s to promise the region's members accelerated economic growth and technological advancement. As illustrated by the ODA-financed New AID Plan and the ASEAN-Japan Development Fund scheme, Japan's bilateral ODA performs in distinctive ways to advance Japan's economic and political interests in Asia. In effect, it is using ODA to help institutionalize a new set of Asian political and economic hierarchies. The following points emphasize that not only do these explicit and implicit hierarchies put Japan at the top, but they also alter the organization of the international system and create new possibilities.

First, ODA is a means of helping Japan rationalize its industrial structure and turn the rest of Asia into a subcontracting production base. By forecasting its own economy's loss of comparative advantage and matching this with the economic profiles of Asian ODA recipients, Japanese economic planners can help move Japanese firms to appropriate overseas locations where their competitiveness can be restored. As in the case of the Eastern Seaboard project in Thailand, Japanese ODA infrastructure projects can be built in anticipation of future needs to transfer industrial production through FDI. ODA-financed technical assistance under the principle of three-into-one ODA serves this same interest.

For Japan to have a policy to make the rest of Asia responsive to Japan's own industrial policy needs, a political mechanism is needed to supplement ordinary market forces. If the promise of Japanese ODA, FDI, and market access induces policy consultations with developing countries over which types of Japanese ODA, private investment, and trade are mutually satisfactory, then a mechanism is at hand. In fact, this is what the New AID Plan, first announced in 1987, has accomplished. It has organized bilateral consultations with individual recipients to decide which Japanese industries will be injected into their countries using ODA and FDI. The payoff for recipients is new comparative advantage in export-oriented industrialization. The negotiation process assigns complementary subcontracting roles to the East Asian developing economies, and the resulting reorganization of investment, production,

and trade flows enhances the region's interdependencies. In this sense a har-
monious division of labor is created in targeted sectors. But this also means
that informal consultations between Japan and recipient governments will
guide the development of production and trade flows.

This Asian division of labor concept goes back to the economic cooperation policy of the 1950s. In a 1956 foreign ministry report on economic cooperation, the godfather of Japan's economic cooperation, Okita Saburo,
wrote: "If every country would try to pursue the same pattern of industrialization there may arise wasteful use of capital resources, or undesirable contraction in foreign trade or, in some cases, excessive competition in the export
market." By the mid-1980s Okita, as a former foreign minister, was arguing
that Japan should be the leader of a "flying geese" pattern of East Asian development, providing appropriate capital, technology, and market access to
its followers to ensure complementary and orderly development. In a speech
inaugurating a new Japan Studies Center in Kuala Lumpur, he stated: "I think
that Japan's role in the region is to contribute to their economic development
by combining the three elements of trade, investment, and ODA."[378]
Summing up this kind of East Asian policy orientation, the *Wall Street
Journal* quoted a foreign ministry official who quipped: "Laissez-faire cannot
be recommended. . . . Careful utilization of market forces is always the
ideal."[379]

One consequence of such an approach is that the emerging East Asian
political economy is becoming focused on managing investment flows, and
Japan's ODA has shown itself to be effective in this task. GATT does not
outlaw this approach to regulating international economic relations—it does
not even anticipate it. Nonetheless, the economic and commercial interests of
other states wishing to gain market share in Asia could be affected. As early
as 1989 U.S. vice-president Dan Quayle was sent on a Southeast Asian tour
where he had to bring up (1) an Indonesian telecommunications project taken
away from AT&T by Japanese firms backed by ODA financing and (2) a
Thai refusal to allow a U.S. firm to start glass production in Thailand in competition with a prior investment approval given to Asahi Glass of Japan.
Although in theory the benefits of Japanese ODA should be available to all,
in practice they are tailored and most responsive to Japanese agendas.

Finally, Japanese ODA promotes the growth of regional organizations
devoted to economic cooperation. Whether it is the Asian Development
Bank, the Pacific Economic Cooperation Conference (PECC), the International Committee for the Reconstruction of Cambodia (ICORC), or the
officially sponsored Japan-ASEAN dialogue, Japanese ODA directly or indirectly finances the activities of these organizations. As these organizations
begin to define regional agendas, Japan assumes a leadership role in promoting economic development from a regional perspective. 252

At the bilateral level Japanese ODA creates considerable leverage over
recipient governments. Whether it is yen-denominated official debt due to

past ODA loans, dependence on ODA to finance ongoing projects and programs, or the desire to retain Japanese financing for future projects or financial crises, recipient governments have strong incentives to find ways of currying favor with Japan. This can be utilized in a number of ways to support Japanese agendas in regional and global regimes.

The ODA-financed effort to build a stronger economic and political foundation for Japan in Asia incorporates economic planning structures as well as a diplomatic corps in policymaking. Japan's strategic economic agenda is defined by the need to enhance Japan's international competitiveness. ODA enhances Japan's exports of capital goods and financial services to Asia and provides new offshore export platforms for Japan's declining industries. This economic agenda strengthens the MFA's diplomacy, for at the global level the MFA presents this as a contribution to collective OECD interests and the management of global issues, while at the regional level Japan's ODA consolidates Japan's political relations with Asia. Thus, Japan's bilateral ODA creates a stronger basis for regional as well as global leadership.

From the Japanese standpoint the best result would be the realization of a hierarchically organized Asian production zone. Although Japanese economic and political predominance is not intended to be hegemonic in the traditional sense, Japanese ODA will still give Japan a strategic advantage over Western liberal states in an era of geo-economic rivalry. Using its ODA networks Japan will generate more and better economic intelligence on the Asian economies. Together with its financial resources, this will help Japan guide recipient government development plans in ways that will complement Japan's own strategic needs. As a matter of course Japanese firms will reap a competitive advantage in gaining the most valuable investment and trade positions in the world's most important growth markets. And Japan's ODA will nurture regional regimes that will set regional agendas that will respond to Japanese leadership.

Japan's Prospects

Japan has much to offer the rest of East Asia. First, it can generate capital surpluses that can then be channeled by the Japanese government and corporations to meet regional needs for infrastructure, industrial technology, employment, and export revenue. Second, it can supply key technologies needed by the region for industrial upgrading. Third, affiliation with its corporate groupings gives industrializing Asian economies access to Japanese and Western markets. Fourth, the liberalization of the Japanese market and the growth of consumerism in Japan promises to absorb more Asian exports. Finally, Japan openly sympathizes with the difficulties East Asian governments experience with human rights and democratization, and though it does not condone repression, it does give priority to economic relations. Coprosperity without military or ideological predominance is what Japan promises, and this is what the region's governments want before talk of democracy and human rights. ⌡ 253-4

⌐Although most East Asian governments are cautious about Japanese leadership of any kind, they do want regional growth to continue, and they cannot shun Japanese overtures when the prospects for Western aid, trade, and investment growth are limited. The new process of deepening and widening the European Union begun in 1985, the opening of Eastern Europe and the former Soviet Union from 1989, and the U.S. decision in 1990 to widen NAFTA to include Mexico have naturally led the East Asian states to consider what can be done to make them less dependent on other regions for growth. The fact that in 1991 East Asia continued to grow rapidly even though the United States was in recession and Europe was growing only slowly proved that although the region still relied on the West, its intraregional growth was strong enough to sustain the region's overall growth momentum. Meanwhile, slow growth and the domestic ills of the West have cast doubt on the Western model of liberal politics and political economy. For these reasons Prime Minister Mahathir bin Mohammed of Malaysia has held Japan up as a model of success for Malaysia under his Look East initiative, and he has persistently called for an East Asian Economic Caucus (EAEC) to promote economic interdependence among the East Asian states since late 1990. For fear of antagonizing the United States, Canada, Australia, and New Zealand, who would be excluded from such a group, Thailand offered the idea of an ASEAN Free Trade Area (AFTA) as a partial substitute for the EAEC proposal, and the subregional AFTA proposal was approved by ASEAN in 1992. But interestingly enough, neither ASEAN nor Japan have categorically repudiated the EAEC idea. A broader Asian Pacific Economic Cooperation (APEC) forum was formed in 1989, but its diverse membership of governments in North America, Latin America, Australasia, and East Asia entails a lack of internal consensus that only highlights the advantages of a less formalized and more homogeneous East Asian grouping. An awareness of a distinct regional interest and identity is growing out of actual and proposed regional economic cooperation schemes, and this will create new possibilities for more autonomous regional structures. ⌡ 254

There are limits to what Japan and the region can consider doing at present. Continuing security dependence on the United States and trade dependence on other regions force East Asia to find "open" formulas for regional cooperation. At the same time, territorial disputes and barriers to the peaceful reunification of China and Korea hinder broad regional cooperation in diplomatic and security affairs. Meanwhile, the legacy of Japan's wartime behavior creates resistance to the idea of Japanese rearmament.

⌐ Nonetheless, we should not be surprised if Japan continues to be successful at using its ODA to organize and strengthen regional institutions, above all in Asian economic cooperation, but also extending to political and security affairs. In economic cooperation Japan is likely to achieve what it requires, namely, a large share of the benefits of Asian economic growth and stronger institutions designed to support this objective. In the areas of politics and security a declining U.S. presence is likely to give Japan and others incentives to provide substitutes for U.S. military capabilities and commitments. To some extent economic interdependence and institutionalized economic cooperation may spill over into regional cooperation in political and security areas. Japan's ODA can help facilitate this process, but multilateral regimes will never be a perfect substitute for U.S. hegemony. To the extent that Japan can convince its neighbors of its peaceful intentions—and this is a key aspect of its ODA diplomacy—military rearmament and an enhanced international security role for Japan could become feasible if or when the need arises. Actual outcomes will be heavily influenced by decisions made in Europe and North America. j 25 r

In conclusion, familiarity with Japan's ODA policy making and implementation structures reveals how a capitalist state can be both strong and smart through the organizational inclusion of the private sector. Methods feature an implicit division of labor in the project cycle, interpenetration through exchange of personnel, shingikai to manage policy consensus at peak and sectoral levels, trade associations active in both policymaking and implementation issues, and implementing agencies that reduce the cost and risk to the private sector when the latter acts in the state's developmental interest. Based on the structure of bureaucratic authority in this policy area, and stabilized by the underlying postwar coalition of conservative interests, the ODA system still integrates the private sector into a state-managed economic and political agenda. Inclusion gives the private sector informal sources of leverage and enough benefits to continue active cooperation, but it cannot match the power and authority of the bureaucracy, which continues to use the private sector as agents of the national interest.

The case of Japan's bilateral ODA also illustrates why Japan has difficulty changing its developmental orientation even after it has reached economic maturity and can afford to pursue nongrowth objectives. The system has produced marginal, incremental change toward nongrowth objectives, but Japan's postwar institutions are premised on the promotion of growth, and the institutionalized links between the state and private sector continue to structure behavior even after core actors have developed more divergent interests and agendas and external stakeholders have become more numerous and important.

Finally, the case of Japanese ODA makes certain points about Japan's rise in the international system. First, it illuminates how the Japanese state plans and implements a market-rational developmental agenda. The network of public-private collaboration, combined with official funding and other policy measures, works to reduce information costs, install suitable infrastructure and regulatory environments in targeted economies, and socialize trade and investment risk. This has helped Japan change its comparative advantage and preserve the integrity of keiretsu by relocating member firms of these corporate groupings that have failing competitiveness. In recent years it has allowed Japan to change the comparative advantage of its ODA recipients as well. The example of the New AID Plan represents the ability to project Japan's own industrial policy needs onto recipient economies, and to restructure Japan's trade and investment relations with Asia to upgrade its position in the international division of labor. By doing so the Japanese state diversifies its dependence on overseas resources and markets, improves its international competitiveness and growth prospects, and raises its position in international economic and political hierarchies.

English-Language Acronyms

ADB	Asian Development Bank
AFTA	ASEAN Free Trade Area
AJDF	ASEAN-Japan Development Fund
AID	Agency for International Development
AOTS	Association for Overseas Technical Scholarships
APEC	Asian Pacific Economic Cooperation
APIC	Association for the Promotion of International Cooperation
ASEAN	Association of South East Asian Nations
BAAC	Bank for Agriculture and Agricultural Cooperatives
BHN	basic human needs
BOB	Bureau of the Budget
BOI	Board of Investment
BOT	Bank of Thailand
CIEC	Council on International Economic Cooperation
DAC	Development Assistance Committee
DAG	Development Assistance Group
D/D	detailed (project) design
DLF	Development Loan Fund
DTEC	Department of Technical and Economic Cooperation
EAEC	East Asian Economic Caucus
ECFA	Engineering Consulting Firms Association
EPA	Economic Planning Agency
ESB	Economic Stabilization Board
ESB	Eastern Seaboard
FDI	foreign direct investment
FILP	Fiscal Investment and Loan Program
F/S	feasibility study
GATT	General Agreement on Tariffs and Trade
G-5	Group of Five
IAEA	International Atomic Energy Agency
ICORC	International Committee for the Reconstruction of Cambodia
IDA	International Development Association
IDC	International Development Center
IDE	Institute for the Developing Economies
IFC	International Finance Corporation

IMF	International Monetary Fund
JAIC	Japan-ASEAN Investment Corporation
JAIDO	Japan Industrial Development Organization
JAL	Japan Air Lines
JCCI	Japan Chamber of Commerce and Industry
JCI	Japan Consulting Institute
JDB	Japan Development Bank
JEMIS	Japan Emigration Service
JEPIC	Japan Overseas Electric Power Industry Council
JERC	Japan Economic Research Center
JETRO	Japan External Trade Recovery Organization
JICA	Japan International Cooperation Agency
JIIA	Japan Institute of International Affairs
JMEA	Japan Machinery Exporters Association
JNR	Japan National Railways
JODC	Japan Overseas Development Corporation
JOEA	Japan Overseas Enterprise Association
JSP	Japan Socialist Party
LDC	less developed country
LDP	Liberal Democratic Party
LLDC	least less developed country
LME	London Metals Exchange
MAFF	Ministry of Agriculture, Forestry, Fisheries
MCA	Management and Coordination Agency
MEd	Ministry of Education
MFA	Ministry of Foreign Affairs
MHW	Ministry of Health and Welfare
MITI	Ministry of International Trade and Industry
MMAJ	Metals and Mining Agency of Japan
MOC	Ministry of Commerce
MOF	Ministry of Finance
MOL	Ministry of Labor
MOT	Ministry of Transportation
M/P	master plan
MPT	Ministry of Posts and Telecommunications
MSAC	most seriously affected country
NEDA	National Economic and Development Authority
NEDO	New Energy Development Organization
NESDB	National Economic and Social Development Board
New AID Plan	New Asian Industrial Development Plan
NIE	Newly Industrialized Economy
NIEO	New International Economic Order
NPT	Nuclear Nonproliferation Treaty
ODA	official development assistance

OECD	Organization for Economic Cooperation and Development
OECF	Overseas Economic Cooperation Fund
OEEC	Organization for European Economic Cooperation
OISCA	Industrial Development Cooperation Association
OOF	other official flows
OTCA	Overseas Technical Cooperation Agency
PARC	Policy Affairs Research Council
PECC	Pacific Economic Cooperation Conference
PKO	peacekeeping operation
P/S	prefeasibility study
PVO	private voluntary organization
R&D	research and development
REAL	Reconsider Aid Citizen's League
SAL	structural adjustment loan
SDF	Self-Defense Forces
S/W	scope of work
TDRI	Thai Development Research Institute
TMOF	Thai Ministry of Finance
UNCTAD	UN Conference of Trade and Development
UNDP	United Nations Development Programme
UNGA	UN General Assembly
UNHCR	UN High Commissioner for Refugees
WEIS	World Economic Information Service

Notes

1. Charles P. Kindleberger, *Power and Money: The Economics of International Politics and the Politics of International Economics* (New York: Basic Books, 1970), 133.

2. Alan Rix, *Japan's Economic Aid: Policymaking and Politics* (London: Croom Helm, 1980).

3. Dennis Yasutomo, *The Manner of Giving: Strategic Aid and Japanese Foreign Policy* (Lexington, MA, 1986).

4. Robert M. Orr, Jr., *The Emergence of Japan's Foreign Aid Power* (New York: Columbia University Press, 1990).

5. Bruce Koppel and Robert M. Orr, Jr., eds., *Japan's Foreign Aid: Power and Policy in a New Era* (Boulder, CO: Westview Press, 1993); also, Shafiqul Islam, ed., *Yen for Development: Japanese Foreign Aid and the Politics of Burden-Sharing* (New York: Council on Foreign Relations, 1991).

6. William L. Brooks and Robert M. Orr, Jr., "Japan's Foreign Economic Cooperation," *Asian Survey*, 25(3) (March 1985), 339.

7. Marjory Ensign, *Doing Good or Doing Well? Japan's Foreign Aid Program* (New York: Columbia University Press, 1992).

8. *Insight: Australian Foreign Affairs and Trade Issues,* 2(13) (August 2, 1993), 16.

9. Adam Smith, *Wealth of Nations* (New York: Modern Library, 1937), 431; quoted in Albert O. Hirschman, *National Power and the Structure of Foreign Trade* (Berkeley, CA: University of California Press, 1980), 5.

10. Albert O. Hirschman, *National Power and the Structure of Foreign Trade* (Berkeley, CA: University of California Press, 1980).

11. George Liska, *The New Statecraft: Foreign Aid in American Foreign Policy* (Chicago: University of Chicago Press, 1960).

12. As defined in 1969 by the Development Assistance Committee (DAC) in *Recommendation on Financial Terms and Conditions,* ODA refers to "those flows to developing countries and multilateral institutions provided by official agencies" that are: (a) "administered with the promotion of the economic development and welfare of developing countries as its main objective," and (b) "concessional in character and contain a grant element of at least 25 percent." See Rutherford M. Poats, *Twenty-five Years of Development Cooperation: A Review* (Paris: OECD, 1986), 171. The "developing countries," or LDCs (less developed countries), are all countries and areas in Africa excepting South Africa; in America except Canada and the United States; in Asia except Japan; in Oceania except Australia and New Zealand; and the following countries in Europe: Cyprus, Gibraltar, Greece, Malta, Portugal, Turkey, and Yugoslavia.

13. Klaus Knorr, *Power of Nations* (New York: Basic Books, 1975), 166–206.

14. Charles Wolf, Jr., *Foreign Aid: Theory and Practice in Southern Asia* (Princeton, NJ: Princeton University Press, 1960), 284.

15. Edward S. Mason, "U.S. Interests in Foreign Economic Assistance," in Gustav Ranis, ed., *The United States and the Developing Economies* (New York: W.W. Norton & Co., 1964), 14–15.

16. Ranald S. May, Dieter Schumacher, and Mohammed H. Malek, *Overseas*

261

Aid: The Impact on Britain and Germany (New York: Harvester Wheatsheaf, 1989), 5.

17. Hans J. Morgenthau, "Preface to a Political Theory of Foreign Aid," in Robert A. Goldwin, ed., *Why Foreign Aid?* (Chicago: Rand McNally, 1963), 74.

18. P. T. Bauer, *Equality, the Third World, and Economic Delusion* (Cambridge, MA: Harvard University Press, 1981), 86.

19. Edward C. Banfield, "American Foreign Aid Doctrines," in Robert A. Goldwin, ed., *Why Foreign Aid?* (Chicago: Rand McNally, 1962), 10–31.

20. David Wall, *The Charity of Nations* (New York: Basic Books, 1973), 58.

21. Paul Mosely, *Foreign Aid: Its Defense and Reform* (Lexington, KY: University Press of Kentucky, 1987), 234.

22. Robert Cassen & Associates, *Does Aid Work? Report of an Intergovernmental Task Force* (Oxford: Clarendon Press, 1986).

23. Edward S. Mason, *Foreign Aid and Foreign Policy* (New York: Council on Foreign Relations, 1964).

24. Max Millikan and W. W. Rostow, "A Proposal: Key to an Effective Foreign Policy," in U.S. Senate, Special Committee to Study the Foreign Aid Program, *Compilation of Studies and Surveys* (Washington, D.C.: GPO, 1957).

25. P. N. Rosenstein-Rodan, "International Aid for Underdeveloped Countries," in J. Bhagwati and R. S. Eckhaus, eds., *Foreign Aid* (London: Penguin, 1970).

26. B.E. Bond-Harrel, *Imposing Aid: Emergency Assistance to Refugees* (Oxford: Oxford University Press, 1986); Anders Wojkman and Lloyd Timberlake, *Natural Disasters: Acts of God or Acts of Man?* (London: Earthscan, 1984).

27. Harry S Truman, Inaugural Address, 1949.

28. P. T. Bauer, op. cit.

29. *North-South: A Programme for Survival, the Report of the Independent Commission on International Development Issues* (Cambridge, MA: MIT Press, 1980).

30. *Report from the Select Committee on Overseas Aid*, House of Commons, Session 1970–71 (London: Her Majesty's Stationery Office, March 1971), paragraphs 10 and 11; cited in David Wall, op. cit., 47.

31. Hans J. Morgenthau, "A Political Theory of Foreign Aid," *The American Political Science Review*, 56 (1962), 301–309; Edward C. Banfield, op. cit.

32. George Liska, op. cit., 6.

33. Milton Friedman, "Foreign Economic Aid: Means and Objectives," in Gustav Ranis, ed., op. cit., 24–38.

34. P. T. Bauer, op. cit., 100.

35. Charles P. Kindleberger, op. cit., 146.

36. Melvyn Krauss, *Development Without Aid: Growth, Poverty and Government* (New York: McGraw-Hill, 1981).

37. Goran Ohlin, *Foreign Aid Policies Reconsidered* (Paris: Development Centre, OECD, 1966), 25.

38. John D. Montgomery, *The Politics of Foreign Aid* (New York: Praeger, 1962), 209–210.

39. John Dower, *Empire and Aftermath: Yoshida Shigeru and the Japanese Experience, 1878–1954* (Cambridge, MA: Harvard University Press, 1979).

40. E. Herbert Norman, *Japan's Emergence As a Modern State: Political and Economic Problems of the Meiji Period* (New York: International Secretariat, Institute of Pacific Relations, 1940), 197.

41. Yoshida Shigeru, *Kaisō jūnen*, vol. 1 (Tokyo: Shichōsha, 1957), quoted in Kosaka Masataka, *A History of Postwar Japan* (Tokyo: Kodansha, 1982), 106–107.

42. John M. Maki, "The Role of the Bureaucracy in Japan," *Pacific Affairs*, 20 (December 1947), 393.

43. Chalmers Johnson, *MITI and the Japanese Miracle* (Stanford, CA: Stanford University Press, 1982), 44.

44. Okita Saburō, ed., *Postwar Reconstruction of the Japanese Economy* (Tokyo: University of Tokyo Press, 1992).

45. Gaimushō Chōsakyoku, *Nihon keizai saiken no kihon mondai* [Fundamental issues in reconstructing Japan's economy], (Tokyo: Gaimushō, March 1946). See also Okita Saburo, *Nihon no keizai seisaku* [Economic policy in Japan] (Tokyo: Yūki Shōbō, 1961), 13–25.

46. Okita Saburō, *Japan's Challenging Years: Reflections on My Lifetime* (Canberra: Australian National University, Australia-Japan Research Centre, 1983), 34.

47. Quoted in Iida Tsuneo, et al., *Gendai nihon keizai-shi: sengō sanjūnen no ayumi* [The economic history of contemporary Japan], Vol. 1 (Tokyo: Chikuma Shobo, 1976), 114–115.

48. Ibid., 116.

49. For an account of this process inside MITI, see Chalmers Johnson, *MITI and the Japanese Miracle* (Stanford, CA: Stanford University Press, 1982).

50. Eleanor Hadley, *Antitrust in Japan* (Princeton, NJ: Princeton University Press, 1970).

51. Iida Tsuneo, et al., op. cit., 77–82.

52. Chalmers Johnson, *MITI,* op. cit., 206.

53. Ibid., 225.

54. Kajima Heiwa Kenkyūjo, *Taigai keizai kyōryoku taikei* [A History of Overseas Cooperation] Vol. 5 (Tokyo: Kajima Heiwa Kenkyūjo, 1975), 31.

55. Hasegawa Sukehiro, *Japanese Foreign Aid: Policy and Practice* (New York: Praeger, 1975), 38.

56. Tsūsho Sangyō Gyōsei Kenkyūkai, *Tsūshō sangyō (II) Gendai gyōsei zenshū, 15* [Commerce and Industry, vol. II, Survey of Contemporary Administration, no. 15] (Tokyo: Gyōsei, 1983), 107.

57. Uchino Tatsuro, *Japan's Postwar Economy: An Insider's View of Its History and Its Future* (Tokyo: Kodansha, 1983), 68–79.

58. Chalmers Johnson, *MITI,* op. cit., 230.

59. Okita Saburō, *The Rehabilitation of Japan's Economy and Asia* (Tokyo: Ministry of Foreign Affairs, 1956).

60. Okita Saburō and Hara Kakuten, *Ajia Keizai to Nihon* [The Asian Economies and Japan] (Tokyo: Iwanami Shoten, 1952).

61. Ajia Kyōkai, *Ajia kyōkai—sono mokuteki to jigyō* [The Asia Association: aims and tasks] (Tokyo: March 1959).

62. For the text see ibid.

63. Lawrence A. Olson, *Japan in Postwar Asia* (London: Pall Mall Press, 1970), 38.

64. Hasegawa Sukehiro, op. cit., 49.

65. Ushiba Nobusuke and Hara Yasushi, *Nihon keizai gaikō no keifu* [The pedigree of Japan's economic diplomacy] (Tokyo: Asahi Shimbusha, 1979), 252.

66. Kajima Heiwa Kenkyūjo, op. cit., 8–9.

67. The personnel of Chōsen Dengyō had regrouped after returning to Japan to form the engineering consulting firm Nihon Kōei, now the largest such firm in Japan.

68. Ushiba and Hara, op. cit., 252–254.

69. Arisawa Hirōmi, ed., *Shōwa keizai-shi* [A history of the Showa economy] (Tokyo: Nihon Keizai Shimbusha, 1976), 357.

70. Ibid., 359–360.

71. Ibid., 358.

72. Ibid., 359.

73. Baishō Mondai Kenkyūjo, *Nihon no Baishō* [Japan's war reparations] (Tokyo: Sekai Janaru, 1963), 87–105.

74. Ajia Kyōkai, "Japan's War Reparations—Achievements and Problems," *Asian Affairs,* 4: 99–111.

75. Shinohara Myōhei, *Kōdō seichō no himitsu* [The secret of high-speed growth] (Tokyo: Nihon Keizai Shimbunsha, 1961), 20.

76. For an explanation of this rationale, see Myohei Shinohara, "Patterns and Change in Postwar Growth," in Lawrence Klein and Kazushi Ohkawa, eds., *Economic Growth: The Japanese Experience Since the Meiji Era* (Homewood, IL: Richard D. Irwin, Inc., 1968), 278–301.

77. Quoted in Uchino Tatsuro, op. cit., 83.

78. Okita Saburo, "Asian Prosperity and Japanese Economy," *Asian Affairs* 4(2) (March 1960), 9.

79. Quoted in Lawrence A. Olson, op. cit., 33.

80. Gaimushō, *Waga gaikō no kinkyō* (Tokyo: Gaimushō, September 1957), 7.

81. Yamamoto Mitsuru, *Nihon no keizai gaikō: sono kiseki to tenkaiten* [Japan's economic diplomacy: its development and turning points] Tokyo: Nihon Keizai Shimbunsha, 1973), 90.

82. Matsuo Taiichiro, "Structural Analysis of Japan's Trade with Southeast Asia," *Asian Affairs,* 3(1) (March 1958), 26–27.

83. Ibid., 35–36.

84. Ministry of International Trade and Industry (MITI), *Foreign Trade of Japan 1958* (Tokyo: JETRO, 1958), 21.

85. Ibid., 34.

86. MITI, *Keizai kyōryoku no genjō to mondaiten, . . . 1958* [The present status and issues in economic cooperation, 1958] (Tokyo: Tsūshō sangyōshō, 1958), 8.

87. Ibid., 8–11.

88. Ibid., 23–24.

89. Quoted in Lawrence A. Olsen, op. cit., 41.

90. This facilitated the resettlement of Japanese colonists displaced from Manchuria and Korea in remoter areas of Paraguay, an issue placed within the scope of Japan's economic cooperation.

91. Kajima Heiwa Kenkyūjo, op. cit., 41.

92. Ibid., 40.

93. Rinji Gyōsei Chosakai, *Kyokan kyōsō no kaikaku ni kan suru iken* [On the reform of interministerial competition] (Tokyo: Prime Minister's Office, September 1964).

94. The name was changed to Pertamina under Suharto.

95. Sakurai Masao, *Waga kuni no keizai kyōryoku* [Our economic cooperation] (Tokyo: Ajia Keizai Kenkyūjo, 1972), 2–9.

96. Shishido Toshio, *Tōnan Ajia enjō o kangaeru* [On aid to Southeast Asia] (Tokyo: Tōyō Keizai Shimpōsha, 1973), 6.

97. Max Millikan and W. W. Rostow, "A Proposal: Key to an Effective Foreign Policy," in *Foreign Aid Program, Compilation of Studies and Surveys,* U.S. Senate, Special Committee to Study the Foreign Aid Program (Washington, D.C.: GPO, 1957).

98. *Twenty-five years of development co-operation: a review: efforts and policies of the members of the Development Assistance Committee* / report by Rutherford M. Poats (Paris: Organisation for Economic Co-operation and Development, 1985).

99. Yamamoto Mitsuru, *Nihon no keizai gaikō* [Japan's economic diplomacy] (Tokyo: Nihon Keizai Shimbunsha, 1973), 353.

100. Ibid., 148.

101. John White, *Japanese Aid* (London: Overseas Development Institute, 1964).

102. Leon Hollerman, *Japan's Dependence on the World Economy: The Approach Toward Economic Liberalization* (Princeton, NJ: Princeton University Press, 1967).

103. Martha F. Loutfi, *The Net Cost of Japanese Foreign Aid* (New York: Praeger, 1973).

104. Hasegawa Sukehiro, op. cit., 13.

105. Lawrence A. Olson, op. cit.; John K. Emmerson, *Arms, Yen & Power: The Japanese Dilemma* (New York: Dunellen, 1971).

106. Nagasu Kazuji, *Nanshin suru Nihon shihon shugi* [Japanese capitalism advancing south] (Tokyo: Mainichi shimbunsha, 1971), 356–357.

107 Onishi Akira, *Teikaihatsukoku to Nihon* [The less developed countries and Japan] (Tokyo: Nihon kanzei kyōkai, 1969); Kawata Tadashi, *'Sho-nihonshugi' no susume* (Tokyo: Daiyamondo-sha, 1972).

108. Kawata Tadashi, op. cit., 76.

109. Taigai Keizai Kyōryoku Shingikai, *Taigai keizai kyōryoku shingikai kankei sankō shiryo-shu* [Reference materials pertaining to the Overseas Economic Cooperation Deliberation Council] (Tokyo: Naikaku Sōridaijin Kanbō Shingishitsu, May 1976), 4–5.

110. Sakurai Masao, *Waga kuni no keizai kyōryoku* [Our economic cooperation] (Tokyo: Ajia Keizai Kenkyūjo, 1972), 173–174.

111. Taigai Keizai Kyōryoku Shingikai, op. cit., 13.

112. Ibid., 123–124.

113. Sakurai Masao, op. cit., 161–162.

114. Ibid., 126–127.

115. Ibid., 180–183.

116. Sangyo Kōzō Shingikai, Kokusai Keizai Bukai, *Nihon no taigai keizai seisaku* [Japan's overseas economic policy] (Tokyo: Daiyamondōsha, 1972).

117. Ibid., 29.

118. Ibid.

119. Nagasu Kazuji, op. cit., 353.

120. Ibid., 355–356.

121. Shishido Toshio, op. cit.

122. Sankei Shimbun Ajia Shuzaihan, *Rinjin-tachi no sugao—baishō to enjō no tanima de* [The shape of our neighbors—in the valley between reparations and aid] (Tokyo: Sankei Shimbunsha, 1971), 229.

123. Yamamoto Mitsuru, op. cit., 191.

124. Ibid., 193.

125. Mikanagi Kiyohisa, former MFA Economic Cooperation Bureau Director-General, interview with author, June 16, 1988.

126. Alan Rix, op. cit., 49–80.

127. Taigai Keizai Kyōryoku Shingikai, *Kongō no kaihatsu kyōryoku no suishin ni tsuite (chūkan tōshin)* [On the further promotion of development cooperation (interim report)] (Tokyo: Sōrifu, August 18, 1975), 9.

128. Ibid., 210.

129. Yamashita Shōichi, "Ohgata enjo purojekuto no keizai hakyū kōka—Asahan purojekuto o hitotsu no jirei to shite" [The economic impact of large-scale aid projects—the case of the Asahan project], *Nenpō Keizaigaku* (March 1986).

130. Matsui Ken, *Keizai kyōryoku—towareru Nihon no keizai gaikō* [Economic cooperation—Japan's dubious economic diplomacy] (Tokyo: Yuhikaku, 1983), 86.

131. *Asahi Shimbun,* August 4, 1988, 9.

132. Asahi Shimbun 'Enjo' Shuzaihan, *Enjo Tojōkoku Nippon* [Japan the developing country in aid] (Tokyo: Asahi Shimbunsha, 1985), 85.

133. Sangyō Kozō Shingikai Kagaku Kōgyo Bukai, *Kongō no Kagaku Hiryō Kōgyo no Susumubeki Hōkō Oyobi Sono Shisaku no Arikata* [The desired direction for the further promotion of the chemical fertilizer industry and those policy measures] (Tokyo: MITI, May 1978), quoted in Asahi Shimbun 'Enjo' Shuzaihan,1985, op. cit.

134. The other projects in this class include: the Japan-Singapore petrochemical complex (joint venture contract signed in 1977 worth ¥117.4 billion); the Amazon aluminum project (1978; $2.57 billion); the Brazil paper pulp project (1973; $398 million); the Saudi Arabia petrochemical complex (1981; ¥278 billion); the incomplete Iran-Japan petrochemical complex (1974; ¥730 billion); the Usiminas Brazilian iron and steel project (1958–1986; ¥157 billion). See MITI, *Keizai kyōryoku no genjō-to mondaiten,* 1986 [The present status and issues in economic cooperation, 1986] (Tokyo: Tsūshō sangyō shō, 1986), 401–412.

135. *1986 MITI Yearbook,* op. cit. 401–402.

136. Briefing by Japanese and Indonesian on-site Inalum project directors, November 25, 1987.

137. Nihon Keizai Shimbunsha, Keizai Kaisetsu-bu, *Baishō no hanashi* [The story of reparations] (Tokyo: Nihon Keizai Shimbunsha, 1957), 51.

138. Nihon Kōei Kabushiki Kaisha. *Nihon Kōei 35-nen shi* [The 35-year history of Nihon Kōei] (Tokyo: Daiyamondo-sha, 1981), 176.

139. Jūkagaku Kōgyō Tsūshin-sha, *Nihon no kaigai shigen kaihatsu* [Japan's overseas natural resource development] (Tokyo: Jūkagaku Kōgyō Tsūshin-sha, 1976), 199.

140. Ibid.

141. Nobutoshi Akao, "Introduction," in Akao, ed., *Japan's Economic Security* (New York: St. Martin's Press, 1983), 38.

142. Others started just after the first oil shock were located in the United States, Brazil, New Zealand, and Venezuela.

143. MITI, *Keizai kyōroyoku no genjō to mondaiten, 1979* [The present status and issues in economic cooperation, 1979] (Tokyo: Tsūshō sangyō shō, 1979), 183.

144. MITI, *Keizai kyōroyoku no genjō to mondaiten, 1958* [The present status and issues in economic cooperation, 1981] (Tokyo: Tsūshō sangyō shō, 1981), 61.

145. Samejima Shinsuke, *Nihon no taigai enjo seisaku: shanai hokoku 192* [Japan's overseas aid policy: internal report 192]. (Tokyo: Asahi Shimbunsha Chōsa Kenkyushitsu, 1982), 97.

146. Ibid.

147. These allegations were made by knowledgeable Indonesian officials interviewed by the author.

148. "Japan to Invest Extra ¥24 bn in Indonesia Plant," *Financial Times,* February 27, 1987.

149. "Nihon e no shukka chūshi" [Shipments to Japan interrupted], *Yomiuri Shimbun,* August 17, 1988.

150. "Kongo no tai'o kuro" [Difficult way ahead], *Nihon Keizai Shimbun,* August 21, 1988.

151. Kokusai Kaihatsu Sentaa, *Makuro keizai enjo koka hyoka ni tsuite no chosa* [Evaluation of macroeconomic impact of aid] (March 1984), 5.

152. Ajia Keizai Kenkyūjo, *ASEAN shokoku no keizai kaihatsu keikaku to waga kuni keizai kyōryoku no arikata* [Economic development planning in the ASEAN countries and how our nation's economic cooperation should be] (March 1986), 145.

153. Suthy Prasartset and Kongsak Sonteperkswong, "Structural Forces Behind Japan's Economic Expansion and the Case of Japanese-Thai Economic Relations," in Pasuk Phongpaichit, et al., eds., *The Lion and the Mouse? Japan, Asia, and Thailand:*

Proceedings of an International Conference on Thai-Japan Relations (Bangkok: Chulalongkorn University, 1986), 189–192.

154. A team research survey published by Khien Theeravit, "Japan in Thai Perspective," cited in Likhit Dhiravegin, "Thai-Japanese Postwar Relations," *Thai Japanese Studies, Special Issue* (March 1984), 20–21.

155. Likhit Dhiravegin, "Thai-Japanese Postwar Relations," *Thai Japanese Studies, Special Issue* (March 1984), 21–23.

156. H. Shigeta, "Economic Relations Between Japan and Thailand," in Likhit Dhiravegin, op. cit., 41–42.

157. Ichiro Komatsu, "Comments on Paper VI," in Pasuk Phongpaichit, et al., eds., op. cit., 346–347.

158. Khien Theeravit, *Research Report on Danish, German and Japanese Assistance to Agricultural Development in Thailand: A Comparative Study* (Bangkok: Chulalongkorn University, Institute of Asian Studies, 1984), 58.

159. Viroj Arunprapan, "White Paper from Thai Construction Industry Association to NESDB," published in *Ruan Prachachart,* December 6, 1985. Cited in Pasuk Phongpaichit, et al., eds., op. cit., 194.

160. Pasuk Phongpaichit, et al., eds., op. cit., 196.

161. Surichai Wanchao and Associates, *Japanese Aid to Thailand: Implementation and Development Impacts* (Bangkok: Asian Studies Institute, Chulalongkorn University, May 31, 1987), vi–vii.

162. Suthy Prasartset and Kongsak Sonteperkswong, op. cit., 191.

163. Montri Chenvidyakarn, in Pasuk Phongpaichit, et al., eds., op. cit., 354.

164. Khien Theeravit, "Comments on Paper III," in Pasuk Phongpaichit, et al., eds., op. cit., 210–214.

165. Bank of Thailand, *Quarterly Bulletin,* 27(1) (March 1987), 48–49.

166. William Dawkins, U.S. commercial attaché, Bangkok, interview with author, November 19, 1987.

167. Itoga Shigeru, "Infurasutorakuchâ" [Infrastructure], in Suzuki Nagatoshi, ed., *Nihon no keizai kyōryoku* [Japan's economic cooperation] (Tokyo: 1989), 83–96.

168. Prasert Chittiwatanapong, *Japanese Official Development Assistance to Thailand: Impact on Thai Construction Industry* (unpublished, undated mimeo), 46.

169. Ajia Keizai Kenkyūjo, *ASEAN shokoku no keizai kaihatsu keikaku to waga kuni keizai kyōryoku no arikata* [Economic development planning in the ASEAN countries and how our nation's economic cooperation should be] (Tokyo: Ajia Keizai Kenkyūjo, March 1986), 145.

170. Ibid., 145.

171. "A Time to Build on Friendship," *Bangkok Post,* September 25, 1987.

172. "Whither the Thai-Japanese Unequal Relationship?" *The Nation,* 2 (November 1987).

173. Pasuk Phongpaichit, et al., eds., op. cit., 192–193.

174. BAAC, *Summary of Reports on the Study of the Impact of OECF Subloans in BAAC Clients (From Ist to Vth Survey),* Bangkok, May 26, 1987, Tables 2 and 4.

175. JETRO Bangkok Office, *Current Trend of Japanese Investment in Thailand and Its Prospect* (Bangkok: JETRO, August 1987), 2.

176. The World Bank, "Thailand: Managing Public Resources for Structural Adjustment," *World Bank Country Study Report* (June 1984), xxxi.

177. Ibid., xxii.

178. Pasuk Phongpaichit, et al., eds., op. cit., 192.

179. Interview with NESDB official, November 17, 1987.

180. JETRO, *Current Trend,* 11.

181. Ajia Keizai Kenkyūjo (March 1986), op. cit.

182. Ibid., 345.

183. Prasert Chittiwatanapong, "Japan's Role in the Asia-Pacific Region: Political Dimension," paper delivered at the Japan Institute of International Affairs conference, The Pacific Century: Problems and Prospects, Tokyo, March 3–4, 1988, 20.

184. William L. Brooks and Robert M. Orr, Jr., "Japan's Foreign Economic Cooperation, *Asian Survey,* 25(3) (March 1985), 339.

185. Shafiqul Islam, "Beyond Burden-Sharing: Economics and Politics of Japanese Foreign Aid," in Shafiqul Islam, ed., *Yen for Development: Japanese Foreign Aid and the Politics of Burden-Sharing* (New York: Council on Foreign Relations Press, 1991), 210.

186. DAC, OECD, *Report by the Secretariat and Questions on the Development Assistance Efforts and Policies of Japan* (restricted to participants) (Paris: DAC, December 22, 1986).

187. Ibid., 2–5.

188. Michael Hofmann, *Japan's Development Assistance: A German View* (Tokyo: Institute of Developing Economies, January 1985), i.

189. Krisda Piampongsant, *The Politicization and Commercialization of Foreign Aid: Do People Benefit?* paper presented at the first conference organized by the Research Assistance Program for ASEAN Scholars in International Affairs (RAPAS), The Japan Institute of International Affairs, Tokyo, March 1987, 18–19.

190. NEDA, Cover Memorandum, *Japan's Official Development Assistance to the Philippines,* dated August 10, 1988 (mimeo), 2.

191. Sankei Shimbun Ajia Shuzaihan, op. cit.; Yamamoto Mitsuru, op. cit.

192. Yamamoto Mitsuru, op. cit., 102.

193. Asahi Shimbun 'Enjo' Shuzaihan, *Enjo tojōkoku Nippon* [Japan: the developing country in aid] (Tokyo: Asahi Shimbunsha, 1985). See also the special confidential Asahi Shimbun "Enjo' Shuzaihan study that was a precursor to that volume: *Samejima Shinsuke, Nihon no taigai enjo seisaku: shanai hokoku 192* [Japan's overseas aid policy: internal report 192] (Tokyo: Asahi shimbunsha chosa kenkyushitsu, 1982).

194. *Report of the Commission of Inquiry into Aspects of the Timber Industry in Papua New Guinea* [The Barnett Report] (Hobart, Australia: The Asia-Pacific Action Group, November 1990).

195. See *Ampo,* 15(3–4) (1983).

196. "Marukosu Giwaku: Japanese Firms Lead; Economic Aid for Whom?" *Asahi Shimbun,* May 7, 1986, 22.

197. "Marukosu Giwaku: Pandora's Box Won't Open? 'Cannot Make Public'; 'Under Investigation,'" *Asahi Shimbun,* May 4, 1986, 22.

198. "Changes in Japan ODA Policies Seen," *Business Day* (Manila), July 21, 1986, 3.

199. Diet record quoted in Doi Takako, Murai Yoshinori, and Yoshimura Keiichi, *ODA Kaikaku* [literal translation: ODA Reform; English title: For Whose Benefit?] (Tokyo: Shakai Shisōsha, 1990), 21.

200. Mainichi Shimbun, Shakaibu, ODA Shuzaihan, *Kokusai enjo bijinesu— ODA was doo tsukawarete iru ka* [The international aid business—how is ODA being used?] (Tokyo: Yaki Shōbo, 1990).

201. "Japan Group Raising Funds for Negros," *Business Day* (Manila), July 29, 1986, 3.

202. Nishikawa Jun, ed., *Enjo to jiritsu—Negurosu shima no keiken kara* [International cooperation and self-reliance: experience of Negros Island] (Tokyo: Dōbunkan, 1991).

203. Kitazawa Yōko, ed., *Hitobito wa kokkyo wo koete mirai wo tsukuru—ODA*

Ajia taiheiyō to Nihon [People crossing borders and building the future—ODA, the Asia Pacific, and Japan], Proceedings of the Kanagawa International Symposium: People's Plan 21st Century (Tokyo: Daisan Shōbō, 1991).

204. This author attended the first meetings of REAL. When he asked why information disclosure and policy change could not be accomplished through normal judicial or legislative procedure as might be done in the United States, the response was incredulity at the naiveté of the question.

205. Murai Yoshinori, et al., *Musekinin enjo ODA taikoku Nippon* (Japan: the irresponsible ODA superpower) (Tokyo: JICC Shuppankyoku, 1989).

206. Doi Takako, Murai Yoshinori, and Yoshimura Keiichi, op. cit.

207. Murai Yoshinori, ed., *Kensho: Nippon no ODA* (Testimony: Japan's ODA) (Tokyo: Gakuyō Shōbō, 1992).

208. *Asahi Shimbun,* September 11, 1989.

209. Sumi Kazuo, ed., *Noo moa ODA baramaki enjo* [No more wasted ODA] (Tokyo: JICC Shuppankyoku, 1992), 79.

210. Ibid.

211. Sōmucho, *Keizai kyōryoku (seifu kaihatsu enjo) ni kan-suru gyōsei kansatsu (dai-ichi ji) kekka ni motozuku kankoku* [Administrative inspection of economic cooperation (ODA) first report of results] (Tokyo: Sōmucho, July 1988).

212. Nishimura Masaki, "Seifu kaihatsu enjo (ODA) no genjo to kadai ni tsuite," *Kikan Gyōsei Kanri Kenkyū,* No. 44 (December 1988), 47–60.

213. Sōmucho, Gyōsei Kansatsu Kyoku, *Gyōsei kansatsu nenpō, FY1989* [Annual record of administrative inspections, FY 1989] (Tokyo: Gyōsei Kanri Kenkyû Sentaa, 1993), 419–420. For official responses to the 1987 report on grant aid, see the FY 1988 *nenpō,* 555–589.

214. *Asahi Shimbun,* December 4, 1992, 1.

215. Keizai Dōyūkai, *Kokusai kyōryoku no arata na tenkai o motomete* [Toward a new direction in international cooperation] (Tokyo: Keizai Doyûkai, June 19, 1987).

216. Rinji Gyōsei Kaikaku Chōsakai, *Kyokan kyōgō jimu no kaikaku in kan suru iken* [Opinion relating to reform of interministerial competition in official activities] (Tokyo: Prime Minister's Office, September 1964).

217. Dai-niji Rinji Gyōsei Kaikaku Chosakai, *Gyōsei kaikaku ni kan-suru daisanji tōshin—kihon tōshin* [Third report on administrative reform] (Tokyo: Prime Minister's Office, July 30, 1982).

218. Rinji Gyōsei Kaikaku Suishin Shingikai, *Kokusaika tai'o—Kokumin seikatsu jyûshi no gyōsei kaikaku ni kan-suru dai-ichiji tōshin* [Responding to internationalization—the first report on administrative reform valuing the people's life] (Tokyo: Prime Minister's Office, July 4, 1991).

219. *KKC Brief, No. 43: A Blueprint for Upgrading Foreign Aid* (Tokyo: Keizai Kōhō Center, August 1987).

220. "Resolution of the 51st General Meeting—Our Resolve to Create a New Corporate Concept: Acting in Step with Communities," *Keidanren Review,* No. 123 (June 1990), 2–3.

221. Keidanren, *Waga-kuni no enjo rinen to kongō no seifu kaihatsu enjo no arikata ni tsuite* [Japan's ODA: its philosophy and future development] (Tokyo: Keidanren, June 26, 1990).

222. DAC, *Aid Review 1990/1991: Report by the Secretariat and Questions for the Review of Japan* (Paris: OECD, 1991), 7.

223. Keidanren, *Kokusai koken no tame no kongō no keizai kyōryoku no arikata—Seifu kaihatsu enjo taikō no sakutei in mukete* [Economic cooperation for international contributions—toward the drafting of an ODA program outline] (Tokyo: Keidanren, March 24, 1992), 4.

224. Taigai Keizai Kyōryoku Shingikai, *Waga kuni taigai keizai kyōryoku no*

suishin ni tsuite [On the promotion of our overseas economic cooperation], (Tokyo: Prime Minister's Office, May 8, 1992).

225. Kawakami Takaro, "21 seiki ni muketa Nihon no enjo seisaku" [Japanese aid policy toward the 21st century], *Gaikō Forum* (March 1993), 4–15.

226. "Nihon no enjo taisei wa jûbun ka" [Is Japan's aid system adequate?], *Nihon Keizai Shimbun*, June 17, 1993, 2.

227. Charlotte Elton, "New Dimensions of Japanese Policy: A Latin American View of Japanese Presence," in Tsuneo Akaha and Frank Langdon, eds., *Japan in the Posthegemonic World* (Boulder, CO: Lynne Rienner, 1993), 240.

228. *JETRO Sensaa,* July 1988, 62–63.

229. "Recent Trends in International Monetary and Trade Issues and Japanese Responses Thereto," *Business Japan—Special Issue,* December 1, 1987, 15.

230. "IDJ Interview: Ajia no kōgyōka seisaku ni sofuto-men shutai de kyōryoku" [Cooperation in soft areas of Asia's industrialization policies], *Kaihatsu Janaru,* 368 (July 1987), 30–31.

231. Ibid., 32.

232. Kokusai Kaihatsu Sentaa, *Makuro keizai enjo kōka hyōka ni tsuite no chōsa* (March 1984), 146–150.

233. Suehiro Akira, "Kōgyo hatten" [Development of manufacturing], in Suzuki Nagatoshi, ed., *Nihon no keizai kyōryoku* [Japan's economic cooperation] (Tokyo: Ajia Keizai Kenkyūjo, 1989), 70.

234. *Kaihatsu Janaru* (July 1987), op. cit., 32.

235. Ibid.

236. MITI, *Keizai kyōryoku no genjo to mondaiten,* 1986 [The Present Status and Issues in Economic Cooperation, 1986] (Tokyo: Tsūshō sangyōshō, 1986), 183.

237. *Mitsubishi Bank Review,* 19(7) (July 1988), 1, 108.

238. "Kankei kinmitsuka suru Nihon to ASEAN" [Increasingly intimate relations between Japan and ASEAN] *JETRO Sensaa (* July 1987), 83.

239. Medhi Krongkaew, "ASEAN Economic Cooperation After the Manila Summit: A New Breakthrough?" paper delivered at the Pacific Century Conference, Tokyo, March 3–4, 1988, 34.

240. Mutiah Alagappa, "Japan's Political Role in the Region," paper delivered at the Pacific Century Conference, Tokyo, March 3–4, 1988, 34–35.

241. Taigai Keizai Kyōryoku Shingikai, *Waga kuni keizai kyōryoku no suishin ni tsuite* [On the promotion of our nation's economic cooperation] (Tokyo: Office of the Prime Minister, May 15, 1987).

242. The institutions represented in the group's senior membership were: Tokyo Electric Power Corp. (board director); Tokyo University (professor emeritus); Japan Development Bank (vice-president); Keizai Dōyūkai (senior director); Industrial Bank of Japan (vice-chair of the board); Japan Steel Corp. (vice-chair); Hitachi Ltd. (board director); Bank of Tokyo (senior director); Japan Life Insurance Co. (vice-president); Keidanren (senior director); IDC (director); Overseas Consulting Enterprises Association of Japan (senior director). *Kaihatsu Janaru* (September 1987), 18.

243. *Kaihatsu Janaru* (April 1988), 92.

244. Ibid., 90.

245. Keidanren, *Keizai kyōryoku bunya ni okeru waga kuni no koken* [Our nation's contributions in the area of economic cooperation] (Tokyo: Keidanren, May 19, 1987). Similar points were echoed by the Keidanren in KKC Brief No. 43, "A Blueprint for Upgrading Foreign Aid" (Tokyo: Keizai Koho Center, August 1987).

246. "Kore kara no keizai kyōryoku" [Future economic cooperation], *Tsūsan Janaru* (May 1988), 17.

247. "Tojōkoku e kuroji kanryū rainen 4-gatsu ni shin kaisha" [New company to recycle surpluses from April], *Asahi Shimbun,* June 24, 1988.

248. "Body to Offer Aid to Developing Countries," *Japan Times,* May 31, 1988.

249. *Nihon Keizai Shimbun,* March 18, 1993 (morning), 5.

250. Taigai Keizai Kyōryoku Shingikai, *Waga kuni keizai kyōryoku no suishin ni tsuite,* op. cit.

251. "Measures to Encourage Business Dealings with Debtor Nations," *Japan's ODA Outlook* [published by *Kaihatsu Jānāru*] (July 1988), 9.

252. "Toshi fando dai-ichi-go: Nihon-ASEAN tōshi (kabu)," [The first investment fund: Japanese-ASEAN investment (equity)] *Kaihatsu Janaru* (March 1988), 44–45.

253. Keiji Kitajima, deputy director of the Fourth Division, Loan Department III, OECF, interview with author, October 19, 1988.

254. Ibid.

255. Ibid.

256. "Tōshi fando dai-ichi-go: Nihon-ASEAN toshi (kabu)," [The first investment fund: Japanese-ASEAN investment (equity)] *Kaihatsu Jānāru* (March 1988), 44–45.

257. "Keizai Kyōryoku," *Tsūsan Janaru* (May 1988), 15–16.

258. "Tsūsan Hakushō: Ajia kyōryoku zenmen ni" [MITI Whitepaper: Asian Cooperation to the fore] *Asahi Shimbun,* June 7, 1988, evening edition; "MITI White Paper Calls for Int'l Policy Coordination," *Japan Times,* June 8, 1988.

259. Keizai Kyōryoku Kyoku, Gaimushō, *Waga kuni no seifu kaihatsu enjo* [Our official development assistance], Vol. I (Tokyo: Kokusai Kyōryoku Suishinkai, 1987), 168.

260. MFA, "The Fourth Medium-Term Target of the Japanese Government of Official Development Assistance (ODA)," June 14, 1988.

261. Keizai Kikakucho, *Sekai to tomo ni ikiru Nihon: Keizai un'ei 5 ka nen keikaku* [Japan living with the world: five-year economic management plan] (May 1988), 26.

262. Ibid., 27–28.

263. Okita Saburo and Toshio Watanabe, *Nishi taiheiyō keizai o yomu* [Understanding the economy of the Western Pacific] (Tokyo: Puranetto Bukkusu, 1991); Toshio Watanabe and Takeshi Aoki, *Ajia shin keizai chizu no yomikata* [How to read Asia's new economic map] (Tokyo: PHP, 1991).

264. Lu Zhongwei, "Tojōkoku kara no hatsugen: Chūgoku" [Responses of developing countries: China], in Suzuki Nagatoshi, ed., *Nihon no keizai kyōryoku: Tojō- koku keizai hatten no shiten kara* [Japan's economic cooperation: from the standpoint of developing countries' economic development] (Tokyo: Ajia Keizai Kenkyūjo, 1989), 207–209.

265. Nihon Sōgō Kenkyūjo, *Kokusai keizai kankyo gekihen shita ni okeru sōgō- teki keizai kyōryoku suishin chosa hōkokushō—Ajia Nettowaku no kochiku in mukete,* FY 1987 study commissioned by EPA, March 1988.

266. *Dantai meikan 1985–1986* [Directory of organizations], Vol. 2 (Tokyo: Shiba, Ltd., 1987), 430.

267. *Gendai Nihon no jinmei roku* [Who's who in contemporary Japan] (Tokyo: Nichigai Asoshietsu, 1987), 512.

268. Nihon Sōgō Kenkyūjo, op. cit., 1.

269. Ibid., 126–127.

270. Ibid., 129.

271. Ibid., 135.

272. Ibid.

273. Kiyoshi Kojima and Terutomo Ozawa, *Japan's General Trading Companies: Merchants of Economic Development* (Paris: OECD, 1984), 28.

274. The operation of the "injection system" was confirmed by various Thai, Philippine, Indonesian, U.S., and Japanese officials interviewed on background by the author.

275. Indonesian director of the Bureau of Inland Transportation, interview with author, November 24, 1987.

276. These practices were recommended to the bureaucracy in the mid-1960s by the Provisional Council on Administrative Reform. See Chapter 5, "Keizai kyōryoku gyōsei ni kansuru kaizen saku," in Rinji Gyōsei Chōsakai, *Kyokan kyōgō jimu no kaikaku in kansuru iken* [Opinion relating to reform of interministerial compeition in official activities] (Tokyo: Prime Minister's Office, September 1964).

277. Although there are no published data on this pass-through ratio, both JICA and OECF officials quoted this estimate in separate interviews with the author.

278. Cf. JICA, "Infrastructure Survey Report for the Huanzala Mine in the Republic of Peru, vol. I" (Tokyo: JICA, February 1984), Chapters 1 and 4.

279. See, for example, "Puranto kyōkai de kaigai nyūsatsu 'dango'," [Overseas bid-rigging by Plant Exporters' Association] *Mainichi Shimbun,* May 15, 1987, Tokyo evening edition, 13. According to confidential records revealed to the public, the Japan Consulting Institute (JCI; formerly known as the Japan Plant Exporters Association, with a membership of the thirty-one largest plant manufacturers) organized its members into two groups: one for electric power plants and one for other industrial plants. The groups would meet once a month to rig bids on ODA project contracts among its members. Successful bidders would pay 0.2–0.4 percent of the contract amount to the group. A MITI official claimed in Diet testimony that as far as MITI knew (MITI is the ministry supervising JCI), the groups were purely for information exchange, and then complained about how the JCI's records became public. See "Hi no hōritsu ni mo ihan," *Mainichi Shimbun,* May 16, 1987, Tokyo evening edition, 10.

280. "Tesūryo, hansu no 6-sha ga 15%," [Payoffs: six companies give 15%] *Yomiuri Shimbun,* May 13, 1987, Tokyo morning edition, 1.

281. *Mainichi Shimbun,* May 11, 1987, Tokyo morning edition, 23. Confidential records of JETRO meetings were revealed in which it was shown that JETRO sponsored a regular meeting for machinery and plant exporters at which major trading company employees appeared as lecturers on the subject of bribing foreign officials to gain ODA loan procurement contracts. These records allegedly showed that JETRO officials knew of and condoned bribery and the rigging of bids through dango.

282. See Chapter IX, "Employment of Consultants," in *OECF Loans and Loan Procedures* (Tokyo: The Overseas Economic Cooperation Fund, n.d., probably 1987).

283. Filologo Pante, Jr., and Romeo Reyes, *Japanese and U.S. Development Assistance to the Philippines: A Philippine Perspective* (Manila: Philippine Institute for Development Studies, 1989), 25.

284. *Puranto yushutsu nenkan, 1988* (Tokyo: Jyūkagaku Kōgyō Tsushinsha).

285. In the 1975–1980 period, 70 percent of government-sponsored bills passed the Diet, and of this amount only 21 percent were amended. See T. J. Pempel, "The Unbundling of 'Japan, Inc.': The Changing Dynamics of Japanese Policy Formation," *Journal of Japanese Studies,* 13 (1987), 286.

286. Suzanne Berger, *Organizing Interests in Western Europe: Pluralism, Corporatism, and the Transformation of Politics* (Cambridge: Cambridge University Press, 1981).

287. The Recruit scandal is a case in point. The public prosecutor, who is under the direction of the justice minister, is left to conduct the investigation of alleged

wrongdoing even when senior bureaucrats and past and present Cabinet ministers are implicated.

288. Frank K. Upham, *Law and Social Change in Postwar Japan* (Cambridge, MA: Harvard University Press, 1987), 16.

289. Ichirō Ogawa, "Administrative and Judicial Remedies Against Administrative Actions," in Kiyoaki Tsuji, *Public Administration in Japan* (Tokyo: University of Tokyo Press, 1984).

290. Frank K. Upham, op. cit., 169.

291. Kiyoaki Tsuji, op. cit., 16.

292. Article 2, Paragraphs 1 and 2. Quoted in Isao Sato, "The Cabinet and Administrative Organization," in Kiyoaki Tsuji, op. cit., 23.

293. Article 7, Item 6 states: "The establishment of such Divisions and Offices and their jurisdiction shall be determined by a Cabinet Order within the limits of applicable laws." Cf. Appendix III, Kiyoaki Tsuji, op. cit.

294. Matsui Ken, *Keizai Kyōryoku — towareru Nihon no keizai gaikō* [Economic cooperation—Japan's dubious economic diplomacy], (Tokyo: Yuhikaku, 1983), 85–86.

295. Ibid., 92.

296. Administrative Management Agency, "Staff Number Control," in Kiyoaki Tsuji, op. cit., 71.

297. Administrative Management Agency, "Public Corporations," in Kiyoaki Tsuji, op. cit., 35–52.

298. DAC, Confidential Aid Review (mimeo), (Paris: OECD, 1986).

299. Kankai Editorial Board, "Geography of Personnel Veins in Bureaucratic World: Economic Planning Agency," *Kankai,* February 1988.

300. DAC, *Aid Review 1990/1991: Report by the Secretariat and Questions for the Review of Japan* (Paris: OECD, 1991), 50.

301. Leonard H. Lynn and Timothy J. McKeown, *Organizing Business: Trade Associations in America and Japan* (Washington, D.C.: American Enterprise Institute, 1990), 13.

302. Keidanren (May 19, 1987), op. cit.

303. Nihon Bōeki Kai, "Saimukuni no keizai kyōryoku ni shōsha no nohau no katsuyo wo," *Kaihatsu Jānāru* (July 1988), 124–25.

304. MITI, *Japan's Technical Cooperation* (Tokyo: The International Development Journal, 1984), 14.

305. *Kaihatsu Janaru,* No. 375 (March 1988), 15.

306. Matsui Ken, op. cit., 89–91.

307. Peter A. Gourevitch, "The Second Image Reversed: The International Sources of Domestic Politics," *International Organization,* 34(4) (Autumn 1978), 880–911.

308. Mancur Olsen and Richard Zeckhauser, "An Economic Theory of Alliances," *Review of Economics and Statistics,* 48(3) (August 1966).

309. Kenneth B. Pyle, *The Japanese Question: Power and Purpose in a New Era* (Washington, DC: American Enterprise Institute, 1992), 26.

310. Kikuchi Kiyoaki, *Namboku mondai to kaihatsu enjo* (Tokyo: Kokusai Kyōryoku Suishinkai, 1978), 168–170.

311. Uchino Tatsuro, op. cit., 172–176.

312. Kikuchi Kiyoaki, op. cit., 355–360.

313. Joseph C. Wheeler, *Development Cooperation: Efforts and Policies of the Members of the Development Assistance Committee, 1986* (Paris: OECD, 1987), 60–61.

314. MITI, *Keizai kyōryoku no genjo to mondaiten,* 1979 [The present status and

issues in economic cooperation, 1979] (Tokyo: Tsūshō sangyōshō, 1979), (Tokyo: Tsusho gyonsho), 181.

315. Tsūsanshō, Sangyō Kōzō Shingikai, *80-jūnen-dai no tsūshō sangyō seisaku no bijyon* [Commercial and industrial policy vision for the 1980s] (Tokyo: MITI, March 17, 1980).

316. Ibid., 500–501.

317. Tsushō Sangyō Gyōsei Kenkyūkai, op. cit., 494.

318. Ohira Sōri no Seisaku Kenkyūkai, Sōgō Anzen Hoshō Kenkyū Gurūpu, *Sōgō Anzen Hoshō Kenkyūkai Gurûpu Hōkokusho* [Report of the study group on comprehensive security] (Tokyo: Naikaku Kanbō Naikaku Shingishitsu Bunshitsu, July 2, 1980), 7.

319. Ibid., 23–24.

320. Ibid., 40–41.

321. Taigai Keizai Kyōryoku Shingikai, *Kongō no keizai kyōryoku no arikata ni tsuite* [The future of economic cooperation] (Tokyo: Sōrifu, November 12, 1980), 4–5.

322. Gaimushō Keizai Kyōryokukyoku, *Keizai Kyōryoku Kenkyukai, Keizai kyōryoku no rinen—seifu kaihatsu enjo wa naze okonau no ka* [The concept of economic cooperation: why give official development assistance?] (Tokyo: Kokusai Kyoryoku Suishin Kyokai, 1981).

323. Ibid., Foreword (unpaginated).

324. Ibid., 75.

325. Ibid., 83.

326. Kikuchi Kiyoaki, op. cit., 706.

327. "Official Says Japan Will Need Nuclear Arms If N. Korea Threatens," *Los Angeles Times,* July 29, 1993, A4.

328. David Arase, "A Militarized Japan?" *Journal of Strategic Studies,* Special Issue (Winter 1994).

329. Robert A. Dahl, *Who Governs?* (New Haven, CT: Yale University Press, 1961).

330. G. John Ikenberry, "Conclusion: An Institutional Approach to American Foreign Economic Policy," in G. John Ikenberry, David A. Lake, and Michael Mastanduno, eds., *The State and American Foreign Economic Policy* (Ithaca, NY: Cornell University Press, 1988), 220.

331. Stephen Krasner, *Defending the National Interest* (Princeton, NJ: Princeton University Press, 1978).

332. Daniel I. Okimoto, *Between MITI and the Market: Japanese Industrial Policy for High Technology* (Stanford, CA: Stanford University Press, 1989), 195.

333. Mainichi Shimbun, Shakai-bu, ODA Shuzaihan, *Kokusai enjo bijinesu—ODA was doo tsukawarete iru ka* [The international aid business—how is ODA being used?] (Tokyo: Aki shobo, 1990); Doi Takako, Murai Yoshinori, Yoshimura Ken'ichi, *ODA kaikaku* [literal translation: ODA reform; English title: For Whose Benefit?] (Tokyo: Shakai Shisosha, 1990); Murai Yoshinori, *Musekinin enjo taikoku Nippon* [Japan: the irresponsible ODA superpower] (Tokyo: JICC Shuppankyoku, 1989).

334. Graham Allison, *Essence of Decision: Explaining the Cuban Missile Crisis* (Boston: Little, Brown and Company, 1971), 32–35.

335. Robert Jervis, *Perception and Misperception in International Politics* (Princeton, NJ: Princeton University Press, 1976).

336. Graham Allison, op. cit.

337. Roger Hilsman, *The Politics of Policymaking in Defense and Foreign Affairs: Conceptual Models and Bureaucratic Politics* (Englewood Cliffs, NJ: Prentice-Hall, 1987).

338. Graham Allison, op. cit.; Herbert A. Simon, *Administrative Behavior: A Study of Decisionmaking Processes in Administrative Organizations* (New York: Macmillan Co., 1947).

339. Alan Rix, op. cit.

340. Peter J. Katzenstein, ed., *Between Power and Plenty: The Foreign Economic Policies of Advanced Industrial States* (Madison, WI: University of Wisconsin Press, 1977), 15.

341. Kenneth Waltz, *Theory of International Politics* (New York: McGraw-Hill, 1979); Robert Gilpin, *War and Change in World Politics* (Cambridge: Cambridge University Press, 1981).

342. David A. Lake, *Power, Protection, and Free Trade: International Sources of U.S. Commercial Strategy, 1887–1939* (Ithaca, NY: Cornell University Press, 1988), 3.

343. Barrington Moore, *Social Origins of Dictatorship and Democracy: Lord and Peasant in the Making of the Modern World* (Boston: Beacon Press, 1966).

344. Peter Gourevitch, "International Trade, Domestic Coalitions, and Liberty: Responses to the Crisis of 1873–1896," *The Journal of Interdisciplinary History,* 8 (1977–1978), 281–313.

345. Nicos Poulantzas, *Political Power and Social Classes* (London: New Left Books, 1973), 285–286; quoted in Eric A. Nordlinger, *On the Autonomy of the Democratic State* (Cambridge, MA: Harvard University Press, 1981), 121. See also Claus Offe, "Laws of Motion of Reformed State Policies" (mimeo, 1976), quoted in Martin Carnoy, *The State and Political Theory* (Princeton, NJ: Princeton University Press, 1984), 133.

346. Theda Skocpol, "Bringing the State Back In: Strategies of Analysis in Current Research," in Peter B. Evans, Dieter Rueschmeyer, and Theda Skocpol, eds., *Bringing the State Back In* (Cambridge: Cambridge University Press, 1985), 9.

347. Peter Evans, *Dependent Development* (Princeton, NJ: Princeton University Press, 1979); Alice Amsden, *Asia's Next Giant* (New York: Oxford University Press, 1989); Robert Wade, *Governing the Market: Economic Theory and the Role of Government in East Asian Industrialization* (Princeton, NJ: Princeton University Press, 1990).

348. Peter Hall, *Governing the Economy: The Politics of State Intervention in Britain and France* (New York: Oxford University Press, 1986), 233.

349. Peter Gourevitch, op. cit.

350. G. John Ikenberry, op. cit., 223–243.

351. Peter J. Katzenstein, "Conclusion," in Peter J. Katzenstein, ed., op. cit., 305.

352. John Zysman, *Governments, Markets, and Growth: Financial Systems and the Politics of Industrial Change* (Ithaca, NY: Cornell University Press, 1983), 300.

353. Peter J. Katzenstein, *Small States in World Markets: Industrial Policy in Europe* (Ithaca, NY: Cornell University Press, 1985).

354. Peter J. Katzenstein, "Introduction," in Peter J. Katzenstein, ed., *Between Power and Plenty,* op. cit., 19.

355. Peter Hall, op. cit., 259.

356. Samuel Brittan, "The Economic Contradictions of Democracy," *British Journal of Political Science,* 5 (1975), 129–159.

357. Albert O. Hirschman, op. cit.

358. C. P. Kindleberger, "The Rise of Free Trade in Western Europe, 1820–1875," *Journal of Economic History,* 35 (1975), 20–55.

359. Max Weber, *From Max Weber: Essays in Sociology,* translated and edited by H. H. Gerth and C. W. Mills (New York: Oxford University Press, 1958), 280.

360. Judith Goldstein, "The Impact of Ideas on Trade Policy: The Origins of U.S.

Agricultural and Manufacturing Policies," *International Organization,* 43 (1989), 32.

361. Judith Goldstein, op. cit., 71; C. P. Kindleberger, "The Rise of Free Trade in Western Europe, 1820–1875," op. cit.

362. Nakane Chie, *Japanese Society* (Berkeley, CA: University of California Press, 1964).

363. Robert Ward, *Japan's Political System* (Englewood Cliffs, NJ: Prentice-Hall, 1978), 58–73; Nobutaka Ike, *Japanese Politics: Patron-Client Democracy* (New York: Alfred A. Knopf, 1972).

364. Chalmers Johnson, op. cit.

365. Eleanor M. Hadley, "The Diffusion of Keynesian Ideas in Japan," Peter A. Hall, ed., *The Political Power of Economic Ideas* (Princeton, NJ: Princeton University Press, 1989), 309.

366. Chalmers Johnson, op. cit., 306.

367. Daniel I. Okimoto, op. cit., 226.

368. T. J. Pempel, "The Unbundling of 'Japan, Inc.': The Changing Dynamics of Japanese Policy Formation," *Journal of Japanese Studies,* 13(1987), 271–306.

369. Daniel I. Okimoto, op. cit., 226, 228.

370. Kenneth Pyle, *The Japanese Question: Power and Purpose in a New Era* (Washington, D.C.: American Enterprise Institute, 1992).

371. Peter J. Katzenstein, *Between Power and Plenty.*

372. J. Mark Ramseyer and Frances M. Rosenbluth, *Japan's Political Marketplace* (Cambridge, MA: Harvard University Press, 1993).

373. Herbert A. Simon, *Administrative Behavior: A Study of Decisionmaking Processes in Administrative Organizations,* 3d ed. (New York: The Free Press, 1976).

374. Michio Muramatsu and Ellis Krauss, "Bureaucrats and Politicians in Policymaking: The Case of Japan," *The American Political Science Review,* 78 (1984), 126–146.

375. Max Weber, "Bureaucracy," in H. H. Gerth and C.W. Mills, eds., op. cit., 214–215.

376. Charles Lindblom, *Politics and Markets: The World's Political and Economic Systems* (New York: Basic Books, 1977).

377. Alice Amsden, op. cit.; Robert Wade, op. cit.; Stephan Haggard, *Pathways from the Periphery: The Politics of Growth in the Newly Industrializing Countries* (Ithaca, NY: Cornell University Press, 1990).

378. Okita Saburō, "Japan's Strategies for and Future Commitment to the Changing World," *Japan Lecture Series* (Kuala Lumpur: Institute of Strategic and International Studies, 1991).

379. *Wall Street Journal,* August 20, 1990, 1.

Select Bibliography

Abegglen, James C., and George Stalk, Jr. *Kaisha, the Japanese Corporation*. Tokyo: Charles E. Tuttle Company, Inc., 1988.

Aberbach, Joel D., Robert D. Putnam, and Bert A. Rockman. *Bureaucrats and Politicians in Western Democracies*. Cambridge, MA: Harvard University Press, 1981.

Aberbach, Joel D., and Bert A. Rockman. *The Administrative State in Industrialized Societies*. Washington, D.C.: American Political Science Association, 1985.

Administrative Management Agency. "Public Corporations." In *Public Administration in Japan*, edited by Tsuji Kiyoaki. Tokyo: University of Tokyo Press, 1984.

———. "Staff Number Control." In *Public Administration in Japan*, edited by Tsuji Kiyoaki. Tokyo: University of Tokyo Press, 1984.

Aida, Toshio, and Kobayashi Hideo, eds. *Seichō suru ajia to nihon sangyō* [Growing Asia and Japanese industry]. Tokyo: Daigetsu Shoten, 1991.

Ajia Keizai Kenkyūjo (Institute for Developing Economies). *ASEAN shokoku no keizai kaihatsu keikaku to waga kuni keizai kyōryoku no arikata* [Economic development planning in the ASEAN countries and how our nation's economic cooperation should be]. Tokyo: Ajia Keizai Kenkyūjo, March 1986.

———. *Keizai kyōryoku handobukku, 1987* [Economic cooperation handbook, 1987]. Tokyo: Ajia Keizai Kenkyūjo, 1987.

Ajia Kyokai (Asia Association). *Ajia kyokai—sono mokutei to jigyō* [The Asia Association: aims and tasks]. Tokyo: Ajia Kyokai, March 1959.

———. "Japan's War Reparations—Achievements and Problems." *Asian Affairs*, 4: 99–111.

Akaha, Tsuneo, and Frank Langdon, eds. *Japan in the Posthegemonic World*. Boulder, CO: Lynne Rienner, 1993.

Akao, Nobutoshi, ed. *Japan's Economic Security*. New York: St. Martin's Press, 1983.

Alagappa, Mutiah. "Japan's Political Role in the Region." Paper presented at JIIA Conference, Tokyo, March 3–4, 1988.

Allison, Graham T. *Essence of Decision: Explaining the Cuban Missile Crisis*. Boston: Little, Brown & Co., 1971.

Amsden, Alice. *Asia's Next Giant: South Korea and Late Industrialization*. New York: Oxford University Press, 1989.

Anchordoguy, Marie. "The Public Corporation: A Potent Japanese Policy Weapon." *Political Science Quarterly*, 103 (1988): 707–724.

Anderson, Perry. *Lineages of the Absolutist State*. London: NLB, 1974.

Applebaum, Richard P., and Jeffrey Henderson, eds. *States and Development in the Asian Pacific Rim*. London: Sage Publications, 1992.

Arase, David. "U.S. and ASEAN Perceptions of Japan's Role in the Asian Pacific." In *Japan, ASEAN, and the United States*, edited by Harry H. Kendall and Clara Joewono. Berkeley, CA: Institute of East Asian Studies, 1991.

———. "Japanese Policy Toward Democratization and Human Rights in Asia." *Asian Survey*, 23, 10 (October 1993): 935–952.

———. "A Militarized Japan?" *Journal of Strategic Studies, Special Issue* (Winter 1994).

Arisawa, Hiromi, ed. *Shōwa keizai-shi* [A history of the Showa economy]. Tokyo: Nihon Keizai Shimbusha, 1976.

Arndt, H. W. *Economic Development: The History of an Idea.* Chicago: University of Chicago Press, 1987.

Arunprapan, Viroj. "White Paper from Thai Construction Industry Association to NESDB," published in *Ruan Prachachart*, December 6, 1985.

Asahi Shimbun 'Enjo' Shuzaihan. *Enjo Tojōkoku Nippon* [Japan the developing country in aid]. Tokyo: Asahi Shimbunsha, 1985.

ASEAN Centre. *ASEAN-Japan Statistical Handbook.* Tokyo: ASEAN Centre, 1988.

Association for the Promotion of International Cooperation (APIC). *Keizai Kyōryoku no Rinen—Seifu Kaihatsu Enjo wa Naze Onkonau no ka* [The concept of economic cooperation: why give official development assistance?]. Tokyo: APIC, 1981.

Ayres, Robert L. *Banking on the Poor: The World Bank and World Poverty.* Cambridge, MA: MIT Press, 1983.

Baishō Mondai Kenkyūjo. *Nihon no Baishō* [Japan's war reparations]. Tokyo: Sekai Janaru, 1963.

Baldwin, David A. *Economic Development and American Foreign Policy, 1943–1962.* Chicago: University of Chicago Press, 1966.

————. "Interdependence and Power: A Conceptual Analysis." *International Organization,* 34, 4 (Autumn 1980), 471–506.

Banfield, Edward C. "American Foreign Aid Doctrines." In *Why Foreign Aid?* edited by Robert A. Goldwin. Chicago: Rand McNally, 1962.

Bank for Agriculture and Agricultural Cooperation. *Summary of Reports on the Study of the Impact of OECF Subloans in BAAC Clients (From Ist to Vth Survey),* Bangkok, May 26, 1987.

Bank of Thailand. *Quarterly Bulletin.* 27, 1 (March 1987).

Barnhart, Michael A. *Japan Prepares for Total War: The Search for Economic Security, 1919–1941.* Ithaca, NY: Cornell University Press, 1987.

Bauer, P. T. *Equality, the Third World, and Economic Delusion.* Cambridge, MA: Harvard University Press, 1981.

Baum, Warren C., and Stokes M Tolbert. *Investing in Development: Lessons of World Bank Experience.* New York: Oxford University Press, 1985.

Beasley, W. G. *Japanese Imperialism, 1894–1945.* New York: Oxford University Press, 1987.

Beer, Samuel H. "Political Overload and Federalism." *Polity 10* (1977), 5–17.

Bellah, Robert. *Tokugawa Religion: The Values of Pre Industrial Japan.* New York: Free Press, 1957.

Berger, Suzanne. *Organizing Interests in Western Europe: Pluralism, Corporatism, and the Transformation of Politics.* Cambridge: Cambridge University Press, 1981.

Bisson, T. A. *Japan's War Economy.* New York: Institute of Pacific Relations, 1945.

Black, Cyril E., et al. *The Modernization of Japan and Russia.* New York: Free Press, 1975.

Bond-Harrel, B. E. *Imposing Aid: Emergency Assistance to Refugees.* Oxford: Oxford University Press, 1986.

Borg, Dorothy, and Okamoto Shumpei, eds. *Pearl Harbor as History: Japanese American Relations 1931–1941.* New York: Columbia University Press, 1973.

Bowie, Alasdair. *Crossing the Industrial Divide.* New York: Columbia University Press, 1991.

Brittan, Samuel. "The Economic Contradictions of Democracy." *British Journal of Political Science,* 5 (1975): 129–159.

Brooks, William L., and Robert M. Orr, Jr. "Japan's Foreign Economic Assistance." *Asian Survey,* 25 (1985): 322–340.

Calder, Kent E. *Crisis and Compensation: Public Policy and Political Stability in Japan.* Princeton, NJ: Princeton University Press, 1988.

Calleo, David P. *Beyond American Hegemony: The Future of the Western Alliance.* New York: Basic Books, 1987.

Campbell, John Creighton. *Contemporary Japanese Budget Politics.* Berkeley, CA: University of California Press, 1977.

Caporaso, James A. "The State's Role in Third World Economic Growth." *Annals of the American Academy of Political and Social Science,* 459 (January 1982): 103– 111.

———, ed. *The Elusive State: International and Comparative Perspectives.* Newbury Park, CA: Sage Publications, 1989.

Carnoy, Martin. *The State and Political Theory.* Princeton, NJ: Princeton University Press, 1984.

Cary, Pete, and Lewis M. Simons. "Profits and Power: Japan's Foreign Aid Machine." *San Jose Mercury News,* April 19–21, 1992.

Cassen, Robert & Associates. *Does Aid Work? Report to an Intergovernmental Task Force.* Oxford: Clarendon Press, 1986.

Cassen, Robert, Richard Jolly, John Sewell, and Robert Wood, eds. *Rich Country Interests and Third World Development.* New York: St. Martin's Press, Institute of Development Studies (Sussex), 1982.

Chilcote, Ronald H. *Theories of Development and Underdevelopment.* Boulder, CO: Westview Press, 1984.

Chittiwatanapong, Prasert. "Japan's Role in the Asia-Pacific Region: Political Dimension." Paper presented at Japan Institute of International Affairs conference, The Pacific Century: Problems and Prospects, Tokyo, March 3–4, 1988.

———. *Japanese Official Development Assistance to Thailand: Impact on Thai Construction Industry.* Unpublished, undated mimeo.

Clark, Rodney. *The Japanese Company.* New Haven, CT: Yale University Press, 1979.

Cohen, Theodore. *Remaking Japan: The American Occupation as New Deal.* New York: Free Press, 1987.

Conolly, T., E. J. Conlon, and S. J. Deutsch. "Organizational Effectiveness: A Multiple Constituency Approach." *Academy of Management Review* 5, pp. 211– 217.

Crowley, James B. *Japan's Quest for Autonomy: National Security and Foreign Policy 1930–1938.* Princeton, NJ: Princeton University Press, 1966.

Curtis, Gerald L. *Election Campaigning, Japanese Style.* New York: Columbia University Press, 1971.

———. *The Japanese Way of Politics.* New York: Columbia University Press, 1988.

Dahl, Robert A. *Who Governs?* New Haven, CT: Yale University Press, 1961.

Dahrendorf, Ralf. *Class and Class Conflict in Industrial Society.* Stanford, CA: Stanford University Press, 1959.

Dai-niji Rinji Gyōsei Kaikaku Chōsakai. *Gyōsei kaikaku ni kan-suru dai-sanji tōshin—kihon tōshin* [Third report on administrative reform]. Tokyo: Prime Minister's Office, July 30, 1982.

Dantai meikan 1985–1986. Vol. 2 (Tokyo: Shiba, Ltd., 1987).

Darby, Phillip. *Three Faces of Imperialism: British and American Approaches to Asia and Africa, 1870–1970.* New Haven, CT: Yale University Press, 1987.

Dernberger, Robert F., and Richard S. Eckaus. *Financing Asian Development 2: China and India.* Lanham, MD: University Press of America, 1988.

Deyo, Frederic C., ed. *The Political Economy of the New Asian Industrialism.* Ithaca, NY: Cornell University Press, 1987.

Dhiravegin, Likhit. "Thai-Japanese Postwar Relations." *Thai Japanese Studies*, Special Issue (March 1984).

Diamond, Larry, Juan J. Linz, and Seymour Martin Lipset, eds. *Democracy in Developing Countries, Vol. Three: Asia*. Boulder, CO: Lynne Rienner, 1989.

Doi Takato, Murai Yoshinori, Yoshimura Keiichi. *ODA Kaikaku* [literal translation: ODA reform; English title: For whose benefit?]. Tokyo: Shakai Shisosha, 1990.

Dore, Ronald. *Flexible Rigidities: Industrial Policy and Structural Adjustment in the Japanese Economy, 1970–1980*. London: Althone Press, 1986.

Dower, John. *Empire and Aftermath: Yoshida Shigeru and the Japanese Experience, 1878–1954*. Cambridge, MA: Harvard University Press, 1979.

Dowling, J. M. and Ulrich Hiemenz. "Biases in the Allocation of Foreign Aid: Some New Evidence." *World Development,* 13 (1985): 534–541.

Drifte, Reinhard. *Japan's Foreign Policy*. New York: Council on Foreign Relations Press, 1990.

Drucker, Peter F. "Japan's Choices." *Foreign Affairs,* 65 (1987): 924–941.

Duus, Peter, Ramon H. Myers, and Mark R. Peattie. *The Japanese Informal Empire in China, 1895–1937*. Princeton, NJ: Princeton University Press, 1989.

Elton, Charlotte. "New Dimensions of Japanese Policy: A Latin American View of Japanese Presence." In *Japan in the Posthegemonic World,* edited by Tsuneo Akaha and Frank Langdon. Boulder, CO: Lynne Rienner, 1993.

Emmerson, John K. *Arms, Yen & Power: The Japanese Dilemma*. New York: Dunellen, 1971.

Ensign, Margee. *Doing Good or Doing Well? Japan's Foreign Aid Program*. New York: Columbia University Press, 1992.

Esman, Milton J., and Daniel S. Cheever. "Japanese Administration: A Comparative View." *Public Administration Review,* 7 (Spring 1947): 100–112.

———. *The Common Aid Effort: The Development Assistance Activities of the Organization for Economic Cooperation and Development*. Columbus, OH: Ohio State University Press, 1967.

Evans, Peter. *Dependent Development: The Alliance of Multinational, State, and Local Capital in Brazil*. Princeton, NJ: Princeton University Press, 1979.

———, Dieter Rueschmeyer, and Theda Skocpol. *Bringing the State Back In*. Cambridge, MA: Cambridge University Press, 1985.

Friedman, Milton. "Foreign Economic Aid: Means and Objectives." In *The United States and the Developing Economies*, edited by Gustav Ranis. New York: W. W. Norton & Co., 1964.

Fruin, W. Mark. *The Japanese Enterprise System: Competitive Strategies and Cooperative Structures*. Oxford: Oxford University Press, 1992.

Fukui, Haruhiro, "Introduction." In *Politics and Policy in Japan,* edited by T. J. Pempel. Philadelphia: Temple University Press, 1982.

Fukuyama, Francis, and Kongdan Oh. *The U.S.-Japan Security Relationship After the Cold War*. Santa Monica, CA: Rand, 1993.

Gaimushō (Ministry of Foreign Affairs). *Waga gaikō no kinkyō* [Circumstances of Japan's diplomacy]. Tokyo: Gaimushō, September 1957.

———, Keizai Kyōryoku Kyoku. *Waga kuni no seifu kaihatsu enjo* [Our official development assistance], vol. I. Tokyo: Kokusai Kyōryoku Suishin Kyokai, 1987.

———, Keizai Kyoryoku Kyoku, Keizai Kyōryoku Kenkyūkai. *Keizai kyōryoku no rinen—seifu kaihatsu enjo wa naze okonau no ka* [The concept of economic cooperation: why give official development assistance?]. Tokyo: Kokusai Kyōryoku Suishin Kyōkai, 1981.

———, Kokusai Kyōryoku Kenkyūkai. *Kokusai kyōryoku handobukku* [International cooperation handbook]. Tokyo: Gaimusho, 1983.

Gaimusho Chōsakyoku. *Nihon keizai saiken no kihon mondai* [Fundamental issues in reconstructing Japan's economy]. Tokyo: Gaimusho, 1946.

Galbraith, John Kenneth. *The New Industrial State.* Boston: Houghton Mifflin, 1967.

"Geography of Personnel Veins in Bureaucratic World: Economic Planning Agency." *Kankai* (February 1988).

Gerlach, Michael. *Alliance Capitalism: The Social Organization of Japanese Business.* Berkeley, CA: University of California Press, 1992.

Gerschenkron, Alexander. *Economic Backwardness in Historical Perspective.* Cambridge, MA: Belknap Press, 1962.

Gilpin, Robert. *U.S. Power and the Multinational Corporation: The Political Economy of Foreign Direct Investment.* New York: Basic Books, 1975.

———. *War and Change in World Politics.* Cambridge: Cambridge University Press, 1981.

———. *The Political Economy of International Relations.* Princeton, NJ: Princeton University Press, 1987.

Goldstein, Judith. "Ideas Institutions and Trade Policy." *International Organization* 42 (1988): 179–217.

———. "The Impact of Ideas on Trade Policy: The Origins of U.S. Agricultural and Manufacturing Policies." *International Organization,* 43 (1989): 31–71.

Gourevitch, Peter A. "International Trade, Domestic Coalitions, and Liberty: Comparative Responses to the Crisis of 1873–1896." *The Journal of Interdisciplinary History* 8 (1977–1978): 281–313.

———. "The Second Image Reversed: The International Sources of Domestic Politics." *International Organization,* 34, 4 (Autumn 1978): 880–911.

Hadley, Eleanor M. *Antitrust in Japan.* Princeton, NJ: Princeton University Press, 1970.

———. "The Diffusion of Keynesian Ideas in Japan." In *The Political Power of Economic Ideas: Keynesianism Across Nations*, edited by Peter A. Hall. Princeton, NJ: Princeton University Press, 1989.

Haggard, Stephan. *Pathways from the Periphery: The Politics of Growth in the Newly Industrializing Countries.* Ithaca, NJ: Cornell University Press, 1990.

———, and Chung-in Moon, eds. *Pacific Dynamics: The International Politics of Industrial Change.* Boulder, CO: Westview Press, 1989.

Hall, Peter. *Governing the Economy: The Politics of State Intervention in Britain and France.* New York: Oxford University Press, 1986.

Halperin, Morton H., with the assistance of Priscilla Clapp and Arnold Kanter. *Bureaucratic Politics and Foreign Policy.* Washington, D.C.: The Brookings Institution, 1974.

Hartmann, Frederick H., and Robert L. Wendzel. *Defending America's Security.* Washington, D.C.: Pergamon-Brassey's International Defense Publishers, Inc., 1988.

Hasegawa, Sukehiro. *Japanese Foreign Aid: Policy and Practice.* New York: Praeger, 1975.

Haseyama, Takahiko, et al. "New Issues of Economic Cooperation: Summary." Paper presented at Institute of Developing Economies sponsored conference, the Tokyo Conference on Global Adjustment and the Future of the Asian-Pacific Economy, Tokyo, May 11–13, 1988.

Hayao, Kenji. *The Japanese Prime Minister and Public Policy.* Pittsburgh, PA: University of Pittsburgh Press, 1993.

Hayter, Teresa, and Catharine Watson. *Aid: Rhetoric and Reality.* London: Pluto Press, 1985.

Held, David. *Models of Democracy.* Stanford, CA: Stanford University Press, 1987.

Herbert, Norman E. *Japan's Emergence As a Modern State: Political and Economic Problems of the Meiji Period*. New York: International Secretariat, Institute of Pacific Relations, 1940.

Hilsman, Roger. *The Politics of Policy Making in Defense and Foreign Affairs: Conceptual Models and Bureaucratic Politics*. Englewood Cliffs, NJ: Prentice-Hall, Inc., 1987.

Hirschman, Albert O. *National Power and the Structure of Foreign Trade*. Berkeley, CA: University of California Press, 1980.

Hofmann, Michael. *Japan's Development Assistance: A German View*. Tokyo: Institute of Developing Economies, January 1985.

Hollerman, Leon. *Japan's Dependence on the World Economy: The Approach Toward Economic Liberalization*. Princeton, NJ: Princeton University Press, 1967.

———, *Japan, Disincorporated: The Economic Liberalization Process*. Stanford, CA: Hoover Institution Press, 1988.

Howell, Thomas R., et al. *The Microelectronics Race: The Impact of Government Policy on International Competition*. Boulder, CO: Westview Press, 1988.

Hrebenar, Ronald J. *The Japanese Party System: From One-Party Rule to Coalition Government*. Boulder, CO: Westview Press, 1986.

Igarashi, Takeshi, ed. *Nihon no ODA to kokusai chitsujo* [Japan's ODA and the international order]. Tokyo: Japan Institute of International Affairs, 1990.

Iida, Tsuneo, et al. *Gendai nihon keizai-shi: sengo sanjūnen no ayumi* [The economic history of contemporary Japan: thirty postwar years], vol. 1. Tokyo: Chikuma Shōbō, 1976.

Ike, Nobutaka. *Japanese Politics: Patron-Client Democracy*. New York: Alfred A. Knopf, 1972.

Ikenberry, G. John, David A. Lake, and Michael Mastanduno, eds. *The State and American Foreign Economic Policy*. Ithaca, NY: Cornell University Press, 1988.

Inada, Juichi. "Nihon gaikō ni okeru enjo mondai no sho sokumen" [Several aspects of the aid problem in Japan's diplomacy]. In *Kokusai Mondai,* 326 (May 1987): 2–20.

Independent Commission on International Development Issues (The Brandt Commission). *North-South: A Programme for Survival: Report of the Independent Commission on International Development Issues*. Cambridge, MA: MIT Press, 1980.

Inoguchi, Takashi. *Japan's Foreign Policy in an Era of Global Change*. New York: St. Martin's Press, 1993.

———, and Iwai Tomoaki. *"Zokugiin" no kenkyū: Jimintō Seiken o gyujira shuyaku-tachi*. Tokyo: Nihon Keizai Shimbunsha, 1987.

Insight: Australian Foreign Affairs and Trade Issues, 2(13). August 2, 1993.

Iriye, Akira, and Warren I. Cohen, eds. *The United States and Japan in the Postwar World*. Lexington, KY: University Press of Kentucky, 1989.

Ishida, Takeshi, and Ellis S. Krauss, eds. *Democracy in Japan*. Pittsburgh, PA: University of Pittsburgh Press, 1989.

Islam, Shafiqul, ed. *Yen for Development: Japanese Foreign Aid and the Politics of Burden-Sharing*. New York: Council on Foreign Relations Press, 1991.

———. "Beyond Burden-Sharing: Economics and Politics of Japanese Foreign Aid." In *Yen for Development: Japanese Foreign Aid and the Politics of Burden-Sharing*, edited by Shafiqul Islam. New York: Council on Foreign Relations Press, 1991.

Itagaki, Hidenori. *'Zoku' no kenkyū*. Tokyo: Keizaikai, 1987.

Jansen, Marius B., ed. *Changing Japanese Attitudes Toward Modernization*. Princeton, NJ: Princeton University Press, 1965.

Japan External Trade Organization (JETRO), Bangkok Office. "Current Trend of

Japanese Investment in Thailand and Its Prospect." Bangkok: JETRO, August 1987.

Japan International Cooperation Agency (JICA). "Infrastructure Survey Report for the Huanzala Mine in the Republic of Peru, vol. I." Tokyo: JICA, February 1984.

———. *Study on the Economic Development of the Argentine Republic, Final Report, Executive Summary.* Tokyo: JICA, January 1987.

———, Country Study Group for Development Assistance to the Republic of the Philippines. *Country Study for Development Assistance to the Republic of the Philippines: "Basic Strategy for Development Assistance."* Tokyo: JICA, April 1987.

Jervis, Robert. *Perception and Misperception in International Politics.* Princeton, NJ: Princeton University Press, 1976.

Jeshurun, Chandran, ed. *China, India, Japan and the Security of Southeast Asia.* Singapore: Institute of Southeast Asian Studies, 1993.

Johnson, Chalmers A. "Japan: Who Governs? An Essay on Official Bureaucracy." *Journal of Japanese Studies,* 2 (Autumn 1975): 1–28.

———. *Japan's Public Policy Companies.* Washington, D.C.: American Enterprise Institute, 1978.

———. *"Omote* (Explicit) and *Ura* (Implicit): Translating Japanese Political Terms." *Journal of Japanese Studies,* 6 (Winter 1980): 89–115.

———. *MITI and the Japanese Miracle.* Stanford, CA: Stanford University Press, 1982.

———, Laura D'Andrea Tyson, and John Zysman, eds., *Politics and Productivity: The Real Story of Why Japan Works.* Cambridge, MA: Ballinger, 1989.

Jūkagaku Kōgyō Tsūshin-sha (JCI). *Nihon no kaigai shigen kaihatsu, 1976* (Gentei ban) [Japan's Overseas Natural Resource Development, 1976]. Tokyo: Jūkagaku Kōgyō Tsūshin-sha, 1976.

———. *Puranto yushutsu nenkan, 1988* [Plant Export Yearbook, 1988]. Tokyo: Jukagaku Kogyo Tsushin-sha, 1988.

Kajima Heiwa Kenkyūjō. *Taigai keizai kyōryoku taikei,* 5, (8–9). Tokyo: Kajima Heiwa Kenkyūjo, 1971.

Kaplan, Eugene. *Japan: The Government-Business Relationship.* Washington, D.C.: U.S. Bureau of International Commerce, 1972.

Kataoka, Tetsuya, and Ramon H. Myers. *Defending an Economic Superpower: Reassessing the U.S.-Japan Security Alliance.* Boulder, CO: Westview Press, 1989.

Katzenstein, Peter J., ed. *Between Power and Plenty: The Foreign Economic Policies of Advanced Industrial States.* Madison, WI: University of Wisconsin Press, 1977.

———. "Introduction." In *Between Power and Plenty: The Foreign Economic Policies of Advanced Industrial States,* edited by Peter J. Katzenstein. Madison, WI: University of Wisconsin Press, 1977.

———. "Conclusion." In *Between Power and Plenty: The Foreign Economic Policies of Advanced Industrial States.* Edited by Peter J. Katzenstein. Madison, WI: University of Wisconsin Press, 1977.

———. *Small States in World Markets: Industrial Policy in Europe.* Ithaca, NY: Cornell University Press, 1985.

Kaufman, Burton I. *Trade and Aid: Eisenhower's Foreign Economic Policy, 1953– 1961.* Baltimore, MD: Johns Hopkins University Press, 1982.

Kawai, Kazuo. *Japan's American Interlude.* Chicago: University of Chicago Press, 1960.

Kawakami Takaro. "21 seiki ni muketa Nihon no enjo seisaku" [Japan's aid policy toward the 21st century]. *Gaikō Forum,* (March 1993): 4–15.

Kawata Tadashi. *'Sho-nihonshugi' no susume* [The way of modest Japanese nationalism]. Tokyo: Daiyamondo-sha, 1972.

Keehn, E. B. "Managing Interests in Japan's Bureaucracy: Informality and Discretion," *Asian Survey*, 30, 11 (November 1990), pp. 1021–1037.

Keidanren (Keizai Dantai Rengōkai) (Federation of Economic Organizations). *Kokusai koken no tame no kongo no keizai kyōryoku no arikata-Seifu kaihatsu enjo taikō no sakutei in mukete* [Economic cooperation for international contribution]. Tokyo: Keidanren, March 24, 1992.

———. "Keizai kyōryoku bunya ni okeru waga kuni no koken." Tokyo: Keidanren, May 19, 1987.

———. "Resolution of the 51st General Meeting—Our Resolve to Create a New Corporate Concept: Acting in Step with Communities." *Keidanren Review*, No. 123 (June 1990): 2–3.

———. *Waga-kuni no enjo rinen to kongō no seifu kaihatsu enjo no arikata ni tsuite* [Japan's ODA: its philosophy and future development]. Tokyo: Keidanren, June 26, 1990.

Keizai Dōyūkai (Japan Committee for Economic Development). *Kokusai kyōryoku seisaku no arata na tenkai o motomete* [In search of a new direction in international cooperation policy]. Tokyo: Keizai Dōyūkai, June 19, 1987.

Keizai Kikakucho (Economic Planning Agency). *Sekai keizai hakusho* [White paper on the global economy]. Tokyo: Okurashō Insatsukyoku, annual.

———. *Sekai to tomo ni ikiru Nihon: Keizai un'ei 5 ka nen keikaku* [Japan living with the world: five-year economic management plan]. Tokyo: Keizai Kikakucho, May 1988.

Keizai Kōhō Center. Brief, No. 43: "A Blueprint for Upgrading Foreign Aid." Tokyo: Keizai Kōhō Center, August 1987.

Keohane, Robert O. *After Hegemony: Cooperation and Discord in the World Political Economy*. Princeton, NJ: Princeton University Press, 1984.

———, ed. *Neorealism and Its Critics*. New York: Columbia University Press, 1986.

Kikuchi, Kiyoaki. *Namboku mondai to kaihatsu enjo* [The North-South problem and development assistance]. Tokyo: Kokusai Kyōryoku Suishinkai, 1978.

Kim, Kwang Suk, and Michael Roemer. *Studies in the Modernization of the Republic of Korea: 1945–75*. Cambridge, MA: Harvard University Press, 1979.

Kindleberger, Charles P. *Power and Money: The Economics of International Politics and the Politics of International Economics*. New York: Basic Books, 1970.

———. "The Rise of Free Trade in Western Europe, 1820–1875." *Journal of Economic History*, 35 (1975): 20–55.

Kitazawa, Yōko, ed. *Hitobito wa kokkyo wo koete mirai wo tsukuru—ODA Ajia taiheiyō to Nihon* [People crossing borders and building the future—ODA, the Asia Pacific, and Japan] (Proceedings of the Kanagawa International Symposium: People's Plan 21st Century). Tokyo: Daisan Shōbō, 1991.

Knorr, Klaus. *Power of Nations*. New York: Basic Books, 1975.

Kohama, Hirohisa, ed. *Chokusetsu tōshi to kōgyōka: Nihon NI, NIES, ASEAN* [Direct investment and industrialization: Japan, NIEs, and ASEAN]. Tokyo: JETRO, 1992.

———. *ODA no keizaigaku* [The economics of ODA]. Tokyo: Nihon Hyōronsha, 1992.

Kojima, Kiyoshi. *Japanese Direct Foreign Investment: A Model of Multinational Business Operations*. Tokyo: Charles E. Tuttle Company, Inc., 1982.

———. *Japan and a New World Economic Order*. Tokyo: Charles E. Tuttle Company, Inc., 1984.

Kojima, Kiyoshi, and Terutomo Ozawa. *Japan's General Trading Companies: Merchants of Economic Development*. OECD: Paris, 1984.

Kokusai Kaihatsu Sentaa (International Development Center). *Makuro keizai enjo kō-ka hyōka ni tsuite no chōsa* [Evaluation of macroeconomic impact of aid]. Tokyo: Kokusai Kaihatsu Sentaa, March 1984.

Kono, Toyohiro. *Strategy and Structure of Japanese Enterprises*. London: Macmillan, 1984.

Koppel, Bruce, and Robert M. Orr, Jr., eds. *Japan's Foreign Aid: Power and Policy in a New Era*. Boulder, CO: Westview Press, 1993.

Kosaka, Masataka. *A History of Postwar Japan*. Tokyo: Kodansha International Ltd., 1982.

Krasner, Stephen D. *Defending the National Interest*. Princeton, NJ: Princeton University Press, 1978.

———. "Approaches to the State: Alternative Conception and Historical Dynamics." *Comparative Politics* (January 1984): 223–246.

———. *Structural Conflict: The Third World Against Global Liberalism*. Berkeley and Los Angeles: University of California Press, 1985.

Krauss, Elli and Isabel Coles. "Built-In Impediments: The Political Economy of the U.S. Japan Construction Dispute." In *Japan's Economic Structure: Should It Change?* edited by Kozo Yamamura. Seattle, WA: Society for Japanese Studies, 1990.

Krauss, Ellis, and Takeshi Ishida, eds. *Democracy in Japan*. Pittsburgh, PA: University of Pittsburgh Press, 1989.

Krauss, Melvyn. *Development Without Aid: Growth, Poverty and Government*. New York: McGraw-Hill, 1981.

Krongkaew, Medhi. "ASEAN Economic Cooperation After the Manila Summit: A New Breakthrough?" Paper presented at JIIA Conference, Tokyo, March 3–4, 1988.

Kreuger, Anne O., Constantine Michalopoulos, and Vernon Ruttan, with Keith Jay et al. *Aid and Development*. Baltimore, MD: John Hopkins University Press, 1989.

Kubota, Akira. *Higher Civil Servants in Postwar Japan: Their Social Origins, Educational Backgrounds, and Career Patterns*. Princeton, NJ: Princeton University Press, 1969.

Kuznets, Simon. "Growth and Structural Shifts." In *Economic Growth and Structural Change in Taiwan,* edited by Walter Galenson. Ithaca, NY: Cornell University Press, 1979.

Kyogoku, Jun-ichi. *The Political Dynamics of Japan*. Translated by Nobutaka Ike. Tokyo: University of Tokyo Press, 1983.

Lake, David A. *Power Protection and Free Trade: International Sources of U.S. Commercial Strategy, 1887–1939*. Ithaca, NY: Cornell University Press, 1988.

Lappé, Frances Moore, Joseph Collins, and David Kinley. *Aid as Obstacle: Twenty Questions About Our Foreign Aid and the Hungry*. San Francisco: Institute for Food and Development Policy, 1980.

Lehmbruch, Gerhard. "Liberal Corporatism and Party Government." *Comparative Political Studies,* 10 (1977): 91–126.

Lewis, W. Arthur. *The Evolution of the International Economic Order*. Princeton, NJ: Princeton University Press, 1978.

Lijphart, Arend. *Democracies: Patterns of Majoritarian and Consensus Government in Twenty-One Countries*. New Haven, CT: Yale University Press, 1984.

Lincoln, Edward J.. *Japan's Economic Role in Northeast Asia*. Lanham, MD: University Press of America, 1987.

———. *Japan's Unequal Trade*. Washington, D.C.: The Brookings Institution, 1990.

Lindblom, Charles. *Politics and Markets: The World's Political and Economic Systems.* New York: Basic Books, 1977.

Liska, George. *The New Statecraft: Foreign Aid in American Foreign Policy.* Chicago: University of Chicago Press, 1960.

Little, Ian, M.D. *Economic Development: Theory, Policy and International Relations.* New York: Basic Books, Twentieth Century Book Fund, 1982.

Lockwood, William. *The Economic Development of Japan: Growth and Structural Change, 1868–1938.* London: Oxford University Press, 1955.

Loutfi, Martha F. *The Net Cost of Japanese Foreign Aid.* New York: Praeger, 1973.

Lu, Zhongwei. "Tojokoku kara no hatsugen: Chugoku" [Responses of developing countries: China]. In *Nihon no keizai kyoryoku: Tojokoku keizai hatten no shiten kara* [Japan's economic cooperation: from the standpoint of developing countries' economic development], edited by Suzuki Nagatoshi. Tokyo: Ajia Keizai Kenkyujo, 1989.

Lynn, Leonard H., and Timothy J. McKeown. *Organizing Business: Trade Associations in America and Japan.* Washington, D.C.: American Enterprise Institute, 1991.

Mainichi Shimbun Shakai-bu ODA Shuzaihan. *Kokusai enjo bijinesu: ODA was doo tsukawarete iru ka* [The international aid business—how is ODA being used?]. Tokyo: Yaki Shōbo, 1990.

Maki, John M. "The Role of the Bureaucracy in Japan." *Pacific Affairs,* 20 (1947): 391–406.

Makin, John H. and Donald C. Hellman, eds. *Sharing World Leadership? A New Era for America & Japan.* Washington, D.C.: American Enterprise Institute, 1989.

Marshall, Byron K. *Capitalism and Nationalism in Prewar Japan: The Ideology of the Business Elite, 1868–1941.* Stanford, CA: Stanford University Press, 1967.

Maruyama, Masao. *Thought and Behavior in Modern Japanese Politics.* London: Oxford University Press, 1963.

Mason, Edward S. *Foreign Aid and Foreign Policy.* New York: Council on Foreign Relations, 1964.

————, et al. *The Economic and Social Modernization of the Republic of Korea.* Cambridge, MA: Harvard University Press, 1980.

————. "U.S. Interests in Foreign Economic Assistance." In *The United States and the Developing Economies*, edited by Gustav Ranis. New York: W. W. Norton & Co., 1964.

Masumi, Junnosuke. *Postwar Politics in Japan, 1945–1955.* Translated by Lonny E. Carlile. Berkeley, CA: Institute of East Asian Studies, University of California, Berkeley, Center for Japanese Studies, 1985.

Matsui, Ken. *Keizai Kyōryoku—towareru Nihon no keizai gaikō* [Economic cooperation—Japan's dubious economic diplomacy]. Tokyo: Yuhikaku, 1983.

Matsuo, Taiichiro. "Structural Analysis of Japan's Trade with Southeast Asia." *Asian Affairs,* 3, 1 (March 1958): 26–27.

Matsushita Seikei Juku, ed. *Nihon no Keizai Kyōryoku to Sekai Keiei* [Japan's economic cooperation and global management]. Tokyo: Sōgō Gyōsei Shuppan, 1989.

May, Ranald S., Dieter Schumacher, and Mohammed H. Malek. *Overseas Aid: The Impact on Britain and Germany.* New York: Harvester Wheatsheaf, 1989.

McCormack, Gavan, and Yoshio Sugimoto. *Democracy in Contemporary Japan.* Armonk, NY: M. E. Sharpe, Inc., 1990.

McKinlay, R. D. "The Aid Relationship: A Foreign Policy Model and Interpretation of Official Bilateral Economic Aid of the United States, the United Kingdom, France, and Germany, 1960–1970." *Comparative Political Studies,* 11 (1979): 411–463.

"Measures to Encourage Business Dealings with Debtor Nations." *Japan's ODA Outlook*. Tokyo: Kaihatsu Janaru, July 1988.

Medhi Krongkaew. "ASEAN Economic Cooperation After the Manila Summit: A New Breakthrough?" Paper delivered at the JIIA Conference, Tokyo, March 3–4, 1988, 34.

Michels, Robert. *Political Parties: A Sociological Study of the Oligarchical Tendencies of Modern Democracy.* Translated by Eden and Cedar Paul. New York: Free Press, 1968.

Miliband, Ralph. *The State in Capitalist Society.* New York: Basic Books, 1969.

Millikan, Max, and W. W. Rostow. "A Proposal: Key to an Effective Foreign Policy." In *Foreign Aid Program, Compilation of Studies and Surveys.* U.S. Senate, Special Committee to Study the Foreign Aid Program. Washington, D.C.: GPO, 1957.

Ministry of Foreign Affairs (MFA). *Diplomatic Bluebook, 1986 Edition: Review of Recent Developments in Japan's Foreign Relations.* Tokyo: MFA, 1986.

———. *Japan's ODA.* Tokyo: APIC, annual.

Ministry of International Trade and Industry (MITI) *Foreign Trade of Japan 1958.* Tokyo: Tsūshō Sangyōshō, 1958.

———. *Japan's Technical Cooperation.* Tokyo: The International Development Journal, 1984.

———. *MITI Yearbook on Economic Cooperation.* Tokyo: Tsūshō Sangyōshō, annual.

Mitroff, I. I. *Stakeholders of the Organizational Mind.* San Francisco: Jossey-Bass, 1983.

Mitsubishi Bank Review, 19, 7 (July 1988).

Moltz, James Clay. "Divergent Learning and the Failed Politics of Soviet Economic Reform." *World Politics,* 45 (1993): 301–325.

Montgomery, John D. *The Politics of Foreign Aid.* New York: Praeger, 1962.

Moore, Barrington. *Social Origins of Dictatorship and Democracy: Lord and Peasant in the Making of the Modern World.* Boston: Beacon Press, 1966.

Morgenthau, Hans J. "A Political Theory of Foreign Aid." *The American Political Science Review,* 56 (1963): 301–309.

———. "Preface to a Political Theory of Foreign Aid." In *Why Foreign Aid?* edited by Robert A. Goldwin. Chicago: Rand McNally, 1963.

Morley, James W., ed. *Dilemmas of Growth in Prewar Japan.* Princeton, NJ: Princeton University Press, 1971.

Mosely, Paul. *Foreign Aid: Its Defense and Reform.* Lexington, KY: University Press of Kentucky, 1987.

Murai, Yoshinori, ed. *Kenshō: Nippon no ODA* [Testimony: Japan's ODA]. Tokyo: Gakuyō Shōbō, 1992.

———, et al. *Musekinin enjo ODA taikoku Nippon* [Japan: the irresponsible ODA superpower]. Tokyo: JICC Shuppankyoku, 1989.

Muramatsu, Michio, and Ellis Krauss. "Bureaucrats and Politicians in Policymaking: The Case of Japan." *The American Political Science Review,* 78 (1984): 126–146.

———. "The Conservative Policy Line and the Development of Patterned Pluralism." In *The Political Economy of Japan, Volume 1: The Domestic Transformation,* edited by Kozo Yamamura and Yasukichi Yasuba. (Stanford, CA: Stanford University Press, 1987), 516–554.

———, Itō Mitsutoshi, and Tsujinaka Yutaka. *Sengo nihon no atsuryoku dantai* [Pressure groups in postwar Japan]. Tokyo: Tōyō Keizai, 1986.

Nagasu, Kazuji. *Nanshin suru Nihon shihon shugi* [Japanese capitalism advancing south]. Tokyo: Mainichi shimbunsha, 1971.

Nakane, Chie. *Japanese Society.* Berkeley, CA: University of California Press, 1964.

Nathan, James A., and James K. Oliver. *Foreign Policy Making and the American Political System.* Boston: Little, Brown & Co., 1987.

National Economic Development Authority (NEDA), Republic of the Philippines.

Cover Memorandum, Japan's Official Development Assistance to the Philippines, dated August 10, 1988 (mimeo), 2.

―――. *Philippine Development Report 1987*. Manila: NEDA, 1988.

Ng, C. Y., R. Hirono, and Narongchai Akrasanee. *Industrial Restructuring in ASEAN and Japan: An Overview*. Singapore: Institute of Southeast Asian Studies, 1987.

Nichigai Asoshietsu. *Gendai Nihon no jinmeiroku* [Personnel register of contemporary Japan]. Tokyo: Nichigai Asoshietsu, 1987.

Nihon Bōeki Kai (Japan Foreign Trade Council). "Saimukuni no keizai kyōryoku ni shōsha no nohau no katsuyō wo." *Kaihatsu Janaru* (July 1988): 124–25.

Nihon Bōeki Shinkōkai (Japan External Trade Organization). *Sekai to nihon no kaigai chokusetsu tōshi* [Foreign direct investment of Japan and the world]. Tokyo: Nihon Boeki Shinokai, annual.

―――. *NIES, ASEAN de no nikkei kigyo (seizōgyō) no katsudō jōkyo* [Activities of Japanese firms (manufacturing) in ASEAN and the NIEs]. Tokyo: Nihon Bōeki Shinkokai, 1992.

Nihon Keizai Shimbunsha, Keizai Kaisetsu-bu. *Baishō no hanashi* [The story of reparations]. Tokyo: Nihon Keizai Shimbunsha, 1957.

Nihon Kōei Kabushki Kaisha. *Nihon Kōei 35-nen shi* [The 35-year history of Nihon Kōei]. Tokyo: Diamond-sha, 1981.

Nihon Sōgō Kenkyūjo (Japan Research Institute). *Kokusai keizai kankyō gekihen shita ni okeru sōgō-teki keizai kyōryoku suishin chōsa hokokushō—Ajia Nettowaku no kochiku in mukete* [Report on the promotion of comprehensive economic cooperation under an international economic environment in transition: toward the construction of an Asian network]. (FY 1987 study commissioned by the EPA). Tokyo: Nihon Sōgō Kenkūjo, March 1988.

Nishikawa, Jun, ed. *Enjo to jiritsu—Negurosu shima no keiken kara* [International cooperation and self-reliance: experience of Negros Island]. Tokyo: Dōbunkan, 1991.

Nishimura, Masaki. "Seifu kaihatsu enjo (ODA) no gEnjo to kadai ni tsuite," *Kikan Gyōsei Kanri Kenkyū*, No. 44 (December 1988), 47–60.

Nordlinger, Eric A. *On the Autonomy of the Democratic State*. Cambridge, MA: Harvard University Press, 1981.

Ogawa, Ichiro. "Administrative and Judicial Remedies Against Administrative Actions." In *Public Administration in Japan*, edited by Kiyoaki Tsuji. Tokyo: Tokyo University Press, 1984.

―――. "The Legal Framework of Public Administration." In *Public Administration in Japan*, edited by Kiyoaki Tsuji. Tokyo: Tokyo University Press, 1984.

Ohlin, Goran. *Foreign Aid Policies Reconsidered*. Paris: Development Centre, OECD, 1966.

Ohtake, H. *Gendai nihon no seiji kenryoku keizai kenryoku* [The political economy of contemporary Japan]. Tokyo: Sanichi Shobo, 1979.

Okano, Kanki. *Nihon baishō ron* [Theories of Japanese reparations]. Tokyo: Tōyō Keizai Shimposha, 1958.

Okimoto, Daniel I. *Between MITI and the Market: Japanese Industrial Policy for High Technology*. Stanford, CA: Stanford University Press, 1989.

Okita Saburō. "Asian Prosperity and Japanese Economy." *Asian Affairs*, 4, 2 (March 1960).

―――. *Postwar Reconstruction of the Japanese Economy*. Tokyo: University of Tokyo Press, 1992.

―――. *Japan's Challenging Years: Reflections on My Lifetime*. Canberra: Australian National University, Australia-Japan Research Centre, 1983.

―――. "Japan's Strategies for and Future Commitment to the Changing World." *Japan Lecture Series*. Kuala Lumpur: Institute of Strategic and International Studies, 1991.

————. *Nihon no keizai seisaku* [Economic policy in Japan]. Tokyo: Yūki Shobo, 1961.

————. *The Rehabilitation of Japan's Economy and Asia.* Tokyo: Public Information and Cultural Affairs Bureau, Ministry of Foreign Affairs, 1956.

Okita, Saburō, et al. "The Potential of the Japanese Surplus for World Economic Development." *WIDER (World Institute for Development Economics Research) Study Group.* Helsinki: WIDER, April 1986.

————, Mobilizing International Surpluses for World Development: A WIDER Plan for a Japanese Initiative," *WIDER Study Group.* Tokyo: WIDER, May 1987.

————, and Toshio Watanabe. *Nishi taiheiyō keizai o yomu* [Understanding the economy of the Western Pacific]. Tokyo: Puranetto Bukksu, 1991.

Olsen, Mancur. *The Rise and Decline of Nations.* New Haven, CT: Yale University Press, 1982.

————, and Richard Zeckhauser. "An Economic Theory of Alliances." *Review of Economics and Statistics,* 48, 3 (August 1966): 266–279.

Olson, Lawrence A. *Japan in Postwar Asia.* New York: Council on Foreign Relations, 1970.

Olson, Lawrence A. *Ambivalent Moderns: Potraits of Japanese Cultural Identity.* Savage, MD: Rowman & Littlefield Publishers, Inc., 1992.

Onishi, Akira. *Teikaihatsukoku to Nihon* [The less developed countries and Japan]. Tokyo: Nihon kanzei kyōkai, 1969.

Organization for Economic Cooperation and Development (OECD). Confidential Aid Review (mimeo). Paris: OECD, 1986.

————. *Report by the Secretariat and Questions on the Development Assistance Efforts and Policies of Japan.* (restricted to participants). Paris: OECD, December 22, 1986.

————. *Financial Resources for Developing Countries: 1986 and Recent Trends.* (OECD press release). Paris: OECD, June 19, 1987.

————, Development Assistance Committee. *Aid Review 1990/1991: Report by the Secretariat and Questions for the Review of Japan.* Paris: OECD, 1991.

————. *Development Cooperation.* Paris: OECD, various years.

————. *Geographical Distribution of Financial Flows to Developing Countries.* Paris: OECD, various years.

Orr, Robert M., Jr. *The Emergence of Japan's Foreign Aid Power.* New York: Columbia University Press, 1990.

Overseas Economic Cooperation Fund (OECF). *OECF 20-nen shi* [20-year history of the OECF]. Tokyo: OECF, 1982.

————, Chōsa Kaihatsu-bu, Dai–2 ka. *Indoneshia kantorii sekutaa chōsa hokokushō* [Report on a country-sector survey of Indonesia]. Tokyo, March 1982.

————. (Kaigai Keizai Kyōryoku Kikin). *Annual Report for Fiscal 1985.* Tokyo: OECF, 1986.

————. *OECF Loans and Loan Procedures.* Tokyo: OECF, n.d.

Ozawa, Terutomo. *Multinationalism, Japanese Style: The Political Economy of Outward Dependency.* Princeton, NJ: Princeton University Press, 1982.

Pante, Filologo, Jr., and Romeo A. Reyes. *Japanese and U.S. Development Assistance to the Philippines: A Philippine Perspective.* Manila: Philippine Institute for Development Studies, 1989.

Park, Yung H. *Bureaucrats and Ministers in Contemporary Japanese Government.* Institute of East Asian Studies, University of California, Berkeley, Center for Japanese Studies, 1986.

Pastor, Robert A. *Congress and the Politics of U.S. Foreign Economic Policy.* Berkeley, CA: University of California Press, 1980.

Patrick, Hugh, and Henry Rosovsky, eds. *Asia's New Giant: How the Japanese Economy Works.* Washington, D.C.: Brookings Institution, 1976.

Peattie, Mark R. *Ishiwara Kanji and Japan's Confrontation with the West.* Princeton, NJ: Princeton University Press, 1975.

Pempel, T. J. "Bureaucratization of Policymaking in Postwar Japan." *American Journal of Political Science,* 18 (1974): 647–664.

———, ed. *Policymaking in Contemporary Japan.* Ithaca, NY: Cornell University Press, 1977.

———. "The Unbundling of 'Japan, Inc.': The Changing Dynamics of Japanese Policy Formation." *Journal of Japanese Studies,* 13 (1987): 271–306.

Phongpaichit, Pasuk. *The New Wave of Japanese Investment in ASEAN: Determinants and Prospects.* Pasir Panjang, Singapore: Institute of Southeast Asian Studies, 1990.

———, Busaba Kunasirin, Buddhagarn Rutchatorn, eds. *The Lion and the Mouse? Japan, Asia, and Thailand: Proceedings of an International Conference on Thai-Japan Relations.* Bangkok: Chulalongkorn University, 1986.

Piampongsant, Krisda. "The Politicization and Commercialization of Foreign Aid: Do People Benefit?" Paper presented at the first conference organized by the Research Assistance Program for ASEAN Scholars in International Affairs (RAPAS), The Japan Institute of International Affairs, Tokyo, March 1987, 18–19.

Poats, Rutherford M. *Twenty-five Years of Development Co-operation: A Review, Efforts and Policies of the Members of Development Assistance Committee: 1985 Report.* Paris: OECD, 1985.

Prasartset, Suthy, and Kongsak Sonteperkswong, "Structural Forces Behind Japan's Economic Expansion and the Case of Japanese-Thai Economic Relations." In *The Lion and the Mouse? Japan, Asia, and Thailand: Proceedings of an International Conference on Thai-Japan Relations,* edited by Pasuk Phongpaichit, et al. Bangkok: Chulalongkorn University, 1986.

Puckett, Robert H., ed. *The United States and Northeast Asia.* Chicago: Nelson-Hall, 1993.

Putnam, Robert D. "Diplomacy and International Politics: The Logic of Two-Level Games." *International Organization,* 42 (1988): 427–460.

Pyle, Kenneth B. *The Japanese Question: Power and Purpose in a New Era.* Washington, D.C.: American Enterprise Institute, 1992.

Ramseyer, J. Mark, and Frances McCall Rosenbluth. *Japan's Political Marketplace.* Cambridge, MA: Harvard University Press, 1993.

Randall, Vicky, and Robin Theobald. *Political Change and Underdevelopment: A Critical Introduction to Third World Politics.* Durham, NC: Duke University Press, 1985.

Report of the Commission of Inquiry into Aspects of the Timber Industry in Papua New Guinea (Summary). Hobart, Australia: The Asia-Pacific Action Group, November 1990.

Research Institute for Peace and Security. *Asian Security 1989–90.* McLean, VA: Brassey's (US) Inc., 1989.

Reyes, Romeo A. *Official Development Assistance to the Philippines: A Study of Administrative Capacity and Performance.* Manila: NEDA, 1985.

Riddell, Roger C. *Foreign Aid Reconsidered.* Baltimore, MD: Johns Hopkins University Press, 1987.

———. *Foreign Aid Reconsidered.* Baltimore, MD: Johns Hopkins University Press, 1987.

Rinji Gyōsei Chōsakai. *Kyōkan kyōgō jimu no kaikaku in kan suru iken* [Opinion relating to reform of interministerial competition in official activities]. Tokyo: Prime Minister's Office, September 1964.

Rinji Gyōsei Kaikaku Suishin Shingikai. *Kokusaika tai'o—Kokumin seikatsu jy ūshi no gyōsei kaikaku ni kan-surudai-ichiji tōshin* [Responding to internationalization—the first report on administrative reform: valuing the people's life]. Tokyo: Prime Minister's Office, July 4, 1991.

Rix, Alan. *Japan's Economic Aid: Policymaking and Politics*. London: Croom Helm, 1980.

Rondinelli, Dennis A. *Development Projects as Policy Experiments: An Adaptive Approach to Development Administration*. New York: Methuen, Inc., 1983.

Rosecrance, Richard, and Stein, Arthur A., eds. *The Domestic Bases of Grand Strategy*. Ithaca, NY: Cornell University Press, 1993.

Rosenstein-Rodan, P. N. "International Aid for Underdeveloped Countries." In *Foreign Aid*, edited by J. Bhagwati and R. S. Eckhaus. London: Penguin, 1970.

Rostow, W. W. *Eisenhower, Kennedy, and Foreign Aid*. Austin, TX: University of Texas Press, 1985.

Rozman, Gilbert, ed. *The East Asian Region: Confucian Heritage and Its Modern Adaptation*. Princeton, NJ: Princeton Unversity Press, 1991.

Saito, Shiro. *Japan at the Summit: Japan's Role in the Western Alliance and Asian Pacific Cooperation*. London: Routledge, 1990.

Saito, Shiro, and Takano Hajime, eds. *Shinseiki no ajia: Nihon ga motsubeki shinario* [Asia toward the twenty-first century: Japan's role in the scenario]. Tokyo: Saimaru, 1991.

Sakai, Hidekichi. "The ASEAN Economy: Current State and Problems." In *Pacific Economic Outlook: Dynamism and Adjustment*. Tokyo: Japan National Committee for Pacific Economic Cooperation, May 1988.

Sakurai, Masao. *Waga kuni no keizai kyōryoku* [Our economic cooperation]. Tokyo: Ajia Keizai Kenkyūjo, 1972.

Samejima, Shinsuke. *Nihon no taigai enjo seisaku: shanai hokoku 192* [Japan's overseas aid policy: internal report 192]. Tokyo: Asahi Shimbunsha Chōsa Kenkyūshitsu, 1982.

Samuels, Richard J. *The Business of the Japanese State—Energy Markets in Comparative and Historical Perspective*. Ithaca, NY: Cornell University Press, 1987.

Sankei Shimbun Ajia Shuzaihan. *Rinjin-tachi no sugao—Baishō to Enjo no tanima de* [The shape of our neighbors—in the valley between reparations and aid]. Tokyo: Sankei Shimbunsha, 1971.

Sato, Isao. "The Cabinet and Administrative Organization." In *Public Administration in Japan,* edited by Kiyoaki Tsuji. Tokyo: Tokyo University Press, 1984.

Satō, Seizaburō, and Matsuzaki, Tetsuhisa. *Jimintō Seiken* [LDP rule]. Tokyo: Ch ūō Kōronsha, 1986.

Saxonhouse, Gary R. "Industrial Restructuring in Japan." *Journal of Japanese Studies,* 5 (Summer 1979): 273–320.

Scalapino, Robert A. *The Politics of Development: Perspectives on Twentieth-Century Asia*. Cambridge, MA: Harvard University Press, 1989.

———. *Major Power Relations in Northeast Asia*. Lanham, MD: University Press of America, 1987.

———. *Asian Political Institutionalization*. Institute of East Asian Studies, University of California, Berkeley, 1986.

Scalapino, Robert A., ed. *Foreign Policy of Modern Japan*. Berkeley, CA: University of California Press, 1977.

Scalapino, Robert A., and Junnosuke Masumi. *Parties and Politics in Contemporary Japan*. Berkeley, CA: University of California Press, 1962.

Scalapino, Robert A., Seizaburo Sato, and Jusuf Wanandi. *Asian Economic*

Development—Present and Future. Institute of East Asian Studies, University of California, Berkeley, 1985.

Schmitter, Phillippe C., and Gerhard Lehmbruch, eds. *Trends Toward Corporatist Intermediation.* Beverly Hills, CA: Sage Publications, 1979.

Schumpeter, Joseph A. *Capitalism, Socialism and Democracy.* New York: Harper & Row, 1976.

Schwartz, Herman M. *States Versus Markets: History, Geography, and the Development of International Political Economy.* New York: St. Martin's Press, 1994.

Seisaku Kenkyūkai, Sōgō Anzen Hoshō Kenkyūkai Gurūpu. *Sōgō Anzen Hoshō Kenkyūkai Gurūpu Hōkokusho* [Report of the study group on comprehensive security]. Tokyo: Naikaku Kanbō Naikaku Shingishitsu Bunshitsu, July 2, 1980.

Shigeta, H. "Economic Relations Between Japan and Thailand." *Thai Japanese Studies*, Special Issue (March 1984).

Shinoda, Yujiro. *Economic Organizations and Business Leaders in Postwar Japan.* Tokyo: Socio-Economic Institute, Sophia University, 1973.

Shinohara, Myōhei. "Patterns and Change in Postwar Growth." In *Economic Growth: The Japanese Experience Since the Meiji Era*, edited by Lawrence Klein and Kazushi Ohkawa. Homewood, IL: Richard D. Irwin, Inc., 1968.

———. *Kōdō seichō no himitsu* [The secret of high-speed growth]. Tokyo: Nihon Keizai Shimbunsha, 1961.

———, Toru Yanagihara, and Kwang Suk Kim. *The Japanese and Korean Experiences in Managing Development.* (World Bank Staff Working Papers, No. 574). Washington, D.C.: The World Bank, 1983.

Shishido, Toshio. *Tonan Ajia enjo o kangaeru* [On aid to Southeast Asia]. Tokyo: Tōyō keizai shimpōsha, 1973.

Shonfield, Andrew. *Modern Capitalism: The Changing Balance of Public and Private Power.* London: Oxford University Press, 1965.

Simon, Herbert A. *Administrative Behavior: A Study of Decisionmaking Processes in Administrative Organizations*, 3d ed. New York: The Free Press, 1976.

Simon, Sheldon W. *East Asian Security in the Post–Cold War Era.* Armonk, NY: M. E. Sharpe, Inc., 1993.

Skocpol, Theda. *States and Social Revolutions.* Cambridge: Cambridge University Press, 1979.

———. "Bringing the State Back In: Strategies of Analysis in Current Research." In *Bringing the State Back In*, edited by Peter B. Evans, Dieter Rueschmeyer, and Theda Skocpol. Cambridge: Cambridge University Press, 1985.

Sōmucho (Management and Coordination Agency). *Keizai kyōryoku (seifu kaihatsu Enjo) ni kan-suru gyōsei kansatsu (dai-ichi ji) kekka ni motozuku kankoku* [Administrative inspection of economic cooperation (official development assistance) with recommendations]. Tokyo: Sōmucho, July 1988.

Sōmucho, Gyōsei Kansatukyoku. *Gyōsei kansatsu nenpō FY1989* [Yearbook of Administrative Inspection, FY1989]. Tokyo: Gyōsei Kanri Kenkyū Sentaa, 1993.

———. *FY 1988 Nenpō*

Stockwin, J.A.A. "Dynamic and Immobilist Aspects of Japanese." In *Dynamic and Immobilist Politics in Japan*, edited by J.A.A. Stockwin, et al. London: Macmillan Press, 1988.

Stokke, Olav, ed. *European Development Assistance, Volume 1: Policies and Performance.* Tilburg: European Association of Development Research and Training Institute; Oslo: Norwegian Institute of International Affairs, 1984.

Sudo, Sueo. *The Fukuda Doctrine and ASEAN: New Dimensions in Japanese Foreign Policy.* Singapore: Institute of Southeast Asian Studies, 1992.

Suehiro, Akira. "Kōgyō hatten" [Development of manufacturing]. In *Nihon no keizai kyōryoku* [Japan's economic cooperation]. Edited by Suzuki Nagatoshi. Tokyo: Ajia Keizai Kenkyūjo, 1989.

Suh, Cang-chul. *Growth and Structural Changes in the Korean Economy, 1910–1940)*. Cambridge, MA: Harvard University Press, 1978.

Sumi, Kazuo, ed. *Noo moa ODA baramaki enjo.* [No more wasted ODA]. Tokyo: JICC Shuppankyoku, 1992.

Sun, Kungtu C. *The Economic Development of Manchuria in the First Half of the Twentieth Century.* Cambridge, MA: Harvard University Press, 1969.

Surichai, Wanchao and Associates. *Japanese Aid to Thailand: Implementation and Development Impacts.* Bangkok: Chulalongkorn University, Asian Studies Institute, May 31, 1987.

Sutihardjo, Hinu. "Role of Economic Cooperation of Japan in Indonesian Development." Paper presented at the ASEAN Economic Development Symposium, Tokyo, October 5–6, 1987.

Suzuki, Nagatoshi. *Nihon no keizai kyōryoku (to jōkoku keizai hatten no shiten kara)* [Japan's economic cooperation (and the economic development of developing countries)]. Tokyo: Ajia Keizai Kenkyūjo, 1989.

Suzuki, Yoshio. "The Future Role of Japan as a Financial Centre in the Asian-Pacific Area." Paper presented at the Tokyo Conference on Global Adjustment and the Future of the Asian-Pacific Economy, Tokyo, May 11–13, 1988, sponsored by the Institute of Developing Economies.

Taigai Keizai Kyōryoku Shingikai (Foreign Economic Cooperation Advisory Council). *Kongo no kaihatsu kyōryoku no suishin ni tsuite (chūkan tōshin)* [On the further promotion of development cooperation (interim report)]. Tokyo: Sōrifu, August 18, 1975.

———. *Taigai Keizai Kyōryoku Shingikai kankei sankō shiryo-shu* [Reference materials pertaining to the Foreign Economic Cooperation Advisory Council]. Tokyo: Naikaku Sōridaijin Kanbō Shingishitsu, May 1976.

———. *Kongo no keizai kyōryoku no arikata ni tsuite* [The future of economic cooperation]. Tokyo: Sōrifu, November 12, 1980.

———. *Waga kuni keizai kyōryoku no suishin ni tsuite* [On the promotion of our nation's economic cooperation]. Tokyo: Prime Minister's Office, May 15, 1987.

Tendler, Judith. *Inside Foreign Aid.* Baltimore, MD: Johns Hopkins University Press, 1975.

Thayer, Nathaniel B. *How the Conservatives Rule Japan.* Princeton, NJ: Princeton University Press, 1969.

Theeravit, Khien. *Research Report on Danish, German and Japanese Assistance to Agricultural Development in Thailand: A Comparative Study.* Bangkok: Chulalongkorn University, Institute of Asian Studies, 1984.

———. "Comments on Paper III." In *The Lion and the Mouse? Japan, Asia, and Thailand: Proceedings of an International Conference on Thai-Japan Relations*, edited by Pasuk Phongpaichit, et al. Bangkok: Chulalongkorn University, 1986, 210–214.

Tokunaga, Shojiro, ed. *Japan's Foreign Investment and Asian Economic Interdependence: Production, Trade, and Financial Systems.* Tokyo: University of Tokyo Press, 1992.

Toyohiro Kono. *Strategy and Structure of Japanese Enterprises.* London: Macmillan, 1984.

Tsuji, Kiyoaki, ed. *Public Administration in Japan.* Tokyo: University of Tokyo Press, 1984.

Tsūshō Sangyō Gyōsei Kenkyūkai. *Tsūshō sangyō (II) Gendai gyosei zenshu, 15.* Tokyo: Gyōsei, 1983.

Tsūshō Sangyōshō (Ministry of International Trade and Industry). *Keizai kyōryoku no genjō to mondaiten,* Tokyo: Tsūshōshō Sangyō, annual since 1958.

———, Sangyō Kōzō Shingikai (Industrial Structure Council). *80-jūnen-dai no tsū-shō sangyō seisaku no bijyon* [Commercial and industrial policy vision for the 1980s]. Tokyo: Tsūshō Sangyōshō, March 17, 1980.

———, Sangyō Kōzō Shingikai Kokusai Keizai Bukai (Subcommitee on the International Economy). *Nihon no taigai keizai seisaku* [Japan's overseas economic policy]. Tokyo: Daiyamondo-sha, 1972.

———, Kagaku Kōgyo Bukai (Subcommittee on Chemical Industries). "Kongo no Kagaku Hiryō Kōgyo no Susumubeki Hōkō Oyobi Sono Seisaku no Arikata" [The desired direction for the further promotion of the chemical fertilizer industry and those policy measures]. Tokyo: Tsūshō Sangyōshō, May 1978.

Uchino, Tatsuro. *Japan's Postwar Economy: An Insider's View of Its History and Its Future.* Tokyo: Kodansha, 1983.

Upham, Frank. *Law and Social Change in Postwar Japan.* Cambridge, MA: Harvard University Press, 1987.

Ushiba, Nobusuke, and Hara Yasushi. *Nihon keizai gaikō no keifu* [The pedigree of Japan's economic diplomacy]. Tokyo: Asahi Shimbusha, 1979.

Vogel, Ezra F., ed. *Modern Japanese Organization and Decision-Making.* Tokyo: Charles E. Tuttle Company, Inc. 1985.

Wade, Robert. *Governing the Market: Economic Theory and the Role of Government in East Asian Industrialization.* Princeton, NJ: Princeton University Press, 1990.

Wall, David. *The Charity of Nations.* New York: Basic Books, 1973.

Waltz, Kenneth. *Theory of International Politics.* Reading, MA: Addison-Wesley Publishing Co., 1979.

Wanandi, Jusuf, and Kumao Kaneko, eds. *Toward a Closer ASEAN-Japan Partnership*: Proceedings of the Japan-ASEAN Conference 1987. Tokyo: Japan Institute of International Affairs, 1988.

Wanchao Surichai and Associates. *Japanese Aid to Thailand: Implementation and Development Impacts.* Bangkok: Asian Studies Institute, Chulalongkorn University, May 31, 1987.

Ward, Barbara. *The Rich Nations and the Poor Nations.* New York: W. W. Norton & Company, 1962.

Ward, Robert. *Japan's Political System.* Englewood Cliffs, NJ: Prentice-Hall, 1978.

Watanabe, Toshio, and Takeshi Aoki. *Ajia shin keizai chizu no yomikata* [How to read Asia's new economic map]. Tokyo: PHP, 1991.

Weber, Max. *The Theory of Social and Economic Organization.* Edited by Talcott Parsons, translated by A. M. Henderson and Talcott Parsons. New York: Oxford University Press, 1947.

———. "Bureaucracy" In *From Max Weber: Essays in Sociology,* translated and edited by H. H. Gerth and C. Wright Mills. New York: Oxford University Press, 1958.

Weiner, Myron, and Samuel P. Huntington. *Understanding Political Development.* Boston: Little, Brown & Co., 1987.

Wheeler, Joseph C. *Development Co-operation: Efforts and Policies of the Members of the Development Assistance Committee, 1986 Report.* Paris: OECD, 1987.

———. *Development Co-operation: Efforts and Policies of the Members of the Development Assistance Committee, 1987.* Paris: OECD, 1988.

White, John. *Japanese Aid.* London: Overseas Development Institute, 1964.

Wilber, Charles K., and Kenneth P. Jameson. *The Political Economy of Development and Underdevelopment.* New York: McGraw-Hill, 1992.

Wilson, Dick. *A Bank for Half the World: The Story of the Asian Development Bank, 1966–1986.* Manila: Asian Development Bank, 1987.

Wilson, James Q. *Political Organizations*. New York: Basic Books, 1973.

————. "The Rise of the Bureaucratic State." *The Public Interest*, 41 (Fall 1975): 77–103.

Wojkman, Anders, and Lloyd Timberlake. *Natural Disasters: Acts of God or Acts of Man?* London: Earthscan, 1984.

Wolf, Charles, Jr. *Foreign Aid: Theory and Practice in Southern Asia*. Princeton, NJ: Princeton University Press, 1960.

The World Bank. "Thailand: Managing Public Resources for Structural Adjustment." *World Bank Country Study Report*. Washington, D.C.: World Bank, June 1984.

Yamamoto, Mitsuru. *Nihon no keizai gaikō: sono kiseki to tenkaiten* [Japan's economic diplomacy: its development and turning points]. Tokyo: Nihon Keizai Shimbunsha, 1973.

Yamamura, Kozo. *Economic Policy in Postwar Japan*. Berkeley, CA: University of California Press, 1967.

————, and Yasukichi Yasuba. *The Political Economy of Japan, Volume 1: The Domestic Transformation*. Stanford, CA: Stanford University Press, 1987.

Yamashita Shōichi. "Ohgata Enjo purojekuto no keizai hakyū kōka—Asahan purojekuto o hitotsu no jirei to shite." [The economic impact of large-scale aid projects—the case of the Asahan project]. *Nenpō Keizaigaku* (March 1986).

Yanaga, Chitoshi. *Big Business in Japanese Politics*. New Haven, CT: Yale University Press, 1968.

Yano, Tōru, ed. *Tōnan Ajia to Nihon* [Japan and Southeast Asia]. Tokyo: Kyōbundō, 1991.

Yasutomo, Dennis. *The Manner of Giving: Strategic Aid and Japanese Foreign Policy*. Lexington, MA: Lexington Books, 1986.

Young, Alexander K. *The Sogo Shosha: Japan's Multinational Trading Companies*. Tokyo: Charles Tuttle Company, Inc., 1986.

Zysman, John. *Governments, Markets, and Growth: Financial Systems and the Politics of Industrial Change*. Ithaca, NY: Cornell University Press, 1985.

Index

About the Book
and the Author

Japan's use of its bilateral foreign aid to help achieve the strategic objectives of its economic and foreign policies is the focus of this original analysis.

Japan has learned well how to use its ODA to facilitate both the structural transformation of its domestic economy and the construction of an international division of labor that supports its continued interests. The Japanese formula is also a diplomatic success, Arase concludes. But the foreign policy burden the country is assuming in the post–Cold War era will prove to be too heavy for ODA alone to sustain. The emphasis of Japanese foreign policy inevitably will shift to other kinds of policy initiatives, especially in the area of security.

DAVID ARASE is lecturer in the Department of Political Studies at the University of London's School of Oriental and African Studies.